bei R.

ist eine rein innere. Im Grunde kann
man keine Teile wirklich verstehen, wenn
man nicht das Ganze dieses Lebens gegen-
wärtig hat. Ich meine als Grundhaltung
denn die Engel sind ja überall die Flammen
am Rande. Jetzt erst erfasse ich ganz
die einzige große Tragik von Rilkes Dasein:
den ganzen törlichen Ernst, mit dem
er die Schönheit lebte - Und das in unserer Zeit. Denn unsere Zeit ist wohl
darin, u. doch ist Rilke der einzige
Mensch dieser Zeit, der das Recht hatte,
vollkommen unpolitisch zu sein - ja,
die Pflicht.

Aber ich umschreibe mit alledem
das Eigentliche nur, weil ich darüber
durchaus mit Ihnen sprechen muß.
- des Gundolf wegen. Oder hätten Sie
es dann lieber gleich schwarz auf weiß?
Aber leicht wird das nicht sein. -

Es ist merkwürdig und schön, wie
das Meer mit seinen großen Wellen, auch

German Literature, Jewish Critics

Studies in German Literature, Linguistics, and Culture

Edited by James Hardin
(*South Carolina*)

GERMAN LITERATURE, JEWISH CRITICS

The Brandeis Symposium

Edited by
Stephen D. Dowden and
Meike G. Werner

CAMDEN HOUSE

First published 2002
by Camden House

Camden House is an imprint of Boydell & Brewer Inc.
PO Box 41026, Rochester, NY 14604–4126 USA
and of Boydell & Brewer Limited
PO Box 9, Woodbridge, Suffolk IP12 3DF, UK

ISBN: 1–57113–158–2

Library of Congress Cataloging-in-Publication Data

German Literature, Jewish critics: the Brandeis symposium / edited by
Stephen D. Dowden, Meike G. Werner.
    p. cm. — (Studies in German literature, linguistics, and culture)
Papers presented at a symposium held in 1997 at Brandeis University.
Includes bibliographical references and index.
ISBN 1–57113–158–2 (alk. paper)
    1. German literature — History and criticism. 2. Jews — Germany —
Intellectual life. 3. Germany — Civilization — Jewish influences. 4. Jews
in literature. I. Dowden, Stephen D. II. Werner, Meike. III. Studies in
German literature, linguistics, and culture (Unnumbered)

PT91 .G47 2002
830.9'00089'924—dc21

2002022299

A catalogue record for this title is available from the British Library.

This publication is printed on acid-free paper.
Printed in the United States of America.

Peter Heller
In Memoriam

Contents

3: A Tradition in Ruins

4: German-Jewish Double Identity

5: Embattled Germanistik

6: German Literature in the Public Sphere

7: Peter Demetz: On Marcel Reich-Ranicki

Illustrations

Acknowledgments

A DEBT OF GRATITUDE IS DUE to the German-American Academic Council for the grant that made the conference and the publication of these proceedings possible. Thanks are due also to Brandeis University and its Center for German and European Studies, under whose auspices the conference took place. As always, the Goethe Institut Boston was a valuable partner, and we are grateful to Jürgen Keil, its then director, for his advice, assistance, and financial support. After Meike Werner left Brandeis University, her new home institution, Vanderbilt University, continued to support the project. A special word of thanks goes to Karin Grundler-Whitacre, Administrative Assistant in the Department of Germanic and Slavic Languages at Brandeis University. Her able management of virtually every phase of organizing the conference and then in preparing the manuscript have been invaluable. Frau Viktoria Fuchs of the Deutsches Literaturarchiv Marbach graciously helped us find the Margarete Susman letter that we have used as endpapers for this book, and Susman's son, Erwin von Bendemann, has kindly allowed its reproduction. We are grateful to Jim Hardin and Jim Walker of Camden House for their friendly support and, especially, their long-suffering patience. Peter Heller, a lively interlocutor and a fine scholar, did not live to see these proceedings published. We dedicate this volume to his memory.

S. D.
M. W.
October 2001

Introduction: Positions to Defend

GERMAN LITERATURE, Jewish Critics — the title announces a tension. German literature — its writing, reception, and canonization — has long been bound up in an uneasy, often exclusionary relationship to German-Jewish history. "In the course of its historical development," Egon Schwarz wrote in his memoirs, "German literature and culture has always stood in a certain tension to Judaism."[1] For many Jews this tension became acute in the wake of the Holocaust. "The study of German literature and culture," Schwarz notes with respect to his own turn to the field in 1949, "demands an explanation, perhaps even a justification, from a Jew who speaks and writes German, especially when it comes so soon after the Second World War and the massacre of Jews by Germans."[2] On the one hand there is, then, a literature with a specific history of exclusion, and an event, the catastrophe itself, which for many Jews changed everything. But the matter is neither so simple nor one-sided. For German literature was also an opening, a point of identification, a world German Jews could enter and consider theirs, even if its language was also the language of the perpetrators.[3]

The second part of the dyad — Jewish critics — is also problematic, especially since in racist thought it was the Germans who created literature and Jews who criticized it.[4] This opposition rested upon a still older idea according to which non-Jewish Germans worked and produced and eked out a living by the sweat of their brows while Jews were parasitic upon the labor of others. At first glance, the opposition German literature-Jewish critics would seem to reproduce this old trope of the anti-Semitic imagination.

Still, we must be mindful and not let our understanding of the past be sabotaged by a poisoned language. Trauma must not be allowed to close the gates of experience. There is a relationship between German literature and Jewish critics; it is complex and overdetermined; it has a history and it carries a burden; and it is constitutive for our field. This volume seeks to understand this relationship and to illuminate its intricacies.

I

The discovery, primarily in the 1980s, of the Holocaust as both a traumatic event and a scholarly subject, constituted the central axis around which thinking about Jewish critics and German literature turned.[5] This was true, in the first order, with respect to the problem posed by German, the sullied language of the perpetrators; it also influenced thinking about the position from which critics, especially Jewish critics, explored German literature.

The pollution of language posed a general as well as a specific problem. In the first decades after the war, silence seemed to many critics — if not necessarily to poets such as Paul Celan, Nelly Sachs, and Rose Ausländer — the appropriate response to the Holocaust. "The world of Auschwitz lies outside speech as it lies outside reason," George Steiner wrote in an essay on Kafka published in 1963: "To speak of the *unspeakable* is to risk the survivance of language as creator and bearer of humane, rational truth. Words that are saturated with lies or atrocity do not easily resume life."[6] Like Adorno's famous verdict on poetry after Auschwitz, Steiner's dictum focused on the inability of a diseased language to express traumatic experience. But Steiner's insight that silence constituted the most defensible response to the Holocaust was also more specific. "The thing that has gone dead is the German language," he had written in a still earlier essay.[7] By the 1980s, this position, which Steiner had himself revised, no longer seemed tenable, for it necessarily remained deaf to the spoken utterances and the written testimony of the survivors of the Holocaust.

The importance of these voices, even when spoken in German, could no longer be repressed. A complicated reorientation took place in which silence gave way to language. There were many cultural landmarks of this transition: Lawrence L. Langer's explications of the literary structure of Holocaust literature (already published in the mid seventies);[8] the airing in 1979 of the American television series, *Holocaust;*[9] the founding of the U.S. Holocaust Memorial Museum (chartered in 1980 and opened in 1993); the establishment of the Fortunoff Video Archive for Holocaust Testimonies at Yale University in 1981; and the production of Claude Lanzmann's epic film of Holocaust testimony, *Shoah* in 1985. The turn away from silence and toward language involved increasing attention to testimony, which offered the possibility, as Shoshana Felman and Dori Laub wrote with respect to Lanzmann's *Shoah,* of "a return and a repossession of the living voice."[10] This mandate to recover the voice, however fractured and distant, also underlies Geoffrey Hartman's plea that we listen to testimony. "The survivors' experience as experienced, their personal story and individual memories," he urged, "was only beginning to be heard."[11]

Experience, as we know, does not come unmediated. The question of who spoke and with whose voice remained a profound problem that would divide generations and significantly alter the ground that made Jewish criticism of German literature possible. Here the shift was from the universalizing assumptions of the Enlightenment to truth claims derived from positions of subordination or difference, truth, in other words, with an attribute.[12] A measure of the gulf separating the two positions can be gleaned from the stances of two eminent critics: Peter Demetz and Sander Gilman. In his essay "On Auschwitz, and on Writing in German: A Letter to a Student," Demetz confesses his sympathy for those European liberals who had "great difficulty in perceiving human beings in closed terms of groups, collectives, classes, national loyalties, or ethnic determinants" and instead argues for seeing in each Jew or Gypsy murdered "a *reiner Mensch* (pure human being) in the sense of the eighteenth century."[13] Demetz's cosmopolitan reluctance to affix religious and ethnic labels to the voices of survivors is consistent with an earlier generation's conviction that the Holocaust, far from being the endpoint of the "Enlightenment project," represents the overturning of the values of the European Enlightenment. A later generation, the one that came of academic age in the 1960s, was more sympathetic to the Frankfurt School and less interested in an earlier formal criticism that eschewed the potentially ideological valuation of literature. By the 1980s prominent scholars of this generation increasingly insisted that morally responsible literary reflection, especially with respect to German literature, must place the Holocaust at the conscious center of its work. "It is from the centrality of the Holocaust in the study of German culture that we must move," writes Sander Gilman in his *Inscribing the Other.* "The Holocaust remains for me . . . the central event of modern German culture, the event toward which every text, every moment in German history and, yes, culture, inexorably moved."[14] Unlike Demetz, Gilman did not attempt to return to the voice of the "pure human being." Rather, and consonant with parallel attempts to establish the epistemological possibilities inherent in identity and difference, Gilman privileged the voice of the "outsider."

Criticism — Jewish criticism — did not entail neutrality but rather meant "to burn with those fires which define you as the outsider."[15]

Gilman emphasized the Jewish "I" of the critic. More precisely, he underscored the perspective of a Jewish critic of Eastern European background, and indeed *Inscribing the Other* is dedicated to the memory of his Jewish-Polish and Jewish-Russian grandparents. This manifest emphasis on particular identity constituted a departure from earlier Jewish critics who tended to identify with Jewish authors and, in doing so, indirectly underscored the particular value of the outsider's critical gaze. Harry Zohn, who in 1939 at the age of fifteen was forced to emigrate from Vienna, self-confidently wrote about, and translated, Jewish authors at a time when few Jewish scholars of German literature writing in the United States focused on the specifically Jewish tradition within German literature.[16] As a professor of German literature at Brandeis University from 1951 to 1996, Zohn understood himself as mediating between the world of Austrian and Jewish literature and the literary culture of the United States.[17] In addition to his immensely important translations of Walter Benjamin, Theodor Herzl, and Gershom Scholem, he also drew attention to the critical edge of authors — such as Stefan Zweig, Kurt Tucholsky, and Karl Kraus — who did not occupy the center of the German literary canon in the postwar years. In Germany, Marcel Reich-Ranicki's book, *Über Ruhestörer: Juden in der deutschen Literatur,* which appeared in 1973, thematized the role of German-Jewish writers — including Ludwig Börne, Heinrich Heine, Jakov Lind, and Jurek Becker, among many others — as occupying a position as outsiders and provocateurs who, precisely because of their marginal status as Jews, can offer privileged and challenging insight. In *Aussenseiter,*[18] which appeared in 1975, Hans Mayer likewise took up this theme and argued that it was precisely this marginal position that led to a certain species of insight, and that this was not only true for Jews but also for women and homosexuals. If this held for writers, the argument could be made for critics as well, especially since both works — Marcel-Reich Ranicki's *Über Ruhestörer* and Hans Mayer's *Aussenseiter* — possessed highly autobiographical undertones.

By the 1980s, these early forays found wider scholarly resonance so that one could, in the words of Konrad Feilchenfeldt, talk about the "rediscovery of the 'Jew' in contemporary German literary scholarship."[19] This rediscovery occurred in an international context, as the German world of Germanistik developed increasingly close ties not only with the United States but also with Israel. Thus, for example, one of the first efforts to understand the place of Jewish writers in the German literary canon emerged from a conference in Jerusalem (undertaken by the University of Göttingen and the Hebrew University of Jerusalem), whose proceedings were published by Suhrkamp as *Juden in der deutschen Literatur: ein deutsch-israelisches Symposion*.[20] The "rediscovery" was also marked by the publication of a number of important essay collections, including a two-volume work edited by Heinz-Dieter Weber and bearing the title *Juden in der deutschen Literatur* (1984–85),[21] and a collection edited by Gunter E. Grimm and Hans-Peter Bayerdörfer entitled *Im Zeichen Hiobs: Jüdische Schriftsteller und deutsche Literatur im 20. Jahrhundert* (1985). These works, and there were others as well,[22] signaled the beginning of a scholarly concern that was long overdue.

Yet these works concentrated on the place of Jews both as writers of and figures in German literature. They did not explicitly address the role of Jewish critics, whether inside or outside the academy. This line of research did not begin in earnest until the early nineties. In the context of a conference held in 1991 in Marbach am Neckar on the "Influence of Exile Scholars in the Germanistik of the Host Countries," German and Austrian Jews who had been forced into exile and who had subsequently shaped Germanistik in their respective countries were invited to discuss their experiences.[23] These exile scholars — such as Hans Eichner, Paul Hoffmann, Hans Reiss, Henry Remak, and Guy Stern — seemed to represent the academic parallel of the "other Germany" and the conference, organized by Walter Schmitz in cooperation with the German Literary Archive in Marbach, marked the beginning of systematic research on the "scholarship of the exile community."[24] But the conference focused on how the experience of exile influenced scholarship and not the specifically Jewish dimension of scholarship in exile. The first work to take up this specific question was written by David Suchoff, who in a special issue of the *Weimarer Beiträge* on "Germanistik in den USA" considered the place of "Jewish critics within American Germanistik," and asked "what it means to be a Jew in postwar America and write on German literature."[25] Suchoff addressed this question not just at the biographical level but also within the works of the critics themselves. Focusing especially on Erich Heller's *The Disinherited Mind* and Heinz Politzer's *Franz Kafka: Parable and Paradox,* Suchoff showed the way in which the Holocaust and post-Holocaust debates on Jewish identity might be traced in the writings of these Jewish critics of German literature.[26]

II

Suchoff's essay represents a fresh and significant turn. For, at least since Gadamer, we know that the perspective from which one views a literature and its history will have a bearing on critical or interpretive practices and their outcome. The presuppositions that inform the questions one puts to literature — the pressures exerted by historical circumstance, the life experiences shared by individual critics, experiences that had a bearing on what it meant to be Jewish or German (or more complexly: German-Jewish) — shape the framework that structures critical vision. The story of when, where, and how Jewish-German exiles or other Jewish critics may have reformulated their thinking and writing about German literature is part of the history of Germanistik. The same may be said of the still more difficult question of whether, how, and to what effect these views have influenced the practice of German literary and cultural studies.

With these questions in mind, the editors invited a diverse set of speakers and respondents to a symposium held in 1997 at Brandeis University. We sought individuals as speakers, respondents, and panelists who would potentially represent a wide range of generational, critical, and national perspectives within the discipline of German literary and cultural studies. The audience of between three and four hundred listeners proved to be an additional resource. Many of them took advantage of the time offered for open discussion to contribute valuable observations.[27] The present volume comprises the lectures and responses from that symposium, and it includes nearly all the purely oral contributions that were spontaneous on the part of invited participants and listeners in the audience. The lectures have been published from the speakers' own prepared texts, as have the prepared comments of the designated respondents. But the rest — that is, panelists' commentaries, discussion from the floor, and the banquet speaker's after-dinner speech — were recorded and transcribed from audio tapes. In addition, the editors have provided annotations at various points in the oral commentary in the hope that they will prove informative to the readers of these pages.[28]

In the first session Hinrich Seeba explores potential links between contemporary cultural criticism of a literary bent — "cultural poetics" — and the practice of German-Jewish literary critics in flight from Nazi Europe. In his lecture, he proposes that these figures — critics such as Heinz Politzer, Erich Heller, and Egon Schwarz — were longstanding outsiders to the world of conventional scholarship on literature in Germany and Austria and, as such, were the intellectual descendants of writerly critics such as Heinrich Heine and Karl Kraus. Seeba emphasizes the difference between his training in German scholarship at postwar West German universities and the re-education he experienced at the University of California under the mentorship of Viennese émigré Heinz Politzer. He finds that Politzer and other critics of similar intellectual provenance (more often Austrian than German) championed a mode of critical discourse honoring not only conventional standards of scholarship but drawing also in equal measure on a special sensitivity to language. This sensitivity, Seeba suggests, was rooted in the particularities of Jewish assimilation in the German-speaking world as well as in a sense that criticism is itself a creative act. Moreover, he points out that the thought of figures such as Karl Lamprecht, Ernst Cassirer, and Georg Simmel — work that the generation of displaced intellectuals knew — found its way into the writings of the émigrés and anticipated the cultural poetics of today in a nontheoretical form.

In his complementary response to Seeba's lecture, Egon Schwarz offers his own experiences of extraterritoriality as a crucial and typical piece of the puzzle. Jewish critics, as perennial outsiders in Germany and Austria, were in a position to have a special perspective on German literature. Once again, Kraus and Heine serve as exemplars of the outsider as critic and gadfly, but so could figures as different as Adorno and Reich-Ranicki, or Gershon Shaked, Andrew Jaszi, and Ruth Klüger. The émigrés of Schwarz's generation, as exiles from their homelands and characteristically less than fully accepted and integrated members of the countries in which they sought sanctuary, continued (and in some instances still continue) to be what he calls UFOs: unidentified foreign outsiders. This standing suggests the potential relevance of personal biography to the history of Germanistik.[29]

This question of the relevance of individual circumstance, or "positionality," to literary criticism incited much discussion. To some degree, one's point of view frames the standards of relevance for an interpretive act, and no point of view stands outside a particular time and place and set of historical circumstances. The question then becomes: To what degree did the experience of exile — to name only one of many contingencies — frame the view entertained by the important Jewish critics of German literature, who in turn helped shape the discipline as we have come to know it? In the case of Egon Schwarz, these experiences were of plain importance. He was drawn to

German literature not least by a curiosity about the historical forces that had so drastically affected his life. But Schwarz also emphasizes the ways in which the American context helped shape German studies. The student rebellion of the sixties and the decline of foreign language requirements also pushed forward the trend toward sociohistorical and cultural studies in German departments. As a result the émigré generation and their successors found themselves well placed to explore the meanings of their own experience, at least until the preoccupation with theory once again marginalized their characteristic essayism.

In the subsequent discussion, Peter Demetz and Dorrit Cohn — two émigré critics known for their formalist leanings — wonder aloud about how relevant the more personal contingencies may have been for the practice of literary criticism in general. They point out that they were at least not aware of so framing their own critical priorities, either as scholars or as teachers and mentors.[30] Other commentators recall a self-conscious reluctance among some members of the exile generation to call attention to themselves and their experience in the practice of criticism. Still, it is at least possible that these experiences affected the individuals who underwent them more than they consciously realized: for example, in choice of texts singled out for special study (one thinks of Demetz's exemplary edition of Lessing's *Nathan der Weise*),[31] in figures included or excluded from their version of the German canon (Cohn began with a book about the fiction of Hermann Broch,[32] then a nearly forgotten figure), in choice of interpretive method,[33] guidance of graduate students and so forth.

In the second session, Christoph König turns to the difficulties of Jewish literary scholars in the nineteenth century.[34] He focuses attention on the case of Ludwig Geiger, founder of the *Goethe-Jahrbuch*. Quoting from letters and other primary sources, König is able to show in vivid detail exactly what Geiger was up against and how poorly he judged the full extent of the forces arrayed against him. Geiger placed his faith in the values of the Enlightenment, and its light blinded him to the darker elements around him. König portrays him as a victim of his own faith in the universality of German high culture. An unconverted Jew, he sought refuge from the grosser elements of German anti-Semitism in the seeming meritocracy of the German university, in the universal ideals of science and scholarship, in Germany's high culture. He understood high culture in a rationalistic and cosmopolitan sense derived from the Enlightenment, as a sphere opposed to the nationalistic sensibility that associated the word "Kultur" with the cultivation of those characteristics and accomplishments that bear German identity. This tradition has made *Kultur* particularistically *German,* meaning not French, not English, and — perhaps most emphatically — not Jewish. Here one thinks of Thomas Mann's pitched battle against his brother Heinrich over German "Kultur," which he depicted as dark and profound and opposed to the rationalistic, superficial, merely democratic French concept of civilization. Geiger's misprision of the character of German *Kultur* in his time is striking. Unable to become a regular professor in Berlin despite the help of so powerful an ally as Wilhelm Scherer, Geiger sought to enter the realm of public letters via the *Goethe-Jahrbuch,* though even here his authority and legitimacy were contested.

Responding to König, Amir Eshel explores the parallel figure of Michael Bernays, a Jewish Wagnerite and German nationalist who converted and found a measure of success through assimilation. But Eshel approaches the topic from the interesting angle of his own schooling in Israel, where no representative of Jewish Enlightenment in Germany was given a hearing. Eshel seems to suggest that always and only to judge these figures from the perspective of the Holocaust — as if they are to be viewed with pity or disdain for not having been able to predict the future — is too limiting. He concludes with an extraordinary anecdote concerning the relationship between two of the most important German-Jewish intellectuals: Peter Szondi, who survived Bergen-Belsen, and Gershom Scholem, who proclaimed the German-Jewish symbiosis a pernicious fantasy and helped shape the views of Israeli and other concerned intellectuals toward the German world and its Jewish history. When offered a chair in Comparative Literature at Hebrew University, Szondi respectfully declined. Though he felt at home in Jerusalem, he wrote to Scholem, this feeling of being at home was one he could not bear. Just why Szondi returned to German literature and Europe is hard to say, but it may well have been simply his refusal to be driven out. When Walter Benjamin's friends were pleading with him to leave before it got to be too late, he replied that there were still positions to be defended in Europe. Like Benjamin, Szondi committed suicide. But this does not mean that they were wrong. It is probably true that Geiger's vision of the German culture was too optimistic — König suggests that Marcel Reich-Ranicki resembles him in this way — but the same cannot be said of Benjamin and Szondi. Their hard unblinking eye defines them as critics.

In the session entitled "Tradition in Ruins," Barbara Hahn focuses attention on three women: Hannah Arendt, Margarete Susman, and Bertha Badt-Strauss. Each was forced into exile, and each carried with her the broken pieces of a life and a tradition. Arendt and Badt-Strauss went to the United States and Susman went to Switzerland. It is Susman who provides the gripping image that Hahn offers as an embodiment of the experience of exile for Jewish intellectuals who were also emphatically German intellectuals. In her powerful confrontation with the fate of German Jewry and its path into the future, *Das Buch Hiob und das Schicksal des jüdischen Volkes,* Susman tells the story of a Jewish Germanist who in 1933 flung himself in front of an oncoming train and was torn to pieces. So it was figuratively with many German Jews, especially those who most fully invested themselves and their identity in the German tradition: writers, actors, cultural journalists, scholars of German language and literature. To compel a German to cease being German — to compel anyone to cease being what she is — destroys the self, tears it to bits. In Susman's vision, this soul-destroying coercion captures the fate of German Jews.

In American exile Hannah Arendt and Bertha Badt-Strauss continued to cultivate the German tradition, or what was left of it after the National Socialists seized control of it. So also did Susman in Switzerland. This much they had in common with the men who shared their fate. But Hahn calls our attention to the fact that these women more actively set about redefining that tradition. They were drawn not only to figures such as Lessing and Heine but also to Rahel Levin Varnhagen, Rosa Luxemburg, Charlotte von Stein and other women who were never quite taken seriously in a profession dominated by men. Work on forgotten or marginal women served at least in part as a kind of work on the self, a way of patching the broken bits of identity into a serviceable whole and at the same time as a way of redefining the scope of German culture and literature for the future. It is perhaps this point that must be stressed: along with grief, rage, and sorrow for a broken tradition and lives lost — what Germanists have conventionally thought of as literary "Trauerarbeit" — the work of Susman, Arendt, and Badt-Strauss is simultaneously creative and future-oriented. It has helped to enlarge, sharpen, and redefine our contemporary vision of the range and intellectual responsibility of Germanistik.

Gesa Dane responds to Hahn's lecture with an illuminating, and for the American audience overdue, portrait of Käte Hamburger's achievement. Somewhat younger than Susman, Arendt, and Badt-Strauss, Hamburger had aimed at an academic career in Germany, and unlike them she returned to Germany after the war. Evidently she too, like Benjamin and Szondi, believed there remained important tasks for Jews in the German world. Still, the metaphor of a self torn to pieces may not be out of place in her case either. Dane emphasizes that Hamburger entertained no doubts about the end of the German-Jewish symbiosis — if it ever was a symbiosis. The nature of her writing before and after the Second World War shows distinctive differences of emphasis. Because her great work, *Die Logik der Dichtung,* is basically formalist in nature (a direct result, Dane points out, of Hamburger's work as a teacher of German language while in Swedish exile), one might be tempted to align her with the text-immanent school of criticism in the postwar German academy and its attempt to evade history and politics by focusing on the work or art as a phenomenon outside of time and place. Bracingly, Hamburger has a strong say on figures as diverse as Heine and Else Lasker-Schüler, Nelly Sachs, and of course Rahel Levin Varnhagen. Her reading of Levin Varnhagen takes sharp issue with that of both Susman, who aligns her with Romanticism in its gloomy Christian orientation toward death, and with Arendt, who places her in a tradition of Jewish suffering that culminates in the Holocaust. Hamburger's Rahel Levin Varnhagen is a life-affirming, non-Christian humanist, in spirit a kinswoman of Goethe. In this picture of Rahel lies a clue to Hamburger's critical disposition. Her criticism belongs not to the tradition of bloodless formalism but to that of liberal humanism which, as Ritchie Robertson points out, has a sharp critical edge that is revealed in her historically tempered criticism of Thomas Mann and Goethe.

Another figure who believed that there were still Jewish positions to defend in Germany and Europe was Hermann Levin Goldschmidt. In session four, Willi Goetschel discusses the place of this crucial figure in the history of modern Jewish letters. At a time when the modifier "German-Jewish" seemed a self-evident contradiction — as it still seems to many people — Goldschmidt argued eloquently and powerfully for a critical cultivation of German Jewry's legacy. Perhaps it is true that the expression "German-Jewish" entails a contradiction, but Goldschmidt is a theorist of contradiction — *Widerspruch* — as a form of discourse. He insists on the historical particularity and the autonomy of Jewish identity in the German-speaking world. Moreover, Goldschmidt refused to accept negative versions of Jewish identity, that is, definitions of Jewish identity imposed from the outside, whether as principal victim of Nazi genocide, as non-Christian, or as non-German. To be a Jew is first of all an affirmative mode of being. He saw it as the task of Jewish intellectuals, including literary intel-

lectuals, to face Jewish-German history squarely — including its contradictions — and, by working up a dialogue with the past, to assert a
positive Jewish-defined vision of what it means to be a Jew in the second half of the twentieth century. Being Jewish is not to be defined
against the background of some supposedly paradigmatic normalcy,
Christian or otherwise, as if Judaism were a deviation from some salu-
brious ideal — like an illness that needs a cure. Historically, the "cure"
for this condition has gone by different names, including expulsion,
assimilation, baptism, repression, and Auschwitz. Jewish identity, any
collective identity, should be a matter of self-determination, and literature is one of the scenes of such self-determination.

It is curious that Goldschmidt is not better known, given the sanity and clarity of his thought. Responding to Goetschel, Thomas Sparr
offers a possible reason for this. Goldschmidt called for dialogue at a
time when hardly anybody, German or Jewish or German-Jewish, was
willing to talk. In fact, Sparr's deliberations suggest that the prospects
for dialogue still remain feeble on the German side of the divide.
While some interest may be generated for the way in which Jews read
German literature, he sees the lack of interest among German critics in
Jewish literature as an unpropitious sign. And where there is interest — he cites the reception of Paul Celan and Nelly Sachs[35] — the specifically Jewish legacy remains misunderstood.

But just what the legacy of German Jewry should mean for the literary critic remains a point of heated contention. In session five, Walter Sokel gives a frank and candid account of his early years and
motives for becoming a professor of German literature. As a refugee
from Vienna to the United States, Sokel was drawn to the study of
German not least of all by the realization that his memories, his roots,
his very self were inseparable from the language and literature in
which he had been reared. Living in a wartime America deeply hostile
to the German culture with which he so strongly identified, Sokel experienced the potential annihilation of Germany as a threat to his own
being. Consequently, he developed what might fairly be described as a
sense of mission. He intended and intends in his work to demonstrate
that the German-Jewish symbiosis was not a myth but an unrealized
dream, that much of value has come from the German cultural sphere,
that the Nazis were illegitimate interlopers, and that the Jewish contribution to German culture was and remains crucial. However many
of his kith and kin the Nazis may have murdered, Sokel does not in-
tend to let them kidnap German cultural history and the German-
Jewish legacy as well.

During the response and discussion of Sokel's lecture, a conspicuous rift comes into view. Marc Weiner pointedly wonders whether Sokel may be considered in any way typical of Jewish critics, whether literature and culture may be legitimately taken to be the vehicle of German values, and whether Sokel's "unabashed investment in the Enlightenment project as based on a belief in its goals of ethical-moral enhancement and improvement through education" might not be doomed from the start by what has become known as the dialectic of Enlightenment. Susanne Klingenstein expresses surprise that Sokel did not identify with the Jews but instead with their German oppressors. Sokel writes that the Allied bombing of German cities angered him more than the news of Nazi genocide. Conversely, news of the Holocaust filled him, as he writes, with "an abysmal sadness." Some Jewish professors of German literature — the example of Sol Liptzin is mentioned — abandoned the study of German literature altogether. Would this constitute an abandonment of the German Jewish legacy? Is an everlasting line of division between Germans and Jews to be upheld? Is "German-Jewish" as a modifier simply an oxymoron or, at best, a historical fantasy? These questions are not so pointedly asked, but they hang in the air, demanding an answer that is not forthcoming.

In the final session Ritchie Robertson explores the work of three prominent literary intellectuals who emigrated from Europe to Britain: Siegbert Prawer, J. P. Stern, and George Steiner. Interestingly, none of the three is a native German: Prawer comes from Poland, Stern from Czechoslovakia, and Steiner — though of Viennese roots — was raised in France and then educated in the United States before settling in Britain and Switzerland. Like Hinrich Seeba, Robertson emphasizes the elegant, essayistic character of the work they have done — he focuses on a major book by each figure — and hence their contribution to the intellectual public sphere. Each of the three, but especially Steiner, has been involved in literary journalism, transcending the narrowness of conventional scholarship. Robertson notes that their cosmopolitan reach of interest and experience contrasts markedly with the earlier provincialism typical of British Germanistik, some of which also demonstrated an element of hostility to Jews. But the exact meaning of Jewishness for Steiner, Stern, and Prawer, personally or for the practice of their criticism, is harder to specify. Each is a Central European émigré with a strong orientation to German literature and cultural tradition, with perhaps an overriding sense of commitment to a liberal humanism in the tradition of Lessing, Marx, Freud, Kafka, and Schoenberg. Each suffered at the hands of Germany, the source of that tradition, because of his Jewish background. As different as they are individually as Jews, historical circumstance has forced them into a common context.

As exiles, their simultaneous detachment from and involvement in German literary tradition is perhaps one key among others to their critical accomplishments. Each has such a distinctly different sense of his own Jewishness and its relation to criticism that they evince little in common other than the experience of exile from their original homelands. Still, as David Suchoff observes in his response to Robertson, these are critics whose exile might conventionally seem to place them either in the tradition of the Wandering Jew or of assimilated figures in denial of their identities. One might suppose that each suffered from a sense of dividedness, a rift within that drives imaginative ambition. On the contrary, Suchoff observes in them a manifest commitment to confronting and exploring "a contradictory legacy that participates in and dissents from the notion of the German itself." The problem is not Jews who are divided against themselves so much as a German tradition that is schizophrenic in its dealing with Jews.

In the category of public intellectual, no Jewish critic of German literature, indeed, no literary critic of any sort is more of a public figure than Marcel Reich-Ranicki. Peter Demetz's discussion of Reich-Ranicki and his work concludes our volume. Like a good many of the critics under discussion at this conference, Reich-Ranicki is emphatically a liberal humanist; he is secular and Jewish in no sense other than that imposed upon him by family experience and conventional prejudice. Still, his longtime associate ventures the opinion that Reich-Ranicki's Jewish affiliation may fairly be defined by a sense of "solemn loyalty to his kin and his continued solidarity with those, past and present, who have been humiliated, disadvantaged, persecuted, and killed." In his book, *Über Ruhestörer: Juden in der deutschen Literatur,* published in 1973, Reich-Ranicki was one of the first postwar intellectuals to explore and affirm the specific role of Jewish writers, intellectuals and other disturbers of the German peace. Both Reich-Ranicki and Demetz himself could be included under the telling rubric of Ruhestörer. Like the critics he describes, Reich-Ranicki (along with Demetz) belongs to the tradition of German and European Enlightenment, with its confidence in skeptical critique, reasoned engagement, and public discourse.

In his lecture on Ludwig Geiger, Christoph König notes in passing that Reich-Ranicki's confidence in the enlightened liberalism of German culture may be misplaced. Is there now a place for Jews in

Germany, or did Jews who returned there fall victim to an illusion about a German culture that has never really existed? Many participants of the conference referred to the existence of a German-Jewish symbiosis as a delusion, a one-way street, a lie. Perhaps high culture invidiously masks the true state of affairs in German life. On the other hand, as a refugee from Nazi terror in wartime Poland — both as an internee of the Warsaw ghetto and later on in hiding — Reich-Ranicki doubtless knows a good deal about German culture, both high and low. His return to Germany and to the German public sphere, as Demetz remarks, suggests a man determined to transform himself from the object of history into a shaper of the modern world. And in Germany, Reich-Ranicki has indeed become an extraordinarily influential shaper of public discourse about literature. But he was not the only one. Taken as a group, Jewish critics of German literature have powerfully shaped modern intellectual life, both inside and outside the university.

— THE EDITORS

Notes

[1] Egon Schwarz, *Keine Zeit für Eichendorff: Chronik unfreiwilliger Wanderjahre*, 2nd ed., with a new epilogue and an essay by Hans-Albert Walter (Frankfurt am Main: Büchergilde Gutenberg, 1992; first published in 1979), 276.

[2] Egon Schwarz, *Keine Zeit für Eichendorff*, 276. Similar statements can be found in Ruth Klüger, *weiter leben: Eine Jugend*, 4th ed. (Munich: dtv, 1995), 202; or Hans Eichner and Walter Sokel, quoted in *Lebenswege und Lieblingslektüren österreichischer NS-Vertriebener in den USA und Kanada*, ed. Beatrix Müller-Kampel in cooperation with Carla Carnevale (Tübingen: Niemeyer, 2000), 13.

[3] See the overviews in Hans Schütz, *Juden in der deutschen Literatur: Eine deutsch-jüdische Literaturgeschichte im Überblick* (Munich: Piper, 1992); *Yale Companion to Jewish Writing and Thought in German Culture, 1096–1996*, edited by Sander L. Gilman and Jack Zipes (New Haven and London: Yale UP, 1997); and Dieter Lamping, *Von Kafka bis Celan: Jüdischer Diskurs in der deutschen Literatur des 20. Jahrhunderts* (Göttingen: Vandenhoeck & Ruprecht, 1998). — For a recent critical discussion of the discourse on German-Jewish literature with suggestions for further reading, see Andreas B. Kilcher, "Was ist 'deutsch-jüdische Literatur'? Eine historische Diskursanalyse," *Weimarer Beiträge* 45 (1999): 485–517; and Amir Eshel, "Schreiben auf Jüdisch? Writing in Jewish?" *Germanic Review* 75 (2000): 91–98.

[4] See for example Adolf Bartels, *Kritiker und Kritikaster: pro domo et pro arte. Mit einem Anhang: Das Judentum in der deutschen Literatur* (Leipzig: Avenarius, 1903). On Bartels, the most prominent anti-Semitic literary critic, see Steven

Nyole Fuller, *The Nazis' Literary Grandfather: Adolf Bartels and Cultural Extremism, 1871–1945* (New York: Peter Lang, 1996).

[5] A telling marker of this late discovery by the scholarly community is the publication history of Raul Hilberg's magisterial *The Destruction of the European Jews*, which was first published in the United States in 1961 but received little attention. It was a book, the political philosopher Judith Sklar supposedly said, that "had been published too early" (see Raul Hilberg, *The Politics of Memory: The Journey of a Holocaust Historian* [Chicago: Ivan R. Dee, 1996], 123). Hilberg revised, expanded, and republished the English edition as a three-volume work in 1985; in Germany, a translation of the original did not appear until 1982 (by a small publishing house) and no major German publisher saw it into print until S. Fischer Verlag brought out the expanded version in 1990.

[6] George Steiner, "K" (1963), in *Language and Silence: Essays on Language, Literature, and the Inhuman* (New York: Atheneum, 1967), 123.

[7] George Steiner, "The Hollow Miracle," in *Language and Silence: Essays on Language, Literature, and the Inhuman* (New York: Atheneum, 1967), 96. For a discussion of the controversy ignited by this essay, which was written in 1959, see Amir Eshel, "Die hohle Sprache: Die Debatte um George Steiners 'Das hohle Wunder,'" in *Deutsche Nachkriegsliteratur und der Holocaust*, ed. Holger Gehle, Doron Kiesel, Hanno Loewy, and Stephan Braese (Frankfurt am Main and New York: Campus, 1998), 317–30.

[8] Lawrence L. Langer, *The Holocaust and the Literary Imagination* (New Haven and London: Yale UP, 1975); *The Age of Atrocity: Death in Modern Literature* (Boston: Beacon P, 1978); *Versions of Survival: The Holocaust and the Human Spirit* (Albany: State U of New York P, 1982); more recently *Art from the Ashes: A Holocaust Anthology* (New York and Oxford: Oxford UP, 1995) and *Preempting the Holocaust* (New Haven and London: Yale UP, 1998).

[9] It is indicative, for example, that directly after the television series "Holocaust," the *New German Critique* in 1980 devoted three special issues to "Germans and Jews."

[10] Shoshana Felman and Dori Laub, "Foreword," in *Testimony: Crises of Witnessing in Literature, Psychoanalysis, and History* (New York and London: Routledge, 1992), xix. The argument is elaborated in the same volume in Felman's penetrating article "The Return of the Voice: Claude Lanzmann's *Shoah*" (204–84).

[11] Geoffrey H. Hartman, "Introduction" to the volume he edited on the occasion President Ronald Reagan's visit in 1985 to the military cemetery in Bitburg, *Bitburg in Moral and Political Perspective* (Bloomington: Indiana UP, 1986), 2. The volume is dedicated to "all who have contributed to the Video Archive for Holocaust Testimonies at Yale." In his "Polemical Memoir" Hartman also reflects on his own support of Jewish Studies since the 1980s as "a variant of 'opening of the canon'" (Geoffrey Hartman, "Polemical Memoir," in *A Critic's Journey: Literary Reflections, 1958–1998* [New Haven and London: Yale UP, 1999], xi–xxxi, here xxvii).

[12] For one key text defining this position see Gayatri Chakravorty Spivak, "Can the Subaltern Speak?" in *Marxism and the Interpretation of Culture*, ed. Cary Nelson and Larry Grossberg (Urbana: U of Illinois P, 1988), 271–313.

[13] Peter Demetz, *After the Fires: Recent Writing in the Germanies, Austria, and Switzerland* (San Diego, New York, and London: Harcourt, Brace, Jovanvich, 1986), 30.

[14] Sander L. Gilman, *Inscribing the Other* (Lincoln and London: U of Nebraska P, 1991), 17. An earlier version of this introduction "How and Why Study the Other?" was published in a special issue of the *German Quarterly* on "Germanistik as German Studies: Interdisciplinary Theories and Methods" as "Why and How I Study the German," *German Quarterly* 62.2 (1989): 192–204, with a critical response by Leslie A. Adelson, "Der, die oder das Holocaust? A Response to Sander L. Gilman's Paper," *German Quarterly* 62.2 (1989): 205–9.

[15] Sander L. Gilman, *Inscribing the Other* (Lincoln and London: U of Nebraska P, 1991), 17.

[16] Zohn wrote his dissertation on "Stefan Zweig as Mediator in Modern European Literature" (Ph.D. diss., Harvard University, 1952). See also his *Wiener Juden in der deutschen Literatur: Essays* (Tel-Aviv: Olamenu, 1964), a collection of essays on Arthur Schnitzler, Stefan Zweig, Richard Beer-Hofmann, Peter Altenberg, and Karl Kraus; *Österreichische Juden in der Literatur: Ein bio-bibliographisches Lexikon* (Tel Aviv: Olamenu, 1969); and *". . . ich bin ein Sohn der deutschen Sprache nur . . .": Jüdisches Erbe in der österreichischen Literatur* (Vienna and Munich: Amalthea, 1986).

[17] See Lola Fleck's interview with Harry Zohn in 1993: "Ich habe mir meine Muttersprache nicht vermiesen oder rauben lassen," in *Lebenswege und Lieblingslektüren österreichischer NS-Vertriebener in den USA und Kanada*, ed. Beatrix Müller-Kampel in cooperation with Carla Carnevale (Tübingen: Niemeyer, 2000), 219–54, which also provides an extensive bibliography of Zohn's critical works, translations, and editions.

[18] Hans Mayer, *Outsiders: A Study in Life and Letters*, trans. Denis M. Sweet (Cambridge, MA: MIT P, 1982). German original: *Aussenseiter* (Frankfurt am Main: Suhrkamp, 1975).

[19] Konrad Feilchenfeldt, "Die Wiederentdeckung des 'Juden' in der Neueren deutschen Literaturwissenschaft nach 1945," in *Zeitenwechsel: Germanistische Literaturwissenschaft vor und nach 1945*, ed. Wilfried Barner and Christoph König (Frankfurt am Main: Fischer, 1996), 231–44.

[20] *Juden in der deutschen Literatur: Ein deutsch-israelisches Symposion*, ed. Stéphane Mosès and Albrecht Schöne (Frankfurt am Main: Suhrkamp, 1986).

[21] Vol. 1 issued as *Der Deutschunterricht* 36.4 (1984) and vol. 2 as *Der Deutschunterricht* 37.3 (1985).

[22] See, for example, Claudio Magris, *Weit von wo: Verlorene Welt des Ostjudentums* (Vienna: Europaverlag, 1974); Charlene A. Lea, *Emancipation, Assimilation and Stereotype: The Image of the Jew in German and Austrian Drama, 1800–1850* (Bonn: Bouvier, 1978); Klara Pomeranz Carmely, *Das Identitätsproblem jüdischer Autoren im deutschen Sprachraum: Von der Jahrhundertwende bis zu Hitler* (Königstein/Ts.: Scriptor, 1981); *In den Katakomben: Jüdische Verlage in Deutschland 1933–1938*, ed. Ingrid Belke (Marbach: Marbacher Magazin 25, 1983); Siegbert S. Prawer, *Heine's Jewish Comedy* (Oxford: Clarendon, 1983); *Juden und*

Judentum in der Literatur, ed. Herbert A. Strauss und Christhard Hoffmann (Munich: dtv, 1985).

[23] The proceedings including the discussions were published as *Modernisierung oder Überfremdung? Zur Wirkung deutscher Exilanten in der Germanistik der Aufnahmeländer,* ed. Walter Schmitz (Stuttgart and Weimar: Metzler, 1994). Among the invited scholars were Richard Thieberger, Paul Hoffmann, Hans Reiss, Guy Stern, Egon Schwarz, Friedrich Georg Friedmann, Henry Remak, and Hans Eichner. Three years earlier, in 1988, and on the fortieth anniversary of the "Anschluss," the Österreichische Gesellschaft für Literatur cooperated with Harry Zohn in inviting eleven American Jewish scholars of German literature, who had been forced into emigration from Austria in 1938/39, to a symposium in Vienna. The contributions of the symposium are published in *Leben mit österreichischer Literatur: Begegnung mit aus Österreich stammenden amerikanischen Germanisten 1938/1988,* ed. Dokumentationsstelle für neuere österreichische Literatur and Österreichische Gesellschaft für Literatur, Zirkular, Sondernummer 20, April 1990. The colloquium included the following participants: Wolfgang Kraus, Harry Zohn, Walter A. Sokel, Joseph Fabry, George Wellwarth, Evelyn Torton-Beck, Peter Heller, Carl Steiner, Franz Bäuml, Alfred Hoelzel, Susan E. Cernyak-Spatz, Herbert Lederer, Walter Grossmann, and Egon Schwarz. See also the English translation, *Language and Culture: A Transcending Bond: Essays and Memoirs by American Germanists of Austro-Jewish descent,* ed. Susan E. Cernyak-Spatz and Charles S. Merrill (New York, Berlin, Bern, Frankfurt am Main, Paris, and Vienna: Lang, 1993).

[24] See the treatment, and further references, in Walter Schmitz's "Vorbemerkung," in *Modernisierung oder Überfremdung? Zur Wirkung deutscher Exilanten in der Germanistik der Aufnahmeländer,* ed. Walter Schmitz (Stuttgart, Weimar: Metzler, 1994), vii–xix, here xii. See also Regina Weber, "Zur Remigration des Germanisten Richard Alewyn," in *Die Emigration der Wissenschaften nach 1933: Disziplingeschichtliche Studien,* ed. Herbert A. Strauss, Klaus Fischer, Christhard Hoffmann, and Alfons Söllner (Munich: Saur, 1991), 235–56; Weber, "Der emigrierte Germanist als 'Führer' zur deutschen Dichtung? Werner Vordtriede im Exil," in *Exilforschung: Internationales Jahrbuch,* vol. 13 (Munich: Edition Text und Kritik, 1995), 137–65; Carsten Zelle, "Emigrantengespräch: Ein Brief Richard Alewyns an Karl Viëtor," *Euphorion* 84 (1990): 213–27; Zelle, "Karl Viëtor: Zum Gedächtnis seines 100. Geburtstages," in *Giessener Universitätsblätter,* Dec. 1992, 25–42; Gisela Hoecherl-Alden, "Germanisten im 'Niemandsland': Die exilierten Akademiker und ihre Wirkung auf die amerikanische Germanistik (1933–1955)," (Ph.D. diss. University of Wisconsin-Madison, 1996); and most recently *Lebenswege und Lieblingslektüren österreichischer NS-Vertriebener in den USA und Kanada,* ed. Beatrix Müller-Kampel in cooperation with Carla Carnevale (Tübingen: Niemeyer, 2000), which includes interviews with Walter Sokel, Peter Heller, Herbert Lederer, Hans Eichner, Egon Schwarz, Harry Zohn, Dorrit Cohn, Ruth Klüger, and Evelyn Torton-Beck. See also Meike G. Werner, "Germanistik in the Shadow of the Holocaust. The Changing Profile of the Professoriate, 1942–1970," in *German Studies in the USA: A Historical Handbook,* ed. Peter Uwe Hohendahl et al. (forthcoming).

[25] David Suchoff, "Jüdische Kritik in der amerikanischen Nachkriegsgermanistik," *Weimarer Beiträge* 39.1 (1993): 393–409, here 394.

[26] Erich Heller, *The Disinherited Mind: Essays in Modern German Literature and Thought* (Cambridge: Bowes & Bowes, 1952); Heinz Politzer, *Franz Kafka: Parable and Paradox* (Ithaca, NY: Cornell UP, 1962).

[27] See the review by Thomas Steinfeld, "Gross und klein: Jüdische Germanisten der ersten Stunde in Amerika," in *Frankfurter Allgemeine Zeitung*, Oct. 1, 1997.

[28] The editors would like to thank Hanne Knickmann from the German Literary Archive in Marbach, a member of a collective group of scholars working on an *Internationales Germanistenlexikon,* for her help in procuring information on a number of scholars of German literature. For further information, one may now consult the *Internationales Germanistenlexikon 1800–1950,* ed. Christoph König, in association with Birgit Wägenbaur, and assisted by Andrea Frindt, Hanne Knickmann, Volker Michel, Angelika Reinthal, and Karla Rommel, 3 vols. (Berlin, New York: de Gruyter, 2002). An extended version of the three volumes will be available on CD-ROM.

[29] In addition to Schwarz's autobiography *Keine Zeit für Eichendorff,* published in 1979, see George Steiner, *Errata: An Examined Life* (London: Weidenfeld & Nicholson, 1997); Marcel Reich-Ranicki, *Mein Leben* (Stuttgart: Deutsche Verlags-Anstalt, 1999); and Geoffrey Hartman, "Polemical Memoir," in *A Critic's Journey: Literary Reflections, 1958–1998* (New Haven and London: Yale UP, 1999), xi–xxxi.

[30] Peter Demetz, "On Auschwitz, and On Writing in German: A Letter to a Student," in *After the Fires: Recent Writing in the Germanies, Austria, and Switzerland* (San Diego, New York and London: Harcourt, Brace, Jovanovich, 1986), 18–56. See also Lola Fleck's interview with Dorrit Cohn, "Emigranten, alles Emigranten . . .," in *Lebenswege und Lieblingslektüren österreichischer NS-Vertriebener in den USA und Kanada,* ed. Beatrix Müller-Kampel in cooperation with Carla Carnevale (Tübingen: Niemeyer, 2000), 255–73.

[31] Gotthold Ephraim Lessing, *Nathan der Weise, Vollst. Text Dokumentation,* ed. Peter Demetz (Frankfurt am Main: Ullstein, 1967).

[32] Dorrit Cohn, *The Sleepwalkers: Elucidations of Hermann Broch's Trilogy* (The Hague, Paris: Mouton, 1966).

[33] Egon Schwarz, for example, reflects on this question in his essay "Method and Memoir of the Emigré Scholar: A Viennese Consciousness in the Andes," in *Latin America and the Literature of Exile,* ed. Hans-Bernhard Moeller (Heidelberg: Winter, 1983), 91–96.

[34] In 1999 Christoph König in cooperation with Barbara Hahn and the Marbacher Arbeitskreis für die Erforschung der Geschichte der Germanistik organized a conference on "Jüdische Intellektuelle und die Philologien in Deutschland 1871–1933." The conference proceedings appeared as *Jüdische Intellektuelle und die Philologien in Deutschland 1871–1933,* ed. Wilfried Barner and Christoph König (Göttingen: Wallstein, 2001).

[35] Thomas Sparr, "Zeit der Todesfuge: Rezeption der Lyrik von Nelly Sachs und Paul Celan," in *Deutsche Nachkriegsliteratur und der Holocaust,* ed. Stephan Brae-

se, Holger Gehle, and Hanno Loewy (Frankfurt am Main, New York: Campus, 1998), 43–52.

1: Cultural Poetics

Heinz Politzer on December 31, 1975 in Berkeley

Hinrich C. Seeba and Heinz Politzer,
presentation of the Festschrift *Austriaca*
in December 1975 in Politzer's home in Berkeley

Academic Emigration and Intercultural Criticism: On the Role of Jewish Critics in Exile

Hinrich C. Seeba

PLEASE ALLOW ME TO START MY REMARKS on a personal note: I came to America exactly thirty years ago last week, because of one Jewish critic, Heinz Politzer. He was for me the paragon of a Viennese artist-writer in the tradition of Grillparzer, Nestroy, Karl Kraus, Hofmannsthal, Freud, and Friedrich Torberg. Always guided by Hofmannsthal's somewhat stereotypical juxtaposition of "Preussen und Österreicher," he would help me — the very recent "Dr. phil." from Tübingen, which to him was "jenseits des Limes" if not even "in den masurischen Sümpfen," — distinguish between German "Tüchtigkeit" and Austrian "Menschlichkeit," between German "Abstraktion" and Austrian "Selbstironie."[1] I learned from him, as corny as it may sound, the love of literature, i.e. to look at literature not just in terms of sociological and methodological issues of interpretation, as I had been trained to analyze them, but as a lively process involving a wealth of cultural images and existential experience, as only, so he insisted, a Jewish critic from Vienna could authenticate. While I was in love with California, Heinz Politzer, the typical *Raunzer* in the best Viennese tradition, loved to hate the "verdammte blaue Himmel" because it continued to separate him from his beloved Vienna. The role assigned to me in this uneven friendship, which lasted until his death in 1978, was that of a somewhat suspect German scholar, who eventually advanced to a level of affectionate acceptance because he appeared to adopt some Viennese ways of looking at things, most of all because he started to look at the magic and crisis of language. Thus I learned, metaphorically speaking, *Wienerdeutsch als Fremdsprache* with all its Jewish idiosyncrasies, long before I tried to give papers in the language of my adopted new country — as I am sure you will find out during the next forty-five minutes.

Seen from the distant viewpoint of *Wissenschaftsgeschichte* and its emerging concentration on academic emigration, Jewish critics in the field of German literature are a significant historical phenomenon which certainly needs to be explored historically, i.e. as a generation of Germanists who were driven out of German-speaking countries, who slowly and under great difficulties established themselves in the American academy and, once recognized, shaped the entire field long beyond their retirement, until the so-called successor generation, mostly American-trained and with quite different experiences and expectations, began around 1980 to turn Germanistik into German Studies. As desirable as it may be, such a factual account of what seems to be a bygone era as an "antiquarian" venture in the Nietzschean sense misses an important point. Rather, detached explorations into the mere history of the discipline and into the role Jewish critics from Erich Heller, Oskar Seidlin, Heinz Politzer, Peter Demetz, Walter Sokel to Egon Schwarz played in the eventual divergence of the German and the American brands of literary scholarship, it seems to me, need to be complemented by a more personally involved look into their possible contribution to the current debate on the prospects of German Studies as they are practiced today.

While the study of *Exilliteratur,* begun in the sixties, has inspired quite a number of disciplines, especially in the social sciences,[2] to look into their own history and into the role European exiles played in it, the study of its critical advocates, many of them creative writers themselves and thus closely connected with the practice of *Exilliteratur,* is strikingly absent from recent documents of the emerging public interest.[3] A case in point for this neglect regarding Jewish critics of German literature teaching in American universities is the catalogue for the exhibition (February 23 to May 11, 1997) at the Los Angeles County Museum of Art, *exiles + émigrés: The Flight of European Artists from Hitler.* It presents the exiled artists — painters, musicians, architects, even art historians and, of course, writers such as Thomas and Heinrich Mann, Lion Feuchtwanger and Leonhard Frank — in a larger intellectual context, with references to Hannah Arendt, Reinhard Bendix, Erich Fromm, Leo Lowenthal, Herbert Marcuse and others, but not to any of the leading Jewish critics in German Studies proper.[4] Such obvious oversights certainly call for increased efforts on the part of literary studies to remember and reconsider the lasting contribution of Jewish critics to the American academy. Not the least reason for looking into this question is the surge of conservative cultural criticism claiming, as did Allan Bloom ten years ago, that the perceived demise of American culture can be blamed on "the German connection": "a mix of German refugees from Hitler and of Americans who had either studied in Germany prior to Hitler or who had learned from these émigrés."[5] Obviously Allan Bloom, who after all was the student of an exiled German professor, Leo Strauss, clearly disliked German "professors" of that generation because they infected, he argues, their American students with cultural relativism. Therefore, I will try briefly to sketch the context of the question to which, in my view, another reflection on Jewish critics of German literature between cultures may provide a more positive answer.

These days the concept of *culture* and its terminological derivatives seem to be on everybody's mind, culture with small or capital C as in *New Cultural History,* in terms of *cultural difference* (as a descriptive term for dealing with "otherness"), *minority culture* (as a corrective to national hegemony), *bi-* or *multiculturalism* (as a politically correct philosophy for a new kind of identity formation), *interculturality* (as a methodological principle for decolonized research), and, of course, *cultural studies* (as an institutionalized field of investigation into cultural difference). All of these terms are subsumed under the heading of the historic *cultural turn* each discipline, at least within the humanities, has seemed eager to engage in during the last ten years.

Since Thomas S. Kuhn it has become customary to claim a "paradigm shift" for such turns. Each new critical trend on the horizon has been greeted as a new "paradigm" expected to provide the overriding critical solution to the problems of particular fields of investigation. After a whole array of academic fields have been tested as a possible successor to theology and philosophy in the traditional role as a *scientia princeps* for all scholarship to follow, it is no longer entire disciplines such as sociology, linguistics, psychology and, most recently, anthropology which are celebrated as new paradigms, but, more modestly, only critical approaches as they may relate to limited groups of fields. After a "linguistic turn" was claimed by Richard Rorty for philosophy, W. J. T. Mitchell followed suit by claiming for the humanities a "pictorial turn."[6] While the former, in the tradition of language philosophy, put the focus back on the verbal construction of theoretical discourse, the latter allows also for nonverbal representations of thought. Both of them, however, are devoted to the nonmimetic, i.e. creatively constructive nature of language.

Sprachlichkeit (the principle of the linguistic turn) and *Bildlichkeit* (the principle of the pictorial turn) are, of course, closely related modes

of knowledge and representation which have traditionally been central
to literary studies. They have also been the critical mainstay of Germany's hermeneutic tradition from Herder through Humboldt and
Schleiermacher to Dilthey and Wittgenstein, in which many of the
Jewish critics were raised. According to this tradition language does not
embellish thoughts; instead, it generates them, or as Herder argued in
his dismissal of Kantian epistemology, "Was heißt *Denken? Innerlich
Sprechen*"[7] and "Sprache ist das Kriterium der Vernunft, wie jeder
echten Wissenschaft, so des Verstandes."[8] Herder's notion, stated as
early as in 1768, "Ich rede in Bildern"[9] parallels the fact that language,
especially in its imagistic quality, became topical in the concurrent
treatises on poetics of even nonpoetic genres, for instance in Friedrich
von Blanckenburg's *Versuch über den Roman* (1774): "Auch dann,
wann die Rede von der bloßen Beschreibung einer Wirkung ist, kann
der Dichter nie *bildlich,* nie bestimmt genug seyn. Auch wenn er nur
in Prosa schreibt, ist die erste Forderung an ihn, daß er das Abstrakte
ins Concrete verwandelt; daß er uns das, in einem einzeln Fall zeige,
was er sagen will."[10] To show in images what you want to say in ideas
is, of course, a rhetorical principle generations of aspiring writers and
critics alike had to learn. One would think that in our time literary
criticism, under institutional pressure from more practical — and more
"reality"-prone — fields like business administration and computer
science, would embrace the recent updating of linguistic and imagistic
modes of knowledge and that it would try to incorporate it into the
"cultural turn" which, after all, is only the third in line after the linguistic and the pictorial turns. But literary criticism, as it has been
practiced in the German departments of this country, seems to face a
typical dilemma of a struggle for institutional survival: whereas on the
one hand there may be an implicit need for literary studies, with an
emphasis on philological detail, to provide some guidance in dealing
with the creative process of linguistic and pictorial construction of reality, there has been, on the other hand, the stronger lure of cultural
studies, with an emphasis on generalizing theory, which will expand,
undercut and very likely replace the literary basis of the discipline,
thus — if we don't watch it — eventually eroding the disciplinary
identity of German Studies.[11]

    This dilemma — of retaining the poetics of creative language on
the one hand and aspiring to cultural theory of nonliterary representations on the other — was partly alleviated by a terminological stroke
of genius when in 1988 Stephen Greenblatt called his efforts "poetics
of culture," thus reconciling the literary and the cultural dimensions.

Reading textual traces as signs of cultural practices, Greenblatt has defined cultural poetics as "a study of the collective making of distinct
cultural practices and inquiry into the relation among these practices."[12] The term "negotiations," by now a well-established buzzword
among the growing number of New Historicists, has drawn new attention to the complex relation between sets of collective beliefs and
experiences as they involve literary and non-fictional modes of expression; "negotiation" refers to the process of circulation and exchange
in which art captivates and in turn shapes social energy. By calling the
study of these relations "poetics," Greenblatt has reconfirmed the belief of earlier cultural critics such as Georg Simmel and Ernst Cassirer
in the aesthetic nature of how cultural practices are organized.

New Historicism, named as such not before 1982 and identified
in 1984 as "la scuola di Berkeley,"[13] was greeted and promoted as a
new theoretical paradigm, but it should be remembered that in many
aspects it paralleled the critical practice of German Studies. While, for
instance, in French Studies the tradition of *explication de texte* has
gone unchallenged for a long time, in German Studies close reading
or "werkimmanente Interpretation" — except for a brief period in the
fifties in Germany itself — did not fare so well. For obvious historical
reasons the study of German literature could not be separated for long
from its social, political, and ideological context. The experience of
the Third Reich and the critical observation of its aftermath in postwar
Germany had made it mandatory, especially for Jewish intellectuals
outside of Germany who were most affected by this experience, not to
lose sight of the ideological determinants of literature, not to get lost
again in intrinsic interpretation with little regard for the general cultural context in which literature and its interpretation could be in-
strumentalized to advance ulterior motives.

If the suggestion that New Historicism may have been matched, if
not even been preceded by the practice of sociocultural "negotiations"
in German Studies comes as a surprise, it seems to be even less known
that New Historicism had its predecessor in the similarly committed
school of *New History* which, centered at Columbia University around
1910, dates back to an earlier import from Germany.[14] The fact that it
later evolved into the New School of Social Research which, founded
in 1919, was to become a haven for a whole generation of Jewish exiles in sociocultural studies made the school of New History a historic
moment in academic transfer.

The leading spokesman of New History, James Harvey Robinson,
who later served also as the first director of the New School, wanted

the study of history to reflect the social and cultural process in which
it was involved.[15] He was inspired by Karl Lamprecht, the controversial cultural historian at the University of Leipzig, who with his materialist approach to history emphasized the sociocultural definition of
historical events as well as the creative process involved in their histo-
riographic recording. Thus Lamprecht gave an early testimony to what
can now be termed cultural poetics.[16] Soon after the very name of the
critical school of historians was anticipated in 1898 when the journal
American Historical Review published a review (by Earle Dow) of
Lamprecht's comprehensive *Deutsche Geschichte* (from 1891 in twelve
volumes) under the title "Features of the New History," Robinson
started corresponding with Lamprecht in 1901 and invited him to
Columbia University in 1904 where Lamprecht was awarded an honorary degree. Some of the central ideas of New History, as extolled in
1926 in a famous speech by Carl Becker (another New Historian, at
Cornell University), "What Are Historical Facts?," seem to be taken
directly from Ernst Cassirer's *Philosophie der symbolischen Formen*
(1923/25/29): "The historical fact is not the past event, but a symbol which enables us to recreate it imaginatively."[17] If history is the
symbolic re-creation of what we imagine has happened, even its material underpinnings become fictionalized in historical discourse, comparable to the structure of literary fiction. While Hayden White, who in
our time is credited with the notion of history as a literary artifact,[18]
does not even allude to Carl Becker, he mentions Cassirer only briefly
in terms of Foucault's professed "affinity for the thought of the late
Ernst Cassirer"[19] without realizing the resemblance of his own
thoughts on metahistory to Cassirer's. Evoking both *Sprachlichkeit*
and *Bildlichkeit,* Cassirer's term "symbolic form" indicates imaginative
systems of signification as they are explored in literary criticism as well
as in philosophy or sociology. Cassirer, who after serving as the first
Jewish chancellor of a German university (in Hamburg 1929/30) was
eventually exiled to the United States, teaching first at Yale (1941–
1944) and then, until his death in 1945, at Columbia, is but one early
example in cultural poetics for many important, yet gravely neglected
strands of cultural transfer.

Two more examples may illustrate the philosophical and institutional network for cultural transfer in academic emigration: First,
Lamprecht's most influential student, Aby Warburg, founded in
Hamburg, where he had been a friend of Cassirer's since 1923, the
famous *Kulturwissenschaftliche Bibliothek,* the first of its kind, which
was moved into exile in 1933 to become the Warburg Institute in

London (whose long-time director Ernst Gombrich was an exile from Vienna).[20] The criteria used for the research and publications in the Warburg Library include the following: "Konkrete Arbeit am Detail; philologische Präzision; weitgehende Ablehnung geistesgeschichtlicher Gemeinplätze; Überschreitung von Fachgrenzen, wo immer das jeweilige Problem es erforderte; gleichberechtigte Einbeziehung von Bildern und Texten, wenn es sich als sinnvoll erwies, besonderes Augenmerk auf das diachrone Verfolgen vorgeprägter Ausdrucksformen wie Symbolen, Stereotypen und Denkmotiven."[21] These criteria perfectly describe the approach to cultural poetics as practiced later by Jewish critics in exile. Most clearly, Erwin Panofsky, who as lecturer at the University of Hamburg since 1920 was affiliated with the Warburg Library, followed Cassirer's attention to the symbols of cultural history when he wrote his early theoretical work "Perspektive als 'symbolische Form'" (1924)[22] and developed the iconological method which still guides much of contemporary American research in art history.[23] Second, the American ambassador in Berlin from 1933 to 1938, when most of the emigration of Jewish scholars was arranged, was William E. Dodd, a member of the New History school, who in 1903 had written a seminal article pleading for "Karl Lamprecht and Kulturgeschichte," paving the way for a kind of sociocultural criticism whose future was in the United States rather than in Germany. Calling Lamprecht, who had encountered much hostility among his German colleagues, "our new historian," Dodd was rightly convinced "that the ideas advanced by the new school of German historians find a more general acceptance in our country than in any other."[24] While the ambassador Dodd could probably do little to help those escape who were no longer accepted in Germany, Erwin Panofsky, Ernst Cassirer, Rudolf Arnheim, Siegfried Kracauer, Hannah Arendt, Günther Anders are but a few names of exiled Jewish intellectuals who benefited from his early gesture of welcome in the name of encompassing cultural studies.

It is against this spotty background of academic transfer in general that the role of exiled Jewish critics of German literature in particular can be better understood. It is in this context that the original question can be rephrased to which their contribution to the study of German literature provides a possible answer: How can the field of German Studies — as it probably should — continue to expand its field of investigation into nonliterary and even nonverbal modes of representation and, at the same time, make full use of its germane expertise in the fictional construction of reality?

The hypothetical answer to the question points to Jewish critics who, like Heinz Politzer in Berkeley, emphatically refused to be called scholars in the strict German sense of *Literaturwissenschaft* and who, instead, championed a creative criticism based on artistic sensitivity and stylistic flair against the ever-present background of their own existential crisis. Typically, when leaving his office to teach his class Heinz Politzer would say: "Ich geh jetzt singen," as if he were going to perform on a stage, acting out the role of the mythical figure of all poetry, Orpheus, who with his powerful singing could enchant animals, plants, and even stones.[25] But the redemptive power of singing was characteristically offset by its perilous counterpart, silence. For the author of *Das Schweigen der Sirenen,* the programmatic title of his collected essays (1968), one of the most compelling lines in German literature was that about a singing siren who would lure mariners to eventually destructive fascination: "Und das hat mit ihrem Singen / die Lore-Ley getan."[26] For Politzer the first lines of Heine's poem, "Ich weiß nicht, was soll es bedeuten," mark, as we would say today and as Politzer would never have said it, the deconstruction of the Jewish subject: "Damit deutet der deutsche Jude Heinrich Heine seine Stellung in der Gesellschaft seiner Zeit aufs schlagendste an. Das Ich versucht, sich sichtbar zu etablieren, vermag aber, was es eingeleitet hat, nicht im Gleichgewicht zu erhalten und wird von der Unordnung, die entstanden ist, leicht in seiner führenden Rolle diskreditiert. Ein Dichter, der 'Ich weiß nicht' singt, singt nicht mehr. Er vermag lediglich zu referieren und zu rezensieren."[27] Uncertain of himself and the meaning he can still project, the first-person narrator of the poem becomes a mirror image uniting Heine, the exile in Paris, and Politzer, the exile in Berkeley. But even if the song of Jewish critics was discredited, believable only in its ironic expression of imbalance and turmoil, the teacher's commitment to metaphorical singing could still evoke the utopian power it once commanded. Mourning the modern lure of silence, Heinz Politzer never ceased to believe, in spite of the ironic twist Heine gave it, in the "gewaltige Melodei" of his own verbal gestures, however disguised they were as critical remarks on Heine: "Schon für Heine schwiegen die Sirenen. Er hörte ihren Gesang nicht mehr, er sah ihn bloß in der Gebärde, die ihn begleitete, und beschrieb, was er sah. Sein artistischer Triumph besteht darin, daß er diesem Schweigen eine Melodie abgewann, die als Melodei zu hohem, aber mißverständlichem Ruhm gelangte."[28] Obviously, the commitment to singing is an artistic triumph, also over those who had tried so hard to silence the Jewish voice — by excluding the critics from the university, by chasing them out of their country, and by ignoring their contribution to the German language.

The experience of exile had only intensified the struggle for a Jewish voice. In most of the exiles' writings there is a striking stylistic as well as intellectual brilliance that in the German university system used to be dismissed as "journalistisch." Following Heinrich Heine and Karl Kraus rather than the wooden paragons of Germanistik at the University of Berlin — Wilhelm Scherer, Erich Schmidt, and Gustav Roethe — Jewish critics like Heinz Politzer wrote literary essays and not scholarly tracts, both expounding and employing the creative, even seductive power of language. For in many cases, with Heinz Politzer and Bernhard Blume being the better known examples, they had long been creative writers of poetry, dramas, and feuilletons, fully participating in the "pictorial" paradigm, before the circumstances forced them to join the "linguistic" paradigm and teach German as a foreign language. Most of them came from outside the university, still too young to boast academic credentials when they were forced out of Germany. But even those who had a chance to succeed as up and coming professors were judged by a stylistic standard so common in German universities that those engaging in displays of intellectual esprit were deemed journalistic and thus unfit for the serious business of German scholarship.

When Friedrich Gundolf, a great stylist and one of the very few Jewish Germanists with a successful academic career within the German university system, was considered for a professorship in Berlin in 1920, Gustav Roethe prevented an offer to him by blaming Gundolf (whom he consistently called by his earlier Jewish name Gundelfinger) for being "mehr eine künstlerische als eine wissenschaftliche Natur."[29] Such labeling, of course, has been common to anti-Semitic stereotyping, especially when it comes to the *Feuilleton*, which was generally perceived as a particularly Jewish genre. In his scathing indictment of the "Einbruch des Judentums"[30] into German literature Heinrich von Treitschke called Heine, the paragon of what Karl Kraus later termed "Impressionsjournalistik,"[31] "geistreich ohne Tiefe, witzig ohne Überzeugung."[32] If *Geist* and *Witz* are constructed as the opposites of German *Tiefe*, it becomes easy to call everyone engaged in *esprit* un-German. Along the line of Hitler's charge that the Jewish artist's "Mätzchen und Tricks" cannot cover up his lack of authentic creativity,[33] Alfred Rosenberg, too, found in Jewish art nothing but "Talmi, Technik, Mache, Effekt, Quantität, Virtuosität, alles was man will, nur keine Genialität, keine Schöpferkraft."[34] Intellectual brilliance and artistic virtuosity were cue words with clearly negative connotations that were often used to indict Jewish writers. Therefore, it is quite interesting to see that only now, in German responses to recent attempts at least to remember the role of Jewish critics in the discipline, a certain sense of loss is emerging. To give only the latest example, in the July 1997 *Mitteilungen* of the "Marbacher Arbeitskreis für Geschichte der Germanistik" a book review includes the following statement: "Die Immigranten versuchten, die deutsche Literatur in die Weltliteratur zu integrieren — dadurch gewann ihre Disziplin viel Weitläufigkeit, und in den Essays von Heinz Politzer, Bernhard Blume, Erich Heller (sowie den in dem Band vertretenen Kollegen) einen intellektuellen Glanz, von dem man hierzulande nur träumen kann."[35] The old labeling "intellektueller Glanz" is so painfully acute, even in its positive revaluation, that the fact that most of these exiled stylists were Jews is not mentioned even once. In any case, the belated dream of a brilliance forever lost will likely grow even bigger in view of the demise of intellectual sophistication and stylistic finesse in Germany's public discourse today.

The underlying question of whether a brilliant style appropriate for the *Feuilleton* rather than for a *wissenschaftliche Abhandlung* is a particularly Jewish characteristic, which in Germany may only now be missed as an awkward asset, is a puzzling one, because it just may resemble the essentialist position of racist aesthetics. Historical reasons, however, for a special sensitivity to language among assimilated Jews seem rather obvious. For one, dedication to the German language was the price of emancipation in the early nineteenth century; the Prussian *Emanzipations-Edikt* of 1812 allowed Jews to become "Einländer und Staatsbürger" only on the condition that they renounce their Jewish names, the use of Yiddish, and Hebrew script.[36] Following Moses Mendelssohn, aspiring Jewish writers defied the anti-Semitic speech stereotyping of "mauscheln" or "jüdeln"[37] and toiled to meet and, in most cases, surpass the standards of grammatical correctness and stylistic elegance.

But there is still another side to the special affinity of Jewish critics to the concepts of *Sprachlichkeit* and *Bildlichkeit*. A disproportionate number of them came from Austria (and its former territories) rather than from a strictly German background — for the simple reason that they had five more years, until 1938, to prepare for an academic and/or artistic career before they, too, were forced to leave. Among the better known exiled critics there appear to be more Austrians than Germans: Erich von Kahler (born in 1885, in Prague, but moving to

Vienna in 1900); Leo Spitzer (1887 in Vienna), Marianne Thalmann (1888 in Linz, Professor in Vienna 1932/33). Franz H. Mautner (1902 in Vienna), Heinz Politzer (1910 in Vienna), Walter Naumann (1910 in Aussig), Erich Heller (1911 in Komotau, Bohemia), Walter H. Sokel (1917 in Vienna), Peter Heller (1920 in Vienna), Hans Eichner (1921 in Vienna), Egon Schwarz (1922 in Vienna), Harry Zohn (1923 in Vienna) and Dorrit Cohn (1924 in Vienna). Compare this large contingent from Vienna with the better known Germanists from Germany: Richard Alewyn (1902 in Frankfurt am Main), Wolfgang Paulsen (1910 in Düsseldorf), Oskar Seidlin (1911 in Königshütte, Upper Silesia), Hans M. Wolff (1912 in Berlin), Henry Remak (1916 in Berlin), Guy Stern (1922 in Hildesheim). Even if we add to the German side the non-Jews Karl Viëtor (1892 in Wattenscheid), Bernhard Blume (1901 in Stuttgart), and Victor Lange (1908 in Leipzig), the predominance of the Viennese perspective (with nine names) over any possible Berlin perspective (with only two names) is so striking that we may find in this asymmetry also a demographic reason for the fact that the Austrians' poetic *Bildlichkeit,* to modify Hofmannsthal's contrastive terms with Grillparzer's similar idiosyncrasies,[38] won out over the Germans' philosophical *Begrifflichkeit.* What Leo Spitzer called the German universities' "Fixfingrigkeit im Spekulativen, die bedenkenlose Taschenspielerkunst, mit der geistige Augenblicksgebäude in der Luft errichtet werden konnten," was now contrasted with the Austrian precision of "iconological" observation, "Scharfe der Kontur, klare Fassung der geistigen Sachverhalte, Beweis des Beweisbaren" based on "eine mehr kosmopolitische Dimension" of comparative cultural studies.[39] Sensitive to both the connotative nature of even critical language and the danger of ideological appropriation of half-baked ideas and cloudy rhetoric, these Jewish critics insisted most of all on idiomatic accuracy, thriving on the logic of a well-crafted argument and precise metaphors which would allow more abstraction than a convoluted theoretical statement. The "präzise, liedhaft schlichte Formeln," which Klaus Mann liked so much about Politzer's early poetic renderings of the "Emigrationsluft" among Jewish intellectuals in Prague,[40] would become the model also for Politzer's later critical writings. Like Karl Kraus and Heinrich Heine, he and other Jewish writers were relentless critics of style, without much tolerance for pretense and lack of precision.

But, as the editors of the *Festschrift* for Oskar Seidlin pointed out, such scrutiny was not just a joyride of vicious schoolmasters; it was based on their painful existential experience of a language in danger of being lost — either to the Nazi propaganda or to their own linguistic alienation in the transition from one culture to the other:

> Wer ins Exil gestoßen wird, nimmt seine Sprache mit sich und oft genug nichts als die Sprache. Sie bewahrend, rettet er seine Identität. Sie vermag Heimat nicht zu ersetzen, aber sie repräsentiert sie. Aus den Werken der Dichter klingt ihre Stimme; der Emigrant mag sie als Zuspruch und Tröstung, aber auch als Einspruch gegen seine Vertreibung, als Zustimmung und als Gegenstimme hören. Daran *muß* er sich halten, will er bleiben, der er ist. Aus solcher Erfahrung erwächst dann wohl auch ein auf die Sprache, aber nicht nur auf sie bezogener *Konservativismus*. Er kann, wenn die Trennung vom Lebensbereich des gesprochenen Wortes zu lange währt, antiquarische Formen annehmen; er kann aber auch, wie bei Oskar Seidlin und wie bei Paul Celan, eine besondere Wachheit, ja Überwachheit gegenüber den Bedeutungen und Klängen, besonders gegenüber den falschen Klängen der Worte gewinnen, wenn von der fremden Sprache her die eigene neu wahrgenommen wird.[41]

As the only remaining link between the old and the new world the German language — and the commitment to its untainted preservation — takes on even more significance than it already had in the Austrian context where it was constantly challenged by the increasing demands of a multiethnic and multilingual society. A conscious and responsible handling of the German language became central to forming a new identity between cultures, with the endangered language serving as a fragile vessel of a cultural tradition which had been misappropriated by Germans speaking and, worse, acting in the name of that very language. This dilemma was most compellingly addressed by Ernst Bloch in a famous article published in 1939 in the exile journal *Direction:* "Now as for the German language, it is threatened, together with its culture-world, with a two-fold danger: suffocating inside Nazi Germany, freezing to death outside Germany."[42] Bloch saw the only solution to the dilemma in embracing the critical creativity of linguistic alienation: "Our language-world encounters the explicit and, in many directions, still implicit *otherness* of a young continent."[43] Anticipating a cue word of current theory, Bloch seems to be saying that accepting one's own alterity in the otherness of one's own language is the only therapy for the pain of living as an outsider.

Obviously, the experience of cultural displacement has further sharpened the linguistic sensitivity of Jewish critics in exile and both forced and helped them to practice cultural poetics by combining literary analysis and cultural criticism in an interdisciplinary spectrum that was to become one of the ambitions of German Studies. Devoted to the preservation and cultivation of good style, referring to "language" both literally and metaphorically, they embraced the "cultural" paradigm and looked at the entire German culture, including philosophy (Adorno), psychoanalysis (Freud), political theory (Hannah Arendt), art history (Erwin Panofsky), architecture (Walter Gropius), music (Kurt Weill), and film (Fritz Lang) to establish literature as another much desired but not necessarily privileged antidote to the rampant fascism in Germany.

But while the very term "interdisciplinarity" is a theoretical principle to define a common purpose in the increasingly departmentalized university today, most of the Jewish critics, usually rather skeptical of and uncomfortable with theory, practiced, and often performed with a flair now almost entirely lost, cultural poetics among the disciplines and across departmental lines. Without calling their critical performance "interdisciplinary," they often worked in close contact with other exiles who, too, in their own fields tried to come to terms with the big question of which aspects of German culture could be blamed for not preventing, and for possibly even leading to, fascism and which aspects should be preserved as unblemished highlights. Sharing a similar educational background and the horrors of persecution and the frustrations of living in exile, these Jewish intellectuals formed a community that proved stronger than the disciplinary restrictions of their respective fields. Even after most of them have passed on, there is a generally accepted sense of shared memory which connected, if I may use Berkeley again as a typical example, the Germanists Hans M. Wolff and his successor Heinz Politzer, the Romanists Leonardo Olschki and Yakov Malkiel, the classicist Thomas Rosenmeyer, the art historian Peter Selz, the sociologists Hans Rosenberg, Leo Lowenthal, and Reinhard Bendix, the lawyers Hans Kelsen, Stephan Kuttner, and Richard Buxbaum as well as the publisher in the University of California Press Max Knight. The explicit and implicit interaction of these scholars across disciplinary boundaries accounts in part for the wider and eventually comparative perspective the exiled historian Hajo Holborn has emphasized: "Meine Verwandlung in einen Amerikaner hat mir für alle deutschen Dinge eine weitere Perspektive verliehen. Viele politische und geistige Fragen, über die Deutsche gern streiten, verlieren an Bedeutung, wenn man sie aus der Ferne betrachtet. Aber noch wichtiger war meine zunehmende Neigung, historische Phänomene auf einer vergleichenden Ebene zu beurteilen."[44] Thus the comparative impetus connects the interdisciplinary and the intercultural perspectives: Jewish critics in exile were not just Germanists, but cultural critics of *Weltliteratur* dabbling in several academic disciplines; and they were no longer just Germans (or Austrians), but Americanized Europeans who engaged in cultural criticism from an expressed and reflected-on subject position between the cultures which would have been ill-received in the German academy with its national orientation and its frustrated ideal of scientific objectivity.

The social and academic interaction of exiles, as a living example of groundbreaking interdisciplinary collaboration, merit the kind of historical scrutiny which Paul Rabinow had in mind when he called for an anthropology of academic politics, i.e. an "ethnography of doctoral examinations, tenure meetings, ad hoc committees, and a long list of other such institutionalized practices."[45] The impact of German-speaking exiles, I feel, deserves special attention if it ever comes to such anthropology of academic politics. Reflecting the demands of their own practice of cultural poetics, the Jewish critics who taught in major German departments in the United States, developed new standards of academic excellence, as they could be traced in personnel decisions and other forms of academic politics, standards which certainly cannot be dismissed as irrelevant to the recent history of German Studies.

Incidentally, only a few months after Heinz Politzer died in July, 1978, the cornerstone for Berkeley's Interdisciplinary Summer Seminar in German Studies, held annually since 1979 and the first of its kind to mark the cultural turn, was laid at the MLA Convention in New York. This DAAD-sponsored seminar set up the institutional framework for our efforts to open up the field of literary study by questioning the textual and visual base of cultural change in Germany, be it in national identity formation in the nineteenth century, new cultural paradigms of the Weimar Republic, the ideology of the Third Reich, the postwar reconstruction, or the confrontation with the Nazi past in both West and East Germany. These studies in change were based on the close reading of texts and images involved in the symbolic construction of reality and thus not a far cry from literary analysis. In fact, it was authentic subjectivity coupled with the attention to rhetorical detail and a distinct sensitivity to linguistic difference that my generation had learned from exiles like Heinz Politzer. Their acute awareness of the outsider's position, as Egon Schwarz has pointed out, favors an implicitly autobiographical approach,[46] which, in contrast to traditional Germanistik, takes into account the fundamental perspectivism of knowledge. The experience of the otherness of language and the concept of positionality gleaned from the crisis and chances of intercultural identity proved instrumental in the development of the kind of cultural criticism that has been at the center of German Studies. Yet, recent studies in the history of German Studies have paid little attention, if any, to the decisive role of Jewish critics in our discipline.[47]

For obvious reasons which have to do with the biological clock, *Wissenschaftsgeschichte* of scholarship in exile so far seems to be more concerned with securing a biographical record of exiled individuals rather than with the structure of their academic socialization and their institutionalized impact on the academy — and even less with the theoretical paradigm which could be gathered from this impact. Following the model of bio-bibliographical accounts in earlier studies of *Exilliteratur,* e.g. the volumes on California in John Spalek's *Deutsche Exilliteratur seit 1933* (1976),[48] materials on exiled scholars have been collected and made accessible, e.g. at the Deutsches Literaturarchiv in Marbach, with the papers of Eduard Berend, Erich von Kahler, Siegfried Kracauer, Käte Hamburger, Bernhard Blume, Richard Alewyn, Adolf Klarmann, Hannah Arendt, Heinz Politzer, and others.[49] A series of colloquia and conferences have heeded the call of the exiled writer Hans Sahl, "Fragt uns aus,"[50] and provided a German forum for a number of Germanists in exile like Richard Thieberger, Paul Hoffmann, Hans Reiss, Guy Stern, Egon Schwarz, Henry Remak, and Hans Eichner to tell their own story as it relates "Zur Wirkung deutscher Exilanten in der Germanistik der Aufnahmeländer."[51] But whereas the role of exiled Jewish intellectuals in the social sciences has been studied rather extensively and more systematically, there is still a lot to be done for German Studies.

Future research will probably deal with some of the following questions, which are raised here to indicate the direction in which an answer to the main question of my remarks may be found: How — and, most of all, based on which arguments — were the careers of exiled Germanists furthered or blocked? How were they, most of them Jews, forced once again, now in the American academy, to confront anti-Semitism in their host departments? And how did they assume the institutional power to effectively change the field of German Studies as a cultural project designed to hold up against the Nazi horrors the canonized memory of classical German culture in the name of Lessing, Goethe, Heine, and Thomas Mann and the enlightened humanism they championed? Using which criteria did these exiled scholars agree on the canon of literary masterworks; and how did they see these works interacting with other forms of art and other media of verbal and visual representation? What kind of methodological paradigm did they develop to combine intrinsic literary analysis with the cultural mission to which they were committed as victims of totalitarianism and racism? Which channels of communication did they utilize to cross and transform the boundaries between departments and disciplines?

In asking these and many more such questions students of cultural theory will look beyond the collection and review of largely biographical and often anecdotal data that can be found in individual exiles' correspondence and autobiographies, e.g. Bernhard Blume's *Narziß mit Brille: Kapitel einer Autobiographie* (1985), which was characteristically translated as *A Life in Two Worlds: An Experiment in Autobiography* (1992).[52] The editors of the German original, Fritz Martini and Egon Schwarz, have indeed concentrated on the personal experiment of living in two cultures and purposefully excluded all of Blume's references to the academic experience because "they would hardly interest a large circle of readers."[53] Whereas the material base for historical investigations may prove to be very limited, those committed to cultural theory may agree with Friedrich Schlegel, who, referring to Winckelmann's art historical project, stated that the best theory of a discipline may very well be its own history.[54] With an eye toward such historical legitimation of a theoretical project, advocates of German Studies may want to look for indications, however implicit, of disciplinary concepts emerging from the intercultural experience of exiled Germanists and other cultural critics; thus they may be able to shed some light on both the theoretical framework and the institutional conditions under which interdisciplinary studies became a course of personal survival.

By way of conclusion, I would like briefly to address the concern of some observers that, as any disciplinary history is rewritten to fit a contemporary agenda, the influence of Jewish literary critics in America's German departments, too, may have been exaggerated. To find out to what extent departmental, university, and professional policies were affected by their input, the pertinent documents have to be collected and analyzed, as it is being done in the case of Heinz Politzer by Walter Schmitz in Dresden, for the kind of anthropology of academic politics Paul Rabinow proposed. But if such concern seems warranted by a statement in Bernhard Blume's memoirs that there was hardly any impact to speak of by exiled Germanists,[55] it should be remembered that Blume was talking only about those refugees who —

like Karl Viëtor, Melitta Gerhard, Martin Sommerfeld, Richard Alewyn, Wolfgang Liepe, and Werner Richter — already held university positions in Germany and who, with the exception of the non-Jew Viëtor, did not find comparable teaching positions at American universities. Aside from the fact that Alewyn, Liepe, and Richter returned to German universities after the war, with Alewyn even transforming his American experience in cultural poetics into a Summer School of German Studies he instituted at the University of Cologne,[56] it is important not to forget that most of the Jewish critics, especially the large circle of Austrians, did not spend their formative years in the pursuit of *Literaturwissenschaft* in the German sense but as creative writers who would significantly broaden the notion of scholarship to include interdisciplinary approaches and intercultural perspectives and thus forever change the discipline. If German Studies, as it probably should, continues to expand the field of investigation into nonliterary and even nonverbal modes of representation, it should, at the same time, fully employ its singular expertise in what Cassirer called the symbolic construction of reality; it should remember that the Jewish critics' practice of cultural poetics emerged from their literary sensitivity and that the principles of *Sprachlichkeit* and *Bildlichkeit* gave their cultural turn the specific edge of authenticity. For the constitution of the Jewish subject, as in Heinz Politzer's interpretation of Heine's poem, is always coupled with an existential uncertainty, if not crisis, that has become the hallmark of modernity. This may account for the *Bescheidenheit* which Egon Schwarz so much admired in Bernhard Blume,[57] and the *Takt* which Heinz Politzer placed at the center of literary criticism,[58] two personal qualities for which, if I may also end on a personal note, we are as much indebted to this generation of Jewish critics as for their insistence on linguistic sensitivity.

Notes

[1] Hugo von Hofmannsthal, "Preussen und Österreicher: Ein Schema," *Gesammelte Werke in Einzelausgaben, Prosa III,* ed. Herbert Steiner (Frankfurt am Main: Fischer, 1952), 407–9.

[2] Cf. *Exil — Wissenschaft — Identität: Die Emigration deutscher Sozialwissenschaftler 1933–1945,* ed. Ilja Srubar (Frankfurt am Main: Suhrkamp, 1988); *An Interrupted Past: German Speaking Refugee Historians in the United States after 1933,* ed. Hartmut Lehmann and James J. Sheehan (Washington, D.C.: German Historical Institute, and Cambridge: Cambridge UP, 1991); and, concentrating

on the Frankfurt School, Martin Jay, *Permanent Exiles: Essays on the Intellectual Migration from Germany to America* (New York: Columbia UP, 1986).

[3] This coincides with the earlier notion that the experience of exiled German writers and critics is hardly ever represented in American literature; cf. Guy Stern, "Das Exil und die amerikanische Gegenwartsliteratur," in *Literatur im Exil: Gesammelte Aufsätze 1959–1989* (Ismaning: Hueber, 1989), 393–402.

[4] Stephanie Barron, ed., *exiles + émigrés: The Flight of European Artists from Hitler* (Los Angeles: Los Angeles County Museum of Art, 1997).

[5] Allan Bloom, *The Closing of the American Mind* (New York: Simon & Schuster, 1987), 141–56 ("The German Connection"), here 148. Cf. Egon Schwarz, "Die Exilanten und die heutige amerikanische Universität," *Modernisierung oder Überfremdung: Zur Wirkung deutscher Exilanten in der Germanistik der Aufnahmeländer,* ed. Walter Schmitz (Stuttgart, Weimar: Metzler, 1994), 119–29, who called Bloom's attack "Teil einer breit angelegten Kampagne gegen eine humanistische, liberale, pluralistische und kosmopolitische Weltanschauung an den amerikanischen Universitäten, wohin sie sich geflüchtet hat, seit sie, einst eine Großmacht im öffentlichen Leben des Landes, zu einer kläglichen Minderheit zusammengeschrumpft ist" (127).

[6] After announcing "the pictorial turn" in an article ("The Pictorial Turn," *Artforum International,* 30 March 1992), W. J. T. Mitchell elaborated on it in his recent book *Picture Theory* (Chicago and London: U of Chicago P, 1994): "Whatever the pictorial turn is, then, it should be clear that it is not a return to naive mimesis, copy or correspondence theories of representation, or a renewed metaphysics of pictorial 'presence': it is rather a postlinguistic, postsemiotic rediscovery of the picture as a complex interplay between visuality, apparatus, institutions, discourse, bodies, and figurality. . . . The current revival of interest in Panofsky is surely a symptom of the pictorial turn" (16).

[7] Johann Gottfried Herder, "Aus 'Verstand und Erfahrung': Eine Metakritik zur Kritik der reinen Vernunft (1799)," in *Sprachphilosophie: Ausgewählte Schriften,* ed. Erich Heintel (Hamburg: Felix Meiner, 1980), 181–227, 189. Cf. Hinrich C. Seeba, "Word and Thought: Herder's Language Model in Modern Hermeneutics," in *Johann Gottfried Herder: Innovator Through the Ages,* ed. Wulf Koepke in cooperation with Samson B. Knoll (Bonn: Bouvier Verlag, 1982), 35–40; and "Geschichte als Dichtung: Herders Beitrag zur Ästhetisierung der Geschichtsschreibung," *Storia della Storiografia. Rivista Internazionale* 8 (1985): 50–72.

[8] Herder, "Aus 'Verstand und Erfahrung,'" 227.

[9] Johann Gottfried Herder, "Über Thomas Abbts Schriften: Der Torso von einem Denkmaal, an seinem Grabe errichtet [1768]," in *Sämtliche Werke,* ed. Bernhard Suphan, vol. 2 (Berlin 1877; reprint, Hildesheim: Olms, 1967), 249–94, 265.

[10] Friedrich von Blanckenburg, *Versuch über den Roman,* Faksimiledruck der Originalausgabe von 1774, mit einem Nachwort von Eberhard Lämmert (Stuttgart: Metzler, 1965), 498.

[11] Cf. Hinrich C. Seeba, "Cultural versus Linguistic Competence? Bilingualism, Language in Exile and the Future of German Studies," *German Quarterly* 69.4 (Fall 1996): 401–13.

[12] Stephen Greenblatt, *Shakespearean Negotiations: The Circulation of Social Energy in Renaissance England* (Berkeley and Los Angeles: U of California P, 1988), 5.

[13] Remo Cesarini, "Nuove strategie rappresentative: La scuola di Berkeley," *Belfagor* 39 (November 1984): 665–85.

[14] On the following cf. Hinrich C. Seeba, "New Historicism und Kulturanthropologie: Ansätze eines deutsch-amerikanischen Dialogs," in *Historismus am Ende des 20. Jahrhunderts: Eine internationale Diskussion,* ed. Gunter Scholtz (Berlin: Akademie-Verlag, 1997), 40–54.

[15] Cf. James Harvey Robinson, *The New History: Essays Illustrating the Modern Historical Outlook* (1912; New York: Macmillan, 1922), 25: "The title of this little volume has been chosen with the view of emphasizing the fact that history should not be regarded as a stationary subject which can only progress by refining its methods and accumulating, criticizing, and assimilating new material, but that it is bound to alter its ideals and aims with the general progress of society and of the social sciences, and that it should ultimately play an infinitely more important rôle in our intellectual life than it has hitherto done."

[16] Cf. Karl Lamprecht, "Was ist Kulturgeschichte? Beitrag zu einer empirischen Historik [1896]," in *Alternative zu Ranke: Schriften zur Geschichtstheorie* (Leipzig: Reclam, 1988), 213–72. Cf. Hinrich C. Seeba, "Interkulturelle Perspektiven: Ansätze einer vergleichenden Kulturkritik bei Karl Lamprecht und in der Exil-Germanistik," *German Studies Review* 16 (1993): 1–17.

[17] Carl Becker, "What Are Historical Facts? [1926]," in *Detachment and the Writing of History: Essays and Letters of Carl L. Becker,* ed. Phil L. Snyder (Ithaca, NY: Cornell UP, 1958), 41–64, 47.

[18] Cf. Hayden White, "The Historical Text as Literary Artifact," in *The Writing of History: Literary Form and Historical Understanding,* ed. Robert H. Canary and Henry Kozicki (Madison and London: U of Wisconsin P, 1978), 41–62; also in: Hayden White, *Tropics of Discourse: Essays in Cultural Criticism* (Baltimore and London: Johns Hopkins UP, 1978), 81–100, and Hayden White, *Metahistory: The Historical Imagination in Nineteenth-Century Europe* (Baltimore and London: Johns Hopkins UP, 1973).

[19] Hayden White, "Foucault Decoded: Notes from Underground," in *Tropics of Discourse: Essays in Cultural Criticism* (Baltimore and London: Johns Hopkins UP, 1978), 230–60, 233.

[20] Cf. Dieter Wuttke, "Die Emigration der Kulturwissenschaftlichen Bibliothek Warburg und die Anfänge des Universitätsfaches Kunstgeschichte in Großbritannien," in *Aby Warburg: Akten des internationalen Symposiums Hamburg 1990,* ed. Horst Bredekamp, Michael Diers, Charlotte Schoell-Glass (Weinheim: VCH, Acta Humaniora, 1991).

[21] Heinz Paetzoldt, *Ernst Cassirer: Von Marburg nach New York — Eine philosophische Biographie* (Darmstadt: Wissenschaftliche Buchgesellschaft, 1995), 74.

[22] Erwin Panofsky, "Perspektive als 'symbolische Form,'" in *Vorträge der Bibliothek Warburg* (Leipzig and Berlin, 1927), 258–330; English version: Erwin Panofsky, *Perspective as Symbolic Form,* trans. Christopher S. Wood (Cambridge: MIT P, 1991).

[23] Erwin Panofsky, *Meaning in the Visual Arts: Papers in and on Art History* (Garden City, N.Y.: Doubleday Anchor Books, 1955), 31. Cf. Kevin Parker, Richard Krautheimer, and Erwin Panofsky, in *exiles + emigrés: The Flight of European Artists from Hitler,* ed. Stephanie Barron (Los Angeles: Los Angeles County Museum of Art, 1997), 317–25.

[24] William E. Dodd, "Karl Lamprecht and Kulturgeschichte," *Popular Science Monthly* 63 (1903): 418–24, 420 and 418.

[25] Cf. Ovid, *Metamorphoseon Libri XVI* [8 A.D.], X.

[26] Heinrich Heine, [*Lorelei,* 1824], in *Sämtliche Schriften,* ed. Klaus Briegleb, vol. 1 (Munich: Hanser, 1968), 107.

[27] Heinz Politzer, "Das Schweigen der Sirenen," in *Das Schweigen der Sirenen: Studien zur deutschen und österreichischen Literatur* (Stuttgart: Metzler, 1968), 13–41, 33.

[28] Politzer, 34.

[29] Quoted from Wolfgang Höppner, "Eine Institution wehrt sich. Das Berliner Germanistische Seminar und die deutsche Geistesgeschichte," in *Literaturwissenschaft und Geistesgeschichte 1910 bis 1925,* ed. Christoph König and Eberhard Lämmert (Frankfurt am Main: Fischer, 1993), 362–80, 372.

[30] Heinrich von Treitschke, *Deutsche Geschichte im 19. Jahrhundert* (Essen: Emil Holmer Verlag, n.d.), 459.

[31] Karl Kraus, "Heine und die Folgen [1911]," in *Ausgewählte Werke,* ed. Dietrich Simon, vol. 1: *Grimassen. 1902–1914* (Munich: Kösel, n.d.), 290–312, 291.

[32] Treitschke, *Deutsche Geschichte,* 458.

[33] Adolf Hitler, *Mein Kampf* [1925/27], 3d ed. (Munich: Verlag Franz Eher Nachfolger, 1930), 332.

[34] Alfred Rosenberg, *Der Mythus des zwanzigsten Jahrhunderts: Eine Wertung der seelisch-geistigen Gestaltenkämpfe unserer Zeit* [1930], 13th–16th edition (Munich: Hoheneichen-Verlag, 1933), 365.

[35] Ulrich Wyss, review of *Modernisierung oder Überfremdung: Zur Wirkung deutscher Exilanten in der Germanistik der Aufnahmeländer,* ed. Walter Schmitz (Stuttgart/Weimar: Verlag J. B. Metzler, 1994), *Mitteilungen des Marbacher Arbeitskreis für Geschichte der Germanistik,* Doppelheft 11/12 (15 July 1997): 36.

[36] *Edikt betreffend die bürgerlichen Verhältnisse der Juden in dem Preußischen Staate* (March 11, 1812), in *Dokumente zur deutschen Verfassungsgeschichte,* ed. Ernst Rudolf Huber, vol. 1 (Stuttgart: Kohlhammer, 1961), 45–47, 45: "§1. Die in Unsern Staaten jetzt wohnhaften, mit General-Privilegien, Naturalisations-Patenten, Schutzbriefen und Konzessionen versehenen Juden und deren Familien sind für Einländer und Preußische Staatsbürger zu achten. § 2. Die Fortdauer dieser ihnen beigelegten Eigenschaft als Einländer und Staatsbürger wird aber nur unter der Verpflichtung gestattet: daß sie fest bestimmte Familien-Namen führen, und daß sie nicht nur bei Führung ihrer Handelsbücher, sondern auch bei Abfassung ihrer Verträge und rechtlichen Willens-Erklärungen der deutschen oder einer andern lebendigen Sprache, und bei ihren Namens-Unterschriften keiner andern, als deutscher oder lateinischer Schriftzüge sich bedienen sollen."

[37] Wolfgang Menzel, the anti-Semitic arbiter of German literature in the 1830s, used the derogatory "jüdeln" for Heine's prose (in *Die deutsche Literatur,* 2d ed. [Stuttgart, 1836], quoted from Heinrich Heine, *Sämtliche Schriften,* ed. Klaus Briegleb, vol. 6.2 [Munich: Hanser, 1976], 419), as did Alfred Rosenberg a century later for Mahler's music (*Der Mythus des zwanzigsten Jahrhunderts,* 365).

[38] Franz Grillparzer, "Tagebuch Nr. 303 (1818)," in *Sämtliche Werke,* ed. Peter Frank and Karl Pörnbacher, vol. 4 (Munich: Hanser, 1964), 312: "Die Wissenschaft hat es mit Begriffen zu tun, die Poesie mit Bildern."

[39] Leo Spitzer, "Deutsche Literaturforschung in Amerika (Randbemerkungen zu Karl Viëtor's Aufsatz, *PMLA* LX, 899–916)," *Monatshefte für Deutschen Unterricht* 37.7 (November 1945): 475–80, 477 and 480.

[40] Klaus Mann, *Der Wendepunkt: Ein Lebensbericht* (Reinbek bei Hamburg: Rowohlt, 1984), 327.

[41] Gerald Gillespie and Edgar Lohner, "Vorwort der Herausgeber" to *Herkommen und Erneuerung: Essays für Oskar Seidlin,* ed. Gerald Gillespie and Edgar Lohner (Tübingen: Niemeyer, 1976), ix–xiv, xi.

[42] Ernst Bloch, "Disrupted Language — Disrupted Culture," *Direction* 2.6 (November-December 1939): 16–17, [continued on] 36; 16.

[43] Bloch, 17.

[44] Hajo Holborn, *A History of Modern Germany,* 3 vols. (New York: A. Knopf, 1959, 1964, 1969); deutsche Fassung *Deutsche Geschichte in der Neuzeit,* aus dem Amerikanischen übersetzt von Annemarie Holborn, 3 Bde. (Frankfurt am Main: Fischer, 1981): (Vorwort zur amerikanischen Ausgabe, XII).

[45] Paul Rabinow, "Resolutely Modern," *Recapturing Anthropology: Working in the Present,* ed. Richard G. Fox (Santa Fe: School of American Research P, 1991), 57–71, 71.

[46] Egon Schwarz, *Keine Zeit für Eichendorff: Chronik unfreiwilliger Wanderjahre* (Königstein/Ts.: Athenäum, 1979): "Will man ein Ding verstehen, so genügt es nicht, sich darein zu versenken, sondern man muß einen Beobachtungsposten einnehmen, der außerhalb liegt, den Gegenstand in seiner Umwelt betrachten, die Perspektive, aus der man ihn sieht, mit in Rechnung stellen, mit anderen Worten, es von einer ihm fremden Sphäre her erklären. . . . Und so könnte ich, um die Untrennbarkeit meines professionellen Wirkens von der Geschichte meines Lebens zu betonen, vielleicht etwas überspitzt aussagen, daß ich auf der Suche nach authentischer Selbstverwirklichung eine autobiographische Methode der Literaturbetrachtung entwickeln mußte" (169–70).

[47] Cf. *German Studies in the United States: Assessment and Outlook,* ed. Walter F. W. Lohnes and Valters Nollendorfs (Madison: U of Wisconsin P, 1976); *Teaching German in America: Prolegomena to a History,* ed. David Benseler, Walter F. W. Lohnes, and Valters Nollendorfs (Madison: U of Wisconsin P, 1988); *Germanistik in den USA,* ed. Frank Trommler (Opladen: Westdeutscher Verlag, 1989) — one of the few articles dealing with the role of exiles can be found in this volume: Wulf Koepke, "Germanistik als eine deutsch-amerikanische Wissenschaft" (46–65); *German Quarterly* 62.2 (Spring 1989 — Theme: *Germanistik as German Studies: Interdisciplinary Theories and Methods*); *German Studies in the USA:*

A Critique of "Germanistik"? Proceedings of a DAAD Conference in Scottsdale, Arizona, January 19–22, 1989 (Tempe, Arizona: Consortium for Atlantic Studies, 1989); *The Future of Germanistik in the USA: Changing Our Prospects,* ed. John McCarthy and Katrin Schneider (Nashville: Vanderbilt UP, 1996).

[48] *Deutsche Exilliteratur seit 1933,* ed. John M. Spalek and Joseph Strelka, vol. 1 (in two parts): *Kalifornien* (Bern und Munich: Francke, 1976). Cf. Helmut Pfanner, *Exile in New York: German and Austrian Writers after 1933* (Detroit: Wayne State UP, 1983).

[49] For data on a total of 25,000 exiles and 8,700 short biographical entries cf. Werner Roeder and Herbert A. Strauss, *Biographisches Handbuch der deutschsprachigen Emigration nach 1933,* 3 vols. (Munich, New York et al.: Saur, 1980–83).

[50] Hans Sahl, "Die Letzten (1973)," in *Wir sind die Letzten. Gedichte* (Heidelberg: Lambert Schneider, 1976), 13.

[51] Cf. *Modernisierung oder Überfremdung: Zur Wirkung deutscher Exilanten in der Germanistik der Aufnahmeländer,* ed. Walter Schmitz (Stuttgart and Weimar: Metzler, 1994).

[52] Bernhard Blume, *Narziß mit Brille: Kapitel einer Autobiographie,* ed. Fritz Martini and Egon Schwarz (Heidelberg: Verlag Lambert Schneider, 1985); English version: *A Life in Two Worlds: An Experiment in Autobiography,* trans. Hunter and Hildegarde Hannum (New York: Peter Lang, 1992).

[53] Blume, *Narziß mit Brille,* 296: "Gestrichen wurden Ausführungen über das System der amerikanischen Universitäten, das für Bernhard Blume auf seinem Weg von Mills, einem kalifornischen Mädchen-College, über Columbus, Ohio bis zur Harvard University und zurück nach La Jolla in Kalifornien bedeutsam wurde, und die kaum einen größeren Kreis interessieren dürften."

[54] Schlegel states in 1800 that the projected sequel to his *Geschichte der Poesie der Griechen und Römer* will achieve for the art of poetry "was Winckelmann für die bildende versuchte; nämlich die Theorie derselben durch die Geschichte zu begründen" (*Kritische Friedrich-Schlegel-Ausgabe,* vol. 3: *Charakteristiken und Kritiken II (1802–1829),* ed. Hans Eichner (Paderborn: Schöningh, 1975), 334.

[55] Blume, *Narziß mit Brille,* 238.

[56] Cf. Regina Weber, "Zur Remigration des Germanisten Richard Alewyn," in *Die Emigration der Wissenschaften nach 1933: Disziplingeschichtliche Studien,* ed. Herbert A. Strauss, Klaus Fischer, Christhard Hoffmann, and Alfons Söllner (Munich, London, New York, Paris: Saur, 1991), 235–56, 251.

[57] Schwarz, *Keine Zeit für Eichendorff,* 157.

[58] Heinz Politzer, "Das Handwerk der Interpretation," in *Das Schweigen der Sirenen: Studien zur deutschen und österreichischen Literatur* (Stuttgart: Metzler, 1968).

Egon Schwarz

Reminiscences of a UFO

Egon Schwarz

MY CONTRIBUTION WILL CONSIST OF two parts: my response to Professor Seeba of whose paper I have been shown only a small fraction prior to this session; and, invited to do so by Meike Werner, I shall try to give an account of how I deal with the anti-Semitism in my chosen field of learning.

Professor Seeba, whom I have known for a long time and for whose work I have the highest respect, has sketched the role refugee scholars from Nazi Europe played in our field of learning. One could and should expand this focus to include many other disciplines, for example psychoanalysis, art history, empirical sociology, and many others. It would not be difficult to argue that the atomic bomb that helped establish American hegemony in the world and ushered in a whole new phase in human history was the work of scientists driven out of Europe by the fascists. It is unthinkable what the world would be like had they done this for Germany as many would have without the insane racial phantasies of the Nazis.

With regard to the narrower field of German, Hinrich Seeba is right to say that many of the refugees were uncomfortable with theory. Some of the more prominent ones had been successful or at least frustrated writers of poetry, drama, and fiction in Europe. As such, their guiding principles had been *Bildlichkeit* and *Anschaulichkeit,* the expression of ideas in the form of images and a rhetoric of persuasion. Thus, publications of Bernhard Blume, Oskar Seidlin, Heinz Politzer, and Erich Heller, to name only a few, were jargon-free masterpieces of elegance in addition to their indisputable scholarly merits. It wouldn't harm our profession if their academic great-grandchildren emulated this achievement. Perhaps our much-lamented isolation wouldn't be so complete. Oskar Seidlin and Erich Heller had already made a start breaking down the barriers that separated the field of German from the general intellectual life of America.

I especially endorse Professor Seeba's call for individual biographies. I have my own difficulties with abstract universals. While they are helpful in bringing some order into the chaos of the phenomenal world, they only seem correct in areas we know little about. Where one has a pretty good grasp of what is the case, generalizations seem to pale. Place of origin, social class, upbringing and education, age at the time of arrival in the United States are important individualizing factors. I for example came from Latin America, and I am sure that the essayism prevailing there had a lasting influence on me. Those mature scholars who had earned university degrees in Europe had attitudes different from the younger ones who got their training mainly at American institutions, such as Walter Sokel, Guy Stern, Peter Heller, Harry Zohn, Dorrit Cohn and I, often from teachers who were refugees themselves. The ability to speak accent-free English, largely a function of age, should not be underestimated as a factor shaping a scholar's image and self-understanding.

Maybe it was out of modesty that Mr. Seeba did not include the likes of himself in his survey. The many young Germans who joined American German departments after the war had a great impact on the profession, forming an important link between the Hitler refugees and the present generation of students. I am thinking of scholars such as Richard Exner, Walter Hinderer, Klaus Berghahn, Jost Hermand, Peter Uwe Hohendahl, Herbert Lehnert, Paul Michael Lützeler, and Hans Vaget.

Professor Seeba gave a splendid overview assigning an honorific place to the exiled scholars in the development of the discipline. It is nevertheless possible to see this process through the prism of different categories. Let me try to mention a few of the forces that worked on German studies from without.

The first of these is professionalization. During the early decades of the century and beyond in many departments the main credential of the teachers was their German birth. Tenure was granted on the basis of longevity or the whims of powerful heads of the department without much consultation. The same was true of recruiting with the aid of the "old boys" network. I am not making value judgments. The results may have been the same as today's, and there may have been more room for the so-called "late bloomers." Most institutions required two years of a foreign language. Students chose their languages by simple prejudices: Spanish had the reputation of the easiest to learn, good for business in Latin America; French was supposed to bestow culture on the learner; German was for the budding scientist.

They were taught grammar and a reading knowledge. Tenure and intermittent prosperous times may have encouraged a kind of laziness. Scaling the higher pinnacles of German literature was regarded as a luxury for a few prestige-hungry oddballs or gentleman scholars.

The refugees played various roles in this scene. Some of them reinforced the amateurish character of the field by being amateurs themselves, lacking the proper training, similar to the Cuban lawyers who fled from Castro to become professors of Spanish in this country. But many, whatever their background, injected intellectualism and broad knowledge into their departments, elevating their levels to new heights, asking exciting questions, publishing in reputable journals, cultivating a fine style of writing, and showing a penchant for comparative literature. In Stuart Hughes's words they deprovincialized academic life in America and became players in the bureaucratization and professionalization that was taking place everywhere.

Secondly, de-literarization. The expansion of the curricula into sociohistorical and cultural studies began early for many reasons. Apart from the fact that the refugees had historic experiences they needed to articulate, two of the most important causes were the youth movement and student rebellion of the sixties and seventies on the one hand and the concomitant reduction or complete abandonment of the language requirement on the other. The new catchword was "relevance," and literature alone seemed not enough to produce it. To lure students back, courses on Marx, the Frankfurt School, fascism and National Socialism, the German and Austrian exiles, on Jewish affairs and the Holocaust were offered in many places. It was the time of the area studies and the theorification of the field. In the first phase of these changes many refugees took an active part. The second theoretical wave which brought mainly French influences into the language departments, including feminist and gay approaches to life and letters, no longer engendered the same interest in the refugee scholars. As a matter of fact, since this second phase became the dominant one, the relative non-participation of the refugee scholars contributed to the re-marginalization of some departments, not only in the public sphere, to which they were amply accustomed, but within their own universities.

Finally, Americanization. In this important transformation the exiles played an active role mainly by their disappearance. By this time many had retired, a number had died. Even the German and Austrian colleagues who had come after the war were growing old or had intellectual objections to the new trends. Also academic immigration to the United States had become much more difficult. But in the mean-time, thanks to the expansion of American universities in the fifties and sixties, large numbers of American scholars had been trained, some of course by the refugee scholars themselves and their postwar successors. This new generation had now come of academic age and began entering the field. Today we are witnessing a development that many American scholars had long desired. Uncomfortable with the overwhelming presence of colleagues who were not only born but also trained abroad and therefore did not have and in some cases didn't even seek familiarity with the culture and traditions of their students, these American scholars had called for the development of an autochthonous American Germanistik as it already existed in England, France, Japan and especially in Italy. The older generation of German professors is dying or retiring and the many younger German-born scholars who are still in the field were largely trained in this country and have been "Americanized" in a manner that was unthinkable for their predecessors. In my opinion, an American Germanistik, genera-tionally and methodologically different from its German counterpart, is in the making.

As I said in the beginning, I was invited to this conference to re-port from personal experience how a Jewish scholar came to terms with the strong anti-Semitic strands within German literature which he had chosen as his field of learning. As a preamble to my remarks I should like to say that at the time I came to the United States in 1949 I could have easily taken up and actually did begin a course of studies that would have led to a career in Romance Languages and Litera-tures. I had started my university education in Ecuador and was at least as fluent in Spanish as in German, and my French did not lag much behind. Had I done this I would have had to deal with anti-Semitism in Spain and France since the ideological hatred of Jews is endemic in all Christian societies. But it was the professors in the vari-ous German departments I attended, especially Bernhard Blume and Oskar Seidlin, who took me under their wings, found employment for me and automatically assumed that I was preparing someday to join their ranks. I acquiesced without much reflection not only because it was the way of least resistance but also for inner reasons: after a dec-ade in Latin America I was ready to return to the language and litera-ture of my early upbringing. I am pretty sure that a subconscious curiosity about the historical forces that had uprooted me also influ-enced my choice. Similarly when years later I offered courses on fas-cism and National Socialism many Jewish students enrolled in them, presumably out of a desire to know what had caused the persecution and eviction of their parents and grandparents as well as the annihilation of their entire ancestral culture in Europe.

When I started my studies of German there was indeed reason to be concerned about anti-Semitism not only in my subject matter but also in the profession itself. German nationalism, anti-Semitism, and Nazi sympathies were not overtly articulated. The defeat of Germany in the Second World War had pretty much silenced such voices. But professors who had held such beliefs were still around, and it was not infrequent that one was confronted with these phenomena in the secondary literature. Let me also remind you that anti-Semitism in the United States in the forties was still very strong and not at all the taboo that it is today.

It was easy for our teachers to avoid the subject of anti-Semitism in the classroom because the prevailing theory of literature was a German variant of the New Criticism that dominated literary studies in the United States as a whole. Hermeneutical interpretation of texts that excluded all consideration of history was a rule that one could only disregard at the risk of seeming crude. Thus such unpleasant subjects as the anti-Jewish bias of the German Romantics and the Wagner circle never came up, nor were the prefascist writings of authors like Paul de Lagarde, Eugen Dühring, Adolf Stöcker, Heinrich von Treitschke, Julius Langbehn, and Artur Dinter ever brought to the students' attention. Contemporary literature and the postwar debates going on in Germany at that time were not part of the curriculum. Our minds were fully occupied, in addition to the tasks of teaching German as a language, with studying and having to pass examinations about everything from Gothic to Goethe and even a little beyond.

Things became different once I had gotten my degree. Already in my dissertation on Georg Christoph Lichtenberg, a stalwart of the German Enlightenment, I included a chapter about his dislike of Jews. My first job was at Harvard. The times when this institution had insisted on quotas for Jews were over, and some professors were Jews. In the German Department I was the only one and still encountered some anti-Semitism, albeit in mild form. Times were not conducive yet to a Gentile-Jewish dialogue. Things changed for me when I went to Hamburg in the late fifties and early sixties, first as a Guggenheim Fellow and then as a Visiting Professor. While I was teaching there, the Senate of the city suggested that the faculty devote more energy to the study of literature of the German exiles. This was received with scorn. Why should one study such trash, was the general reaction. This

Egon Schwarz at the entrance to the subway,
New York City, 1949

Egon Schwarz with his wife Dorle and their children
Rudolf and Caroline, Cambridge, Mass., Christmas 1957

attitude enraged me enough to publish, with the cooperation of the progressive Wegner Verlag, two volumes, *Nation im Widerspruch* (1964) and *Verbannung* (1963), one of the first books on the fate and problems of the writers driven into exile by Adolf Hitler.

Back in the United States Guy Stern, I, and others worked hard to introduce these critical subjects into the Modern Language Association and the American Association of Teachers of German as well as into the humanities curricula. I taught courses not only on the exiled writers but also on fascism, National Socialism, anti-Semitism and the so-called Jewish question. I also founded a German Studies Program at Washington University, which I had joined in 1961, thus being among those who began to transform our field from purely one of literary studies into the cultural discipline it is today. But by the end of the sixties these were no longer isolated attempts. The student rebellion and youth movement in the United States and many other countries was in full swing, asking questions about the German past. At that point the idealizing reception of the Jewish scholars in the realm of thinking about German history took place. Jewish thinkers like Theodor Adorno, Max Horkheimer, Walter Benjamin, Herbert Marcuse, followed by Norbert Elias, became the guiding intellectual models for two generations. Sigmund Freud and psychoanalysis, long shunned and vilified by German scholars, were eagerly absorbed into German and Austrian intellectual life. The destinies of exiled Jewish authors of all fields became a study that occupied thousands. The Jewish character of Viennese culture was celebrated in books and seminars. Exile libraries were established, conferences held. Monumental editions of Jewish writers, for example Heine, prospered. Holocaust studies in political science, sociology, and history were financed.

This does not mean that being a Jew in German Studies had entirely ceased to be problematic. The unconstrained intercourse between Jews and Gentiles in Germany and Austria, if it had ever existed, was lost, perhaps forever. The phenomenon of philosemitism erected new barriers. One never knew for sure whether the invitations and honors one received were due to a genuine interest in one's work or a kind of "restitution." Of course, if one has to choose between anti-Semitism and philosemitism the choice is not difficult. I see a parallel in the debate about affirmative action. By and large the situation was a far cry from what it had been at the beginning of my career. Today the theorification of my field of learning has become pervasive and ubiquitous with the result that the concerns of ethnic identity are central to it. The learned journals are full of the controversies, for example, about the anti-Semitism in Wagner's operas or the merits of Daniel Goldhagen's book, with contributions by scholars from both sides of the Atlantic Ocean.

The modest attempts to direct attention to the Jewish question that I undertook in my youth dwindle before this passionate onslaught. It is a passion I cannot fully share. Perhaps one cannot expect a lot of lava from an extinct volcano. But there is more to it. A long time has gone by since questions of national, ethnic, or religious identity have occupied my mind. I grew up in the grey period between the two wars and, while I kept faith with my faithless hometown of Vienna for a long while after I had to leave it, the rush and urge to survive in the harsh environment of the Andes wiped out much of the identification I had brought along into my emigration. In turn, the Latin American "Identifikationsangebot" was very feeble. The possibility of becoming a real "Bolivian" or "Ecuadorian" even in a hundred years of solitude in those countries was practically nil.

All the more was I tempted to become an American after arriving in the United States. The image I had of the country was strongly tinged by Roosevelt's New Deal and his antifascism. This illusion did not last long: McCarthyism, the Vietnam war, the proxy wars in Central America, racism, and more recently the treatment of the poor and the anti-immigrant wave — these and many other events and phenomena made it impossible and even undesirable for me to seek an identification with this society. Israel, a country I had visited only once briefly, didn't come into question either. My thoroughly unreligious and anti-nationalistic orientation precluded any such adoption. The impression of a society of victims turning into oppressors fills me with pessimism, and the use of the "holocaust," a misnomer anyway, as an excuse for dubious practices fills me with grief and indignation. Mostly, I am quite content as a UFO, an "unidentified foreign outsider" wherever I happen to be. I acknowledge the many influences of Jewish, Austrian, Latin American, German, and North American culture in my intellectual and emotional make-up, but I cannot "identify" with any geographic entity. In this respect I am reminded of an ironic phrase, untranslatable without destroying its flavor, that strikes me typically Viennese: *A bissel ungern is ma eigentlich überall!* I feel no inclination to privilege and much less to glorify any of the countries in which I have lived.

Necessarily there arrives the moment when a person feels obsolescent in relation to the society that surrounds him or her. Maybe it is this experience to which I am giving expression. *Panta rhei.* Or to quote a fellow Jewish Viennese author, Arthur Schnitzler: "Sicherheit ist nirgends . . . Wer es weiß, ist klug."

Egon Schwarz at the end of the 1970s among his students — on the left, Bernhard Zimmermann

Panelists' Commentary

REGINA WEBER (STUTTGART): The general view that the exiled Germanists held up against the Nazi horrors — the canonized memory of classical German culture in the name of Lessing, Goethe, Heine, and Thomas Mann — should be modified in the light of research on Jewish concerns today. Jewish scholars such as Michael Brenner and Shulamit Volkov try to define Jewish identity no longer only by the experiences of the Holocaust, but in a larger, more positive context in the past. Against Goldhagen they show that there *was* a German-Jewish symbiosis in Germany prior to 1933, before Hitler.

In Germanics *Geistesgeschichte* was responsible to a certain degree for the development from "Luther to Hitler." In 1945 Karl Viëtor, a famous refugee from the University of Giessen who was Kuno Francke Professor of German Art and Culture at Harvard since 1937, wrote the often quoted essay "Deutsche Literaturgeschichte als Geistesgeschichte: Ein Rückblick" (*PMLA* 60 [1945]), a judgment on *Geistesgeschichte* which passed for the necrology of the German "geistesgeschichtliche Bewegung." But there is a correspondence between Karl Viëtor and Richard Alewyn, professor at Queens College New York since 1939, which dates from 1946, dealing just with this problem.[1] Actually both refugees wanted to rescue to some extent the German *Geistesgeschichte* that had shaped their identities as German scholars. But they followed different paths.

Viëtor's refusal of "Literaturgeschichte als Geistesgeschichte" in the *PMLA* article does not include the German philosopher Hegel, as he himself emphasizes; on the contrary, he wants to rescue Hegel, which means the Protestant development of the *Geistesgeschichte* without the aberrations into Darwinism and relativism of values. He wants to understand German literature "sub quaedam aeternitatis specie." Alewyn, on the other hand, stresses in his letter [written in New York, 29 May 1946] the importance of a boundary in the German-speaking countries, pointing to the contrast between the northern and the southern sphere of culture, —between "Protestantismus und Bürgerlichkeit auf der einen" und "Katholizismus und höfische (sowie volkstümliche) Kultur auf der anderen Seite." He characterizes the northern tradition by the domination of the "Wort," while the southern sphere of culture is attached to the "Bild," to the pictorial way of artistic expression. Alewyn in his own research followed the traces of European culture, beginning with the *Barockforschung* and transcending the limits of the literary studies in writing about the theater, the opera, the garden culture and the *Festkultur* (in *Das grosse Welttheater: Die Epoche der höfischen Feste in Dokument und Deutung* [Hamburg: Rowohlt, 1959]; partly written in 1938/39). He seems to have used the theory of cultural poetics in his time.

I think that the different positions of Viëtor and Alewyn are typical for two ways of self-representation of exiled German scholars: Viëtor is the protagonist of Germanics as a national philology, and Alewyn is a representative of the European culture within the German-speaking countries and beyond them. And I think that it is not a mere accident that Alewyn is of Jewish descent and Viëtor is not; he was only married to a Jewish woman. Viëtor was a professor at Harvard, and one of his successors in the German department of Harvard was the refugee Bernhard Blume, not Jewish either but also married to a Jewish woman. (Before his professorship at Harvard Blume had been a professor at Ohio State University, where there is a letter of recommendation in the university files stressing that "he is not a Jew" [3 August 1944]). Alewyn had greater difficulty in entering the German departments of the United States, which were bastions of German national ideology, including Jewish exiles at that time, a fact to which Egon Schwarz has just testified.

So different personal backgrounds produced different sensibilities, and Alewyn's awareness of the *other* tradition of the German *Geistesgeschichte*, which was not the national one, might have its origin in his Jewishness, though he was a Protestant and seems to have had ties neither to his Jewish descent nor to Jewishness in general, which he never mentioned expressly in his works.

Professor Seeba in his presentation stressed the importance of Austria as the native country of perhaps the majority of the German-Jewish scholars who emigrated to the German departments of the United States. And he showed us that they often were not "scholars" in the limited sense of the word but outsiders to the discipline, authors and artists themselves. Today this tradition seems to be represented by Ruth Klüger, professor at the University of California, who became well known as a writer of literature about the Holocaust. Now she is looking for the traces of German-Jewish symbiosis too, approaching the point of view of Brenner and Volkov. In her article in a

German feminist journal (*Emma*, No. 5, Sept./Oct. 1997) she stresses the importance of the Austrian Catholic region in the past centuries, too, where she discovered more permissiveness and tolerance for women writers, including German-Jewish women writers, than in the northern sphere of culture with its predominant Protestant "Bürgerlichkeit."

In 1945 Alewyn reflected at Queens College in New York about the possibilities of returning to Germany. In a letter to Ernst Beutler he wrote: "Ich gehöre nun einmal in den deutschen Geisteszusammenhang hinein und daran wird sich auch nichts mehr ändern" [New York, 18 August 1946]. It seems to me he had his roots there, as a German and as a Jew.

GISELA HOECHERL-ALDEN (UNIVERSITY OF PITTSBURGH): I want to add too that — because in my own work I looked at the archives at the University of Wisconsin — I must say the records are in a very dismal state.[2] The only reason some of the things survived is because one of the department heads actually didn't know what to do with the papers, and one of the secretaries said, "Why don't you give it to the archives?" Then unfortunately in the fifties the department heads just threw things out. So what we have are letters by Richard Alewyn, for example when he first found out that he was probably going to have to go to America.

These letters are very interesting because they all ended up in Wisconsin since Alexander Hohlfeld, who was at the time the department head, was also the head of the American Association of Teachers of German for a very long time and hence was well known to Germanists also outside of the United States.[3] And that is the only reason they ended up in Wisconsin. You see a lot of letters going to Hohlfeld and from other Germanists and other departments, that write: "We have had an application by soandso. Do you know anything about this person, is he Jewish maybe? Well, we wouldn't mind giving a Jew a position, but in the way our university is structured, we have quotas." These letters are typed and they have a lot of hand-written confidential notices on them. So, unfortunately, as I said, not all these universities kept good records. It is just by accident some of these records are still there. This addresses something that Hinrich Seeba said, namely that we should go into these records and see how on a departmental level this was handled. But unfortunately a lot of these things were destroyed at Madison. And you can see that someone went in there later and x-ed out information. So, nobody knows who it was, and I am sure this is probably what has happened in other departments as well. Which would make what Hinrich Seeba has called for a little difficult.

FRANK TROMMLER (UNIVERSITY OF PENNSYLVANIA): Since I was invited as a respondent, I will respond especially to Hinrich Seeba's very impressive assessment of the Jewish contribution. It is really hard to disagree with Hinrich Seeba in general — but someone has to do the dirty work, Hinrich — so I will disagree now. I see that the gist of your presentation, of your assessment comes retrospectively. It is looking for tradition, for roots, for something that is, let's say, the development in the last twenty years: cultural studies, German studies. You see the roots in the contribution of Jewish immigrants in the thirties and forties. I grant you, you have painted a very good picture of the general contribution back to Cassirer, but I would say the following: I have a somewhat different perspective on this. I also came thirty years ago. I discovered this when I heard you speak. It was thirty years ago that Harvard hired me as a visiting lecturer, in 1967. And I later joined the University of Pennsylvania, and I also had a Jewish mentor, Adolf Klarmann — Klarmann a very good friend of Heinz Politzer's — so, at least, I would like to expand this autobiographical review. You don't have to suffer through too much, but I would say that what you brought up is the enormous contribution, and for me having come to the United States as a journalist, never wanting to be in a German university, it was really thanks to many colleagues, mostly Jewish colleagues, that I stayed here. It was due to Adolf Klarmann (1904–1975) and Henry Remak (b. 1916), and Erich Heller (1911–1990) and also due to Walter Sokel and Peter Demetz — I would include Egon Schwarz — that I felt that there was something to develop for someone who came. It was still sort of on the margins of Germanistics. However, what I learned from the older generation was an enormous love for literature. You mentioned it, Hinrich, and in Politzer's case it's very clear. It was a love of literature. That was something certainly many *Germanisten* had lost, or didn't express — or if they did express it, very often they didn't express very well. But it was expressed very well, as you have said, in many of the essays, the contributions of American or German-Jewish American Germanists. This love of literature is something that I think revitalized the discipline and I think the expansion into comparative literature — to some extent even institutionally with Erich Auerbach (1892–1957) and Leo Spitzer (1887–1960) — that is a contribution that is special.

You made the point that many of the Germanists came from Vienna and from Austria. I see it somewhat differently. I wrote my dissertation on the Austrian novel, and I should say *fortunately:* it was a wonderful entrance ticket with American colleagues. Austria seems to have been in the 1950s, maybe even a little earlier, Austria seems to have been an area where academics in the United States could deal with German affairs without dealing with the Germans. I didn't say *Piefkes,* that would be too strong, however, it was something that could be maintained back to Hofmannsthal, something you have written about, that could be maintained in many ways, without constantly having to address the provocation that the history of German politics presented. And so Austria was "ein dankbares Gebiet." That's what colleagues told me, and so I traveled on it. As a Piefke having looked at Austria also — I probably have to go back — why did I choose Joseph Roth, and Musil, and Broch? Because I wanted this area of literature without the attachments of German politics, especially Nazi politics. I think that Politzer and Klarmann and many others cherished this and integrated it. It was not until the 1960s, the late sixties, Egon Schwarz brought it out in pointing to this generation that came in the 1960s, more or less younger Germanists from Germany who at that time — when the American university opened up toward a lot of social unrest, but also social science, and in the sixties and seventies — that this was more the source for the interdisciplinarity that you are pointing out. Berkeley plays an important role. I mean 1964 to 1974: certain things that came from Berkeley at the time. I wouldn't really bring in too much of the, let's say, specific influence of Jewish immigrants on Germanistik. What I bring to you is a differentiation of what you bring out. A differentiation, meaning that the field and the institution of German in the United States had a particular — let's say — position, was opened up in the 1950s, and also in a contradistinction to German Germanistik, but a lot of other factors really have to do with the developments of the 1970s and 1980s. That is maybe a good way to now respond.

Discussion

HINRICH SEEBA: I would like to take up one point Frank Trommler just made at the very end, namely what I tried to emphasize that the majority of the exiled Germanists or the exiled Jewish critics who have been so influential in the academy here, came from Austria, that this Austrian perspective allowed them to deal with German literature without dealing with Germany. I would see that in a more positive light, not as escaping from social and sociological tendencies, but I would see it more as the biographical basis for their outsiders' position and for their reflection on the outsiders' position. That they were twice removed from German affairs and therefore could develop a critical viewpoint on Germany, which people coming directly from Germany may not have as strongly represented. So I would see the Austrian perspective, especially after the war when Austrians were very proud of not being German and insisted a little bit too much in Austria itself that they had become the first victims of Germany, but I would see that as far as Jewish critics are concerned as an asset and not as a liability, as an asset for developing more socially concerned critical viewpoints on developments in postwar Germany. And that is something which I tried to emphasize very much, that the autobiographical approach which Egon Schwarz emphasized in his own memoirs is a very interesting and very important development that Jewish critics taught us. My generation had grown up excluding "I," the ego, the first person from any scientific statements. To learn to say "I" again — and not only to say "I," "ich" talking about our own anecdotal evidence of our lives and how much this life has affected the way we look at things — but to go beyond that and see it in a more general and even more theoretical perspective, namely the concept of positionality. I think that the recent emphasis on positionality is historically grounded in the experience of those who had to say "I" because their perspective was so much influenced by what they experienced and what they went through. So, I would say it is very important, as Egon Schwarz pointed out in his response, to emphasize the biographical approach, to look at the biographies of Jewish critics. I think much more needs to be done there. Alewyn is an interesting case in point.

Regina Weber has worked on Alewyn and has for instance pointed out that Alewyn — who I think would be a very interesting example — tried at first, to neglect, not only to neglect but to deny his Jewish origin when he was very upset about the fact that he had lost his position.[4] He pointed out in letters — Regina Weber published this excerpt from this letter to the university — that he actually was a conservative German who therefore was done an injustice when he was considered "only" a Jew and therefore had to leave his position. But it would be interesting to look at such details, biographical details, but I would want to go beyond the biographies of individual cases and look into the effect of Jewish Germanists on the perspectives, on the goals, and the methods used in our field. And I think there the impact, even though it may not be as strong in institutional terms, may be much larger, and the autobiographical aspect leading to the concept of positionality is only one example. The other one is, I think, the emphasis on the precision and the "Bildlichkeit," the "Anschaulichkeit," which we had to learn, and what Egon Schwarz pointed out as the jargon-free rhetoric of persuasion. That I think is something that should be not only valued but also which could be and should be emulated.

The other aspect, also something that Regina Weber pointed out in her article, is to see not only the impact of Jewish critics on the development of the field here in America, but also the impact the returnees had on the development of German Germanistik. Alewyn would be just one case in point. That he would start a summer school in German Studies with this English title I think is most interesting for perspectives which had not been common, which had not been used in Germany. That is certainly a reflection on something which he had learned here in America, and I think it is something which goes beyond literature, namely to see literature really in a cultural context. And that's what I wanted to emphasize: that the cultural context of looking at literature and looking at literature not in a privileged manner any more was very important for these exiles. It had an effect on both the American discipline of German Studies or Germanistik as well as on Germany, and it would be interesting to look at that.

Another detail I recollect now from Blume's memoir is the very, very difficult situation exiled Jewish critics were facing when they had to deal in the thirties with officials from Nazi Germany. Bernhard Blume talks about his interaction, or lack of it, with the consul general in San Francisco while he was teaching at Mills. I think that would be very interesting to look at the interaction between Jewish critics at

German departments in the American university system with the officials who represented Germany and tried really to silence these Jewish critics of Germany.

Another aspect that also was brought out by Bernhard Blume: the interaction between such Jewish critics with students who came from Nazi Germany as exchange students. Bernhard Blume talks about one particular student, a very attractive woman student with whom he was very taken, who then later turned out to report on him when she returned to Germany, even though she had been a very friendly and very open and very supportive student in his class. That would be interesting too, because apparently there was an exchange program going on with students coming from Nazi Germany studying at American universities, studying with the Jewish exiles who would confront them with very different views on Germany. I think this is another area that I would like to look into more systematically — or which I would like to see looked into more systematically than has been done so far, even though the material may be somewhat limited. I learned from Walter Schmitz that even looking at the papers of Heinz Politzer in Dresden shows a lot about the process of tenure promotions and personnel actions in Berkeley, which would be very interesting to see — especially if you happen to be one of those looked at.

PETER HELLER (SUNY BUFFALO): Ich möchte etwas kaltes Wasser auf manche dieser Dinge geben, also zum Beispiel dieser Käse, den Alewyn und Viëtor da geistesgeschichtlich konstruieren, wonach Österreich angeblich offener war, denn schliesslich war der Adolf der grösste Österreicher dieses Jahrhunderts, der berühmteste jedenfalls. Diese österreichische *connection,* die da hervorgehoben wird, halte ich für Quatsch. Und genauso wie ich für Quatsch halte, daß man die Linie Luther, Bismarck bis Hitler so zieht, wie das dann in der Propaganda üblich war. Außerdem, wer war dieser Viëtor? Er war ein Mann, der sich 1932 oder 33 in einem berühmten Artikel völlig zum Nationalsozialismus bekannte,[5] ein Jahr später war er dann nicht mehr dieser Ansicht. Wenn wir also diese Beispiele als besonders markante Kontributionen der Refugees in Amerika zur Entwicklung der Germanistik auffassen, glaube ich, da kann ich nicht mit.

JEFF PECK (YORK UNIVERSITY): I wanted to extend Hinrich Seeba's point to another generation that has only been referred to, but I think also has to be taken into consideration, that one might call the grandchildren of the generation being talked about. Or the third generation. The cohort of which I am a member is also an interesting generation in the United States because in some way it's a transition generation between the exiled Germans, the next generation who were Germans who came to the United States who weren't Jewish, and my cohort — of which many are Jewish. If you look at some of the people in that cohort — who are at a number of universities in the United States and who are also practicing cultural studies — I don't think it is coincidental that this group was trained by people who had been trained by these refugees who taught us an appreciation of literature — as Heinz Politzer did to me — but also then were trained in primarily French and also German theoretical traditions and tried to combine those two and move the discipline in a different direction which has now come to be called cultural studies. But it is a different kind of cultural studies and a different kind of appreciation of culture than our so-to-speak grandfathers had taught. And I think that this American-Jewish Germanistik has also contributed in a particular way, which marks it, as I said, as this transition.

In addition, Hinrich has pointed out the notion of positionality. I think one of the things that we want to consider when we talk about positionality is that it's also this generation who had been practicing a form of new cultural studies, who are Americanized Germanists who are Jewish, who have been trained in these two traditions and are also reflecting on their Jewish position differently, I think, than the Jewish critics of the, let's say, grandfather generation. This can be seen as both positive and negative. I mean it can be seen as positive as a way of acknowledging how our own backgrounds are influencing the kind of Germanistik we are practicing; on the other hand it can be part of a general critique that's leveled by people who are against cultural studies beyond Germanistik who would say that there is too much attention brought to reflecting on who one is when one studies. The question is: How explicit should that reflection be about being Jewish? The Goldhagen debate for example has brought this up — not so much in Germanistik but at least in history and in other fields.

DORRIT COHN (HARVARD UNIVERSITY): I know far less about the matter being discussed than Professor Seeba and Professor Schwarz, and I have learned a lot from their presentations. But I feel that two things should be emphasized — and I speak now as a person of the generation that's being talked about but also as a person who studied with the generation that's being talked about. Two things: One is that I wonder whether there is not more emphasis to be put on the symbiosis between Jewish and non-Jewish scholars of the refugee generation as Professor Trommler has emphasized. I for example studied with René Wellek and Karl Viëtor and was not particularly aware of the fact that they were not Jewish — neither of them were — and I have heard here today that Bernhard Blume was not. In other words I really think that perhaps there should be more emphasis on the symbiosis here.

The other point I want to make is that the word New Criticism was mentioned once, I believe in passing, by Egon Schwarz but I think it should be mentioned more often and particularly by way of emphasizing the large range of possibilities that was enacted by the refugee generation. Many of them were New Critics in practice and not in theory, and many of them worked — Professor Wellek for example, who was one of the leaders of this, and certainly Alewyn and Blume — worked very much in the direction of close explication of individual texts. Their work tended to be quite apolitical and also by implication non-intercultural. So these are the two things that I felt need to be emphasized more strongly than they were perhaps emphasized by anyone on the board to this point.

PETER DEMETZ (YALE UNIVERSITY): I have a question, but I don't know whether it *is* a question. I'll be thinking aloud. I was deeply struck by the question of saying "I," and my question is whether this hasn't come very late in the development. I can't remember that anyone of my generation came to the United States beginning to say "I." Is that a virtue or is that a disadvantage? Should we have spoken up earlier, or not at all? One can also ask whether it hasn't taken an inordinate time in America to bring about Holocaust studies. People were silent about it for quite a while. And also this learning to say "I" took a long time, and I am asking myself, since I am feeling myself part of the problem, whether this didn't come from an effort to work in one's profession. As far as I am concerned, I came to this country after experiencing the impossibility of doing what I wanted to do. Suddenly, I come to a country where I am allowed to do what I want to do, and I think it was not a moment of saying "I." It was the moment of looking at some scholarly — let's say — "it," not in the Freudian sense "es," not "ich," and trying to be a scholar, to do what I always wanted to do for a long time before you began to say "I." Before you felt justified of saying "I," justified by your scholarly effort. That's a question probably more than an answer.

Peter Demetz, Neustift, summer 1958

Peter Demetz with his daughter Anne Marie,
Connecticut, fall 1961

HENRY A. LEA (UNIVERSITY OF MASSACHUSETTS): I would like to add a personal footnote to what Professor Trommler said. I was a long-time student of Adolf Klarmann.[6] I entered the University of Pennsylvania in 1938. He was a remarkable man; I was his student for many, many years. He was shabbily treated in that department, mainly because he was both Jewish and Austrian, which meant that he had two strikes against him in a heavily ethnocentrically German-oriented department. He was engaged for much of his career in an epic, long-running feud with an old-time German pedagogue, who was very good in his way, but they were total opposites. The the old-time German professor — with a dueling scar across his face (he really looked the part) — was a very good classroom teacher who categorized and systematized and organized everything heavily almost in a Procrustean manner, but was very well prepared of course.[7] Adolf Klarmann didn't work that way. His mentality was totally different, was not systematic; he was not theoretical. He had an amazing gift for literary interpretation that was not traditional, was unorthodox, and he didn't pay much attention to the secondary literature. He didn't consider Goethe and Schiller deities. When I was in the other man's classroom in a Schiller seminar — I was a senior in college — he threw me out of the class because I smiled at something he said about Schiller: "Verlassen Sie die Klasse." This had never happened to me in my whole life. I was a fairly shy, bashful, retiring young kid. I had to find my way back in his class. I went up to his office with a great deal of trepidation and I said: "Sir, I didn't mean to offend you." He said, you may offend me, but don't you dare to offend Schiller. He had a picture of Schiller up on his wall. He let me come back into class, and I think later when I returned after the war as a graduate student, I don't think he even remembered, and he certainly didn't hold it against me. But Dr. Klarmann — he was fabulous in drama, on figures like Grillparzer and Schnitzler, but also on Kleist and Hauptmann. He really had read afresh these works and he came up with absolutely fresh and humanistic, not academic interpretations, which were memorable. I still remember them because he brought these figures in Grillparzer to life, in a way you won't find these interpretations in the textbooks, in the secondary literature, they were purely his own, but they made absolute sense. He had rethought them based on his rich human experience. I wrote my dissertation with him. It was very difficult, because he didn't give you much help. He wouldn't sit down the way other men would and organize the material for you. The other man would probably even tell you what to say. But Adolf Klarmann left you to figure this out for yourself. In the end they made peace with each other. The older man retired and went back to Germany — Dr. Klarmann told me about this later — and he didn't like what he found in Germany, and he apparently also found out what had happened earlier, which he hadn't been willing to face up to. He wrote a conciliatory letter to his younger colleague from Germany from his retirement, so that eventually this hostility was relieved. But what I was going to say also, which gets really to the heart of the topic of this conference, the main difference between them was — there were many of them — that Klarmann had a sense of humor, a sense of irony. He was self-deprecating, he was always skeptical, inquiring, exploring, he didn't take anything at its face value, whereas the other man was a cultural nationalist. In 1940/41 when the Nazis were in control of all of Europe, except Sweden, Switzerland, and Portugal and only England was still fighting on the Allied side, I took a course with him on nineteenth-century German drama. I was a junior in college, 1940/41, with the German professor. He picked three plays, *Der Prinz von Homburg*, *Agnes Bernauer,* and *Die Jüdin von Toledo*. And the theme was the individual versus the state and in that course — of course it was a long time ago and I don't remember the details — but he emphasized the priority, the prerogatives, the power of the state, when it came to conflict between the individual and the state. You would think that in 1940/41 at the height of Nazi power that a teacher teaching these plays would issue a warning about what happens when the state becomes too powerful, but nevertheless he took the other point of view. So I wanted to pay tribute to Dr. Klarmann as he was my mentor for many years too. I stayed in touch with him after I finished my dissertation, and became his friend.

Adolf D. Klarmann

WULF KOEPKE (TEXAS A&M): Well, could I come back to a little bit more objective things? One of the points that struck me even today is that there is a difference in the writings and the attitudes of the refugee scholars here during the thirties and during the war; where they still largely abstained from the present, and from any sort of problems that would go beyond the text. I have looked for instance at what they were writing about, and it was Goethe. The only twentieth-century writer that began to show up was Thomas Mann. He was the second Goethe. And it was only in the late fifties and the beginning sixties that the present started to creep in with Egon Schwarz's generation. With the generation of the refugees who had served in the American army who came back and who started their studies after the war. I think there is a marked difference of more self-confidence to face the past and the tradition in a different way. Of course for me the reason to look at it was that Germanistik, except for Thomas Mann, never looked at the exiled writers who lived in America during the time that they were here. Except for one little series that Harold von Hofe wrote,[8] nobody ever bothered to contact them — Klarmann was another exception, naturally — let alone write about them while they were here and while they could be contacted and while they could be interviewed. This came much later. And I think this sort of abstention from the present is a remarkable fact, as is the coming together of the exiles and the successor generation from Germany, ours, in starting to confront the past and the present and wanting to deal with it.

JONATHAN SKOLNIK (UNIVERSITY OF OREGON): I would like to pick up on something the previous speaker said, and also on something Dorrit Cohn said. I think Professor Seeba's portrait of German-Jewish intellectual refugees as anticipators of some of the progressive tendencies in criticism should probably also be complemented by what I think is another important chapter, which is the role of intellectuals like Leo Strauss and a few others — also I would probably include some of the people you called the "wooden paragons" of Germanistik — as founders of a certain kind of unique cultural conservatism that rightly or wrongly many of them articulated as a response to their experiences as refugees. They were radically alienated by the student movement in the 1960s, and the feeling was definitely mutual. I think this is something that should also be addressed in the context.

HANS VAGET (SMITH COLLEGE): I would like to offer a comment to what Wulf Koepke just said about the position of Thomas Mann in the thirties and forties in this country. I think it needs to be pointed out that the role he assigned to Thomas Mann in the thirties was actually occupied by Gerhart Hauptmann, not by Thomas Mann. That came much later. It also needs to be pointed out that Thomas Mann was invited by almost every college and university in this country (except my own, alas!), but that he was rarely invited by the German department. It was always the Comparative Literature department, or the English department or some other department, rarely the German department. For good reasons, if you go into the personnel constellations in each of those departments.

One more quick comment to what Peter Demetz said earlier. I share his ambivalence about the imperative now of saying "I" when we act professionally. I think there are cases where it is paramount, where it is necessary to say "I" and to indicate where one stands and where one comes from. There are many other cases where it is unhelpful. Let me add that I remember distinctly that Peter Demetz started saying "I" much earlier than he now remembers. When I had the privilege of sitting in his seminar at Columbia where he was a guest professor at that time, one of the things that impressed me about him, that as a professional critic talking about imagery he would say "I" and that — coming at that time from Tübingen — it impressed me enormously and I have ever since striven to introduce my little "I's" into my comments on literature and imagery.

WALTER SOKEL (UNIVERSITY OF VIRGINIA): I would like to first of all pick up something that Frank Trommler pointed out very well, and I would like to expatiate a little bit on that love of literature. I am talking particularly of people like Heinz Politzer, Erich Heller, Bernhard Blume, and Oskar Seidlin. All these people were displaced writers. This is very, very important. They were creative writers. And because they were creative writers, they were readers of literature, but in a special way. Not like the German scholars of the older school who read literature as scientists, but they read literature identifying with it and so they became excellent teachers, because teachers have to be hams. And the ham is an actor. And as an actor interprets literature, he is the first critic: the actor, the conductor in music and so on. So they were artist teachers and artist scholars. I think this did not come out sufficiently. In placing this generation of 1910: Blume was older, he was born in 1901, but Politzer on New Year's Eve in 1910, Erich Heller two months later, no, nine months later, in September 1911 (I know because of the Festschriften, you see). So they had in common the flair, for — Adolf Klarmann also of course — the flair for the dramatic, for the self-stylization, which is typical of the writer. And I think that differentiates them both from their predecessors, the Germanisten of the old school, but also from their successors, the sociology-minded, textual-minded, very serious scholars. They were not as serious. They were very multi-faceted.

And one more thing, something Hans Vaget brought up, about Thomas Mann being taught. Well, I would say that my own Doktorvater, André von Gronicka, should be mentioned. He did bring Thomas Mann into the curriculum at Columbia University when I was a student there. That was a breath of fresh air. That was just wonderful. Because before that of course Thomas Mann was never mentioned by the other teachers.

Tamara Evans (City University of New York): I would like briefly to comment on Richard Alewyn at Queen's College, linking up with something that Professor Gisela Hoecherl-Alden said. When Regina Weber came to Queen's College in search of traces of Richard Alewyn, maybe five or six years ago, I started to go through old files, through the files that we call "the morgue," and nothing was left of Richard Alewyn except his "Lohnkarte." We were able to reconstruct what his salary was in the forties, and there were annual letters of reappointment but no record of the lectures or the courses that he taught. Regina Weber at that time struck me as somewhat incredulous: "But don't you have notes, lecture notes, anything of his that would remember and honor his activity there as a teacher of literature?" There was nothing there, and I think it's just college bureaucracy rather than malevolence that wiped out all traces, and perhaps ignorance on the part of some people concerning who it was who taught there in the forties.

The other thing I would like to briefly talk about is the fact that I was a student of Oskar Seidlin's at Ohio State and that if it is not presumptuous to say so, after I went on and he went to Indiana University, we stayed friends. There are several things that were mentioned today that remind me of him. First of all what Professor Sokel just referred to, his creative writing. He had published poetry while in exile in Switzerland; he had written two children's novels also published in Switzerland — perhaps just to get some bread and butter. But certainly what we all know him for, the brilliance of his writing and his essays might also be just a transmutation of his creative skills. Second, what Professor Cohn mentioned, the fact, and here I probably disagree with you, Professor Seeba, that not everybody of that generation was really into cultural criticism, at least in seiner Lehre, as I remember Oskar Seidlin, what he taught was politically decontextualized altogether. I am going through old notes that I took on his seminar on young Goethe, and there were no references made to the politics of those times, let alone to the politics of his time. When in private conversation one attempted to hear details, let us say of his exile in Switzerland, which is something that I think I know something about myself, my mother having been a refugee in Switzerland — those were conversations that he ducked. I think German literature also stopped for him with Thomas Mann. I do not say that critically, because he had that passion, that love of literature, which he transmitted to us, and he is responsible for having made us discover the love of words like no one else I could think of.

Finally, what Professor Demetz said, or phrased in terms of a question: when did he and others of his generation learn to say "I"? I cannot remember Oskar Seidlin ever, ever saying in any of his lectures or his seminars "I." Never did he refer to his experience in Germany or thereafter as an exile in the United States, and never did we think as students that he was there teaching as a Jewish scholar. He did not deny it — it was clear who he was — but I do not think that in significant ways this affected his manner of teaching.

BRITTAIN SMITH (BOSTON UNIVERSITY): Not being an official respondent, I was wondering if I could ask a question. It is actually directed to Professor Seeba and it picks up on what Professor Cohn and the last speaker also mentioned. When I read Heinz Politzer on Grillparzer or Kafka, I don't see Sozialkritik, and I wonder if this doesn't teach me somehow about those writers and their works, and I wonder if it doesn't point to, if not a contradiction, at least a tension in what you called their desire to have us read literature not as a privileged discourse, not privilege-based and what you called their Bildlichkeit, or what the Russian formalists would call the literariness of something. It seems to me that there is a way in which they do point to something privileged and special about Bildlichkeit, about literature. I have a hard time seeing them as harbingers or precursors of a kind of wider social perspective, and I was just wondering if you might want to elaborate a little bit on that tension.

HINRICH SEEBA: I can probably confirm some of the impressions which were brought forward here, namely that especially coming from the '68 generation, and I am part of that generation, it was striking to see that these Jewish critics, for me it was mainly Heinz Politzer, were as it was just phrased "politically decontextualized." But I wouldn't say that political decontextualization, which could also be interpreted as political conservatism as in the case of Seidlin, as it was done in the Festschrift introduction I quoted from, that this political decontextualization is identical with an abstinence in the consideration of cultural context. And even Politzer in his Grillparzer study would always — as far as I read his book and as I know it from his talks, from his classes, and from many conversations — would always see the author not only as the anonymous [sic] also of a text, but as a living person in a social-historical-cultural context. But he would not engage political interpretation, you are correct there, and I think all those who have expressed this are very correct in saying that this generation cannot be seen, possibly with the exception of Egon Schwarz, as politically left-leaning, as supporters of causes which were closer to our hearts in the late sixties.

But what I was trying to say was that this generation anticipated many of the positions which have become theoretical positions now. Which have become conceptualized as theoretical positions, but which were never formulated as theoretical positions. Jeff Peck pointed out that positionality is something that is now possibly differently interpreted than it was by these Jewish critics at the time, but nevertheless I would say that we could use the term positionality for understanding the extent to which they have brought in personal experience, at least implicitly, into their dealings with literature. And that is something I would miss even now when we have more theoretical discussions of positionality, that in dealing with German literature and German culture, Austrian literature, Austrian culture, today we miss the involvement of personalities who have been very much formed and been informed by their experience and it was certainly our understanding and our knowledge of the extent to which they were really framed, or by which they were guided, to the extent to which they were guided by this experience of the critical situation, of a critical life, of a crisis in life and I think that helped at least me personally very much to find a totally new approach to literature, not as a merely objective field, as I had learned to study in literary scholarship, *Literaturwissenschaft*, as I was trained in Germany.

ELISABETH KEIL (GOETHE INSTITUT BOSTON): I would like to refer to Dr. Regina Weber. I am German, and I am at the moment a student at Hebrew College. I grew up in Germany after the war and I was

a student of Professor Richard Alewyn, 1963–67. The students admired him and we thought his lectures were great, and I personally
had to make a few attempts for getting grants. So I came to him and I
thought I had to bring out theoretical approaches and critiques and
everything what he said about Hofmannsthal, and then he asked me
"Do you know something from Hofmannsthal by heart? Can you
bring some of his poetry?" And I found that striking. He just showed
us the beautiful language, and he thought this is very important and
the love of the language, that's what he also brought us students. But
that he was Jewish I didn't know, and nobody, I think, not many students knew that he was Jewish; that was not an issue. It might be an
interesting question: the influence of a professor like Richard Alewyn
coming back to Germany and his influence on second generation
Germans again.

WALTER SOKEL: I just want to take issue with the political. There are
two things, very briefly. I do think we have a disagreement here in
general, not just between Herrn Seeba and myself, but I think that the
voices here have voiced some kind of questioning, friendly questioning, very friendly questioning of this excellent talk: namely, a political
disagreement. You see, Heinz Politzer, Erich Heller, and Oskar
Seidlin were cultural conservatives. I know that personally from conversations with them, from my contacts with them, and from their
works. They were really the old tradition of Austrian patriotism, not
Seidlin of course, but Heller and Politzer; they were Kakanian patri-
ots. They were on the right wing, and Oskar Seidlin was passionate in
attacking the '68 generation and became almost very reactionary in his
views around 1970. So I would say that we have to distinguish between the generation of 1910, and the generation of Egon Schwarz of
1922, and Guy Stern who also belongs to this generation. They were
of course left leaning, progressive, and very different and sociologically
oriented, and it was an anathema for Heinz Politzer, but particularly
for Erich Heller and Oskar Seidlin to bring in sociological considerations. I remember how Oskar Seidlin responded to an article of mine,
which I had written for his Festschrift.[9] He was very "befremdet" — I
quote the word — by my approach to Thomas Mann comparing him to
his brother Heinrich Mann. He was "befremdet" by this political act.

LEO LENSING (WESLEYAN UNIVERSITY): I have two comments.
One — this is picking up on what Hinrich Seeba and also Egon
Schwarz said — Heinz Politzer's essayistic work and his scholarly work
does in another sense I think lead to certain present theoretical posi-

tions because of his interest in psychoanalysis and the way that he framed and constructed what you called his existential experience through psychoanalysis and used that certainly in his later criticism to a great extent. But I have a comment that I think will seem a question to Hinrich Seeba and Egon Schwarz. Obviously the documentary and archival work on the problems we are going to talk about today, are just beginning and so I think it's going to be difficult to speak with much authority, certainly from my side today at all, but it seems to me that the influence that the Jewish Germanist had on things like a reading list, and on what used to be the canon, and on what graduate students read, is an extremely important one and I want to offer a provocative thesis. I think that it is clear that the Jewish Germanists came to this country with their own likes and dislikes, their literary taste. I think it is possible that some of them also influenced the canon, or what was read in graduate schools on the basis of a very understandable reaction to Jewish-German and Austrian-German writers who were considered "self-haters," "Jewish self-haters." The two examples that come to my mind are Karl Kraus and Kurt Tucholsky, who for a long time were certainly not on graduate students' reading lists in this country and there are certainly exceptions among the Germanists. Heinz Politzer by the way was interested in a different kind of Kakania. He taught a course at Cornell in 1971 and 1972 which began with *Ein Bruderzwist in Habsburg* and ended with *Die letzten Tage der Menschheit,* so with another kind of Kakania. But I think that many Germanists who came to this country from Germany considered certain German-Jewish writers beyond the pale, and I think this has influenced the writing of literary history up until this day. I mean things are changing now, but it's been a long time coming.

Editors' Annotations

[1] Carsten Zelle, "Emigrantengespräche: Ein Brief Richard Alewyns an Karl Viëtor," *Euphorion* 84 (1990): 213–14.

[2] Gisela Hoecherl-Alden, "Germanisten im 'Niemandsland': Die exilierten Akademiker und ihre Wirkung auf die amerikanische Germanistik (1933–1955)" (Ph.D. diss., University of Wisconsin, 1996).

[3] On Hohlfeld see Cora Lee Nollendorfs, "The First World War and the Survival of German Studies: With a tribute to Alexander R. Hohlfeld," in *Teaching German in America: Prolegomena to a History*, ed. David P. Benseler, Walter F.W. Lohnes, and Valters Nollendorfs (Madison: U of Wisconsin P, 1988), 176–95.

[4] Regina Weber, "Zur Remigration des Germanisten Richard Alewyn," in *Die Emigration der Wissenschaften nach 1933: Disziplingeschichtliche Studien*, ed. Herbert A. Strauss et al. (Munich: K.G. Saur, 1991), 235–56.

[5] Karl Viëtor, "Die Wissenschaft vom deutschen Menschen in dieser Zeit," *Zeitschrift für Deutsche Bildung* 9 (1933): 342–48; teilw. auch in Karl Otto Conrady, *Einführung in die Neuere deutsche Literaturwissenschaft* (Reinbek bei Hamburg: Rowohlt, 1966), 216–20. Vgl. auch Carsten Zelle, "Zum Gedächtnis seines 100. Geburtstages. Mit einem Verzeichnis seiner Schriften und Lehrveranstaltungen," *Giessener Universitätsblätter* 25 (1992): 25–42.

[6] Adolf Klarmann (b. 1904 in Austria, d. 1975 in the United States): A.B. und A.M. New York University 1926 and 1927; University of Munich, 1926/27; Ph.D. University of Pennsylvania, 1930. Klarmann taught at NYU from 1926 to 1928, at University of Rochester 1928/29 and 1930/31. He spent most of his career at the University of Pennsylvania and was best known for his work on Franz Werfel. For a list of publications see *Views and Reviews of Modern Literature: Festschrift for Adolf D. Klarmann*, ed. Karl S. Weimar (Munich: Delp, 1974).

[7] The reference here is to Ernst Jockers (b. 1887 in Germany, d. 1963). He took his degree in German from Strassburg in 1924 then emigrated to the United States in the same year. As of 1929 he was at the University of Pennsylvania until his retirement in 1957. He was also known as a Werfel scholar. In 1930 Klarmann became Jockers's first doctoral student, writing his dissertation on musicality in the work of Franz Werfel. For a list of his writings see *Mit Goethe: Gesammelte Aufsätze* [Festgabe zu Ernst Jockers 70. Geburtstage am 7. Januar 1957] (Heidelberg: Winter, 1957).

[8] Harold von Hofe, "German Literature in Exile: Alfred Döblin," *German Quarterly* 17 (1944): 28–31; "German Literature in Exile: Heinrich Mann," *ibid.*, 88–92; "German Literature in Exile: Thomas Mann," *ibid*, 145–54, "German Literature in Exile: Franz Werfel," *ibid.*, 263–72; "German Literature in Exile: Bruno Frank," *German Quarterly* 18 (1945): 86–92.

[9] Walter H. Sokel, "Demaskierung und Untergang wilhelminischer Repräsentanz: Zum Parallelismus der Inhaltsstruktur von *Professor Unrat* und 'Tod in Venedig,'" in *Herkommen und Erneuerung: Essays für Oskar Seidlin*, ed. Gerald Gillespie und Edgar Lohner (Tübingen: Niemeyer, 1976), 387–412.

2: Jüdische Philologen und ihr Kanon

Ludwig Geiger, February 26, 1891
(© Deutsches Literaturarchiv Marbach).

Aufklärungskulturgeschichte: Bemerkungen zu Judentum, Philologie und Goethe bei Ludwig Geiger

Christoph König

IN DEUTSCHLAND HABEN Wissenschaftler Hemmungen, von *jüdischen* Intellektuellen zu sprechen.[1] Das Motiv erscheint auf den ersten Blick lauter: man möchte nicht erneut Menschen ausschließen, die sich selbst allenfalls sekundär durch ihr Judentum bestimmten, und sie zu einem Untersuchungsgegenstand zusammenfassen, obwohl sie offenbar wenig eint. Die Nationalsozialisten stehen vor ihren Augen und wie sie 1933 viele Deutsche erst zu Juden gemacht haben. Gegen diese Haltung hat sich Gershom Scholem mit großer Entschiedenheit gewandt: "Nachdem sie als Juden ermordet worden sind, werden sie nun in einem posthumen Triumph zu Deutschen ernannt, deren Judentum zu betonen ein Zugeständnis an die antisemitischen Theorien wäre. Welche Perversion im Namen eines Fortschritts, der den Verhältnissen ins Auge zu schauen nach Möglichkeit meidet."[2] Als ob es die Juden und ihre Schwierigkeiten nicht auf eine andere Weise gegeben hätte, als es die Deutschen damals durchsetzten.

Der Hemmung, über jüdische Intellektuelle zu sprechen, kommen die Forscher, die Scholem geisselt, argumentativ nach. Sie sagen: Aufgrund der Schwierigkeiten, die Juden zu definieren, kann man allenfalls die Art untersuchen, in der über sie gesprochen wurde und in der sie selbst über sich gesprochen haben, also die Fremd- und Selbstbestimmungen. Die Diskurs- und Systemtheorie läßt sich dafür benutzen. Sie unterscheidet zwischen den Diskursen und den Menschen. Doch eigentlich anerkennen sie nur die Macht der Diskurse und interessieren sich nicht dafür, ob die Menschen sich den Diskursen widersetzen. Die Menschen, die in den Diskursen (oder Systemen) agieren, tauchen als Größe nur auf, wenn sie sich als Gruppe den Diskursen fügen. Zur Vorstellung von der Macht des Diskurses tritt also die Vorstellung einer faktischen Identität des Gegenstands, ohne die es diesen Gegenstand nicht gibt. Von Juden kann man demzufolge nur sprechen, wenn der Antisemitismus sie durchgreifend und einheitlich geformt hat. Diese Trennschärfe gibt es natürlich nicht. Für diese Forscher schafft die Themenstellung erst den Gegenstand. Als kritische Geister fühlen sie sich verpflichtet, das Thema zu verhindern.

Zu dieser Verdrehung einer kritischen Position kann es nur kommen, wenn man an der *Identität* festhält und glaubt, die Menschen, die es nicht zu dieser Identität gebracht haben, vor den Historikern schützen zu müssen. Doch was tut man mit den Qualen dieser Menschen und ihren Lösungen? Ich bevorzuge daher eine dialektische Vorstellung: die Auffassung, daß auch die Negativität eine Realität hat. Alle diese jüdischen Intellektuellen, die im Kaiserreich und in der Weimarer Republik lebten, handelten in einer bestimmten kulturellen Situation, in der jüdische Traditionen deutschen gegenüberstanden, und sie entschieden sich auf eine bestimmte Weise. Ihre Entscheidungen rechtfertigen nicht, von einer jüdischen Identität zu sprechen, wohl aber ihre *Schwierigkeiten*. Das meine ich mit der Realität der Negation. Natürlich fallen diese Entscheidungen höchst unterschiedlich aus. Daher führen Untersuchungen auf diesem Feld (wie das Marbacher Symposion "Jüdische Intellektuelle und die Philologien in Deutschland" zeigte) zu lauter verschiedenen Biographien, zu Biographien von Leuten, die indes das Problem teilen.

Sind die Historiker, die die Themenstellung ablehnen, Wissenschaftshistoriker, so meinen sie, über ein drittes Argument (nach "Diskurs" und "Identität") zu verfügen: nämlich die Autonomie des Systems Wissenschaft, das "jüdische" Prägungen ausschließe. Die Rede von den jüdischen Intellektuellen habe keinen wissenschaftshistorischen Wert, denn die Schwierigkeiten, die sie als Juden haben (wenn die Schwierigkeiten überhaupt anerkannt werden), prägen weder ihre wissenschaftlichen Methoden, noch ihren Stil, noch die Resultate. Man tritt, so diese Auffassung, in die Halle der Universität und dort ist alles sehr hell. Auch hier muß man sich der Systemtheorie erwehren, die in Deutschland, mehr als in Frankreich, wo man das unter Wissenschaftssoziologen gar nicht versteht, das Sagen hat. Ihre Schwäche besteht darin, nicht erklären zu können, daß in dem einen System Elemente des anderen auftauchen und dort ihre Kraft entfalten. Ich spreche hier von kulturellen Werten und der Kultur im allgemeinen. Die Frage, die ich hier stellen möchte, lautet daher: Welchen Einfluß haben die Schwierigkeiten und die darauf antwortenden Entscheidungen, die die Gelehrten außerhalb der Universität fällen, auf ihr Tun innerhalb der Institution? Eine vorläufige Antwort möchte ich schon jetzt geben.

Die Wissenschaft bildet zu jeder Zeit Alternativen aus, die eine gewisse Festigkeit haben. In den Epochen, von denen ich hier spreche, steht einem philologischen Ansatz im engeren Sinn (den Editionen, biographischen Detailstudien etc.) eine Philologie im weiteren Sinn entgegen, der ich Wilhelm Dilthey und Wilhelm Scherer zurechnen möchte. Sie paarten die Materialkenntnis mit philosophisch-ästhetischen Reflexionen.[3] Daraus entwickelte sich dann auch die Geistesgeschichte zwischen 1910 und 1925.[4] Gleichfalls konnte man verschiedene Autoren zum Gegenstand nehmen (die Frauen, Heine, Goethe). Und im Verhältnis von Wissenschaft und Literaturkritik gab es alle Schattierungen.[5] Dieses Verhältnis war ein Spannungsverhältnis, denn die klugen Gelehrten wußten, daß es einen methodisch notwendigen Zusammenhang zwischen der Kritik (samt den zugehörigen Werten) und der Philologie gab. Die jüdischen Philologen bewegen sich in diesen Alternativen (selten gehen sie darüber hinaus, wie etwa Jacob Bernays[6]), doch welche Wahl sie treffen, geht stets auf ihre Biographie zurück. Jean Bollack hat gezeigt, daß gerade die jüdischen Schüler von Wilamowitz dessen philologisches Programm in verzweifelten Anstrengungen exerzieren, während seine nicht-jüdischen Schüler sich genialisch-spekulative Züge gestatten.[7] Wenn Gelehrte Optionen ihrer Wissenschaft nutzen, so hat das, auch wenn es vorerst im Rahmen der Wissenschaft bleibt, Folgen für die weitere Geschichte dieser Wissenschaft.

Ludwig Geiger, auf den ich mich nun konzentriere, schrieb der deutschen Kultur universalisierende Kraft zu: alles, dessen sie sich bemächtigt, verliere die Vorurteile, auch die antisemitischen. (Diese Naivität findet man noch in Marcel Reich-Ranickis Autobiographie *Mein Leben*. Die Hilflosigkeit des jüdischen Bildungsbürgers, der alles, was Kultur sei, akzeptiert, ist bestürzend.[8]) Die Kultur sieht Geiger auch in der Wissenschaft am Werk und kann daher keine rechte Dialektik von Kulturwerten und Wissenschaft entwickeln. Politisch gesehen, gehört er zu den "Kulturtheoretikern der Assimilation" (Andreas Kilcher).[9] Er wendet sich gegen die Antisemiten und gegen die Zionisten, die jeweils auf ihre Art das Jüdische zu isolieren suchen. Geiger ist mit seiner Leugnung des Antisemitischen in der deutschen Kultur fast ein Vorläufer der Diskurstheoretiker. Zumindest hinsichtlich seines Programms. Doch man erkennt die Grenzen der Diskursanalyse, wenn sich Geiger in seinen Taten über sein Programm hinwegsetzt. Dazu zwingt ihn sein Gegenstand, die Literatur, die mit abfälligen Bemerkungen über die Juden nicht spart. Geiger rechnet sie generell der (universalisierenden) Kultur zu, doch bevorzugt er — darin besteht einer seiner Auswege — bestimmte Dichter wie Lessing und Heine. Mit Goethe tat er sich schwer.

Wenn man daran denkt, daß auch jüdische Intellektuelle innerhalb wissenschaftlicher Optionen sich bewegen, so gilt für Geiger, daß er gerade die *Trennung* von Wissenschaft und Öffentlichkeit, wo der un-kultivierte Antisemitismus zuhause sei, benutzt. Fortschrittlichere For-scher suchen diese Trennung zu überwinden. Geiger bleibt methoden-geschichtlich zurück, weil er sich schützen muß: sich und seine Treue zur jüdischen Konfession. Er tut dies innerhalb der Universität oder als Herausgeber einer wissenschaftlichen Zeitschrift (des *Goethe-Jahrbuchs*). Ich möchte das nun in vier Abschnitten zeigen: anhand 1. seiner Stellung zum Judentum, 2. des "philologischen Dreiecks" von Wissen, Werten und Institutionen,[10] 3. seiner Strategien in der Wis-senschaft, und 4. seiner Studien zu "Goethe und die Juden."

1. Judentum

Ludwig Geiger (1848–1919) veröffentlicht 1910, in der Tradition der Söhne berühmter Gelehrter, die Biographie seines Vaters, des Reform-rabbiners Abraham Geiger. Er teilt darin einen Brief mit, den der Va-ter ihm, dem Siebzehnjährigen, 1866 schrieb, als er sich entschloß, das Studium der Theologie aufzugeben.

> Deine Studien würden, wenn ich Deine Geistesrichtung nicht ganz und gar verkenne, doch keine anderen sein als: Philosophie, alte Sprachen, zumal als die lebendigste Äußerung ihres geistigen Le-bens, Geschichte ihrer Literaturen, Geschichte überhaupt als die Entwicklung des Menschengeistes und zumal die geistige Bewe-gung, welche Juden und Judentum in die Menschheit gebracht. Das ist am Ende auch jüdische Theologie, ob sie theoretisch erkannt, ob sie praktisch geübt wird. Du hast sie in dieser Form nur kennen, we-nigstens als berechtigt ehren gelernt.[11]

Weil Gott sich vorzüglich in "großen Geistestaten" mitteile, und diese aufeinander bauen, besteht die neue jüdische Theologie auf einer auf-geklärten Geschichtsphilosophie, die — auch wenn die Nähe zum deutschen Idealismus groß ist — ihren Ursprung im Judentum habe, denn von da stamme der Gedanke einer "die Einheit der Welt gestal-tenden und lenkenden Geistesmacht."[12] Ohne diesen Gottesgedanken verliere die jeweilige Kultur ihren Sinn: Abraham Geiger spricht von den "Monstrositäten" im Pentateuch, wenn ihn Moses allein ge-schrieben hätte.[13] Daher seine Leichtigkeit, alte Ritualgesetze (Speise-gesetze, die Beschneidung, oder Gebete wie das um eine Rückkehr nach Jerusalem[14]) abzulegen. Während der Rabbiner theoretische und praktische Theologie nicht trennen muß, wird Ludwig Geiger, als Historiker des Judentums und als Philologe, das Programm säkularisieren. Dabei hat er weniger den von Max Weber beschriebenen Prozeß einer Rationalisierung von Religion vor Augen, die in der Moderne sich zur Kultur wandle, als öffentlich der jüdischen Vernunft ihre säkularen Grundlagen zu nehmen,[15] ohne ihren Anspruch aufzugeben. In der Defensive bleibt der Gedanke einer sich selbst aufklärenden Kultur erhalten, wenn sie denn nur Kultur genug sei: am ehesten in der Dichtung und einer vorurteilslos registrierenden Wissenschaft. Kultur bestimmt Geiger nicht mehr als Ausprägung des universalen Gottesgedankens, zu dem der Abstand sich im Lauf der Geschichte verringere — entschieden wird ihr der (politische und schützende) Begriff der "Konfession" entgegengehalten.

Denn die Zeiten haben sich geändert. Geiger argumentiert wie die Mehrzahl der jüdischen nationalliberalen Intellektuellen zu Beginn des Kaiserreichs[16] und gebraucht für sich regelmäßig die Formel eines *deutschen Gelehrten jüdischer Konfession.*[17] Die Assimilation betreffe die Völker und nicht den Glauben. Juden unterschieden sich nicht von den Deutschen, sondern von den Christen. 1912 noch, als der Druck auf die Juden ungleich größer geworden war, antwortet er auf eine Umfrage zu *Judentaufen,*[18] die durch Werner Sombarts Buch *Die Juden und das Wirtschaftsleben* (Leipzig, 1911) ausgelöst wurde und sich an Wissenschaftler und Schriftsteller richtete, die einer anderen, der Generation der Moderne angehörten. Eine der Fragen lautete: "Welches sind die voraussichtlichen Folgen (in geistiger, politischer und wirtschaftlicher Beziehung oder einer dieser) im Falle der Assimilation sämtlicher Juden durch Uebertritte und Mischehen?"[19] Geiger bestritt entschieden, daß dies wünschenswert sei:

> Energisch aber muss ich mich dagegen wenden, als wenn erst durch den Uebertritt oder durch die Mischehe eine Assimilation möglich wäre. Das ist ein Unding, eine schwere Beleidigung gegen alle die deutschen Juden, die wie ihre Vorfahren es etwa seit einem Jahrhundert getan, Deutsche geworden sind, also gar nicht nötig haben, erst Deutsche zu werden. Ist Assimilation — und das kann doch nur der Sinn des Wortes sein — eine Deutschwerdung in Sitte, Sprache, Behaben, Gefühlen, so bedarf es dazu weder der Mischehe noch der Taufe.[20]

Indem Ludwig Geiger den reformjüdischen Gedanken einer aufgeklärten Geschichte des menschlichen Geistes auf die deutsche Kultur verwendet, gerät er in eine heillose Lage. Er verliert die Instanz, die das

Antisemitische dieser Kultur als zeitweilige "Monstrosität" ablehnte, und kann sich nur mit den bescheidenen Mitteln der Philologie gegen sie behaupten.

2. Das philologische Dreieck

Trennen! lautet seine methodische und seine wissenschaftspolitische Devise. Geiger steht in der Geschichte der deutschen Philologie, deren spezifische, Ende des neunzehnten Jahrhunderts sich ausprägende Konstruktion im Dreieck von Wissen, Werten und Institution er — durchaus subversiv — nutzt.

Wie Antisemitismus und Forschung zusammenhängen, ist oft untersucht worden; auf zwei Ansätze möchte ich besonders hinweisen: (a) Eine Soziologie der *Institution* erläutert, welche Werte, die in der Universität selbst vertreten wurden, den Zugang dorthin verlegten;[21] (b) die *Wissen*soziologie will die Entwicklung wissenschaftlichen Wissens erklären und hat etwa für die Naturwissenschaften erforscht, daß Spezialisierung Fortschritt bedeute, und man zur Spezialisierung erst an der Peripherie der Institution (hierarchisch oder geographisch aufgefaßt) gezwungen werde.[22] Ich möchte die beiden Ansätze ausführlicher skizzieren, um zu zeigen, daß sie für eine Wissenschaftsgeschichte jüdischer *Philologen* nicht ausreichen. Man muß beherzigen, daß hier der Gegenstand sprachlich und damit kulturell verfaßt — und so den Werten der Interpreten ausgesetzt ist.

1. Sozialgeschichte.

Monika Richarz wertet in ihrer Untersuchung zur "Sozialgeschichte der jüdischen Intelligenz und der akademischen Judenfeindschaft 1780–1848" (1982) 280 Gutachten aus, in denen sich Wissenschaftler aller Fakultäten dazu äußern, wie die einzelnen preußischen Universitäten 1847 gerüstet wären, das im gleichen Jahr erlassene Judengesetz praktisch anzuwenden. Privatdozenten, außerordentliche und ordentliche jüdische Professoren waren diesem Gesetzentwurf nach zuzulassen, sofern die Statuten einer Universität, namentlich die konfessionellen, dies erlaubten. Insgesamt erwiesen sich die Professoren konservativer als der Landtag und bestritten zur Hälfte, daß selbst eine begrenzte Zulassung mit dem konfessionellen Charakter der Hochschulen vereinbar sei. Ihre Argumente spiegeln die verbreiteten kulturellen Ängste (Konkurrenz, staatliche Mißachtung des eigenen Berufsstandes) und allgemeine Vorurteile, etwa der Vorwurf, daß es den Juden am wirklichen Willen zur Assimilation mangle. Ein Rechtshistoriker schreibt: "Seine [des Juden] Nationalität ist mit seiner Reli-

gion auf das engste verwebt, er kann sich jener nicht entäußern, solange er Jude ist; er wird nicht deutsche Volkstümlichkeit annehmen
oder sich ihr bedeutend nähern und nicht die deutscher Volkstümlichkeit angehörigen Rechte mit gleicher Hingebung, Liebe und Fähigkeit wie der Deutsche ergreifen, pflegen und lehren."[23] Gleichfalls auf
die Kultur bezogen war die — mit einem Hinweis auf die zeitgenössische Literatur gewürzte — Warnung vor einer atheistischen, liberalen
oder revolutionären Zersetzung der Universität durch die Juden. So
wollte man den Zugang zur Universität kontrollieren. Eine Soziologie
der Institution kann das erkennen, doch sie tut sich schwer, wenn sie
beschreiben will, was innerhalb der Universität mit jenen Werten geschieht. Denn die Werte regeln nicht automatisch auch die Forschung. Die Deutsche Philologie gibt sich nach außen als eine
nationale Wissenschaft. Doch im Seminar sieht es gern anders aus,
wilder. Die Deutsche Philologie gilt nicht unbedingt zurecht als das
höchste Ziel der nationalen Assimilation.

2. Wissenssoziologie.

Die Institution schafft einen Innenraum, den bestimmte Wissenschaften nutzen. Shulamit Volkov — sie widmet sich dem Erfolg der Juden
in der Wissenschaft zu Zeiten des Kaiserreichs — geht von dem inneren Universalismus der Universität aus (den Robert Merton als ober-
ste wissenschaftliche Norm formuliert hat) und erkennt darin ihre
große Attraktivität für die Juden. "Aber auf Juden, deren Väter bereits
die Spitze des Erfolgs erklommen hatten, schien die Wissenschaft
doch eine spezielle Anziehungskraft auszuüben. In ihrem zumindest
scheinbaren Universalismus und der Betonung von Verdienst und
Talent lag das Versprechen einer Gemeinschaft ohne Schranken, in
der durch Leistung alles erreichbar war und die keine rassischen oder
religiösen Unterschiede kannte."[24] Weil Volkov sich auf einzelne Naturwissenschaften beschränkt und auch nicht die Forschung selbst
studiert, die Publikationen nicht liest, muß sie sich auf einen Mecha-
nismus verlassen, auf ein institutionelles Gesetz, das man etwa so
resümieren kann: der Fortschritt einer Wissenschaft resultiert aus Spezialisierung. Spezialisierung gibt es nur an der Peripherie, die sich auf
die Hierarchie beziehen oder geographisch gemeint sein kann. Die jüdischen Gelehrten waren zur Spezialisierung gezwungen. Sie mußten
länger Privatdozenten sein als andere, und sie kamen, wenn sie überhaupt einen Ruf erhielten, selten an *große* Universitäten, sondern an
kleine, wo man das eigene Spezialgebiet von früher, als man noch Privatdozent war, ohne große Hindernisse weiter kultivieren konnte.

Nochmals also die Frage: Gilt das auch für die Philologie? Ist Spezialisierung der Quell von institutionellem Erfolg? Trifft nicht vielmehr zu, daß die Überwindung der positivistischen Spezialisierung und die Einführung philosophischer oder kritischer Gesichtspunkte um 1900 den Fortschritt versprechen? Und daß diese Ansätze tatsächlich von den Rändern und Außenbezirken kommen, aber nicht innerhalb der Universität, sondern aus dem kulturellen Raum, den man nicht mehr von der Universität abschotten will? — Mit der Philologie hat es eine eigene Bewandtnis, weil in ihr Wertvorstellungen (gewollt oder nicht) *methodisch* relevant sind. Außerdem prägen zwischen 1910 und 1925 neue philosophische Gesichtspunkte die Wissenschaftsgeschichte ("Fortschritt" ist selten das richtige Wort), die gerade die Spezialisierung *überwinden* sollen.[25] Diese Ansätze kommen tatsächlich von den Rändern und Außenbezirken, aber weniger innerhalb der Universitätslandschaft, sondern aus dem kulturell-literarischen Raum (etwa von einer allgemeinen Philologie Hugo von Hofmannsthals), den man nicht mehr von der Universität abschotten will.[26]

Unter Philologen galt die wissenschaftliche Norm, man dürfe den eigenen Werten und Überzeugungen nicht direkt Eingang in die Forschung gewähren. Im negativen Abdruck von Nietzsches Kritik liest sich das so: "Die historische Bildung ist vielmehr nur im Gefolge einer mächtigen neuen Lebensströmung, einer werdenden Cultur zum Beispiel, etwas Heilsames und Zukunft-Verheissendes, also nur dann, wenn sie von einer höheren Kraft beherrscht und geführt wird und nicht selber herrscht und führt."[27] Programmatisch trennt man zwischen Fakt und Ordnung, ja im philologischen Seminar werden gerne jene Werte ("Goethe der Olympier" etwa) aufgelöst, die nach außen das Fach national legitimieren und die man in Festreden proklamiert. Nietzsches Leben verkommt früh schon national. Scheidet man auch zwischen Universität und Öffentlichkeit, bleibt dies methodisch unbefriedigend, denn die kulturellen Werte finden sich da wie dort und müssen sich, solange sie nicht auf den eigenen Gegenstand bezogen werden, im Innenraum der Institution, gegen ihre philologische Auflösung, unreflektiert Geltung verschaffen, etwa in der Auswahl der Gegenstände. Im Zeitalter des Historismus gilt es vor allem, das heterogene Wissen zu meistern: Geiger vertraut auf eine nach Werten der Aufklärung ordnende Kultur in der Wissenschaft, so daß er die Dialektik einer bevorurteilten deutschen Kultur in ihrem Verhältnis zu den philologischen Wissenschaften nicht erkennt. Nicht weil sie unwissenschaftlich sind, sondern weil sie die Wissenschaft für ihn fundieren, geht er auf seine Werte nicht ein.

Wehrt Geiger sich gegen Antisemitisches, benutzt er die Philologie (und ihre Tricks: etwa die Kanonbildung) somit eher, als daß er sie samt den theoretischen Schwächen überwindet. Statt zu trennen, müßte er vermitteln. Selten wird die für das Trennen erforderliche Disziplin deutlicher als in seiner Rezension von Victor Hehns Buch *Gedanken über Goethe* (Berlin 1887).[28] Geiger unterscheidet zwischen dem, was man im Fachblatt sagen kann, und dem, was vor einem größeren Publikum möglich sei. Nur in der *Nation* könne er Kritik üben, wenn Werte — "Den Juden theilt er [Hehn] Schläge aus, wo er nur kann." — Eingang in die Wissenschaft fänden, in einer wissenschaftlichen Zeitschrift hielte er sich zurück: "Ich selbst, wenn ich das Werk lobe, bin sehr weit davon entfernt, mich mit allen Ansichten desselben einverstanden zu erklären. Aber die Darlegung dieses Gegensatzes gehört mehr in ein Fachblatt."

Doch auch dort könnte er nicht wissenschaftskritisch argumentieren. Denn ihm stehen, wenn die Gegenstände sich gegen ihn richten, nur zwei Auswege offen: der positive einer eigenwilligen Kanonbildung (so widmet Geiger sich früh den Frauen in der Dichtung) oder das simple Registrieren des Abfälligen, als könne er in vornehmer Distanz die Gegenstände kultivieren, die es von sich aus nicht vermochten. Auswahl der Gegenstände und blindes Vertrauen auf eine heteronome Macht der Kultur in der Wissenschaft gehören zu den Identifizierungsformen der sammelnden Philologen. Bei vielen Deutschen ist diese "Kultur" national konnotiert, bei ihm rationalistisch. Geiger verläßt sich auf eine die Vorurteile quasi läuternde Vernunft seiner registrierenden Wissenschaft; ist die Wissenschaft selbst von negativen Stereotypen erfüllt, bleiben Hilflosigkeit und Trauer, denn an die läuternde Beobachtung einer bevorurteilten Wissenschaft glaubt auch Geiger offenbar nicht. "Stände eine solche Tirade in dem Zeitungsartikel eines konservativen oder antisemitischen Heißsporns, so würde man sie gleichmüthig ansehen, vielleicht kaum über dieselbe die Achsel zucken, in dem Buche eines Mannes von der Bedeutung Viktor Hehns, den man gern voll und ganz verehren möchte, liest man sie mit tiefer Trauer."[29]

3. Strategien/Habitus

Geiger hat sich als Historiker (über *Urteile griechischer und römischer Schriftsteller über Juden und Judentum*, 1873) in Berlin habilitiert und verdankt den Zugang zur Universität und zur Germanistik im besonderen der ausdrücklichen Förderung Wilhelm Scherers, der von 1877 bis 1886 in Berlin lehrte und Geiger über sein doppeltes Außenseitertum als Jude und Fachfremder hinweghalf:[30] 1880 sorgt er für Geigers Ernennung zum außerordentlichen Professor.[31] Das war das Maximum für einen nicht konvertierten Juden. Mitten im Zentrum der Nationalphilologie, bei Goethe, verschafft Geiger sich im gleichen Jahr, außerhalb Berlins (in Frankfurt am Main, im jüdischen Verlag Rütten & Löning[32]) und außerhalb der Universität, mit der Gründung des *Goethe-Jahrbuchs* seine Zitadelle.

Erst fünf Jahre später konstituiert sich die Goethe-Gesellschaft in Weimar und bestimmt notgedrungen das *Goethe-Jahrbuch* zu ihrem Organ.[33] Auf den Inhalt hat man keinen Einfluß (immerhin veröffentlicht das Goethe- und Schiller-Archiv regelmäßig aus den Beständen), und gibt doch einen erheblichen Zuschuß. Es ist weniger der Vorstand als Erich Schmidt, Scherer-Schüler und Literarhistoriker in Berlin, der sich mit der so institutionalisierten Machtlosigkeit nicht abfinden kann; er greift Geiger mit über die Jahre hin zunehmender Schärfe an ("Das Jb ist bei Herrn Geiger nicht in den rechten Händen. Ihm fehlt dafür die Persönlichkeit, die Autorität, das Wissen, das Urteil, die Genauigkeit."[34]) und erreicht 1913, wenige Wochen vor seinem eigenen Tod, daß Geiger auf der Jahresversammlung der Goethe-Gesellschaft das Jahrbuch verliert.

Die Attacken des modernen "Damenprofessors" Schmidt fallen in eine antisemitische Welt; Schmidt selbst ist wohl freier von diesen Vorurteilen. Seine beinahe aristokratische Weltläufigkeit wird nach seinem Tod von Gustav Roethe dem jüdischen Kandidaten Richard Moritz Meyer entgegengehalten: Man tut so, als wolle man lieber einen Grafen als einen Juden, und Roethe nimmt — weil es einen zweiten Schmidt nicht gebe — selbst das Amt auf sich. Gustav Roethe schrieb an Wolfgang von Oettingen am 7.5.1913, als man ihm die Präsidentschaft erstmals angetragen hat: "Lieber wäre es mir, Sie nähmen etwa Burdach. Daß Berlin im Vorstand vertreten sein muß, sehe ich ein; daß es durch Rich. Meyer vertreten werde, kann ich nicht wünschen, zumal in diesem Augenblick nicht; Sie verstehen das ohne Ausführungen. So will ich mich in den Vorstand wählen lassen." Und am 10.5.1913: "Sie dürfen nicht vergessen, daß in Erich Schmidt doch auch ein gutes Stückchen, wenn nicht Hof, so doch Weltmann steckte, daß er die Leichtigkeit besaß, die da hin gehört, die aber wir Gelehrten mit gutem Grund in der Regel nicht besitzen." In Wahrheit war Meyer zwar Weltmann, aber — als Jude, den Roethe selbst stets zu verhindern wußte — nicht Professor.[35]

Der Generationenkonflikt zwischen Geiger und Schmidt war zumindest in Teilen ein antisemitisches Artefakt, d.h. methodische Schwäche resultierte aus der Defensive gegen den Antisemitismus. Schmidt ist wegen seiner *Urbanität* bei der traditionsorientierten Gesellschaft, die Geiger stets in Schutz genommen hat, auf Widerstand gestoßen. Er fordert ein populäres Jahrbuch und einen Charakter als Herausgeber, denn die literarische (repräsentierende) Persönlichkeit vermag — so sein nie eingelöstes methodisches Programm — das philologische Wissen zu bündeln.[36] Solchen Charakter spricht er Geiger ab und greift ihn, der in einem philologischen Wahrheitspathos arbeitet, persönlich an. Geiger sucht seine Zitadelle unangreifbar zu halten, indem er auseinanderhält, was Schmidt zu verbinden sucht (auch innerhalb des Jahrbuchs, wo zwei Rubriken einander gegenüberstehen: der allgemeine Essay und die philologische "Critische Untersuchung"). Er hütet sich, offen seine Werte zu vertreten, oder Angriffen *grundsätzlich* zu begegnen und sich so zu schwächen: das lehrt das Studium der Akten in Weimar. Geigers Verhaltensmaxime lautet, stets auf die spezifische Situation und auf die einzelne Sache bezogen zu antworten. Sie entspringt dem diszipliniert-defensiven Habitus des Trennens, der einem auch in der Rezension von Hehns antisemitischem Buch begegnet.

4. Goethe und die Juden[37]

Will Geiger *persönlich* über seine philologischen Gegenstände sprechen, drängt er nach außen. Zur Verteidigung erklärt er vorab: "Ich spreche nicht als Jude, sondern als Literarhistoriker. Als Jude bin ich Partei, als Literarhistoriker bin ich parteilos."[28] Unausgesprochen bleibt seine Überzeugung, daß die Literatur die dumpfen Vorurteile läutere, die ihre Voraussetzungen bilden. Solche Universalität soll ihn über die Parteiungen hinwegheben. Doch der Gegenstand selbst leistet dem nicht Folge. Von dieser Diskrepanz zeugen Geigers Abhandlung über "Faustsage und Faustdichtung vor Goethe," die 1889/90 in *Westermanns Illustrierten Deutschen Monatsheften* erschien,[39] als auch die im Wintersemester 1904/05 an der Berliner Universität gehaltene öffentliche Vorlesung über *Die deutsche Literatur und die Juden* samt dem Goethe gewidmeten Abschnitt.[40]

Der Gedanke einer allgemeinen *Aufklärungskulturgeschichte*, in die der Dichter tritt, prägt Geigers Methode. Das Werk sei nicht dem Autor und nicht seiner Kultur entgegenzusetzen, denn das Werk hebe den reinen und das heißt: vernünftigen Kern des Autors und seiner

Kultur ans Licht. Weil Geiger Literatur mit Vernunft (in der Geschichte) gleichsetzt, kann er die "Literatur" (im Sinn einer höheren Potenz) von den einzelnen Werken nicht unterscheiden. Weil er keinen Werkbegriff hat, kennt er keine unterschiedliche Ausprägung der Vernunft von Werk zu Werk, und — was die Autonomie des Werks angeht — jede Äußerung des Autors in seinen Werken muß ihm als wertvoll gelten. Gerade Geigers Universalitätswille verkennt, wie wenig ein ästhetischer Gegenstand partikular ist, wenn er sich dem allgemeinen Vorurteil nähert; mit anderen Worten: daß er nur als partikularer universal ist. Denn das ästhetisch Besondere ergibt sich aus vielen kleinen klugen Schritten. Noch ist es weit in der Wissenschaftsgeschichte, bis sich Vernunft solcherart ummünzen läßt in die Kritik einer "Logik des Produziertseins" (Peter Szondi).[41]

Von den Werken her kann man so weder ihre Vernunft noch ihre Unvernunft begründen. Dunkle Werke und dunkle Worte des Dichters muß Geiger daher exoterisch, das heißt von außen her, umdeuten oder rechtfertigen. Der Umdeutung und der Rechtfertigung gelten meine abschließenden Bemerkungen.

Umdeutung. Die *Historia von D. Johann Fausten* gilt Geiger als Kompilation umlaufender Geschichten, schlecht komponiert und in barbarischer Sprache; die Puppenspieler schließlich haben einen herrlichen Stoff "dem niedrigsten Teile des Volkes" dargeboten, selbst "Komödianten der allertraurigsten Sorte, Menschen ohne Bildung und ohne Geist."[42] Der Sinn des Stoffes liege im faustischen Charakter Fausts, den der Drang nach Wissen auszeichne; Geiger liest Goethes Faustdichtungen wie Lessings Faust-Fragmente (1759); ein von oben bewirkter Untergang war auszuschließen. Etwas wissen wollen durfte in der Aufklärung nicht mehr als Hybris bestraft werden. Lessing wollte daher sein Stück mit der Rettung Fausts durch "eine Erscheinung der Oberwelt" beschließen. Doch Goethe hatte — wie wir wissen — anderes im Sinn als Lessing.

In seiner Naturtheologie hält Goethe die Wißbegier am Zügel. Die eigene Wißbegier und die seiner Figuren. Er verfügt, darin ist er wie später Hofmannsthal ein moderner Dichter, frei über die Traditionen. Diese Freiheit verdankt er der spekulativen Konstruktion seiner Naturphilosophie. Der Freiheit hält er die Begrenzung entgegen, denn sein Ziel ist die individuelle Gestalt, die die Traditionen *meistert* und ihnen "gemessenen" Sinn respektive *Berechtigung* gibt. Individualität setze, so der Gedanke, eine von der Natur gegebene Vielfalt voraus (das ist die Wißbegier), innerhalb der bestimmte Züge privilegiert werden. Das geschieht auf Kosten von Wissensbeständen, die nicht bedacht werden. Denn alles zu wissen verhindert die Form. Die Entscheidung erzeugt die unterscheidbaren Gestalten. Die Grenzen ("Fortifikationen" sagt Goethe) lassen sich von ihm hinausschieben. Daher ist die Geschichte Goethes Gegner: sie hat für ihn keine Gestalt. Er rechnet sie zu dem dem Menschen fremden Großen, das außerhalb seiner Kreise bleibt und ihn zerstört. Um die Welt zu gestalten, unterstellt er die Traditionen aus dieser Welt seiner naturphilosophischen Konstruktion, die auch den *Faust, Zweiter Teil* bestimmt: treibt die Heteronomie auf einen Punkt zu, wo sie unlösbar wird, greift die *Natur* (als Schlaf, Ohnmacht, Tod) ein, die Szene wechselt, das Geschehen geht anders weiter. Man denke an das Gespräch zwischen Helena und Phorkyas, die der Helena all die Geschichten unter die Nase hält, die von ihr im Umlauf sind: Helena klärt daraufhin nicht den Zusammenhang dieser Geschichten, sondern fällt in Ohnmacht. Das ist ein ästhetischer Akt des Autors, der so zu interpretieren ist: Goethe negiert das aufgeklärte Verlangen, *alles* mit den gehörigen Unterschieden hinzunehmen (und zu wissen).[43] Das hat Geiger nicht wahr haben wollen und liebt in Goethe seinen Lessing.

Rechtfertigung. In seiner Vorlesung über "Goethe und die Juden" registriert Geiger Einschlägiges[44]: Goethes Hebräischstudium, seine Bibelkenntnis, die eine oder andere Bekanntschaft, die Verehrung durch die Berliner Jüdinnen, des Dichters Respekt vor Spinoza und Mendelssohn, aber ebenso Goethes Zustimmung zu restriktiver Judengesetzgebung, die frühe "Judenpredigt" und antijudaistische Äußerungen wie die in *Wilhelm Meisters Wanderjahren.* Geiger registriert und fragt nicht weiter, darauf vertrauend, daß allein die literarische Beschäftigung Goethes mit dem Judentum diesem schließlich zugute kommen werde; oder er schiebt es schlicht auf Goethes schlechte Laune, wenn der sich zornig gegen Juden geäußert hat.

Geiger stützt sich auf Goethe — und beide haben Unrecht. Denn die Kultur ist zu schwach, um sich gegen ihren eigenen Antisemitismus zu wehren. Tatsächlich trennt Goethe zwischen jüdischer Kulturtradition und Juden, denen er begegnet bzw. von denen er in der jüdischen Geschichte liest: "Jene Mythen, wahrhaft groß, stehen in einer ernsten Ferne respektabel da und unsere Jugendandacht bleibt daran geknüpft. Wie aber jene Heroen in die Gegenwart treten, so fällt uns ein, daß es Juden sind und wir fühlen einen Kontrast zwischen den Ahnherren und den Enkeln, der uns irremacht und verstimmt."[45] Die jüdische Tradition ist in die deutsche Kultur abgesunken und kann so von Goethe akzeptiert werden. Zugrunde liegt der Gegensatz von menschlicher Beschränkung und kultureller Universalität. Doch

bei genauerem Hinsehen wird klar, daß Goethe die jüdischen Geschichten innerhalb seiner eigenen christlichen Kultur deutet. Meist
nach den Gegensätzen "partikular vs. universal," "Gesetz vs. Liebe,"
"außen vs. innen."[46] Die Hierarchie steht für ihn — wie man in der
Pädagogischen Provinz der *Wanderjahre* (II/2) leicht nachlesen
kann — fest. In Goethes Werken herrscht eine Konstruktion, ein Gedanke, der von der Beschränkung in der Vielfalt ausgeht. Gedanken
sind universal, doch wenn aus ihnen literarische Werke geschaffen werden, kehrt das Leben mit seinen Vorurteilen wieder ein. Sie sind zu
schwach, sich dagegen zu wehren. Heteronome kulturelle Werte, die
in die Texte aufgenommen werden, behalten viel von ihrem alten
Sinn.

Geigers Haltung in den Berliner Vorlesungen ist ebenso verzweifelt wie trotzig. Seine Überzeugung: Die *Literatur* scheidet den
Dichter vom Pöbel, gilt selbst bei Goethe nur mit Einschränkungen.

Anmerkungen

[1] Diese Überlegungen nehmen kritisch Argumente auf, die zu den Vorbereitungen des von mir gemeinsam mit einer Projektgruppe des Marbacher Arbeitskreises für Geschichte der Germanistik konzipierten internationalen Marbacher Symposions "Jüdische Intellektuelle und die Philologien in Deutschland. 1871–1933" (16.-19.6.1999, Deutsches Literaturarchiv) gehörten und auch das Symposion selbst prägten: die Akten der Tagung sind unter demselben Titel erschienen, hrsg. v. Wilfried Barner und Christoph König (Göttingen: Wallstein, 2001). Der Beitrag ist bereits erschienen auf Englisch in *Goethe in German-Jewish Culture,* ed. Klaus L. Berghahn and Jost Hermand (Rochester, NY: Camden House, 2001), 65–83. Die Position, gegen die ich hier ausdrücklich und freundlich streite, vertritt etwa Jürgen Fohrmann, dessen Nähe zu Niklas Luhmann auch Jürgen Kaube ("Jenseits der Identität," *Frankfurter Allgemeine Zeitung,* 30.6.1999) teilt. Vgl. auch Christoph König, "Jüdische Gelehrte und die Philologien, 1871–1933," *Mitteilungen,* hrsg. v. der Arbeitsstelle für die Erforschung der Geschichte der Germanistik, Heft 9/10 (1996): 10–16.

[2] Gershom Scholem, "Juden und Deutsche," in *Judaica II* (Frankfurt am Main: Suhrkamp, 1970), 22.

[3] Vgl. Wilfried Barner, "Literaturgeschichtsschreibung vor und nach 1945: alt, neu, alt/neu," in *Zeitenwechsel: Germanistische Literaturwissenschaft vor und nach 1945,* hrsg. v. Wilfried Barner und Christoph König (Frankfurt am Main: Fischer, 1997), 119–49; Nikolaus Wegmann, "Was heißt einen 'klassischen Text' lesen? Philologische Selbstreflexion zwischen Wissenschaft und Bildung," in *Wissenschaftsgeschichte der Germanistik im 19. Jahrhundert,* hrsg. v. Jürgen Fohrmann und Wilhelm Voßkamp (Stuttgart, Weimar: Metzler, 1994), 334–450.

[4] *Literaturwissenschaft und Geistesgeschichte 1910 bis 1925,* hrsg. v. Christoph König und Eberhard Lämmert (Frankfurt am Main: Fischer, 1993).

[5] Christoph König, "Hofmannsthal. Ein moderner Dichter unter den Philologen" (Göttingen: Wallstein, 2001).

[6] Jean Bollack, *Jacob Bernays: Un homme entre deux mondes* (Villeneuve d'Ascq: Presses universitaires du Septentrion, 1998).

[7] Jean Bollack, "Die klassische Philologie und die Juden vor 1933," Beitrag zur Tagung "Jüdische Intellektuelle und die Philologien in Deutschland" (Anm. 1).

[8] Marcel Reich-Ranicki, *Mein Leben* (Stuttgart: Deutsche Verlags-Anstalt, 1999).

[9] Andreas B. Kilcher, "Was ist 'deutsch-jüdische Literatur'? Eine historische Diskursanalyse," *Weimarer Beiträge* 45 (1999): 485–517, Zitat 494.

[10] Cf. Christoph König, "Wissen, Werte, Institutionen," in *Zeitenwechsel,* 361–84.

[11] Ludwig Geiger, *Abraham Geiger: Leben und Lebenswerk. Mit einem Bildnis* (Berlin: Reimer, 1910), 178–79.

[12] Cf. Ludwig Geiger, *Geschichte der Juden in Berlin: Festschrift zur zweiten Säkular-Feier. Anmerkungen, Ausführungen, urkundliche Beilagen und zwei Nachträge 1871–1890* (1871, Nachdr., mit Vorwort von Hermann Simon, Berlin: Arani,

1989); darin widmet sich Geiger ausführlich der Wissenschaft des Judentums und sagt über Immanuel Wolf: "Das Judenthum, so definirte er, bezeichnet die Idee der göttlichen Einheit, die während der alten Zeit und im jüdischen Volke lebendig war, wenn sie auch Einwirkungen von anderen Völkern erhielt und sich von hier aus anderen mittheilte. Die mosaische Theokratie war der Körper zu diesem geistigen Inhalt" (177).

[13] Ludwig Geiger, *Geschichte der Juden in Berlin,* 180.

[14] Cf. Ludwig Geigers Erinnerung an die zweite Rabbinerversammlung in Frankfurt am 21.7.1845 (Ludwig Geiger, "Eduard v. Bauernfeld und die Frankfurter Rabbinerversammlung," *Allgemeine Zeitung des Judentums,* 1.11.1895), wo sein Vater den Vorsitz führte. A. Geiger unterschied ewige Sittengesetze von Ritualgesetzen, die Mittel zu religiösen Zwecken waren, jedoch kein Selbstzweck (d.i. Gottes Wille).

[15] 1910 warnt er etwa in einer öffentlichen Vorlesung vor Übertreibungen, die auf jüdischer Seite vorkommen, und meint unter anderem die "Überhebung der eigenen, d. h. der jüdischen Leistungen" (Ludwig Geiger, *Die Deutsche Literatur und die Juden* [Berlin: Reimer, 1910], 7).

[16] Cf. Jacob Toury, *Die politischen Orientierungen der Juden in Deutschland: Von Jena bis Weimar* (Tübingen: Mohr, 1966), 122. Sie hießen aufgrund konstitutioneller Zugeständnisse Bismarcks erfolgreiche Außenpolitik gut und durften national empfinden.

[17] Cf. z. B. Geiger, *Die Deutsche Literatur und die Juden,* 11.

[18] Werner Sombart et al., *Judentaufen* (München: Georg Müller, 1912).

[19] Sombart et al., 6.

[20] Sombart et al., 45.

[21] Monika Richarz, "Juden, Wissenschaft und Universitäten. Zur Sozialgeschichte der jüdischen Intelligenz und der akademischen Judenfeindschaft 1780–1848," in *Gegenseitige Einflüsse deutscher und jüdischer Kultur von der Epoche der Aufklärung bis zur Weimarer Republik,* hrsg. von Walter Grab (Tel-Aviv: Nateev Print. and Publ. Enterprises, 1982), 55–73.

[22] Shulamit Volkov, "Soziale Ursachen des Erfolgs in der Wissenschaft. Juden im Kaiserreich," *Historische Zeitschrift* 245 (1987): 315–42.

[23] Richarz, "Juden, Wissenschaft und Universitäten," 70.

[24] Volkov, "Soziale Ursachen des Erfolgs in der Wissenschaft. Juden im Kaiserreich," 328–29.

[25] Cf. *Literaturwissenschaft und Geistesgeschichte 1910 bis 1925.*

[26] Cf. Christoph König, "Wahrheitsansprüche. Goethes, Nietzsches und Hofmannsthals Ideen für eine allgemeine Philologie um 1905," in *Konkurrenten in der Fakultät. Kultur, Wissen und Universität um 1900,* hrsg. v. Christoph König und Eberhard Lämmert (Frankfurt am Main: Fischer, 1999), 44–58.

[27] Friedrich Nietzsche, "Unzeitgemäße Betrachtungen. Zweites Stück: Vom Nutzen und Nachtheil der Historie für das Leben," *Werke. Kritische Gesamtausgabe,* 3. Abt., Bd. 1, hrsg. v. Giorgio Colli und Mazzino Montinari (Berlin, New York: de Gruyter, 1972), 239–330.

[28] In *Die Nation* 4, Nr. 38 (1886/87): 569–70, hier 570.

[29] *Die Nation* 4, Nr. 38 (1886/87): 570.

[30] 1877 möchte er ihn etwa als Beiträger zu der von Elias Steinmeyer gemeinsam mit ihm und Karl Müllenhoff herausgegebenen *Zeitschrift für deutsches Alterthum und deutsche Literatur* gewinnen; er schreibt am 31.10.1877 an Steinmeyer: "Dr. Ludwig Geiger hat mich besucht, u. ich ihn. [...] Noch wichtiger schiene mir allerdings, wenn ihm ein regelmäßiger Bericht über humanistische Litteratur für den Anzeiger übertragen würde." Zu Scherers kritischer Haltung im Antisemitismus-Streit vgl. Jürgen Sternsdorff, *Wissenschaftskonstitution und Reichsgründung: Die Entwicklung der Germanistik bei Wilhelm Scherer. Eine Biographie nach unveröffentlichten Quellen* (Frankfurt am Main: Lang, 1979), 215–17.

[31] Geiger erinnert sich 1918, fast vierzig Jahre später: "Scherer . . . ging in seiner Liebenswürdigkeit, und ich darf wohl auch hinzufügen, in der Wertschätzung meiner Person und meiner Leistung, so weit, daß er, alsbald nach seiner Uebersiedlung, mir und andern erklärte, er wolle dafür Sorge tragen, daß mir eine Professur gewährt würde. Bei diesem wahrhaften und offenen Manne war Wort und Tat eins" ("Ranke und Scherer. Aus den Lebenserinnerungen von Ludwig Geiger," *Vossische Zeitung*, 20.6.1918).

[32] Cf. Michael Brenner, Stefi Jersch-Wenzel und Michael A. Meyer: *Emanzipation und Akkulturation 1780–1871*, Bd. 2 von *Deutsch-jüdische Geschichte der Neuzeit* (München: Beck, 1996), 274.

[33] Cf. Norbert Oellers, "Elf Bemerkungen zum Beitrag von Karl Robert Mandelkow," in *Literaturwissenschaft und Geistesgeschichte 1910 bis 1925*, 356–61.

[34] Aus einem Antrag Erich Schmidts an die Goethe-Gesellschaft vom 4.4.1894 (Goethe und Schiller-Archiv Weimar GSA 149/959, S. 313 Rückseite).

[35] Beide Dokumente GSA 149/968. Vgl. Roland Berbig, "'Poesieprofessor' und 'literarischer Ehrabschneider.' Der Berliner Literaturhistoriker Richard M. Meyer," *Berliner Hefte* 1 (1996): 37–99; Hans-Harald Müller, "'Ich habe nie etwas anderes sein wollen als ein deutscher Philolog aus Scherers Schule.' Hinweise auf Richard Moritz Meyer," Beitrag zur Tagung "Jüdische Intellektuelle und die Philologien in Deutschland" (Anm. 1).

[36] Vgl. Volker Ufertinger, "Erich Schmidt. Philologie und Repräsentation im Kaiserreich" (Magisterarbeit, Universität München, 1995).

[37] Cf. Wilfried Barner, "Jüdische Goethe-Verehrung vor 1933," in *Juden in der deutschen Literatur: Ein deutsch-israelisches Symposion*, hrsg. v. Stéphane Moses und Albrecht Schöne (Frankfurt am Main: Suhrkamp, 1986), 127–51.

[38] Geiger, *Die Deutsche Literatur und die Juden*, 81.

[39] Ludwig Geiger, "Faustsage und Faustdichtung vor Goethe," *Westermanns Illustrierte Deutsche Monatshefte* 67 (1889/1890): 752–67; vgl. Hans Mayer, "Faust, Aufklärung, Sturm und Drang," *Sinn und Form* 13, H. 1 (1961): 101–20.

[40] Geiger, "Goethe und die Juden," in *Die Deutsche Literatur und die Juden*, 81–101.

[41] Cf. Christoph König, "Loslösungsakte. Zur Vernunft in literarischen Werken," in *Literaturwissenschaft und politische Kultur: Für Eberhard Lämmert zum 75. Ge-*

burtstag, hrsg. v. Winfried Menninghaus und Klaus R. Scherpe (Stuttgart, Weimar: Metzler, 1999), 268–73.

[42] Geiger, "Faustsage und Faustdichtung vor Goethe."

[43] Cf. Christoph König, "Wissensvorstellungen in Goethes *Faust II,*" *Euphorion* 93 (1999): 227–49.

[44] Zu dieser Frage vgl. Julius Bab, *Goethe und die Juden* (Berlin: Philo-Verlag, 1926); Heinrich Teweles, *Goethe und die Juden* (Hamburg: Gente, 1925); Günter Hartung, "Goethe und die Juden," *Weimarer Beiträge* 40 (1994): 398–416 (vgl. auch dessen Artikel "Judentum," in *Goethe Handbuch,* Bd. 4/1: *Personen, Sachen, Begriffe A-K,* hrsg. v. Hans-Dietrich Dahnke und Regine Otto [Stuttgart, Weimar: Metzler, 1998], 581–90). Bab wendet sich als erster gegen eine aufgezwungene äußerliche Fragestellung; die Isolation eines Aspekts mißachte Goethes integrale Persönlichkeit. Doch das Leben Goethes ist ebenso exoterisch wie eine kulturgeschichtliche Idee.

[45] An Carl Friedrich Zelter, 19. Mai 1812, in *Briefe der Jahre 1805–1821,* Bd. 3 von *Goethes Briefe und Briefe an Goethe. Hamburger Ausgabe in 6 Bänden,* hrsg. v. Karl Robert Mandelkow unter Mitarbeit von Bodo Morawe (München: Beck, 1988), Nr. 961, 193.

[46] Vgl. Johann Wolfgang Goethe, "Zwo wichtige bisher unerörterte biblische Fragen (1772/73)," in *Ästhetische Schriften 1771–1805,* hrsg. v. Friedmar Apel (Frankfurt am Main: Deutscher Klassiker-Verlag, 1998), 131–40.

Peter Szondi and Gershom Scholem, Berlin 1971
(© Marlene Schnelle-Schneyder, Bochum)

Vom wahren Weg: Eine Respondenz

Amir Eshel

ALS ICH DIE AUFGABE ÜBERNAHM, hier auf Christoph Königs Vortrag über Ludwig Geiger und (wie ursprünglich auch vorgesehen) Michael Bernays zu respondieren, erinnerte ich mich an meine Geschichtslehrerin am Staatlichen Gymnasium von Haifa. Sehr deutlich sehe ich auch heute noch, wie die zierlich wirkende Dame im langen braunen Rock beim Sprechen über Strömungen im deutschen Judentum des neunzehnten Jahrhunderts plötzlich Züge einer mythologischen Furie annahm. Mit donnernder Stimme ließ diese Schülerin Gershom Scholems an den Ansichten von Leopold Zunz, Moritz Steinschneider und Abraham Geiger nichts, aber auch gar nichts gelten. Nicht nur hatten diese allzu gebildeten Wissenschaftler das Judentum nie richtig verstanden, sondern ihr Weg hatte, wenn nicht direkt, so doch zumindest über einige unwesentliche Umwege zum Niedergang des europäischen Judentums, ja gar zur Reichspogromnacht geführt. Das Werk dieser falschen Propheten einer gefährlichen Wissenschaft, dieser Vertreter einer fraglichen Reformbewegung, sei Teufelswerk gewesen und trage Schuld an beinahe allen historischen Folgen.

Solche Urteile dürfen niemanden wundern. Liest man, wie sich Gershom Scholem selbst über die Schriften von Moritz Steinschneider und Leopold Zunz äußert, so fällt sofort der dialektische Charakter, die eigentümliche Mischung aus Bewunderung und Abneigung, aus Hochschätzung und Verachtung, die seine Position bestimmen, auf. "Wie viel Kälte herrscht in diesen Wissenspalästen. Beim Lesen dieser Werke meint man plötzlich das Antlitz der Medusa erblickt zu haben. Etwas vollkommen Unmenschliches schaut einen an, und läßt durch Halbsätze und Nebenbemerkungen das Herz versteinern."[1]

Die Erinnerung an meine Lehrerin ließ mich neugierig in der *ha'Enzyklopedia ha'iwrit,* der großen hebräischen Enzyklopädie, nachschlagen. Unter dem Stichwort Ludwig Geiger las ich folgendes: "Ludwig Geiger. Literatur- und Kulturhistoriker . . . war ein extremer

Anhänger der Assimilation (*mitbolel kitzoni*) und sein Hauptziel war
es, die wissenschaftliche und gesellschaftliche Anerkennung der deutschen Gesellschaft . . . zu erlangen." Michael Bernays wird in der Enzyklopädie nur unter dem Stichwort Jizchak Bernays erwähnt, nämlich
als der zum Christentum übergetretene Sohn des großen Hamburger
Rabbiners.

Was mag zu solchen Bewertungen geführt haben? Wie dürfen sie
im Hinblick auf den literarischen Kanon dieser Gelehrten verstanden
werden? Und worauf deutet der jeweilige Kanon zwei der bedeutendsten Philologen jüdischer Herkunft in der zweiten Hälfte des neunzehnten Jahrhunderts? Ich möchte bereits jetzt eine vorläufige
Antwort auf diese Fragen wagen, um diese im folgenden ausführen zu
können. Ich möchte argumentieren, daß im jeweiligen Kanon dieser
beiden Gelehrten ein charakteristisches Spannungsverhältnis zwischen
Erinnern und Vergessen, Bewahren und Verdrängen, Lernen und
Verlernen aufscheint. Ein Spannungsverhältnis, welches vor dem
Hintergrund ihrer eigenen Person, zugleich aber auch ihres Kollektivs
betrachtet werden soll. Anders fomuliert: Mir scheint die Frage nach
dem Kanon *auch* die nach dem Ort der Philologie als Ausdruck des
kulturellen Gedächtnisses zu sein. — Warum eigentlich?

Die Biographien Ludwig Geigers (1848–1919) und Michael Bernays' (1834–1897) stellen mehr als den Gegenstand geschichtlich-
philosophischer Studien dar. Die Lebenswege von Geiger und Bernays
sind geprägt durch die zentralen Fragen im Leben eines jeden deutsch-
jüdischen Intellektuellen seit der Haskala und das mit zunehmendem
Nachdruck nach der Emanzipation. Im Mittelpunkt dieser Überlegungen stand der Widerstreit zwischen dem jüdischen kulturellen
und religiösen Erbe einerseits und den Theoremen und Lebensformen
der Moderne andererseits. Bezeichnend für diese beiden Philologen
sind die unterschiedlichen Versuche, diesen Widerstreit zu lösen. Und
die Lösung? Diese schlug sich eindeutig auch in ihren wissenschaftlichen Interessen, in ihrem literarischen Kanon nieder.

Michael Bernays stammt aus der Familie des Rabbiners *Chacham*
Isaak Bernays, der als erster in der Hamburger Talmud-Tora-Schule
neben der Religionslehre auch profane Fächer einführte. Seine Welt-
offenheit war indes bedingt, sie sollte vielmehr den Sog der Reformer-
ziehung eindämmen. *Chacham* Isaak Bernays stemmte sich gegen jede
liturgische Änderung im orthodoxen Ritual, gegen jede Reform-
bestrebung im Leben der Gemeinden. Über das Gebetbuch der Re-
formanhänger soll er gesagt haben, daß es sich zwar um ein Gebetbuch handle, nicht aber um ein jüdisches. Sein Schüler Samson

Raphael Hirsch wurde der bedeutendste Vertreter der deutschen Orthodoxie im neunzehnten Jahrhundert.

Man kann aus heutiger Sicht die Tiefe des Bruchs, den Michael Bernays durch seine Taufe 1856 vollzog, kaum überschätzen. Sie bedeutete die bewußte, eindeutige Trennung von der Welt seiner Eltern, von seiner Vergangenheit. Dem entspricht in verblüffender Konsequenz sein Kanon. Man kann sich kaum des Eindrucks erwehren, daß es sich dabei um die Tilgung jeder Spur seiner Herkunft handelt: die Klassik, besonders Homer, Goethe, Schiller, Shakespeare, Herder, Schlegel, Haller, Wieland und Klopstock und immer wieder Goethe.

Reste verlorener Welten sucht man bei dem Münchner Professor Michael Bernays, wie aus seinen Briefen deutlich wird, vergeblich. Ein bezeichnendes Beispiel dafür bietet seine Verehrung für Richard Wagner. Im Oktober 1877 besucht er den Verfasser des 1850 erschienenen *Die Juden in der Musik* in der Villa Wahnfried. Mit Cosima Wagner spricht er über den persönlichen Wert und Einfluß der Wagnerianer.[2] Zutiefst gerührt vom Plaudern mit dem großen Meister und dessen Frau schreibt Bernays an Hermann Uhde und Frau über Wagners *Parsifal,* nicht ohne eine persönliche Auslegung des Plots hinzufügen: In der Figur der Cundrie/Kundry sieht Bernays "eine Art von ewiger Jüdin." Diese Cundrie wird, weil sie lachte, als sie den Heiland am Kreuze sieht, "zu ewigem Lachen verdammt, wird von dem Zauberer Klingsohr als Werkzeug der Verführung gebraucht und findet weinend den ersehnten Tod, da Parsifal ihr durch die Taufe den Glauben an den Erlöser giebt." Viel entschiedener als bei Wolfram ist bei Wagner, so Bernays, "die christliche Weltidee, die bewegende Kraft des Ganzen."[3]

Michael Bernays verband seine Ansichten über Literatur mit politischen Grundsätzen. Zum Deutsch-Französischen Krieg schreibt er am 18. September 1870 an den Bremer Bürgermeister Otto Gildemeister:

> Die endlich aufleuchtende Sonne deutscher Herrlichkeit blendet fast zu sehr. Vor der Erkenntnis, daß durch die Thaten unseres Volkes, das seine lange verhüllte Größe vor aller Welt Augen offenbart, von nun an der Geschichte Europas neue Bahnen vorgeschrieben werden, daß die europäischen Geschicke von jetzt an ihren Schwerpunct in Deutschland finden, vor dieser Erkenntnis schwindet jede andere Betrachtung. . . . Das deutsche Volk verliert den zweideutigen Titel der Dichter und Denker. . . . Auch dem Blödsichtigen muß es einleuchten, daß an unserer Literattur, deren Entwicklung gleichzeitig

ist mit der steigenden Größe Preußens, sich das Nationalgefühl wieder aufgebaut hat.[4]

Der Rabbinersohn, der ohne die Ideen des Liberalismus sein Leben wahrscheinlich im Ghetto verbracht hätte, zeigt sich nach den Wahlen in München im Sommer 1878 über die Vermehrung der Sozialdemokraten geradezu erschrocken. Hermann Uhde und Frau gibt er zu bedenken, daß der "vulgäre, despotische, aller tieferen Lebensauffassung abgewandte Liberalismus" seit langem den Untergang verdiene, darüberhinaus sei er vollkommen unfähig, diesen abzuwehren.[5]

Vergessen, Verdrängen, Verlernen: In dem mit dem Jahr 1857 einsetzenden detaillierten Verzeichnis der Publikationen Michael Bernays' — erstellt von Georg Witkowski — versucht man vergebens nach Zeichen, die auf die Jahre vor 1856 einen Hinweis geben könnten.

Im turbulenten Jahr 1848, acht Jahre also vor der Taufe Bernays', erblickt Ludwig Geiger das Licht der Welt in Breslau. Sein Vater Abraham Geiger, seit fünf Jahren — nach erbitterten Auseinandersetzungen mit den Orthodoxen — Oberrabbiner der Breslauer Jüdischen Gemeinde, gehörte zur ersten Generation der *Wissenschaft des Judentums*. In der Orthodoxie sah Abraham Geiger nicht nur die Folge geistiger Versteinerung, sondern auch eine Gefahr für den Prozeß der gesellschaftlichen Assimilierung der Juden. Sein religiös-gesellschaftliches Programm bestand darin, das Judentum zu einem Bestandteil der allgemeinen, d.h. europäischen Kultur zu machen. Unter diesem Aspekt könnte auch sein theologischer Eifer, der von einem bezeichnenden philologischen Interesse begleitet war, verstanden werden. Beides stellte Abraham Geiger unter Beweis in seiner *Urschrift und Übersetzung der Bibel* (1857) und in seinen Übersetzungen aus dem Werk Ibn Gabirols (1867) und Jehuda Halevis (1851).

Abraham Geigers Sohn Ludwig setzte diese Linie auf seine Art fort. In der Vorrede zu dem 1910 erschienenen *Die Deutsche Literatur und die Juden* schrieb er: "Das Interesse für die Literaturgeschichte der Juden, mir durch meinen Vater eingeflößt, erfüllte mich von früher Kindheit an."[6] Weder in seinem beruflichen Werdegang noch in seinen wissenschaftlichen Interessen kann Ludwig Geiger eine gleichgültige Haltung seiner kulturellen Herkunft gegenüber attestiert werden. Daß sich der Philologe dem Humanismus, der italienischen Renaissance und Goethe widmete, ist bekannt und bereits angesprochen worden. Ich möchte mein Augenmerk darauf richten, daß der 34-fache Herausgeber des *Goethe-Jahrbuches* ein stetes Interesse an historisch-jüdischen Themen zeigte. Dieses erstreckte sich von Themen

wie die *Urteile griechischer und römischer Schriftsteller über Juden und
Judentum* (1873) über das *Studium der hebräischen Sprache im
Deutschland des 15. und 16. Jahrhunderts* (1870) bis hin zur *Geschichte
der Juden in Berlin* (1871). Letztere schrieb Geiger im Auftrag der
Berliner Jüdischen Gemeinde, in der er mehrere Ehrenämter beklei-
dete. Mir scheint an der Person Ludwig Geigers gerade dies interes-
sant zu sein, daß er sowohl über Petrarca (1874) und Reuchlin (1871)
als auch über Mendelssohn, Zunz, Michael Sachs und nicht zuletzt
Abraham Geiger schrieb. Bezeichnend für den Gelehrten Geiger ist
auch, daß er sich nicht von den gesellschaftlichen, gar tagespolitischen
Belangen des öffentlichen jüdischen Lebens im Deutschland seiner
Zeit fernhielt. Der überzeugte Anhänger der Reformbewegung und
Verfechter des Liberalismus, der sich entschieden gegen den Zionis-
mus wandte — was wahrscheinlich zu dem bösen Urteil in der ein-
gangs erwähnten Enzyklopädie führte — war Herausgeber der *Allge-
meinen Zeitung des Judentums* und der *Zeitschrift für die Geschichte der
Juden in Deutschland,* eine Zeitschrift, die er selbst gegründet hatte.

Auch im Umgang mit dem literarischen Kanon blieb seine Haltung *umfassend,* nichts ausschließend. *Umfassend* meine ich auch im
Sinne von nicht vergeßlich: Als Geigers Aufsatz über *Goethe und die
Juden* erschien, wurde ihm von jüdischer Seite entgegengehalten, er
habe mit seiner Schrift dazu beigetragen, daß "die Judenfrage" als etwas anderes "als allgemeine Frage der Humanität, der bürgerlichen
Gerechtigkeit oder der Konfession" betrachtet werden könne.[7] Diese
Haltung, nämlich über "Jüdisches" soweit es geht, wenig und unauf-
fällig zu sprechen, kommentiert Geiger wohlwollend, aber unmißver-
ständlich als einen "sogenannte[n] philosophische[n] Standpunkt,"
der mit dem "historischen" nicht verwechselt werden dürfe. An die
Adresse derjenigen Juden, die befürchteten, Goethe könnte durch seinen Aufsatz die Gestalt eines Judenfeindes annehmen, richtet Geiger
einen naiv-empirischen, dennoch durchdachten und klugen Satz: "Wir
wollen vergangene Dinge und Menschen sehen, wie sie gewesen sind,
Ihr [*sic*] wollt sie uns vorführen, wie sie hätten sein sollen."[8] Viele Juden, fährt er fort, fürchten, "daß durch die Aufhellung der Vergangenheit, durch Erzählung der Leiden ihrer Glaubensgenossen . . . die
neueren Judenfeinde in ihren Ansichten bestärkt werden. . . . Ich,"
schließt Geiger, "theile diese Furcht nicht."[9] Diese Antwort aus dem
Jahre 1887 bezeichnet einen eindeutig *anderen* Standpunkt im Spannungsverhältnis von Erinnern und Vergessen, Bewahren und Verdrängen, als der eines Michael Bernays. Fünfzig Jahre vor der Reichspogromnacht, als das Ziel einer gelungenen gesellschaftlichen Einglie-

derung der Juden noch greifbar zu sein schien, war Ludwig Geiger offensichtlich nicht bereit — trotz Goethe-Verehrung und fundiertem Interesse an der europäischen Kultur — seinen eigenen Standpunkt, sein *eigenes* kulturelles Gedächtnis aufzugeben.

In seinem Aufsatz "Die Wissenschaft des Judentums damals und heute" (*chochmat jsrael bajamin habem hubazntan hase*) aus dem Jahre 1961 wirft Gershom Scholem unter anderem die Frage auf, wie das Programm der Wissenschaft des Judentums angesichts der Shoah bewertet werden kann. Scholem hält fest: "Die Shoah machte zu Null und Nichte einen Standpunkt, der nur vor ihr möglich gewesen war. Nach der Shoah kann man das Judentum nicht anders betrachten als in der Kontinuität eines gesellschaftlichen Kollektivs, das zwar mit der Inspiration großer Ideen hadert, sich aber von ihnen nie völlig leiten oder verknechten läßt."[10] Das Hadern um die Form des kulturellen Gedächtnisses blieb auch nach der Shoah, wenn auch unter anderen Voraussetzungen, fundamental; bedeutende jüdische Philologen, die *nach* der Shoah wirkten, rangen und ringen darum. Ein charakteristisches Beispiel dafür bietet ein hervorragender Vertreter der deutschen Philologie unseres Jahrhunderts. Ich meine Peter Szondi, dessen Briefe uns Christoph König und Thomas Sparr auf eine so bemerkenswerte Weise vorgelegt haben. Peter Szondi, ein aus Ungarn gebürtiger Jude, der 1944 nach Bergen-Belsen deportiert wurde und nur durch das Kaziner-Abkommen gerettet werden konnte, folgte sowohl in seinem literarischen Kanon als auch in klaren politisch-menschlichen Positionen (erinnert sei an den Fall Staiger und an Hans Egon Holthusen) Scholems tiefsinniger Erkenntnis. Neben der intensiven Beschäftigung mit Shakespeare, Hölderlin und Kleist legte Szondi einzigartige Celan-Lektüren vor, und er setzte sich unermüdlich für das Werk Walter Benjamins ein. Wie sehr Peter Szondi in seiner Person und Biographie den Widerstreit zwischen den Ideen und Lebensformen der Moderne einerseits und der Suche nach einem eigenen "Fixpunkt der inneren Geographie"[11] andererseits repräsentierte, belegt sein Briefwechsel mit Gershom Scholem.

Scholems Anfrage, ob er den Lehrstuhl für Komparatistik an der Hebrew University übernehmen wolle, beantwortete Peter Szondi in einem Brief vom 26. Februar 1970 abschlägig: "Wenn ich vorhin sagte, daß Sie und Ihre Frau genau wissen, was in einem vorgeht, der in meiner Lage ist, dann meinte ich es nicht nur allgemein. Sie haben einmal in Jerusalem mit einem in seiner Hellsichtigkeit zwar nicht überraschenden, aber unvergesslichen Satz gesagt, warum ich in Deutschland lebe und wohl hier bleiben werde: weil ich es verlernt habe, zu Hause zu sein. . . . Das ist eine Krankheit, die man vielleicht mit der Rosskur einer, aus welchem Grund auch immer, notwendig werdenden Emigration heilen könnte; aus freiem Willen bringe ich die Kraft zu diesem Schritt umso weniger auf, als ich in Jerusalem vor zwei Jahren ja nicht nur empfand, dass ich dort zu Hause bin, sondern auch, dass ich das nicht ertrage."[12]

Es gibt nur wenig mir bekannte Zeugnisse, die ähnlich dokumentieren, welchen persönlichen und fachlichen Widerstreit jüdische Philologen, besonders nach der Shoah, auszuhalten haben. Dies gilt besonders für diejenigen, die sich der Germanistik zuwandten, aber auch für die jüdischen Lyriker, die weiterhin deutsch schrieben. Zwischen Lernen und Verlernen, auf der Suche nach einem nie ganz erreichbaren Fixpunkt der inneren Geographie: Jüdische Philologen, die sich weder in ihrem Kanon noch in ihrem Leben verleugnen, versuchen sich dem Widerstreit auszusetzen, sie versuchen den Weg zu gehen, den Franz Kafka als den "wahre[n] Weg" aufspürte: "Der wahre Weg geht über ein Seil, das nicht in der Höhe gespannt ist, sondern knapp über dem Boden. Es scheint mehr bestimmt stolpernd zu machen, als begangen zu werden."[13]

Anmerkungen

[1] Gershom Scholem, "Mitoch hirhurim al chochmat jsrael" (Aus Reflexionen zur Wissenschaft des Judentums), in *Dwarim be'go* (Explications and Implications: Writings on Jewish Heritage and Renaissance) (Tel Aviv: Am Oved Publishers, 1990), 385–403, hier 392.

[2] Vgl. *Briefe von und an Michael Bernays* (Berlin: B. Behr's Verlag, 1907), 28.

[3] *Briefe von und an Michael Bernays,* 30.

[4] *Briefe von und an Michael Bernays,* 94–96.

[5] *Briefe von und an Michael Bernays,* 50.

[6] Ludwig Geiger, *Die Deutsche Literatur und die Juden* (Berlin: Druck und Verlag von Georg Reimer, 1910), VII.

[7] Ludwig Geiger, "Goethe und die Juden," in *Vorträge und Versuche: Beiträge zur Litteratur-Geschichte von Ludwig Geiger* (Dresden: Verlag von L. Ehlermann, 1890), 215–80, hier 256.

[8] Geiger, "Goethe und die Juden," 261.

[9] Geiger, "Goethe und die Juden," 261.

[10] Gershom Scholem, "Die Wissenschaft des Judentums damals und heute" (Chochmat jsrael bajamin hahem hubazman hase), in *Od dawar* (Explications and Implications: Writings on Jewish Heritage and Renaissance, vol. 2) (Tel Aviv: Am Oved Publishers, 1989), 133–42, hier 139–40.

[11] Szondi an Gershom Scholem, Berlin, 3. Mai 1969, *Peter Szondi: Briefe,* hrsg. v. Christoph König and Thomas Sparr (Frankfurt am Main: Suhrkamp, 1993), 266–67.

[12] Szondi an Gershom Scholem, Berlin-Grunewald, 26. Februar 1970, *Peter Szondi: Briefe,* 301–3.

[13] Franz Kafka, [Fragment], in *Nachgelassene Schriften und Fragmente,* hrsg. v. Jost Schillemeit, Bd. 2 (Frankfurt am Main: S. Fischer Verlag, 1992), 113.

Panelists' Commentary

HANNE KNICKMANN (DEUTSCHES LITERATURARCHIV, MARBACH):
Herr König hat in seinem Vortrag am Beispiel von Ludwig Geiger gezeigt, wie schwierig es ist, nach Gemeinsamkeiten unter jüdischen
Philologen zu fragen. Sein Vorschlag dazu ist eine kritische Fachge-
schichte, die die vom Philologen getroffene Wahl des Gegenstandes
als Wertung versteht.

Dazu eine generelle Anmerkung: Mir scheint, daß in der Beschäftigung mit der deutsch-jüdischen Kulturgeschichte die Diskussion um die
"richtigen" Fragen mindestens so viel Raum einnimmt wie die um die
Antworten. Mich interessiert also die Art und Weise, wie die deutsch-
jüdische Kulturgeschichte befragt wird. Man stößt da schnell auf eine
stereotype Struktur: zuerst wird die Dringlichkeit des Themas bestätigt
und dann folgt meistens ein Einwand, daß aber die Fragen in der ge-
genwärtigen Formulierung dem Thema nicht gerecht werden können.
Sie werden demontiert und neu formuliert, und erst dann folgen Antworten und Stellungnahmen. Ein Beispiel dafür ist der Band *Judentaufen*, den Herr König erwähnt hat.[1] Es sind die gesammelten Antworten auf eine Umfrage, mit der man sich aus Anlass von Sombarts
1911 erschienenem Buch *Die Juden und das Wirtschaftsleben* an Reprä-
sentanten des kulturellen Lebens gerichtet hatte.[2] Auch hier haben die
meisten die ihnen vorgelegten Fragen zuerst einmal kritisiert und um-
formuliert, bevor sie sie beantworteten. Ein anderes Beispiel wäre auch
der 1994 erschienene Band mit Gesprächen über *Jüdisches Denken in
Frankreich* von Elisabeth Weber.[3] Die Reaktionen gingen wieder in die
gleiche Richtung: das Thema sei wichtig, die Fragen müssten beant-
wortet werden, aber sie seien nicht richtig gestellt.

Zurück zu Herrn Königs Vorschlag, die Wahl des Gegenstandes
als Wertung zu verstehen. Ich möchte hier zum Vergleich kurz auf
Eduard Berend (1883–1973) eingehen, der fast im Alleingang die historisch-kritische Jean Paul Ausgabe bewerkstelligt hat.[4] Es gibt einen
Brief an Karl Wolfskehl, in dem Berend schrieb: "Eine Gesamtausgabe
gibt ja aber nur den Gott selbst, den dann jeder nach seiner Weise an-
beten mag."[5] Berend wollte damit der grundsätzlich anderen Klassi-
ker-Verehrung im Georgekreis begegnen. Hier läßt sich ein Bogen

spannen zu dem ersten Teil unserer heutigen Diskussion, als es um das "Ich" des Philologen ging. Denn mit dieser Äußerung, die durchaus programmatisch gemeint war, trat Berend mit seiner Person hinter den Autor zurück, den er edierte. Das ging nur, weil er erstens auf Jean Paul und zweitens auf die Möglichkeit einer objektiven Edition vertraute. Einige, die Berend persönlich gekannt haben, haben mir erzählt, er habe sein Lebenswerk wohl auch deshalb Jean Paul gewidmet, weil Jean Paul einer der wenigen deutschen Autoren gewesen sei, von denen es keine antisemitischen Äußerungen gibt.

Eduard Berend and Käte Hamburger
(© Deutsches Literaturarchiv Marbach).

Bei Goethe ist das nicht so. Wir haben gehört, wie Ludwig Geiger versuchte, damit umzugehen. Auch Michael Bernays (1834–1897) hat einen bedeutenden Teil seines Lebenswerks Goethe gewidmet. Anders als Geiger wollte er ihn aber nicht interpretieren, sondern in der Edition seiner Schriften selbst sprechen lassen. Ähnlich wie Berend glaubte Bernays, daß sich ein "wahrer" Text herstellen läßt, und er ging noch weiter, wenn er meinte, damit auch eine wahre Literaturgeschichte konstruieren zu können. Geiger interpretierte Goethe in der Nachfolge Lessings aufklärerisch. Bei Bernays, der sich 1856 evangelisch taufen ließ, steht Goethe in der langen und programmatischen

Einleitung seiner Edition der Schriften des jungen Goethe zwar im historischen Kontext der Aufklärung, aber der Begriff "Aufklärung" fällt nirgends.[6] Er scheint ihn regelrecht zu vermeiden. Für Bernays ist Goethe das große Vorbild der persönlichen Selbstbestimmung und der persönlichen Befreiung von der Geschichte. Aufklärung bedeutete Befreiung von der Tradition. Vor dem Hintergrund seiner eigenen Biographie fällt auf, wie ausführlich sich Bernays mit diesem Goethe-bild auseinandersetzte, freilich ohne auch nur anzudeuten, was Goethe hier für ihn persönlich bedeutet haben mochte. Im Vergleich zu seinen Briefen und dem, was eben in der Responsion über sie gesagt wurde, findet man in Bernays' wissenschaftlichen Publikationen keine persönlichen oder gar politischen Äußerungen.

Noch ein Wort zur Rolle der Editionsphilologie. Auch sie kann zu einem der Randgebiete werden, in denen Fortschritt möglich ist, ähnlich wie es Herr König thematisiert hat. Im Fall von Berend war sie ein Fluchtraum, der ihn gefährlich lange schützte. Bis kurz nach der Reichspogromnacht 1938 hatte er sich trotz ständiger Bedrohung in Deutschland halten können, weil er sich als Herausgeber hinter seinem Autor verbarg. Berend hoffte, seine editorische Arbeit in Deutschland fortsetzen zu können, indem er sich nicht selbst zu Wort meldete und sogar geschehen ließ, daß von ihm edierte Bände nicht mehr seinen Namen trugen. Als institutioneller Fluchtraum fungierte hier die Akademie, nicht die Universität. Berend hatte unmittelbar nach dem Ersten Weltkrieg drei Versuche unternommen, sich zu habilitieren, und ist dreimal abgewiesen worden. Er blieb sein Leben lang Privatgelehrter und edierte Jean Paul auf der Grundlage eines Werkvertrags mit der Preußischen Akademie der Wissenschaften in Berlin. In diesem Zusammenhang noch eine Bemerkung zu Gustav Roethe, der ja nach Geiger Präsident der Goethe-Gesellschaft geworden war. Berend hatte bereits in den Jahren nach 1910 den Plan einer historischen Gesamtausgabe entworfen und sich damit an Roethe gewandt, der vermitteln sollte. Zur Diskussion stand der Münchner Verlag von Georg Müller. Roethe sprach sich mit dem erstaunlichen Argument gegen Georg Müller aus, daß Müller zu national sei — das aus Roethes Mund. Sein Einwand wird erst verständlich, wenn man weiß, daß Georg Müller bayerisch-national, also süddeutsch-partikularistisch eingestellt war. Er hatte Anteil an der Zeitschrift der süddeutschen Partikularisten, den *Süddeutschen Monatsheften,* und finanzierte damit später seinen Verlag. Gegen diesen bayerischen Nationalismus trat Roethe an. Er behauptete zwar, Berends Fähigkeiten als Philologe zu respektieren, machte aber zur Bedingung, daß sich sein Mißtrauen "gegen die betriebsamen Literaturjuden" erst noch "als unberechtigt" erweisen müsse.

Eine letzte Bemerkung zur Rolle des bayerischen Partikularismus. Bernays war ab 1873 der erste außerordentliche und dann 1874–1890 der erste ordentliche Professor für Neuere Sprachen und Literatur in München. Daß sich jemand wie Bernays jahrzehntelang in diesem akademischen Status behaupten und dabei verkünden konnte, die einzige Rettung vor den beiden großen Gefahren des Liberalismus und des Katholizismus liege im Protestantismus, hat mit Sicherheit auch diese politische Komponente des Kulturkampfes zwischen dem preußischen Staat und der katholischen Kirche, der 1871 begonnen hatte.

Barbara Hahn (Princeton University): Ich möchte nur auf zwei Dinge hinweisen, die sich beide noch einmal auf Ludwig Geiger beziehen. Dieses wunderschöne Bild von Kafka mit dem Seil, über das man stolpert, möchte ich noch etwas straffer ziehen und zwei weitere Stolpersteine der deutschen Universität anmerken, die, glaube ich, Ludwig Geiger aus einer anderen Perspektive deutlich machen. Wenn ich es richtig sehe, dann war für jüdische Gelehrte im neunzehnten Jahrhundert das Vergessen sämtlicher jüdischer Gegenstände eine Voraussetzung der Integration in die Hochschule. Diese Auseinandersetzung fing an — ich hoffe, daß ich das jetzt historisch richtig hinkriege — mit der Berufung von Eduard Gans auf einen Lehrstuhl der Berliner Universität.[7] Als Eduard Gans in seine Habilitationsschrift über die Geschichte des Erbrechts auch ein Kapitel über hebräisches Recht integrierte,[8] wurde ihm vorgeworfen, daß dies die Chance zur Habilitation nachhaltig verunmögliche, weil dieses Recht nicht zum europäischen Kulturkontext gehöre, sondern woanders hinführe. Mit anderen Worten, es wurde als Voraussetzung dafür, an einer deutschen Universität Professor zu werden, verlangt, daß man vergißt, wo man herkommt. Die zweite Geschichte, die bei Ludwig Geiger so auffällig ist: Er hat nicht nur nicht vergessen, wo er herkam; er hat diese Gegenstände mitgenommen und sich um Dinge gekümmert, um die sich ein deutscher Professor nicht zu kümmern hatte, wenn er damals etwas werden wollte an der deutschen Universität. Das war die Literatur von Frauen. Erstens hat er eine Monographie über Therese Huber geschrieben und zweitens eine über Karoline von Günderode.[9] Wenn man sich anschaut, wie in Deutschland, das bis heute im Kanon der Literatur mit sehr wenig Schriftstellerinnen auskommt, im Unterschied zu England und Frankreich, wenn man sich anschaut, wie überhaupt Literatur von Frauen tradiert wurde im neunzehnten Jahrhundert, dann waren es immer Familienangehörige, die sich darum gekümmert haben. Wenn darunter ein Akademiker war, hat die entsprechende Schriftstellerin Glück gehabt und kam in den Kanon der Literatur. Alle anderen wurden bis ins zwanzigste Jahrhundert meistens nur von Doktorandinnen bearbeitet. Doktorandinnen verschwanden nach der Dissertation und haben diese Forschung nicht weitergetrieben, weil die deutsche Universität sich gegen Frauen so sperrte. Wenn man in diesem Feld sich anschaut, was Ludwig Geiger getan hat, dann ist das also doppelt ungewöhnlich. Er hat sich nicht nur um seine Geschichte gekümmert, er hat sich darüber hinaus um etwas gekümmert, was ihn überhaupt nichts anging, wenn er an einer deutschen Universität eine Stimme bekommen wollte. Die beiden Dinge zusammen: Vergiß', daß du ein Jude bist, wenn du an eine deutsche Universität kommst und wenn du das nicht vergißt, dann kümmere dich bitte nicht um Dinge, die dich ebenfalls nichts angehen, machen diese Figur doch noch einmal sehr ungewöhnlich im Kontext der Universität.

BERND WIDDIG (MIT): There are two adjectives that I found emphasized in Christoph König's talk that struck a chord with me when I read yesterday Ludwig Geiger's "Goethe und die Juden." And these are "ausweglos" and "verzweifelt." I just want to quote the first sentence: "Wer über Goethe und die Juden spricht oder schreibt, tut am besten von vorn herein ein Glaubensbekenntnis zu formulieren. Ich spreche nicht als Jude, sondern als Literaturhistoriker. Als Jude bin ich Partei, als Literaturhistoriker bin ich parteilos."[10] And I wonder especially after this morning's discussion how this is possible. When you read this article, Geiger's article, you read the incredible tension, "die Vergeblichkeit," of holding these two things apart and we are coming back to the discussion of this morning of saying "I." I think I realized that it may be an utopian notion of a public sphere, a place where one does not have to say "I." But in a system where identity politics does play a role, it may be ultimately dangerous not to say "I." Something Geiger tried and did not succeed in. Talking about identity politics it became again clear through this talk, how important positionality is. Geiger participated in the establishment of a *Kulturnation,* and he thought, he being in the university, that this would take place in a sphere where one does not have to say "I," where the ultimate project of establishing that *Kulturnation,* of establishing the German canon was all about saying "I," but with the exclusion of certain people who were not to say "I, the German." So, I think Christoph König's talk makes us aware about the tension between the establishment of a *Kulturnation* and a real public sphere. A real public sphere would have created a space where one could say "I." Maybe we can take up the question of the role universities did play in establishing a public sphere in Germany or in ultimately prohibiting a real "Öffentlichkeit" in the terms of Habermas.

Discussion

WALTER SOKEL: I would like to join Mr. Widdig about the question of "I" and the public sphere. We must realize that the Enlightenment and "die vorurteilsfreie Wissenschaft" of the nineteenth century which was based on the Enlightenment was an enormous step forward, but it had to be paid for. It was, to put it in terms of Kafka's "Ein Bericht für eine Akademie," an "Ausweg," but it was not "Freiheit nach allen Seiten." Now what we have to realize is that our identity politics of today is a reaction. Of course it is a justified reaction to a universalism that was not universal. And of course Hitlerism showed where universalism would eventually lead, so we need now this phase, but we mustn't stop here. We have to get back to the nineteenth century in many ways and to the Enlightenment and to a *real* public sphere, where identity politics will no longer be necessary.

BERND WIDDIG: I was very much reminded when I read this little piece by Geiger and I heard the talk, of course of Victor Klemperer's *Tagebücher* and again, if you want to describe these *Tagebücher* it was the "Ausweglosigkeit und Verzweiflung." Someone again, fifty years later, tried to deal with this notion of *Kulturnation* in a quite similar way as Geiger, but very self-consciously actually describes the "Ausweglosigkeit." When you read his dictum of 1934: Die Nazis sind undeutsch. I am the one who is German. They are *undeutsch*. Over the years he slowly had to acknowledge his marginality in this culture.

HASKELL BLOCK (SUNY BINGHAMTON): While going through Max Koch's *Zeitschrift für vergleichende Litteraturgeschichte und Renaissance Litteratur* and also his *Studien,* which he edited about the same time, I came across Ludwig Geiger.[11] Geiger was for a time associated with this project. Max Koch was also Jewish, but a very ardent nationalist.[12] He underwent some of the same tensions that have been discussed here. The battle between nationalism and cosmopolitanism was fought out to some extent in turn-of-the-century Germany over the field of Comparative Literature, which never really got very far in spite of these early efforts of Max Koch, which were somewhat misguided. I think the classic text here is the review by Benedetto Croce in *La*

Critica early in the twentieth century, in which he pointed out the methodological consequences of the journal that Koch and Geiger were editing.[13] But there were other forces also at work. There were Jewish comparatists in the late nineteenth and early twentieth century. One thinks of Georg Brandes (1842–1927), of Louis Paul Betz (1861–1904) in Zurich, and there were others.

Incidentally the allusion to Peter Szondi is I think quite apt here too, because Szondi thought of himself essentially not as a Germanist, but as a comparatist and did very important work in the study of Comparative Literature. I think there is a good article by Gert Mattenklott on "Szondi als Vermittler," which covers this point I think rather well.[14] But in Germany the field had hard going in a large part, because of the pressures of cultural nationalism when someone had the temerity to ask for a chair in Comparative Literature at the turn of the century. Well, we need more chairs for *Germanistik,* how could we afford such a luxury? And this is the story, it seems to me in large part, until shortly after the Second World War when the situation had radically changed. But there was obviously an opportunity missed here. I think the fact that Jewish scholars were drawn toward comparative study — and this has been the case in the United States since the Second World War also to some extent — I think that the awareness of the incentive of a cosmopolitan approach to literature was certainly not limited to Jewish scholars but seized on by them. It may be that their Jewishness rendered them somewhat more disposed to do so.

THOMAS SPARR (JÜDISCHER VERLAG IM SUHRKAMP VERLAG): Nur eine kurze Anmerkung zu dem Kanon. Ich glaube, die schwierigste Frage, vor die uns Ihre Beiträge stellen, ist die: Gibt es eine Gegenstandswahl, gibt es eine Auswahl literarischer Texte, die das Judentum der Autoren spiegeln oder die etwas über jüdische Philologen sagen? Ich glaube, daß man den Blick dann auch erweitern muß für bestimmte institutionelle Zusammenhänge. Das, worauf Hanne Knickmann hingewiesen hat, ist meines Erachtens sehr wichtig, nämlich daß Michael Bernays als protestantischer Professor in der Hochburg des Katholizismus natürlich eine Auseinandersetzung reproduziert hat, die viel mit seinem Judentum zu tun hat. Und die Bücher von Geiger über Therese Huber und Karoline von Günderode müßte man noch einmal lesen, ob nicht darin auch eine Auseinandersetzung mit dem eigenen Judentum stattfindet. Das Judentum wird, glaube ich, nicht nur dann thematisiert, wenn es wirklich ausdrücklich zu Wort kommt, sondern auch in anderen Zusammenhängen.

Editors' Annotations

[1] *Judentaufen,* von Werner Sombart, Matth. Erzberger, Friedrich Naumann, Prof. [Alfred] Weber/Heidelberg, Frank Wedekind, Hanns Heinz Ewers, Heinrich Mann, Prof. Josef Kohler, Fritz Mauthner, Max Nordau, Prof. Ludwig Geiger, Hermann Bahr, Prof. Maybaum, Richard Nordhausen, Richard Dehmel und namhaften Professoren deutscher Universitäten (München: Georg Müller, 1912).

[2] Werner Sombart, *Die Juden und das Wirtschaftsleben* (Leipzig: Duncker & Humblot, 1911).

[3] Elisabeth Weber, Hrsg. *Jüdisches Denken in Frankreich: Gespräche mit Pierre Vidal-Naquet, Jacques Derrida, Rita Thalmann, Emmanuel Levinas, Leon Poliakov, Jean-François Lyotard, Luc Rosenzweig* (Frankfurt am Main: Jüdischer Verlag, 1994).

[4] *Jean Pauls Sämtliche Werke: Historisch-kritische Ausgabe,* hrsg. v. der Preußischen Akademie der Wissenschaften et al. (Weimar: Hermann Böhlaus Nachfolger, 1927–; ab 1952 Berlin: Akademie Verlag). — Für die editorischen Richtlinien vgl.: Eduard Berend, *Prolegomena zur historisch-kritischen Gesamtausgabe von Jean Pauls Werken,* Abhandlungen der Preussischen Akademie der Wissenschaften, Jg. 1927, Phil.-Hist. Klasse. Nr. 1 (Berlin: de Gruyter & Co. in Commission, 1927). — Über Eduard Berend vgl. Hanne Knickmann, "Der Jean-Paul Forscher Eduard Berend (1883–1973). Ein Beitrag zur Geschichte der Germanistik in der ersten Hälfte des 20. Jahrhunderts. Teil 1," in *Jahrbuch 1994 der Jean Paul Gesellschaft,* 7–91; Teil 2, in *Jahrbuch 1995 der Jean Paul Gesellschaft,* 7–104 (mit Schriftenverzeichnis).

[5] Eduard Berend an Karl Wolfskehl, 10. Dezember 1913 (Deutsches Literaturarchiv Marbach).

[6] *Der junge Goethe. Seine Briefe und Dichtungen von 1764–1776, 3 Theile,* hrsg. und mit einer Einleitung von Michael Bernays (Leipzig: S. Hirzel, 1875).

[7] Die Geschichte von Gans' Berufung auf einen Lehrstuhl der Berliner Universität rekonstruiert Johann Braun, *Judentum, Jurisprudenz und Philosophie: Bilder aus dem Leben des Juristen Eduard Gans (1797–1839)* (Baden-Baden: Nomos, 1997), vor allem 46–74.

[8] Eduard Gans, *Das Erbrecht in weltgeschichtlicher Entwicklung,* 4 Bde. (Berlin: Maurersche Buchhandlung, 1824 und 1825, Stuttgart: Cotta, 1829 und 1835).

[9] *Therese Huber, 1764 bis 1829: Leben und Briefe einer deutschen Frau* (Stuttgart: Cotta, 1901); *Karoline von Günderode und ihre Freunde* (Stuttgart, 1895, Neudr. Stuttgart: Deutsche Verlags-Anstalt, 1970).

[10] Ludwig Geiger, "Goethe und die Juden," in *Vorträge und Versuche: Beiträge zur Litteratur-Geschichte von Ludwig Geiger* (Dresden: Verlag von L. Ehlermann, 1890), 215–280, hier 215.

[11] *Zeitschrift für vergleichende Litteraturgeschichte* 1 (1886/87), continued as *Zeitschrift für vergleichende Litteraturgeschichte und Renaissance Litteratur* 1 (1887)–18 (1910).

[12] Max Koch (1855–1931) became an "ordentlicher Professor" at Breslau in 1895. Breslau was one of the few German universities in which it was possible for a Jew to hold this post.

[13] Benedetto Croce, "Varieta: La 'Letteratura Comparata,'" *La Critica,* vol. 1 (1903): 77–80.

[14] Gert Mattenklott, "Peter Szondi als Komparatist," in *Vermittler: H. Mann, Benjamin, Groethuysen, Kojéve, Szondi, Heidegger in Frankreich, Goldmann, Sieburg,* hrsg. v. Jürgen Siess (Frankfurt am Main: Syndikat, 1981), 127–42. Also as: "Peter Szondi comparatiste," in *Figures de médiateurs. De l'Allemagne de Weimar à la France de la Ve,* ed. Victor Leduc (Paris: 1982), 69–84.

3: A Tradition in Ruins

Margarete Susman (© Deutsches Literaturarchiv Marbach)

Trümmer im Gepäck: Margarete Susman, Bertha Badt-Strauss und Hannah Arendt in der Emigration

Barbara Hahn

DREI AUTORINNEN — eine Konstellation, die sich nicht von selbst versteht. Soweit wir wissen, waren die Frauen nicht miteinander bekannt. Sie bewegten sich in unvereinbaren politischen und theoretischen Welten und kannten die Arbeiten der anderen wahrscheinlich nicht. Wir wissen nur, daß Bertha Badt-Strauss in den zwanziger Jahren zwei kurze Aufsätze über Margarete Susman veröffentlichte.[1] Die Texte dieser Autorinnen zu konstellieren, öffnet ein Spektrum überraschender Ähnlichkeiten und gleichzeitig von unvereinbaren Unterschieden. Das beginnt bereits bei einem gemeinsamen Interesse, das die Autorinnen noch in Deutschland entwickelten: Alle drei reflektierten ihr intellektuelles und politisches Verhältnis zum Judentum in der Auseinandersetzung mit zwei Frauen, die in der deutschen Geschichte keinen Platz fanden: Rahel Levin Varnhagen und Rosa Luxemburg.[2] Ihre Urteile könnten unterschiedlicher nicht ausfallen. Doch im Schreiben über deren Texte können sie alles miteinander verweben, was ihren eigenen theoretischen und politischen Ort in Deutschland vor der Emigration bestimmte: Jüdin, Frau, Intellektuelle, Politik, Freundschaft, Liebe, Literatur, Philosophie.

Die Lebensgeschichten der drei Autorinnen zeigen biographische Parallelen, die viele teilen, wenn sie Jüdinnen waren und vor 1933 in Deutschland lebten. In ihre Leben griff die Geschichte mit einer Gewalt ein, der sich keine entziehen konnte. Die älteste, Margarete Susman, wurde 1872, kurz nach der Reichsgründung in Hamburg geboren. Dreizehn Jahre später, und damit in einer ganz anderen Konstellation beginnt das Leben von Bertha Badt-Strauss in Breslau. Als Hannah Arendt 1906 in Hannover geboren wurde, war nur noch wenig Zeit, bis das deutsche Kaiserreich den Ersten Weltkrieg begann. Während zwischen den Geburtsjahren der drei Frauen insgesamt 36 Jahre vergingen, in denen sich Deutschland dramatisch veränderte, liegen die Sterbedaten enger beieinander. Margarete Susman starb 1966 in Zürich, Bertha Badt-Strauss 1970 in Chapel Hill/North Carolina, Hannah Arendt 1975 in New York. Alle drei beendeten ihr Leben in der Emigration; die Flucht aus ihrer Heimat und später das furchtbare Wissen um die Shoah prägte einen langen Abschnitt des Lebens. Der Bruch mit einer Tradition, so unterschiedlich diese auch bestimmt war, durchzieht als Schmerz, als Wunde, als Herausforderung an das Denken die Arbeiten, die diese Autorinnen seit ungefähr 1943 publizierten.

Die Voraussetzungen für intellektuelle Arbeit waren sehr unterschiedlich: Während Margarete Susman keine akademische Ausbildung bekam, weil der Vater ihr diese verbot, wurden die beiden anderen Frauen tief von der deutschen Universität geprägt. Als Bertha Badt-Strauss 1908 in Breslau über Annette von Droste-Hülshoffs Beziehungen zur englischen Literatur promovierte,[3] gehörte sie zu den ersten Doktorandinnen, denn Preußen hatte Frauen gerade erst offiziell zum Studium zugelassen. Hannah Arendts Studienzeit dagegen fällt in die Weimarer Republik, in eine Zeit also, in der der Anteil von Frauen an den Studierenden sprunghaft zunahm. Studium, Promotion — darum mußten Frauen nicht mehr kämpfen. Doch beide bekamen aus unterschiedlichen Gründen nie eine Stelle an einer deutschen Universität. Für Bertha Badt-Strauss wäre die Habilitation — die formale Voraussetzung für eine Professur in Deutschland[4] — ein völlig aussichtsloses Unterfangen gewesen; erst 1918 bekamen Frauen offiziell die Genehmigung dazu. Ob Hannah Arendt mit ihrer großen Studie über Rahel Levin Varnhagen diese Hürde auf dem Weg zur Professur genommen hätte, ist sehr zu bezweifeln.[5] Nach dem Januar 1933 war jegliche Überlegung in diese Richtung hinfällig.

An den Arbeiten der Frauen läßt sich ablesen, daß sie aus der Entfernung von der Universität eine Chance gemacht haben. Die Unabhängigkeit ihrer Sichtweisen ist Indiz dafür, daß der Raum ihres Denkens nicht eingeengt war durch die Vorgaben und Reglementierungen dieser machtvollen Institution des Wissens. Für alle drei waren die intellektuellen Bezüge, die sie sich selbst schufen, weit wichtiger, als eine universitäre Umgebung hätte sein können. Denken und Schreiben wurden nicht zur Profession, sondern blieben Leidenschaften, deren Raum, deren Zeit, deren Ort immer wieder neu und zusammen mit anderen Menschen produziert werden mußten. Es wird im folgenden also um Texte gehen, die nicht im Kontext der Wissenschaft als Beruf, sondern dem eines kritischen Denken als Berufung entstanden sind. Dieser Ort, der nicht ein für alle mal bestimmt werden kann, sondern immer neu erarbeitet werden muß, impliziert auch ein anderes Verhältnis zu Tradition und Überlieferung als das, welches in und durch eine Institution geprägt wird. Auch wenn nach dem Abschied aus Deutschland alles — die Sprache des Schreibens, der kulturelle Kontext, Bezüge zu Tradition und Überlieferung, Thematiken und Schreibweisen — neu zur Disposition stand, öffneten sich nur bestimmte Wege. Margarete Susman und Bertha Badt-Strauss, die vor der Flucht jahrzehntelang in Deutschland publiziert hatten, mußte der Bruch mit diesem Land anders treffen als Hannah Arendt, die am Beginn ihrer Karriere als Autorin stand.

Bei allen Unterschieden finden sich im Gepäck der Frauen andere Bruchstücke als in dem ihrer männlichen Zeitgenossen, und auch der Umgang mit diesen Resten ist anders. Paradigmatisch für diesen Umgang könnte man Anspielungen auf einen Trümmertext par excellence lesen: "Ich sitze hier auf den Trümmern von Jena und suche meine eigenen Trümmer zusammen," schrieb Goethe in einem Brief vom 16. November 1807 an Carl Friedrich von Reinhard.[6] Aus Goethes *Tag- und Jahresheften* wissen wir, in welchen Texten der Schmerz um den Verlust Schillers vor allem bearbeitet wurden: "Pandora sowohl als die Wahlverwandtschaften drücken das schmerzliche Gefühl der Entbehrung aus."[7] Schmerz und Verlust sind die Töne, die Margarete Susman ihrem Buch *Deutung einer grossen Liebe: Goethe und Charlotte von Stein* von 1951 als Motto voranstellt. Aus der *Pandora* zitiert sie Prometheus, der sagt: "Nicht sonderbar soll jedem scheinen, was geschieht, / Vereint er sich Dämonen gottgesendeten."[8] Hannah Arendt dagegen hält sich an Prometheus' Bruder Epimetheus, wenn sie in einem Brief aus Tel Aviv vom 14. Oktober 1955 an Heinrich Blücher in New York paraphrasierend zitiert: "Wer von dem Schönsten zu scheiden verdammt ist."[9] Das Verb der Zeile — "fliehe" — wurde ausgelassen, stehen blieb nur mit "abgewendete[m] Blick." Die übersprungene "Flucht" in dieser Paraphrase läßt sich durchaus symptomatisch lesen: Goethes *Pandora* im Gepäck — und die Emigration ist immer schon "mit dem schmerzlichen Gefühl der Entbehrung" grundiert.

Was aber nehmen die Autorinnen mit aus Deutschland und was zieht in den Jahren nach der Flucht ihre Aufmerksamkeit auf sich? Neben ihrem gemeinsamen Interesse an Rahel Levin Varnhagen und Rosa Luxemburg springt ein weiteres ins Auge, das sie in der Emigration ausprägen: Alle drei publizierten nach 1945 mindestens einen Text, der sich explizit mit der Frage auseinandersetzt, was das Wissen um den Holocaust für die Juden und damit auch für ihre eigene intellektuelle Existenz bedeutet. Ähnlichkeiten zeigen sich ebenso im

Umgang mit zeitgenössischer deutscher Literatur. Wie gebrochen das
Verhältnis zur Muttersprache sich auch immer konstituierte, literarische Texte bildeten nach wie vor eine Art Heimat. Wobei jedoch eine
scharfe Grenze zwischen öffentlichen und privaten Vorlieben gezogen
wird. Eine Zeitgrenze. Denn zeitgenössische Texte hatten nur dann
noch einen Wert, wenn sie sich mit dem Traditionsbruch der Nazizeit
befaßten. Öffentlich äußerten sie sich nur über Arbeiten von Schriftstellern, die die Erfahrung des Exils teilten. Bertha Badt-Strauss
schrieb über Thomas Mann und Karl Wolfskehl.[10] Wie Briefe und Essays von Margarete Susman zeigen, standen diese beiden Schriftsteller
für sie ebenfalls im Mittelpunkt der Aufmerksamkeit.[11] Hannah Arendt
bemühte sich als Mitarbeiterin des Schocken-Verlags um die Veröffentlichung von Wolfskehls Gedichten; und alle drei Autorinnen standen mit ihm im Briefwechsel. Hannah Arendt veröffentlichte darüberhinaus im amerikanischen Exil Essays über Hermann Broch, Walter
Benjamin und Bertolt Brecht. Ebenso wie Bertha Badt-Strauss sah sie
nun einen wesentlichen Teil ihrer Arbeit darin, deutschsprachige
Schriftsteller an die Sprache ihres neuen Landes zu vermitteln. Beide
begannen sehr schnell, auf Englisch zu publizieren. Bertha Badt-
Strauss veröffentlichte seit 1943 regelmäßig in verschiedenen Zeit-
schriften, vor allem im *Jewish Frontier* und im *Reconstructionist*.[12]
1956 erschien ein englisches Buch, eine Skizze von Leben und Werk
der Jessie Sampter.[13] Hannah Arendt publizierte bereits 1942 erste
englische Aufsätze, 1951 legte sie ihr erstes Buch in dieser Sprache
vor.[14] Für beide Autorinnen bedeutete die Emigration einen Perspek-
tivenwechsel. Der Blick geht nicht nur zurück nach Deutschland, sondern richtet sich auf eine neue Sprache, eine neue Kultur.

Sprachwechsel

Wer flieht, hat leichtes Gepäck. Auch wenn von all dem Zurück-
gelassenen — von Büchern und Papieren, Manuskripten und Noti-
zen — später wieder etwas auftauchen sollte, auch wenn dieser Rahmen eines intellektuellen Lebens irgendwann noch einmal wieder
aufgebaut werden kann: der Riß bleibt. Wer flieht, hat schweres Gepäck. Mitgeschleppt werden all die unsichtbaren Lasten, die man nicht
loswird. Am schwersten drückt die Muttersprache, die jeder Erinnerung, jedem Schmerz und jeder Freude ihre besondere Farbe gibt. In
dieser Sprache das ganze Durcheinander im Gedächtnis, von Kinder-
liedern und Gedichten bis zu Passagen aus philosophischen Texten,
von Splittern einer Sprache der Liebe und der Politik bis zu einge-
schliffenen Redeweisen der Alltagssprache.

"Es gibt keinen Ersatz für die Muttersprache," sagt Hannah Arendt im Interview mit Günter Gaus. "Ich schreibe in Englisch, aber ich habe die Distanz nie verloren." Diese Distanz zur anderen Sprache skizziert Hannah Arendt in einer doppelten Bewegung. Sie markiert einen Verlust, weil "die Produktivität, die man in der eigenen Sprache hat,"[15] nicht in den Text der fremden Sprache übertragen werden kann. Und gleichzeitig liegt darin eine Chance. Da die neue Sprache nicht von Erinnerungen an Laute und Rhythmen überschrieben ist — "im Deutschen kenne ich einen ziemlichen großen Teil deutscher Gedichte auswendig," sagt Hannah Arendt zu Günter Gaus —, bietet sie Raum für Fremdheit und Rauhheit. Gerade für das Buch über den Totalitarismus eine unabdingbare Voraussetzung, wie sich zeigen wird.

Margarete Susman war anders als Bertha Badt-Strauss und Hannah Arendt in ein Land emigriert, das mit Deutschland die Schriftsprache teilt. Sie mußte versuchen, in dieser Sprache einen Ton zu etablieren, der Distanz deutlich machte. Dies war einfacher als die Sprache zu wechseln, und gleichzeitig war es viel schwieriger: "Ich sehnte mich noch im Widerstreben nach dem wahren Deutsch, in dem ich alle Werte des Lebens empfangen hatte," schreibt sie 1964 im Rückblick auf diesen komplizierten Prozeß, "ich fühle auch heute noch immer wieder, daß die Kluft zwischen dem warmen, kulturgeprägten Deutsch und dem kalten sterilen Deutsch der Nationalsozialisten noch nicht ganz geschlossen ist."[16] Eine unmögliche, aber notwendige Passage zwischen dem Deutschen und dem Deutschen, das Wagnis der Zweisprachigkeit in einer Sprache, oder wie Erich von Kahler zum 90. Geburtstag von Margarete Susman an diese schrieb: "Aber waren wir Juden . . . , wir unentwegbare Weltbürger, nicht schon von altersher zur seelischen Zweisprachigkeit bestimmt? In ihrem Werk ist sie offenkundig und zugleich überwunden."[17]

Karl Wolfskehl

Im Sommer 1934 traf Margarete Susman im Schweizer Exil mit Karl Wolfskehl zusammen, den sie bereits um die Jahrhundertwende in München im Georgekreis kennengelernt hatte. Die "neue Schicksalsgemeinschaft der Emigration" eröffnete eine ganz neue Begegnung, in der die gemeinsame Gebundenheit an die deutsche Sprache und das unlösbare Problem einer deutsch-jüdischen Identität eine schwierige Liebesbeziehung grundieren. So schwierig, daß Susman in ihrer Autobiographie mehrfach von "Wahnsinn" spricht: "Dazu kam ein Wahnsinn, in dem er mich bestärkte: ich hatte lange das Gefühl, daß wir unter den Menschen völlig allein seien, denn ich allein glaubte ihm in seinem schweren Kampf zu helfen, der um seine neue jüdische Dichtung entbrannte, während er doch von allen, die ich je gekannt habe, die meisten Menschen um sich hatte."[18]

Wolfskehls "jüdische Dichtung," die er 1934 unter dem Titel *Die Stimme spricht* veröffentlichte, wurde selbst wie im "Wahnsinn" produziert. Susman schreibt, daß der Dichter sie "ohne eigenen Willen" schrieb, "nächtlich aus schweren Träumen aufgeschreckt." Umso wichtiger daher eine Instanz, die garantiert, daß diese Dichtung mit ihrer fast unerträglichen Spannung zwischen deutscher Sprache und "jüdischem Schicksal" auch verstanden wird. Doch in dieses neue Verhältnis von Literatur und deren Kritikern ist ein Ungewicht gefügt.[19] Wolfskehl nimmt Susmans Verstehen und betont mehrfach, "was ihre öffentlichen Worte mir an Freude geschenkt haben und an Beruhigung,"[20] doch die umgekehrte Bewegung sucht man in den an die Freundin gerichteten Gedichten und Briefen vergeblich. Er versteht sie nur als Interpretin seiner eigenen Arbeit, nicht als Theoretikerin eigenen Rechts. Dieser "Wahnsinn" der Einseitigkeit zerstört die Liebesbeziehung. Und mit ihr auch ein neues Verhältnis von deutsch-jüdischer Literatur und deren Kritik, das sich gerade zu etablieren begann.

Als Hannah Arendt mit Karl Wolfskehl in Kontakt tritt, ist dessen Dichtung in einen anderen Kreis getreten. Am Horizont seines Schreibens steht nicht mehr Stefan George; die Flucht aus Europa nach Neuseeland, das Wissen um den Völkermord hat diese Bindung an den Rand gerückt. Wolfskehl schreibt wie Margarete Susman und Nelly Sachs sein Kaddisch für die ermordeten europäischen Juden als Umschrift des Buches Hiob: *Hiob oder Die Vier Spiegel*.[21] Hannah Arendt, die als Mitarbeiterin des Schocken-Verlags mit Wolfskehl korrespondiert, ist an der englischen Ausgabe von *Die Stimme spricht* beteiligt, die 1947 unter dem Titel *1933 — A Poem Sequence* erscheint. In einem interessanten Ausweichmanöver entzieht sie sich der Positionierung, die Wolfskehl ihr brieflich bereitet. Am 6. Juni 1947 schreibt er, daß er soeben ihren Kafka-Aufsatz gelesen habe: "Man kann den Fall, den Dichter, seine Stelle in Zeit und Weltraum gar nicht deutlicher, nicht wahrer, ja ich muß sagen auch nicht endgiltiger hinstellen. Ich bin begeistert."[22] Hannah Arendt schlägt die Situierung als Literaturkritiker in ihrem Brief vom 17. Juni 1947 entschieden aus: "Ich habe mich natürlich über Ihre so freundlichen Zeilen außerordentlich gefreut. Haben Sie herzlichen Dank. Nur fürchte ich, daß ich mit dem Kafka-Aufsatz Erwartungen erweckt habe, denen ich schwer werde nachkommen können. Ich schreibe eigentlich nie über literarische Themen und bin gerade damit beschäftigt, ein Buch zu schreiben, so daß ich eigentlich Artikel garnicht mehr veröffentliche."[23]

The Origins of Totalitarianism, das Buch, das Hannah Arendt gerade schreibt, ist nicht das Buch einer Literaturkritikerin. Es ist auch kein Buch, das dichterischer Arbeit wie der Wolfskehls einen Platz geben könnte — die Korrespondenz mit dem blinden Seher wird nicht weitergeführt. Anders Bertha Badt-Strauss. Wolfskehl hatte sie als Übersetzerin seiner Gedichte ins Englische vorgeschlagen.[24] Sie selbst bemühte sich intensiv um Übersetzungen seiner Publikationen: "Es wird mir immer eine wehmütige Freude bleiben, daß Karl Wolfskehl, den ich in den Studententagen in München kennen gelernt hatte und mit dem ich in den Jahren seines Exils in steter Verbindung geblieben war, mir dies Werk als sein 'Vermächtnis' sandte und mich bat, dafür zu sorgen, daß es an die Öffentlichkeit gelange."[25]

Als seine Botin an die Öffentlichkeit spricht Wolfskehl sie auch brieflich an: "Widerhall und Zuruf müssen dem Dichter schönste Bestätigung bringen! Auch von anderer Seite höre ich gelegentlich, daß . . . mein Name bei den deutschen Juden Amerikas anklingt." Damit dieser Klang nicht verebbe, schickt er ihr Auszüge aus dem "neuen Buch," aus *Hiob oder Die Vier Spiegel.* "Es gibt mehrere solcher Runden," so fährt der Brief fort, "auch einen das eigne Leben in die Wirklichkeit hebenden Abschied ans Geburtsland."[26] Eine Frage findet sich nicht im Brief. Die Frage danach, wie die Botin selbst ihren "Abschied ans Geburtsland" bearbeitet.

Das furchtbare Wissen um den Holocaust

Vor ihrer Flucht aus Deutschland hatte sich Bertha Badt-Strauss nie in politische Debatten verwickelt; die Geschehnisse der Zeit wurden in ihren veröffentlichten Arbeiten nicht reflektiert. Unzeitgemäße und übergangene Figuren, vergessene und verborgene Traditionen — dafür interessierte sie sich von ihren frühen bis zu ihren letzten Publikationen.[27] Ein Text jedoch, den sie 1946 veröffentlichte, springt in die Zeit. Es ist keine umfangreiche Studie, wie sie die beiden anderen Frauen nach 1945 vorlegten — dafür war sie möglicherweise schon viel zu krank. Seit vielen Jahren litt sie an Multipler Sklerose und konnte sich eine solche Arbeit sicher nicht mehr zutrauen.[28] Ein kurzer Aufsatz im *Aufbau* ist es, der den Kontext ihrer sonstigen Publikationen umso nachhaltiger sprengt. Mit der Veröffentlichung von "Purim Vincent und Purim . . . Hitler" löste sie ein Gelöbnis ein, das sie 1939, kurz vor ihrer Flucht aus Deutschland, abgelegt hatte. Damals schrieb sie an einem Aufsatz über "das Purim des Jahres 1616," der nicht mehr erscheinen konnte, weil der zuständige Redakteur der Meinung war, allein die Erwähnung des Wortes Purim würde sie alle ins Konzentrationslager bringen. "Da war's, dass ich mir gelobte: wenn einst der Himmel mich aus diesem Abgrund befreite," so wolle sie noch einmal die Pessach Haggadah zitieren, daß "in jedem Geschlecht Einer aufstand, um uns zu verderben. . . . Und der Heilige, gelobt sei ER, befreite uns aus ihrer Hand."[29] Und so verbindet sie die Mahnung, "Gaskammern und Folterungen" nicht zu vergessen, mit der Gewißheit, daß der Mord an den europäischen Juden nicht das Ende jüdischen Lebens ist.

In Margarete Susmans Buch *Das Buch Hiob und das Schicksal des jüdischen Volkes* von 1946 — eines der ersten Bücher überhaupt, das den Holocaust thematisiert — fallen keine solchen Worte. Die ungeheure Eindringlichkeit des Textes beruht vielmehr darauf, daß nichts erzählt und nichts benannt wird. Wir erfahren nicht, wie und wo der Mord an den europäischen Juden geschah; der Text setzt voraus, daß die Leser dies "wissen." Es geht nicht um die Rekonstruktion historischen Geschehens, sondern ähnlich wie im biblischen Buch Hiob um die Frage nach dem Sinn dieses Geschehens. Das Buch ist daher auch nicht von der Suche nach einer Sprache für das Unvorstellbare geprägt, es zeigt vielmehr, daß der Riß in der Geschichte, der "Zusammenbruch," wie Susman sagt, von Kontinuitäten umschlossen bleibt, denen man nicht entrinnen kann. Nur in einer gewaltsamen Geste, die Züge der Selbstzerstörung trägt.

Diese tiefgehende Verletzung stellt Susman in ihrem Buch als "furchtbares Symbol für die Unlösbarkeit der Verknüpfung" von Deutschtum und Judentum dar. Sie erzählt die Geschichte eines "bekannten jüdischen Germanisten, der sich in den Tagen nach der Machtergreifung Hitlers vor einen fahrenden Schnellzug warf und sich mitten auseinanderreissen liess."[30] In diesem drastischen Bild, das im Buch mehrfach auftaucht, kulminiert ihr Verfahren der Parallelisierung unterschiedlichster Geschichten: Margarete Susman liest Hiobs Geschichte als Paradigma der Geschichte des jüdischen Volkes, eines "Hiob unter den Völkern," die wiederum das Muster für die Geschichte der deutschen Juden abgibt.

In der steten Wiederholung der Figur des Zerreißens werden Lesarten aufgestört, die in Susmans Buch gerne eine versöhnende Geste gegenüber den Deutschen, gegenüber den Christen gefunden hätten. Auch wenn Susman immer wieder auf Gemeinsamkeiten im kulturellen Kontext von Christen und Juden in Deutschland, von Juden und Deutschen als Teil Europas oder auch des Abendlandes hinweist, so bleibt doch eine unüberschreitbare Trennungslinie. Die Erfahrung der Wunde, des Risses, einer unheilbaren Verletzung können Deutsche und Juden nicht teilen. Im Völkermord haben auch die Deutschen ihre Tradition, ihre Kultur verloren. Doch der Preis, den sie dafür zu bezahlen haben, wird in Susmans Buch nicht diskutiert. Für diese Reflexion sind andere zuständig — der Prozeß des Durcharbeitens kann nicht geteilt werden. In einer zentralen Passage des Buches wird dies in aller Schärfe deutlich gemacht: "Auf die Frage, ob es ein Zufall war, dass gerade von diesem [dem deutschen] Volk dies Widermenschliche ausgegangen ist, ist die Antwort ein klares Nein: wir vermögen in der deutschen Geschichte, im deutschen Geist, in der deutschen Gesinnung deutlich die Wesenszüge aufzufinden, die — in unausdenkbar tiefem Sturz durch das Zeitgeschehen als Ganzes und durch unerträglich nationales Unglück — in diesen Abgrund hinabführte. Aber daneben stellt sich doch sofort die Frage: Hatten denn nicht wir, die deutschen Juden, an diesem Geist, diesem Wesen teil? Haben wir nicht in jenem Lande mitgelebt, seine Schicksale mitgetragen, seine Gedanken mitgedacht? Sprechen wir nicht seine Sprache? Haben wir nicht alles, was wir wissen und selber sind, in deutscher Sprache empfangen? Nannten wir uns nicht und waren wir nicht Deutsche? Nicht freiwillig, sondern künstlich, gewaltsam, mit den verworfensten Mitteln mussten wir aus diesem Volk ausgesondert werden. Wir mussten uns selbst zerreissen, um nicht mehr Deutsche zu sein, und wir haben es getan."[31]

Der jüdische Germanist, von dem Susman erzählt, jemand, der für die Pflege der deutschen Sprache schon von Beruf aus zuständig ist, wird so zum Symbol einer Trennung, die alle deutschen Juden vollziehen mußten. Einer Trennung, die alle lebendigen Verbindungen zu einer Sprache, einer Tradition zerstört. Mitten auseinandergerissen — das bedeutet, daß es keine Mitte, kein Selbst mehr gibt. Nur noch Teile, die kein Ganzes mehr bilden können. Die in sinnlose Partikel zerbrochen sind, weil die Einzelstücke in keiner Spannung mehr zueinander stehen.

Anders als Margarete Susman und Bertha Badt-Strauss griff Hannah Arendt in ihrem Kaddisch für die ermordeten europäischen Juden nicht auf biblische Traditionen zurück. Auch weist sie ihren Schreibort in *The Origins of Totalitarianism* nie als den einer "Jüdin" aus, wie es die beiden anderen Autorinnen taten. Hannah Arendt entwirft einen politischen Text, der keine Erklärung, sondern eine Theorie des Geschehens entwickelt. Wie Margarete Susman erzählt auch sie nicht vom Mord an den europäischen Juden, weil dabei der Gefahr des pathetischen Sprechens kaum zu entrinnen sei. Pathetik aber bedeute Verharmlosung, bedeute eine Rückübersetzung in immer schon Bekanntes. "Dies nicht," so sagt sie im Interview mit Günter Gaus, "dies hätte nie geschehen dürfen," und hält damit die Suche nach einem Denkraum offen, in dem diese Geschehnisse so auftauchen können, daß sie ihre Ungeheuerlichkeit in der Darstellung nicht verlieren.[32]

Das gelingt gerade auch im Rückgriff auf literarische Texte, die an argumentativ schwierigen Punkten eingeführt werden. Zitiert werden Marcel Proust, Joseph Conrad und Franz Kafka. Abgesehen von Kafkas Romanen scheint der gesamte Kanon deutschsprachiger Literatur unbrauchbar, um sich den brennenden politischen Frage der Zeit zu nähern. Die Texte dieser drei Autoren werden jeweils so eingeführt, daß sie mehr erhellen als theoretische Arbeiten: "Für die Gesellschaftsgeschichte der Juden wie für ihre Rolle in der Gesellschaftsgeschichte des vorigen Jahrhunderts gibt es kaum ein aufschlußreicheres Dokument als die Beschreibung, die Proust uns in 'Sodome et Gomorrhe' hinterlassen hat,"[33] heißt es im ersten Teil des Buches, der den Antisemitismus untersucht. In der Analyse des Rassismus wird Joseph Conrad eingeführt, der das "Entsetzen vor Wesen, die weder Mensch noch Tier zu sein schienen" in seinem Roman *The Heart of Darkness* als "Erfahrungshintergrund" weit besser erhelle, "als die einschlägige geschichtliche oder politische oder ethnologische Literatur."[34] Kafkas Romane schließlich öffnen den Blick auf bürokratische Strukturen, die in theoretischen Texten noch lange nicht auf den Begriff gebracht werden konnten. Kafka begriff die "Grundelemente bürokratischer Herrschaft mit all ihren Konsequenzen . . . ; in dem Verwandlungsprozeß der Wirklichkeit durch die dichterische verdichtete Einbildungskraft entstand ein Modell, das weit über die damalige Erfahrung hinaus gültig und vorbildlich ist."[35]

Ein Vergleich der amerikanischen mit der deutschen Fassung, die Hannah Arendt selbst erstellte, zeigt einen überraschenden Befund: Weit stärker als im Englischen wird im Deutschen die Bedeutung literarischer Texte für die Analyse herausgestellt. Während in der amerikanischen Version unterschiedliche Textformen nebeneinander zitiert werden, stechen in der deutschen die eben zitierten Passagen hervor. Hannah Arendt hat also in der Adressierung ihres Buches an ihre verlorene Heimat einen anderen Akzent gesetzt als in dem Buch, das ihren Namen als Autorin in der neuen Welt etablierte. *Elemente und Ursprünge totaler Herrschaft* enthält damit auch eine Spitze gegen Theoriebildung nach deutscher Weise, nach Art deutscher Universitäten. Denn diese impliziert eine scharfe Trennung theoretischer und literarischer Schreibweisen, eine Hierarchisierung der beiden, die auf der Seite der Theorie zu unverzeihlichen Blindheiten führt. In der amerikanischen Tradition dagegen kann ein literarischer Text auch für theoretische Fragen geöffnet werden, und eine theoretische Arbeit wird nicht mißtrauisch beäugt, wenn sie gut geschrieben ist.

Noch einmal — Schmerz und Verlust Margarete Susman über Goethe und Charlotte von Stein

Zwischen dem *Buch Hiob* von 1946 und der Neuauflage der *Frauen der Romantik* von 1960, zwei Büchern, die deutlich die Signatur der Zeit tragen, veröffentlichte Margarete Susman ein Buch, das merkwürdig zeitlos erscheint. Da es das Verhältnis von Deutschen und Juden nicht explizit berührt, fiel es zwischen alle Stühle. Die *Deutung einer grossen Liebe: Goethe und Charlotte von Stein* von 1951 entwirft die Geschichte einer unmöglichen Liebe. Doch wer liebt wen? Gleich auf der ersten Seite betont Margarete Susman, daß wir nur Goethes Stimme hören, nicht aber die der Charlotte von Stein. Sie verbrannte ihre Briefe an Goethe am Ende ihres Lebens, und daher ist sie so stumm wie die Frau im kulturtheoretischen Modell Europas, das Margarete Susman in den 20er Jahren entworfen hatte.[36] Wie es später in ihrer Autobiographie *Ich habe viele Leben gelebt* heißt, war die Perspektive daher zu Beginn der Arbeit an diesem Buch verschoben; im Mittelpunkt stand Goethe: "Was mich an Goethe überwältigte, war mir in schier unfaßlicher Weise verwandt und wurde mir doch erst in dieser letzten Zeit wirklich klar: seine unerhörte Liebe zur Schönheit in jeder Gestalt. Was mich dann in einem späteren Zeitpunkt zu meinem Buch über Goethe zwang, war das glühende und ernste Leben in seinen Briefen an Charlotte von Stein. . . . Um dieser Briefe, das heißt um seinetwillen habe ich mich bemüht, diese Frau zu erfassen, der er eine so gewaltige Liebe und eine so bittere Enttäuschung brachte und die mir anfangs schwer verständlich war, erst mit ihrer schmerzlichen Grabschrift die Art ihrer Liebe nahebrachte: 'Sie konnte nichts begreifen, / Die hier im Grunde liegt; / Nun hat sie's wohl begriffen, / Da sie sich so vertieft.'"[37]

"Gewaltige Liebe" und im gleichen Zug "bittere Enttäuschung" — als ob Charlotte von Stein in einem Verhältnis zu Goethe gestanden hätte, das — verkleidet und verwandelt — dem von Juden und Deutschen geähnelt hätte. Ein kompliziertes Spiel aus Spiegelungen, aus etablierten und wieder verworfenen Identitäten durchzieht das Buch. Es trägt abwechselnd Züge einer polarisierenden Konstellierung, die mit Konnotationen von "deutsch" und "jüdisch" spielt.

Goethe hat "Jüdisches" an sich; gleichzeitig ist er zutiefst "deutsch":
"Das Schicksal, der Weltgeist hat dem unsterblichen Antlitz Goethes
die Züge des problematischsten Volkes gegeben, das für die Großen
und Übergroßen, die es aus sich hervorgebracht hat, immer so uner-
hört teuer zahlen mußte. Goethe wußte wie wenige um die Gefahren
Deutschlands und des deutschen Wesens."[38]

Charlotte von Stein auf der anderen Seite ist ganz anders mit
Deutschland verbunden als Goethe. Ihr sei jeder Nationalismus fremd
gewesen; während Susman bei den späten Romantikern den "wilde-
sten Nationalismus"[39] fand, wie es in der neuen Einleitung zu den
Frauen der Romantik heißt, war Charlotte von Stein gerade nicht in
diesem Sinne "deutsch." Sie wird als in jeder Hinsicht "menschlich"
beschrieben — frei von Haß, frei von Ab- und Ausgrenzungen. Auch
wenn es Goethe allein ist, der diese unglaubliche Enttäuschung bei ihr
auslöst, so wird er in Susmans Buch nicht verurteilt. Die Beziehung
dieser beiden Menschen wird vielmehr so dargestellt, daß ihre Möglichkeit gerade darin liegt, daß sie keine Dauer ermöglicht. Eine Konstellierung wird entworfen, in der Verhältnisse nicht einfach applizier-
bar sind. Mann-Frau, Deutsche-Juden — alle polarisierenden Zuschrei-
bungen wechseln immer wieder die Plätze. Susman arbeitet mit
verschobenen Darstellungsformen oder besser gesagt: die Darstellung arbeitet mit dem Muster der Verschiebung.

Das Buch über Goethe und Charlotte von Stein, über eine unmögliche Liebe — könnte man es als ein zweites Kaddisch lesen? Aber für wen
oder wofür? Vielleicht ist es ein Abgesang auf das besondere Verhältnis,
in das Deutsche und Juden eingetreten waren.

Wechsel der Schreibweisen nach 1945

Die Wege der drei Autorinnen in der Emigration gehen weit auseinander, wenn wir die Schreibweise ihrer Texte betrachten. Bertha Badt-
Strauss hatte bis zur Flucht aus Deutschland den Schwerpunkt ihrer
Arbeit auf das Bewahren und Weitergeben von Texten gelegt. Durch
ihre Editionen und Aufsätze (Rahel Levin, Moses Mendelssohn,
Hermann Cohen) hatte sie an der Etablierung eines literarischen Ka-
nons mitgearbeitet, in dem gerade auch verborgene und vergessene
Stimmen einen Platz haben sollten. Ein Kanon für Juden in Deutschland. Diesem Kanon sollten Texte und Lektüren eingeschrieben werden, die — wie sich am Beispiel Rosa Luxemburgs zeigt — durchaus
nicht common sense waren. Die Publikationen von Bertha Badt-Strauss
arbeiten an der Stiftung von Gemeinsamkeit, die ausdrücklich kulturell und nicht politisch bestimmt ist. Nie bewegte sie sich schreibend

ins Feld der Politik, nie nimmt sie in diesem Bereich der Öffentlichkeit Partei. Für Bertha Badt-Strauss muß Schreiben diesen Abstand wahren, damit die Spannung zwischen Einzelnen und Gesellschaft nicht verloren geht. Politik erscheint daher als Raum von Differenzen, die mit anderen Mitteln als dem Schreiben ausgetragen werden müssen. Damit Unterschiede im Feld der Politik nicht verschwinden, braucht es einen getrennten Bereich, in dem Wege in der Tradition, zur Tradition erprobt werden können. Kulturtheoretisches Schreiben knüpft Verbindungen, die im Feld der Politik notwendig zerrissen werden müssen. Dieses Modell beruht auf zwei Prämissen: Die Politik muß demokratisch bestimmt sein, und in der Gesellschaft muß Raum für verschiedene kulturelle Identitäten sein. Beide Prämissen wurden 1933 zerstört. Der Wechsel in die USA scheint Bertha Badt-Strauss mit einem neuen Problem zu konfrontieren: Diese Gesellschaft funktioniert nach den Regeln der Demokratie. Doch kulturelle Identitäten scheinen enger mit politischen Parteiungen verbunden zu sein als dies in Deutschland der Fall war. Mit welcher Art des Schreibens darauf zu antworten gewesen wäre — für diese Frage findet Bertha Badt-Strauss keine Lösung mehr.

Anders Margarete Susmans Schreibkonzept. Sie hatte versucht, der chaotischen Vielstimmigkeit der Welt mit einem Schreiben zu begegnen, in dem sich viele treffen können. Seit der Jahrhundertwende reden alle Stimmen durcheinander, so schrieb sie in einem Essay über Georg Simmel.[40] In diesem Gewirr, das alle religiösen und philosophischen Gewißheiten des 19. Jahrhunderts suspendierte, versuchte Margarete Susman mit ihrem Schreiben einen Halt zu finden. Dabei schlägt sie einen besonderen Weg ein. Weder versucht sie, die Fragmente der Welt in ihren Texten wieder zusammenzuführen, noch experimentiert sie mit einem Schreiben, das Darstellungsformen für das Zerstückelte sucht. Sie schreibt, als ob man mit Freunden, mit Gleichgesinnten gemeinsam schreiben und damit der "unendlichen Einsamkeit" entrinnen könnte, die sie den wichtigen theoretischen Büchern des beginnenden 20. Jahrhundert attestiert hatte. Sie liest diese Bücher, als ob sie alle in einem großen Buch stünden. In diesem Buch des Denkens schlägt sie mit ihren Essays eine neue Seite auf und beginnt, in die Gedanken anderer ihre eigenen hineinzuweben. Sie liest und schreibt nicht, um Antworten auf Fragen zu finden; für sie sind Bücher "Fragen auf Fragen," wie Ingeborg Nordmann bemerkt hat.[41]

Für dies Verweben von Gedanken ist die monographische Studie nicht die angemessene Schreibform. Margarete Susmans Bücher sind immer nur Stationen in einem endlosen Prozeß. Jeder einzelne Ge-

danke könnte auch in eine ganz andere Richtung führen; kein Kapitel
ist so fertig und abgeschlossen, daß es nicht doch noch einmal neu
und ganz anders geschrieben werden müßte. Aufsätze gehen den Büchern voraus, die sich zu großen Essays weiten und in Aufsätzen fort-
geschrieben werden.[42]

Bertha Badt-Strauss, 1929

Susmans Schreiben verwebt also die Stimmen anderer Theoretiker und anderer Bücher in ihre eigenen Arbeiten und erzeugt so eine eindrucksvolle Polyphonie. Keiner ihrer eigenen Texte ist jemals fertig, abgeschlossen, erledigt. Und doch liegt in diesem offenen Verfahren eine Begrenzung. Ihre Texte produzieren eine Einheit, so brüchig diese auch ist. Keine Stimme mischt sich ein, deren Dissonanz den Zusammenklang nachhaltig stören würde. Die Welt *ist* im Buch; die Texte können bei aller Offenheit nicht genug Abstände erzeugen. Vor allem nicht zur Politik. Wie Hannah Arendts Arbeiten zeigen, ist dieser Abstand Voraussetzung dafür, daß sich dann wieder Begegnungen zwischen Heterogenem ergeben können. Hannah Arendt trennt Philosophie und Politik, sie trennt Geschichtsschreibung von literarischen Schreibweisen. Sie arbeitet in ihren Texten mit Bruchstücken aus den unterschiedlichsten Diskursen, die in neue und überraschende Kombinationen gebracht werden. Gerade auch in ihren Texten über Rosa Luxemburg und Rahel Levin. Beide sind — wie sie sagt — ein "unwahrscheinlicher Gegenstand" für biographisches Schreiben. Denn beide repräsentieren nichts, beide zeigen, daß ein Individuum in gewissen Abschnitten der Geschichte wie außerhalb der Gesellschaft leben kann — ohne gegebene Vermittlungsinstanzen.

Als Hannah Arendt die Biographie Rosa Luxemburgs von Peter Nettl rezensierte,[43] stellte sie die Analyse dieses Spannungsfeld in den Mittelpunkt. Rosa Luxemburg, eine "Randfigur" der deutschen Sozialdemokratie und Autorin theoretischer Bücher, die immer schon als Abweichungen gelesen wurden. Rosa Luxemburg, die gerade dann unrecht hatte, wenn ihre Meinung mit der der Mehrheit übereinstimmte. So unwahrscheinlich es also ist, gerade ein solches Leben biographisch zu bearbeiten, findet Peter Nettl doch Punkte der Synthetisierung. Seine Biographie ist daher — wie Hannah Arendt zeigt — ein Stück Geschichtsschreibung.[44]

"Unter den Büchern über den Imperialismus ist vielleicht keines von einem so außerordentlichen geschichtlichen Instinkt geleitet wie die Arbeit Rosa Luxemburgs. Da sie im Verfolg ihrer Studien zu Resultaten kam, die mit dem Marxismus weder in seiner orthodoxen noch in seiner reformierten Form in Einklang zu bringen waren, und doch sich von dem mitgebrachten Rüstzeug nicht befreien konnte, ist ihr Werk Stückwerk geblieben; und da sie es weder den Marxisten noch deren Gegnern hatte recht machen können, ist es fast unbeachtet geblieben."[45]

Als Hannah Arendt sich selbst einmal auf das Feld biographischen Schreibens wagt und Rahel Levins Leben beschreibt, vermeidet sie ge-

rade das, was sie an Nettl lobt. Ihr gelingt keine Geschichtsschreibung, wenn sie Rahel Levins Lebens skizziert. Im Vorwort ver-
wirft sie solche Intentionen sogar ausdrücklich. Sie will in ihrem Text
etwas anderes versuchen: "Was mich interessierte, war lediglich, Rahels Lebensgeschichte so nachzuerzählen, wie sie selbst sie hätte er-
zählen können."[46] Ein merkwürdiger Konjunktiv. Es gab ja nichts
Überliefertes, das man Rahels Leben hätte nennen können. Nichts also, was nacherzählbar gewesen wäre. Rahel Levins "Leben" besteht
bis heute nur aus Bruchstücken der Überlieferung. Ihr Nachlaß enthält Briefwechsel, in die sie die unterschiedlichsten Menschen verwik-
kelt hatte. Jeder Brief ist selbst schon eine Mischung aus narrativen
und reflektierenden Momenten, aus philosophischen und politischen
Gedankensplittern, die nie in ein System gebracht werden. Wie also
läßt sich etwas nacherzählen, das sich selbst nur in Bruchstücken gibt?

Hannah Arendt wiederholt in ihrer Biographie genau dieses Bau-
prinzip des Fragmentarischen, wenn nun auch sie Bruchstücke aus den
unterschiedlichsten Diskursen montiert. Biographisches Schreiben
praktiziert sie nicht als Synthesierung, sondern umgekehrt als Ausstel-
len einer Mischung von Kontingenz und Heterogenität, von Indivi-
duellem und Gesellschaftlichem.

So gesehen gibt es also eine Übereinstimmung zwischen dem
überlieferten "Text" Rahel Levins und Hannah Arendts biographi-
schem Verfahren. Arendt schreibt nicht über Rahel Levin, sondern sie
entwickelt eine Lektüre, die deren eigenem Schreiben korrespondiert.
Für eine Lektüre Rosa Luxemburgs wäre dieses Verfahren nicht angemessen gewesen. Rosa Luxemburg trennte Diskurse. In ihren Briefen wird nicht theoretisiert, in ihren theoretischen Texten nichts
erzählt. Es gibt narrative Texte (wie beispielsweise die Einleitung zu
Wladimir Korolenkos Autobiographie) und politische Artikel, in die
narrative Passagen eingefügt sind. Und es gab Leidenschaften, die sich
nicht in die Welt der Texte integrieren liessen. Bilder, Skizzenbücher,
Herbarien. Bei Rosa Luxemburg — so könnte man sagen — waren
gerade diesen scharfen Trennungen Voraussetzung für Produktivität.

Hannah Arendt konnte wie Rahel Levin nicht trennen. Immer
wieder wurde ihr vorgeworfen, daß ihre Texte unsystematisch und in-
konsistent seien. Doch ein Vorwurf kann dies nur sein, wenn voraus-
gesetzt wird, daß theoretisches Schreiben "rein" zu sein hat. Man
könnte aber umgekehrt argumentieren und sagen, daß genau dieses
Schreiben, daß diese Mischung dem Phantasma den Boden entzieht,
ein Text könne alles einfangen. Hannah Arendt stellt Lücken aus, läßt
Unvereinbares aufeinanderprallen. Dieses Textverfahren, das sie aus

der Lektüre Rahel Levin Varnhagens entnahm, ist zeitgemäßer als alle noch so geschlossenen Texte. Es rettet die Bruchstücke einer zerstörten Tradition, die damit nicht in die Geschichte der Sieger eingepaßt werden können. Es knüpft Stränge, die quer zu gegebenen Überlieferungsrastern liegen. Als Hannah Arendt mit ihrer fast abgeschlossenen Rahel Varnhagen-Biographie Europa verließ, hatte sie mehr im Gepäck als das, was ihre akademischen Lehrer sie lehren konnten. Bei Heidegger hatte sie gelernt zu denken, wie sie nach dem Krieg schreibt, und Jaspers' moralische und politische Integrität hatte ihr die Sicherheit gegeben, daß es trotz aller Brüche noch eine Herkunft gab. Doch bei Rahel Levin, die sie einmal ihre beste Freundin nennt, die leider schon über hundert Jahre tot sei, hatte sie etwas anderes gelernt: So zu schreiben, daß Heterogenität ausgestellt und nicht eingeebnet wurde. In Deutschland stieß dies durchaus nicht auf Verständnis. Dies wird in Blick auf eine Passage aus einem Brief Martin Heideggers an Hannah Arendt deutlich. Er las ihre Arbeit der Verknüpfung von Heterogenem ganz anders: "Du Hannah, Das *eigentliche* 'Und' zwischen 'Jaspers und Heidegger' bist nur Du. Es ist schön, ein 'Und' zu *seyn*."[47] Hannah Arendts Texte präsentieren kein schönes "Und." Sie bringen die Trümmer nicht zum Verschwinden, sondern reißen Diskrepanzen auf, die sich der Lesbarkeit immer aufs Neue entziehen.

Trümmer im Gepäck — auf unterschiedliche Weise arbeiten die Texte der drei Autorinnen an einem unlösbaren Problem. An einer Frage ohne Antwort. Eine zerbrochene Tradition ist nicht einfach durch eine andere zu ersetzen. Weder der Sprachwechsel noch die Suche nach einer neuen Sprache in der alten bieten eine Lösung. Daß keine aufscheint, daß der Bruch lesbar bleibt — darin liegt die Stärke ihrer Texte. Den Bruch zu lesen, bleibt immer noch aufgegeben.

Anmerkungen

[1] Vgl. Bertha Badt-Strauss, "Dorothea Mendelssohn und Rahel Levin. Gedanken zu Margarete Susmans Buch *Frauen der Romantik,*" *Bayrische Israelitische Gemeindezeitung* 6 (1930): 330–32, sowie diess., "Margarethe Susmann. Ein Dank zu ihrem 60. Geburtstag," *Bayrische Israelitische Gemeindezeitung* 10 (1934): 478, wo es heißt: "Wer jemals das scharfgeschnittene, wie von einer Gemme stammende Profil dieser Frau gesehen hat — die verwegene Nase, den bohrenden Blick des Auges unter langer Wimper hervor, den schmerzlich geschwungenen Mund — der weiß: hier steht eine ungewöhnliche Frau vor uns. Nur der Geist konnte sich solche Züge bauen." Susman, "diese unbekümmerte Wahrheitssuche-

rin," sei den Weg gegangen "von der Gemeinde der Einsamen zur Gemeinschaft ihres Volkes," so das Resümee des Aufsatzes.

[2] Bertha Badt-Strauss publizierte zwei Ausgaben von Rahel Levin Varnhagens Briefen und Tagebüchern, vgl. *Rahel und ihre Zeit: Briefe und Zeugnisse* (München: Rentsch, 1912); *Rahel Varnhagen: Menschen untereinander* (Berlin: Wettgeist-Bücher, [1928]) und einen Aufsatz über Rosa Luxemburgs Briefe, "Rosa Luxemburg," *Der Jude* 8 (1924): 186–89. Zu ihrer Lektüre dieser beiden Figuren vgl. meinen Aufsatz "Bertha Badt-Strauss (1885–1970). Die Lust am Unzeitgemäßen," in *Frauen in den Kulturwissenschaften: Von Lou Andreas-Salomé bis Hannah Arendt,* hrsg. v. Barbara Hahn (München: Beck, 1994), 152–65 und 330–38. Margarete Susman fuhr auch in der Emigration fort, sich mit diesen beiden Frauen zu beschäftigen; vgl: "Rahels geistiges Wesen," *Neue Jüdische Monatsschrift* 2 (1918): 464–77; "Rahel," *Der Morgen* 4 (1928): 118–38; "Rahel Varnhagen von Ense. Zu ihrem 100. Todestag," *Die literarische Welt* 9, Nr. 10 u. Nr. 11/12 (1933): 7–8 u. 11–12; "Rosa Luxemburgs Briefe," *Der Aufstieg,* 19.1.1923; "Rosa Luxemburg," *Neue Wege* 45 (1951): 435–40. In ihrem Buch *Frauen der Romantik,* das inzwischen vier Auflagen erreicht hat, ist ein Kapitel Rahel Levin gewidmet. Zitiert wird im folgenden aus der vierten Auflage, hrsg. v. Barbara Hahn (Frankfurt am Main: Insel, 1996). Auf Hannah Arendts Beschäftigung mit Rosa Luxemburg und Rahel Levin wird unten genauer eingegangen.

[3] Bertha Badt-Strauss, *Annette von Droste-Hülshoff in ihren Beziehungen zur englischen Literatur* (Leipzig: Quelle & Meyer, 1909); ein Nachdruck erschien 1978 in Ann Arbor/Michigan.

[4] Zur Geschichte des Ausschlusses von Frauen aus deutschen akademischen Institutionen vgl. *Frauen in den Kulturwissenschaften.*

[5] Die Geschichte von Hannah Arendts nie erfolgter Habilitation rekonstruiert Liliane Weissberg in ihrer "Introduction" zur Neuauflage von Hannah Arendts Biographie der Rahel Varnhagen: Hannah Arendt, *Rahel Varnhagen: The Life of a Jewess,* ed. Liliane Weissberg (Baltimore and London: Johns Hopkins UP, 1997), 3–69, hier 39–41.

[6] Johann Wolfgang von Goethe, *Werke,* Weimarer Ausgabe, hrsg. im Auftrage der Großherzogin Sophie von Sachsen, Abt. I-IV, 133 Bde. (Weimar, 1887–1919), hier IV/19, 459.

[7] Goethe, *Werke,* IV/20, 140–41.

[8] Goethe, *Werke,* I/50, 331.

[9] Goethe, *Werke,* I/50, 333. Allerdings sagt Epimetheus hier: "Wer von der Schönen zu scheiden verdammt ist, / Fliehe mit abgewendetem Blick!" Hannah Arendt, Heinrich Blücher, *Briefe 1936–1968,* mit einer Einf. hrsg. v. Lotte Köhler (München, Zürich: Piper, 1996), 411.

[10] Nachdem Bertha Badt-Strauss vor ihrer Flucht aus Deutschland schon mehrere Artikel über Wolfskehl publiziert hatte, zeigt sich nach der Ankunft in den Vereinigten Staaten eine deutliche Konzentration ihrer publizistischen Arbeit auf diesen Dichter sowie auf Thomas Mann; vgl.: "Dichter jüdischen Schicksals. Ein Wort des Dankes für Karl Wolfskehl," *Der Aufbau,* 31.1.1943; "Karl Wolfskehl. Interpreter of Jewish Fate," *Jewish Frontier* 11 (1943): 18–22; "Neue Kunde von Karl

Wolfskehl," *Der Aufbau,* 12.1.1945; "Karl Wolfskehls 'Letztes Wort,'" *Der Aufbau* 30.7.1948; "Karl Wolfskehl's Letters," *Jewish Frontier* 26 (1959): 24. Über Thomas Mann publizierte sie ebenfalls in beiden Sprachen: "Thomas Mann and the Midrash," *The Reconstructionist* 11, H. 5 (1945): 12–16; "Thomas Mann und der Midrasch," *Jüdische Rundschau* 1, Nr. 3 (1946): 22–23.

[11] Vgl. Margarete Susman, "Karl Wolfskehl. Die Stimme spricht," *Der Morgen* 10 (1934): 471–73. Wie aus ihren ungedruckten Briefen an Erich von Kahler hervorgeht, las Margarete Susman vor allem Thomas Manns Joseph-Roman sehr genau. Trotz Kahlers Aufforderung hat sie ihre Reflexionen über dieses Buch nicht veröffentlicht.

[12] Eine ausführliche Bibliographie ihrer Schriften findet sich in *Frauen in den Kulturwissenschaften,* 334–38.

[13] Bertha Badt-Strauss, *White Fire: The Life and Works of Jessie Sampter* (New York: Reconstructionist P, 1956).

[14] Hannah Arendt, *The Origins of Totalitarianism* (New York, Harcourt and Brace, 1951). Die deutsche Ausgabe erschien unter dem Titel *Elemente und Ursprünge totaler Herrschaft* (Frankfurt am Main: Europäische Verlagsanstalt, 1955). Im folgenden wird aus der Taschenbuchausgabe des Ullsteinverlags (Frankfurt am Main, Berlin, Wien, 1980) zitiert. Die beiden Ausgaben unterscheiden sich bekanntlich erheblich; auf die Unterschiede kann hier nur kurz eingegangen werden.

[15] Hannah Arendt, "Was bleibt? Es bleibt die Muttersprache: Ein Gespräch mit Günter Gaus (1964)," in *Ich will verstehen: Selbstauskünfte zu Leben und Werk,* hrsg. v. Ursula Ludz (München, Zürich: Piper, 1996), 44–70, hier 58–59.

[16] Margarete Susman, *Ich habe viele Leben gelebt: Erinnerungen* (Stuttgart: Deutsche Verlags-Anstalt, 1964), 140.

[17] Erich von Kahler, Text zum 90. Geburtstag von Margarete Susman (Deutsches Literaturarchiv Marbach, Nachlaß Susman, Signatur: 91.88.410).

[18] Susman, *Ich habe viele Leben gelebt,* 148.

[19] Susman, *Ich habe viele Leben gelebt,* 147.

[20] Brief Wolfkehls vom 29.1.1935; *"Jüdisch, römisch, deutsch zugleich . . ." Karl Wolfskehl, Briefwechsel aus Italien 1933–1938,* hrsg. v. Cornelia Blasberg (Hamburg: Luchterhand, 1993), 90. Susman hatte *Die Stimme spricht* im *Morgen* rezensiert, vgl. Anm. 11.

[21] Karl Wolfskehl, *Hiob oder Die Vier Spiegel* (Hamburg: Claassen, 1950).

[22] Karl Wolfskehl, *Briefwechsel aus Neuseeland 1938–1945,* hrsg. v. Cornelia Blasberg und mit einem Nachwort von Paul Hoffmann, 2 Bde. (Darmstadt: Luchterhand, 1988), hier Bd. 1, 215. Die englische Fassung von Arendts Rezension war bereits 1944 erschienen; vgl. "Franz Kafka: A Revaluation," *Partisan Review* 11 (1944): 412–22. Wolfskehl hatte die deutsche Version gelesen, "Franz Kafka. Von neuem gewürdigt," *Die Wandlung* I (1946): 1050–62.

[23] Wolfskehl, *Briefwechsel aus Neuseeland 1938–1945,* Bd. 1, 216.

[24] In Wolfskehls Brief vom 30.4.45 an Salman Schocken heißt es über die Übersetzung einiger Zeilen aus seinem Gedicht *Am Sederabend zu lesen,* die Badt-Strauss in ihren Aufsatz über Wolfkehls Dichtung integriert hatte, daß diese

"Umgießung des ersten Seder-Gedichts in rhythmisch bewegter Prosa nicht bloß mir das ausreichend wiederzugeben scheint, was der Dichter in strafferer Haltung ursprünglich gestaltet hat." Wolfskehl, *Briefwechsel aus Neuseeland 1938–1945,* Bd. 1, 212.

[25] Bertha Badt-Strauss, "Studententage in München," in *Vergangene Tage: Jüdische Kultur in München,* hrsg. v. Hans Lamm, 2. erw. u. durchges. Aufl. (München: Langen Müller, 1982), 197–200, hier 199.

[26] Brief vom 10.10.45; Wolfskehl, *Briefwechsel aus Neuseeland 1938–1945,* Bd. 1, 778.

[27] Vgl. dazu genauer meinen Aufsatz "Bertha Badt-Strauss (1885–1970). Die Lust am Unzeitgemäßen," in *Frauen in den Kulturwissenschaften,* 152–65 und 330–38.

[28] Für diese Auskunft danke ich Herrn Professor Albrecht Strauss, dem Sohn von Bertha Badt-Strauss, sehr herzlich.

[29] Bertha Badt-Strauss, "Purim Vincent und Purim . . . Hitler," *Der Aufbau,* 22.3.1946, 16.

[30] Margarete Susman, *Das Buch Hiob und das Schicksal des jüdischen Volkes* (Zürich: Steinberg, 1946, 2. Auflage 1948), nach der im folgenden zitiert wird, hier 77. Angespielt wird auf Hermann Jacobsohn, Professor für Vergleichende Sprachwissenschaft an der Universität Marburg, der am 27.4.1933 Selbstmord beging. Für diesen Hinweis danke ich Dr. Birgit Wägenbaur und Hanne Knickmann vom Deutschen Literaturarchiv, Marbach.

[31] Susman, *Das Buch Hiob,* 218–19.

[32] Arendt, "Was bleibt? Es bleibt die Muttersprache," 59.

[33] Arendt, *Elemente und Ursprünge,* Bd. 1, 142.

[34] Arendt, *Elemente und Ursprünge,* Bd. 2, 106–7. Vgl. auch 111–14, wo Hannah Arendt ausführlich aus diesem Roman zitiert.

[35] Arendt, *Elemente und Ursprünge,* Bd. 2, 194.

[36] Erst nach dem Ersten Weltkrieg, so argumentiert Margarete Susman, "hat die Frau ihr Schweigen gebrochen," erst jetzt beginnt "der Kampf um Sprache und Bild," vgl. "Das Frauenproblem der Gegenwart," in *Das Nah- und Fernsein des Fremden: Essays und Briefe,* hrsg. v. Ingeborg Nordmann (Frankfurt am Main: Jüdischer Verlag, 1992), 143–67, hier 143–44.

[37] Susman, *Ich habe viele Leben gelebt,* 99–100.

[38] Susman, *Deutung einer großen Liebe,* 33.

[39] Susman, *Frauen der Romantik,* 13. Über Charlotte von Stein heißt es in *Deutung einer großen Liebe* dagegen: "Obwohl sie leidenschaftlich deutsch gesinnt war, war ihr aller Nationalismus im heutigen Sinne fremd. Ihr leidenschaftlicher Haß gegen Napoleon, den Goethe, nicht weniger jenseits alles Nationalen, verehrte, war allein der gegen den Störer des Friedens und Stifter immer neuer geschichtlicher Verwirrung. Gegen die Franzosen kannte sie keinen Haß; sie hatte für die armen, vom Heer abgesprengten Franzosen nicht anders als für ihre armen Landsleute immer einen Topf mit warmer Suppe bereitstehen" (186–87).

[40] Margarete Susman, "Die geistige Gestalt Georg Simmels," in *Vom Nah- und Fernsein des Fremden,* 37.

[41] Vgl. Ingeborg Nordmanns Essays über Margarete Susman: "Wie man sich in der Sprache fremd bewegt," in *Vom Nah- und Fernsein des Fremden,* 227–67, hier 241, sowie diess.: "Der Dialog ist Bruch und Beginn. Zu Margarete Susman. Ein Porträt ihres Denkens," in *Zur Geschichte der jüdischen Frau in Deutschland,* hrsg. v. Julius Carlebach (Berlin: Metropol-Verlag, 1993), 203–18.

[42] Vgl. beispielsweise *Frauen der Romantik* (Jena: Diederichs, 1929 und 3. verm. u. veränd. Aufl. Köln: Melzer, 1960), das in vielen Aufsätzen vor- und nachgeschrieben wurde, wie aus der Bibliographie deutlich wird. Dasselbe gilt für *Hiob und das Schicksal des jüdischen Volkes* (Zürich, 1946). Auch Aufsätze, die sich nie zum Buch weiteten, schrieb Margarete Susman immer wieder um; hier sei lediglich auf ihre Texte zu Rosa Luxemburg hingewiesen, vgl. "Rosa Luxemburgs Briefe," *Aufstieg,* 19.1.1923; "Rosa Luxemburg," *Neue Wege. Blätter für den Kampf der Zeit* 45, 11 (1951); 435–40. Wiederabdruck in: Margarete Susman, *Vom Geheimnis der Freiheit. Gesammelte Aufsätze 1914–1964,* hrsg. v. Manfred Schlösser (Darmstadt, Zürich: Agora, 1965), 271–83; "Es darf keine Verdammten geben," *Neue Wege. Blätter für den Kampf der Zeit* 53, 2 (1959): 37–42.

[43] Peter Nettl, *Rosa Luxemburg* (Oxford: Oxford UP, 1966).

[44] Hannah Arendt, "Rosa Luxemburg" (1968), in *Menschen in finsteren Zeiten,* hrsg. v. Ursula Ludz (München, Zürich: Piper, 1989), 49–74.

[45] Arendt, *Elemente und Ursprünge,* Bd. 2, 52.

[46] Hannah Arendt, *Rahel Varnhagen.* Inzwischen liegen verschiedene Lektüren dieser Biographie vor: vgl. Deborah Hertz, "Hannah Arendt's Rahel Varnhagen," in *German Women in the Nineteenth Century: A Social History,* ed. John C. Fout (New York: Holmes and Meier, 1984), 72–87, sowie Liliane Weissbergs bereits zitierte Einleitung zur amerikanischen Neuausgabe des Buches; die interessanteste ist die von Ingeborg Nordmann, *Hannah Arendt* (Frankfurt am Main: Campus, 1994), 29–38.

[47] Hannah Arendt, Martin Heidegger, *Briefe. 1925–1975,* hrsg. v. Ursula Ludz (Frankfurt a.M.: Klostermann, 1998), 110.

Käte Hamburger (© Deutsches Literaturarchiv Marbach)

Eine Klassikerin der Literaturtheorie: Käte Hamburger

Gesa Dane

KÄTE HAMBURGER (1896–1992) ist die wichtigste deutschsprachige Literaturtheoretikerin des zwanzigsten Jahrhunderts, in ihrer
Bedeutung wohl nur mit Walter Benjamin zu vergleichen. Die Ab
handlung, die später ihre Habilitationsschrift werden sollte, *Die Logik
der Dichtung*, verfaßte sie noch in Schweden, wo sie seit 1934 lebte.
In dieser Untersuchung unternimmt Hamburger es, mit philosophisch
streng durchgearbeiteten Begriffen eine "Logik der Dichtung" zu erar-
beiten. Ihre Theorie der Dichtungsarten hat sprachtheoretische Grundlagen: Die Sprache der Dichtung, zu der sie das Drama und den Roman
rechnet, ist kategorial von der Alltagssprache unterschieden — eben
fiktional, d.h. in ihren Wesenszügen von anderen Arten der Rede ver-
schieden, sie hat einen anderen Zeitmodus, andere Referenzbezüge.
Die erzählte Wirklichkeit ist aufgrund dieser "Logik der Dichtung" eine
andere als die Alltagswirklichkeit. Die lyrische Dichtung bildet in Hamburgers System eine Besonderheit. Sie ist keine Fiktion, sondern immer
unmittelbare Aussage eines dichtenden Subjektes.[1] Viel diskutiert und
umstritten waren ihre Thesen, zu empirisch, zu rational, zu gramma-
tisch, so lautete der Tenor. Für die Methodendiskussion im Fach Germanistik war Hamburgers *Die Logik der Dichtung* von großer Wichtig-
keit. Eröffnete doch diese Abhandlung die Möglichkeit, die Grundbe-
griffe des Faches und seines Gegenstandes schärfer zu fassen.[2] Sie gab
auch Perspektiven für eine germanistische Literaturwissenschaft, die sich
vornehmlich auf einfühlend-immanentes Deuten oder formelle Analysen beschränkt hatte, überhaupt wieder Bezüge zwischen der Literatur
und außerliterarischen Bereichen herzustellen, in diesem Fall philosophische Fragestellungen. Hamburgers Verdienst bleibt es, einerseits
die Eigenständigkeit der Dichtung zu denken und andererseits Verbindungen zu anderen Disziplinen herzustellen und es dennoch zu verstehen, ein literarisches Werk nie in einem außerliterarischen System
aufgehen zu lassen.[3]

Jünger als Margarete Susman und etwa dergleichen Generation
wie Hannah Arendt und Bertha Badt-Strauss angehörend, hatte auch
sie die neuen Möglichkeiten der akademischen Bildung für Frauen
wahrnehmen können.[4] Es gibt auch thematische Berührungspunkte
zwischen ihnen. Im Werk Käte Hamburgers nach 1945 ist jedoch keine Untersuchung zu finden, die, vergleichbar mit Susmans Monographie *Das Buch Hiob und das Schicksal des jüdischen Volkes*, als Kaddisch
für die ermordeten Juden zu lesen wäre.[5] Auch setzte sie sich nicht
ebenso dezidiert öffentlich mit politisch-philosophischen Theorien,
Traditionen und Fragen auseinander, wie wir es von Hannah Arendt
kennen. Diese bewegt sich, skizzenhaft gesagt, im Feld zwischen Philosophie und politischer Theorie, eng verbunden mit der Reflexion
über das Schicksal der Juden in Deutschland. Für Hamburger wäre
das vergleichbar zu konturieren mit den Stichworten Philosophie —
Literatur — exemplarische Darstellung des Schicksals von Juden in
Deutschland. Leitmotivisch, wenn auch verstreut in ihren Abhandlungen, geht Hamburger auf das Schicksal der Juden in Deutschland ein.[6] In Texten etwa zu Rahel Varnhagen, Heinrich Heine, Nelly
Sachs oder Else Lasker-Schüler spricht sie von der Verfolgung und der
Vernichtung der Juden oder, allgemeiner, von dem, was ihnen ange-
tan wurde.

In einer Hinsicht unterscheidet sich Hamburger grundsätzlich von
Arendt und Badt-Strauss: Sie strebte seit den zwanziger Jahren eine
wissenschaftliche Laufbahn an einer deutschen Universität an, allerdings vergeblich. Nach dem Studium, zunächst in Berlin, dann in
München und nach der Promotion in München im Fach Philosophie,
lebte sie in ihrer Heimatstadt Hamburg. Dort verdiente sie als Buch-
händlerin ihren Lebensunterhalt. Während dieser Zeit schrieb sie ihre
ersten größeren Aufsätze. Und sie hörte an der neu gegründeten
Hamburger Universität Vorlesungen, u.a. bei Ernst Cassirer.[7] Sie ging
1928 nach Berlin, als Privatassistentin des Philosophen und Privatdozenten Paul Hofmann, also ohne offizielle Anstellung an der Berliner
Universität. Ursprünglich hatte sie den Wunsch, wenn Hofmann ein
Ordinariat erhielte, sich bei ihm zu habilitieren. Während ihrer Arbeit
an der Monographie *Thomas Mann und die Romantik* orientierte sie
sich wieder stärker in Richtung Literaturwissenschaft, fragte sogar
noch 1933 bei Rudolf Unger in Göttingen nach den Möglichkeiten
einer Habilitation an, sie skizzierte ein Projekt mit dem Arbeitstitel
Humanität und Existenz.[8] Von einem Studienaufenthalt in Dijon, begonnen im Herbst 1933, kehrte sie nicht mehr nach Deutschland zu-

rück. Mithilfe von schwedischen Freunden, die sie in Frankreich kennengelernt hatte, konnte sie sich in Göteborg niederlassen.

Anders als Susman, Arendt und Badt-Strauss wollte Käte Hamburger nach Kriegsende in Deutschland arbeiten und leben. Dies gelang ihr erst 1956 trotz bedeutender Fürsprecher wie etwa Walter Rehm und Emil Staiger. Nach Stuttgart kam sie, weil Fritz Martini, der seit 1943 als außerordentlicher und seit 1950 als ordentlicher Professor an der Technischen Hochschule Stuttgart lehrte, sich für sie einsetzte.[9] Er bewirkte, daß sie ihre Habilitationsschrift in Stuttgart einreichen konnte. 1957 wurde Käte Hamburger im Fach Germanistik/Neuere deutsche Literatur von der Philosophischen Fakultät der TH Stuttgart habilitiert — und 1959 als außerplanmäßige Professorin für Allgemeine Literaturwissenschaft angestellt.[10] Für ein Ordinariat, also einen Lehrstuhl, war sie nach dem bundesdeutschen Beamtengesetz bereits zu alt. Dagegen kamen viele ihrer Germanistenkollegen, die zwischen 1933 und 1945 in Deutschland geblieben und inzwischen wieder in Amt und Würden waren, mit diesem Gesetz nicht in Kollision. In der hierarchisch verfaßten Universitätsstruktur war und ist der Unterschied zwischen einer außerplanmäßigen Professur und einem Ordinariat gewaltig — nicht nur, was Prestige und Einkommen angeht. Privatassistentin, außerplanmäßige Professorin — institutionell blieb Käte Hamburger, was sie vor der Emigration gewesen war, eine Außenseiterin. Und das, obwohl sie nach der Publikation ihrer Habilitationsschrift *Die Logik der Dichtung* mehr und mehr Berühmtheit erlangte.

Die philosophische Tradition, an die Hamburger in der *Logik der Dichtung* anknüpft, war die Philosophie der zwanziger Jahre, die Phänomenologie, die Existenzphilosophie und auch die *Philosophie der symbolischen Formen* von Ernst Cassirer.[11] Hinzu kommt eine Tatsache, die viel zu häufig übersehen wird: die Erfahrung des Deutsch-als-Fremdsprache-Unterrichtens in Schweden. Hamburger berichtet, daß sie unzählige Menschen der verschiedensten Altersstufen und Berufsgruppen in der deutschen Sprache unterrichtet habe: "wahrscheinlich hätte ich mich auch niemals für so etwas wie das Imperfekt, das Präteritum interessiert, wäre nie darauf gekommen, daß es sich mit diesem etwas sonderbar verhalten muß, wenn in einem Roman der Satz zu lesen steht 'Morgen war Weihnachten' — ahnte aber nicht, daß dieser Satz . . . der Keim zu einem ganzen Buch werden würde, das ich *Die Logik der Dichtung* betiteln würde."[12]

"Wenn ich Schriften von vor 1933 lese, ist es wie eine ferne Vergangenheit. Damals hatte die Gegenwart, und so auch die damals ge-

genwärtige Wissenschaft, noch ihren Zusammenhang mit der deutschen Geisteskultur. Jetzt ist es wie ein gähnender Abgrund oder wie
lauter abgerissene Fäden, und sinnlos erscheint es mir oft, in der toten
Tradition mich zu bewegen. Ob sie wieder lebendig werden kann?"[13]
Ein Blick auf ihre literaturwissenschaftlichen Arbeiten zeigt, wie sie die
abgerissenen Fäden aufnimmt, freilich nicht ohne die Spuren der Zer-
störung kenntlich zu machen. Wie sich dies in ihrer Forschung aus-
wirkte, läßt sich sehr eindrücklich an ihren Arbeiten über Rahel
Varnhagen, an ihrer Kritik an Thomas Manns *Faustus*-Roman und ihrem Mythos-Buch aufzeigen.

Daß die "Geschichte des deutschen Judentums"[14] hundert Jahre
nach dem Tod von Rahel Varnhagen beendet war, steht für Käte
Hamburger fest. Die Veränderung von Hamburgers Deutung von
Rahel Varnhagen ist hier aufschlußreich, gibt es doch zwei Abhandlungen über sie von Käte Hamburger. Die erste erschien 1934 auf
Französisch in der *Revue Germanique* unter dem Titel "Rahel et Goethe,"[15] die zweite 1968 in der Festschrift für Lieselotte Blumenthal.[16]
Der Text wurde in signifikanter Weise umgearbeitet und erweitert. In
der ersten Abhandlung stand Rahel im Zentrum, ihre Goethe-
rezeption, ihr Verstehen der Schriften Goethes, wie es in den Briefen
Rahels zum Ausdruck kommt. Rahel Varnhagen als Goetheverehrerin
in ihrer Rolle als Mitbegründerin des Goethekultes, das sind die in-
haltlichen Schwerpunkte Käte Hamburgers im Jahr 1933/34. Diese
haben sich 1968 verändert. Hamburger verfolgt nun das Ziel, die Figur Rahel historisch zu positionieren. Denn, so ihre These, Rahels
Goetheverständnis ist nicht nur für die "deutsche Geistesgeschichte,"
sondern auch für die "Geschichte des deutschen Judentums" bedeutsam. Hamburger arbeitet eine Reihe von historischen Fakten über die
Geschichte des deutschen Judentums bis zum Ende des achtzehnten
Jahrhunderts in den Text ein. Was um die Wende vom achtzehnten
zum neunzehnten Jahrhundert in Rahel Varnhagen im Zeichen der
Humanität noch konvergieren konnte, "deutsche Geistesgeschichte"
und "deutsches Judentum," ist jetzt, nach der Shoah, auseinandergerissen. In dieser zweiten Fassung des Rahel Varnhagen-
Aufsatzes geht Käte Hamburger auf Susmans Rahel-Kapitel in deren
Monographie *Frauen der Romantik* und auf Hannah Arendts inzwischen erschienene Rahel-Biographie ein. Insbesondere im Zusammenhang mit Rahel Varnhagens Goetheverständis will Hamburger
Susmans Einordnung von Rahel in die Reihe der Frauen der Romantik korrigieren. Nur die äußeren Lebensdaten und Lebensbedingun-
gen teilt sie mit den anderen in dem Band dargestellten Frauen. Der

nach Hamburgers Ansicht zentrale Grundzug der Romantik, die Sympathie, die Verbundenheit mit dem Tode, die romantische Todessehnsucht, all dies unterscheidet Rahel Varnhagen grundlegend von den anderen: "Aber gerade diese romantische und in dieser Hinsicht christliche Haltung, war nicht diejenige Rahels."[17] Hamburger unterstreicht die Lebenszugewandtheit Rahel Varnhagens, allen äußeren Widrigkeiten zum Trotz, und sieht eben in dieser eine zentrale Affinität zwischen Rahel Varnhagen und Goethe.[18] Geradezu harsch ist ihr Urteil über die Monographie von Hannah Arendt über Rahel Varnhagen. Hamburger würdigt zwar Arendts Unternehmen, die Figur Rahel aus der "Platt- und Schönmalerei"[19] von Varnhagen von Ense herauszulösen. Arendts Deutungsansatz sei aber gleichermaßen eine Verzerrung, weil ihre Perspektive nur die der an der Herkunft leidenden getauften Jüdin sei.

> Jüdin und Schlemihl, Paria und Parvenue sind die Kategorien, unter denen Hannah Arendt Rahels Leben und Wesen interpretiert. Sie hat dieses Rahel mehr oder weniger diffamierende Buch geschrieben, weil sie als bewußte Jüdin in Rahel einen besonders prägnanten Fall der von Anfang an zum Scheitern verurteilten Assimilationsbemühungen des deutschen Judentums sicht. Das Buch ist unter dem Aspekt von 1933 konzipiert, des Antisemitismus überhaupt, und richtet sich durch das Beispiel Rahel hindurch, aus jüdischem Selbstbewußtsein, gegen die Assimilation.[20]

Hier besteht eine fundamentale Differenz zwischen Hamburger und Arendt, eine Differenz, die über die Beurteilung der historischen Figur Rahel Varnhagen hinausgeht. Denn Hamburger teilt nicht die Überzeugung Arendts, der Prozeß der Annäherung zwischen jüdischen und christlichen Deutschen habe zwangsläufig scheitern müssen. Eine Interpretation wie die von Hannah Arendt stellt eine Kontinuität her, durch die, um in der Diktion Hamburgers zu bleiben, der "gähnende Abgrund" an Tiefe verliert.

In eben diesem Horizont sind auch ihre kritischen Fragen an den *Faustus*-Roman von Thomas Mann anzusiedeln. Seine literarischen Werke waren seit dem Ende der zwanziger Jahre Gegenstand ihrer Analysen. Den Roman *Joseph und seine Brüder* hatte Hamburger auch deshalb für gelungen gehalten, weil Joseph dort im Zeichen der Humanität zur Mitmenschlichkeit gebildet wurde.[21] Und nun Hamburgers kritische Skepsis gegenüber dem *Faustus* und dessen, wie sie es nennt, anachronistischer Symbolik. Den Einwand des Anachronismus begründet sie damit, daß in diesem Roman die Traditionen der deutschen Geistesgeschichte, insbesondere der Musik, Theologie und

Philosophie auf die ihnen innewohnenden Voraussetzungen für die
Entstehung des Nationalsozialismus befragt, sogar verantwortlich ge-
macht werden. Es werden — literarisch — Kontinuitäten hergestellt.
Thomas Manns dialektisches Denkmuster, an die *Dialektik der Auf-
klärung* von Horkheimer und Adorno gemahnend, das Böse sei das
fehlgegangene Gute, ist für Hamburger ein völlig unangemessenes
Verfahren: "Denn wenn in der echten Faustepoche ein faustisches
Streben und Leben Versündigung an der theologischen Weltordnung,
Abfall von Gott und Teufelswerk bedeutete, so erscheint eine so di-
rekte Übertragung auf ein künstlerisches Schaffen des zwanzigsten
Jahrhunderts anachronistisch."[22] Ihre skeptischen Fragen gehen über
die Verwendung des Fauststoffes einschließlich der des Teufelspaktes
hinaus. Hamburger stellt gegen Ende ihrer Abhandlung die rhetori-
sche Frage, ob der Roman in einem "freilich vageren und nicht symbolischen Sinn" ein Teufelsroman sein könne. Sie schließt mit der nur
scheinbar lakonischen Bemerkung, "seine [Thomas Manns] Klage,
Dr. Fausti Weheklag, ertönt nicht nur über das deutsche Volk."[23] Hier
lenkt sie den Blick darauf, daß innerhalb des Romans ein Unterschied
zwischen Deutschen und Juden gemacht wird, den der Autor Thomas
Mann selbst nicht mehr machte — ein Unterschied, der sich durchaus
im Horizont der nationalsozialistischen Ideologie bewegt. Aus dieser
Perspektive freilich ist für Käte Hamburger der Roman ein Teufelsroman. Daß sie sich mit dieser Auslegung nicht innerhalb der Intentionen von Thomas Mann bewegte, wußte sie.[24] Ungeachtet Thomas
Manns harscher Reaktion auf ihre Interpretation widmete sie ihm
später die erste Ausgabe der *Logik der Dichtung,* nachdem sie noch
vor seinem Tod sein Einverständnis erhalten hatte.

Daß aus dem Humanitätsideal nicht mit Notwendigkeit Humanität als Verhalten hervorgeht, zeigt Hamburger in ihrer Monographie
*Von Sophokles zu Sartre: Griechische Dramenfiguren antik und mod-
ern.*[25] Diese Studie ist zugleich ein Beispiel für Hamburgers kompara-
tistische Arbeitsweise. Sie dachte nicht in Nationalliteraturen und sie
bezog zeitgenössische, auch nicht kanonisierte Texte in ihre Überlegungen ein. In dieser Arbeit verfolgt sie die These, daß das Selbst-
verständnis der Menschen in einer Epoche oder Zeit auch an der literarischen Bearbeitung von Mythen ablesbar ist. Am Beispiel des
Iphigenie-Mythos läßt sich Hamburgers Argumentation besonders gut
aufzeigen. Hamburger befragt zunächst die griechischen Vorlagen
und stellt fest, daß Iphigenie als Priesterin in Tauris Menschenopfer
gebracht hat. In der deutschen Tradition wurde Goethes Umgestal-
tung des Mythos so wirkungsmächtig, daß das Wissen um diese grau-

samen Seiten des Iphigenie-Stoffes nahezu in Vergessenheit geriet.[26] Bis Gerhart Hauptmann 1942 in seiner *Atridentetralogie* die archaisch-chthonische Seite wieder ins Spiel brachte. Iphigenie wurde hier wieder zur Halbgöttin mit antihumanen Zügen. "Einer humanistischen Zeit konnte der Sieg des delphischen Geistes über den archaischen als ein endgültiger erscheinen, der Glaube gedeihen, daß die Menschheit vom Niederen zum Höheren sich einsinnig fortentwickle. . . . Die brutalen Erfahrungen unserer Zeit haben gelehrt, daß das 'Archaische,' wie immer sublimiert oder 'verdrängt' es sein mag, nicht durchaus überwunden wird, sondern je und je wieder hervorbrechen und furchtbar modern werden kann."[27] Unvorstellbar seit der Klassik erscheint Hauptmanns Iphigenie den modernen Erfahrungen angemessen. So wird aus Iphigenie, dem Symbol für Humanität in der deutschen Tradition seit der Klassik, bei Hauptmann wieder eines für Antihumanität, Tod und Angst.

Der skeptische Blick auf Tradition und Scheitern des Humanitätideals bleibt auch in Käte Hamburgers letzter, einer eher philosophisch-problemorientierten Studie *Das Mitleid* (1985) bestimmend. Es ist dies ein Traktat gegen die Verabsolutierung des Mitleids als einer praktischen Haltung. Mitleid ist für Hamburger ein Affekt, der folgenlos und unverbindlich ist, der nicht in barmherziges, verantwortungsvolles oder sorgenvolles Handeln mündet.

Das alles scheint nur auf den ersten Blick recht weit von der *Logik der Dichtung* entfernt. Denn die begriffliche Schärfe und Präzision, die Hamburger dort zeigte, praktiziert sie auch hier. Spannend werden ihre Interpretationen und Darstellungen, wenn sie sich, fast unmerklich, allmählich von ihrem dichtungslogischen System entfernt und literarische Texte mitsamt ihren Traditionen ausleuchtet und zum Sprechen bringt. In der Auseinandersetzung mit ihren Schriften habe ich so etwas wie ein literaturwissenschaftliches Lieblingsbuch entdeckt — das über den Mythos, ich kann es nur empfehlen.

Käte Hamburger ist am 8. April 1992 in Stuttgart hochgeehrt gestorben.[28] Tradition in Ruinen — sie hatte gewiß ihre ganz eigene Weise, sowohl mit den Traditionen als auch mit den Ruinen zu leben und wissenschaftlich zu arbeiten.

Anmerkungen

[1] Hamburger wiederholt ihre Theorie von der Aussage des lyrischen Ich, das mit dem Ich des Dichters identisch ist, sehr prägnant etwa in ihrer Rezension von Hilde Domins *Wozu Lyrik heute: Dichtung und Leser in der gesteuerten Gesellschaft* (*Poetica* 3 [1978]: 310–15). Wenn alltägliche Wertungen ins Spiel kommen, zeigen sich die Grenzen dieses Lyrikverständnisses, wie Hamburgers Deutung von Else Lasker-Schülers Altersdichtung zeigt. Hamburger kommentiert hier normativ, wenn sie feststellt, daß "seltsamerweise . . . ein großer Teil der Gedichte der alten Frau Liebesgedichte" sind (Käte Hamburger, "Else Lasker-Schüler," in *Es ist ein Weinen in der Welt: Hommage für deutsche Juden unseres Jahrhunderts*, hrsg. v. Hans Jürgen Schulz [Stuttgart: Quell, 1990]), 92.

[2] Vgl. *Um Thomas Mann: Der Briefwechsel Käte Hamburger — Klaus Schröter 1964–1990*, hrsg. v. Klaus Schröter in Zusammenarbeit mit Armin Huttenlocher (Hamburg: Europäische Verlagsanstalt, 1994), 174. Dort finden sich auch Hinweise auf ihr Insistieren auf klare Begriffe und Begriffsverwendung in der Literaturwissenschaft (23).

[3] Der Film als künstlerische Gattung ist für sie eine eher epische Gattung, vgl. "Zur Phänomenologie des Films," *Merkur* 10 (1956): 873–80.

[4] Als Tochter einer jüdischen Bankiersfamilie 1896 in Hamburg geboren, legte sie das Abitur an dem traditionsreichen Johanneum ab, nachdem sie ein Realgymnasium für Mädchen besucht hatte. Das Studium der Fächer Kunstgeschichte, Geschichte und Literaturgeschichte nahm sie zum Sommersemester 1917 in Berlin auf. Ab dem Wintersemester 1918/19 studierte sie in München, ihr Hauptfach wurde die Philosophie. 1922 wurde sie im Fach Philosophie promoviert mit einer Arbeit über *Schillers Analyse des Menschen als Grundlegung seiner Geschichts- und Kulturphilosophie,* in der sie interdisziplinär literaturwissenschaftliche und philosophische Fragen verband.

[5] Vgl. dazu Barbara Hahn, "Hiobsgeschichten. Übersetzungen und Umschriften von Martin Luther und Martin Buber," *DVjs* 71 (1997): 146–63.

[6] Vgl. z.B. Käte Hamburger, "Heine und das Judentum," Vortrag gehalten in Stuttgart, 16. März 1982, Stuttgart 1983; weiter auch "Das transzendierende Ich. Zur Lyrik von Nelly Sachs," in *Kleine Schriften zur Literatur und Geistesgeschichte*, 2. erw. Aufl. (Stuttgart: H.-D. Heinz Akademischer Verlag, 1986), 335–44.

[7] Sie veröffentlichte in dieser Zeit verschiedene Abhandlungen in angesehenen Publikationsorganen: "Novalis und die Mathematik. Eine Studie zur Erkenntnistheorie der Romantik," in *Romantik-Forschungen* (Halle: Niemeyer, 1929), 113–84 und "Das Todesproblem bei Jean Paul," *DVjs* 7 (1929): 446–74.

[8] Vgl. Käte Hamburger an Rudolf Unger, Hamburg, 3. Juli 1932, Bl. 1 (Niedersächsische Landes- und Universitätsbibliothek Göttingen, Nachlaß Unger: Code MS. R. Unger 40); dazu Gesa Dane, "Käte Hamburger," in *Wissenschaftsgeschichte der Germanistik in Portraits,* hrsg. v. Christoph König, Hans Harald Müller und Werner Röcke (Berlin: de Gruyter, 2000), 189–98, hier 193.

[9] Fritz Martini (1909–1991), 1934 promoviert (Berlin), 1939 Privatdozent in Hamburg, 1943 außerordentlicher und seit 1950 ordentlicher Professor an der TH Stuttgart.

[10] Hamburger war nach Melitta Gerhard (1927, Kiel) und Anni Meetz (1944, Kiel) die dritte habilitierte Wissenschaftlerin in diesem Fach, vgl. *50 Jahre Habilitation von Frauen,* hrsg. v. Elisabeth Boedecker und Maria Meyer-Plath (Göttingen: O. Schwartz, 1974), 206–7 und 211. Streng genommen handelt es sich hier nicht um eine Remigration wie im Fall etwa der um wenige Jahre jüngeren Forscher Richard Alewyn oder Werner Milch, Wolfgang Liepe und Werner Richter. Sie waren alle bereits vor der Emigration habilitiert worden, hatten Grundlagen und Ausgangspositionen für eine akademische Laufbahn gelegt, an die sie, wenn auch mit vielen Brüchen und Problemen, zumindest anknüpfen konnten.

[11] Bereits der Titel assoziiert Ernst Cassirers *Zur Logik der Kulturwissenschaften.* Mit Cassirer, dessen Abhandlung 1942 in Göteborg publiziert wurde, stand sie in persönlichem Kontakt. In der Wende zur Sprachphilosophie und Logik folgt sie Cassirers *Philosophie der symbolischen Formen,* wenn sie die Dichtungssprache "logisch" und aus der Sprache heraus begründen will.

[12] Käte Hamburger, "Rede beim Empfang im Senatssaal anläßlich der Ehrenpromotion in Siegen am 25. Juni 1980," in *Ehrenpromotion Käte Hamburger: Dokumentation,* hrsg. v. Johannes Janota und Jürgen Kühnel (Siegen: Universität-Gesamthochschule-Siegen, 1980), 38.

[13] Käte Hamburger an Josef Körner, 12. Mai 1946, zit. nach Petra Boden, "Es geht uns Ganze! Vergleichende Beobachtungen zur germanistischen Literaturwissenschaft in beiden deutschen Staaten 1945–1989," *Euphorion* 91 (1997): 247–75, hier 247.

[14] Käte Hamburger, "Rahel und Goethe," in *Kleine Schriften zur Literatur und Geistesgeschichte,* 2. erw. Aufl. (Stuttgart: H.-D. Heinz Akademischer Verlag, 1986), 164.

[15] Käte Hamburger, "Rahel et Goethe," *Revue Germanique* 25 (1934): 313–30.

[16] Die ausführliche Widmungsadresse an die Weimarer Goethephilologin Lieselotte Blumenthal übernimmt Hamburger auch in dem Wiederabdruck in den *Kleinen Schriften.* Dort stellt sie auf den zweiten Blick erstaunliche Zusammenhänge her: Varnhagen sei keine der "unmittelbaren Vorkämpferinnen des Frauenstudiums gewesen," sie stehe jedoch am Anfang des Weges, "den hundert Jahre nach ihr die Frauen haben betreten können. Es erschien mir doppelt sinnvoll, daß das Goethe-Erlebnis der Rahel Varnhagen der Gegenstand dieses Beitrages ist, ein geistiges, literarisches Erlebnis, das, so subjektiver Art es bei Rahel auch ist, doch in den Bereich der Wissenschaft gehört, der wir, sie und ich, uns gewidmet haben. Sinnvoll also erscheint es mir, daß Ihnen von mir dieser kleine Beitrag über eine Frau dieser Art in der Festschrift, die Ihre große Lebensleistung auf dem Gebiet der Goethezeit ehrt, überreicht wird." (Käte Hamburger, "Rahel und Goethe," in *Kleine Schriften,* 163.)

[17] *Kleine Schriften,* 171.

[18] Ihr geht es weniger um philologisch nachweisbare Korrespondenzen, sondern vielmehr um das Aufzeigen von tieferliegender "Übereinstimmung des Lebens-

gefühls, die gerade in den Äußerungen zutage tritt, die sich nicht gerade auf Goethe und ein Goethewerk beziehen" (*Kleine Schriften,* 172).

[19] *Kleine Schriften,* 181.

[20] *Kleine Schriften,* 181–82.

[21] Hamburgers Wertschätzung des Humanitätsideals in der deutschen Tradition konvergiert mit Cassirers Kulturphilosophie. Wie dieser glaubt sie nicht, daß die Aufklärung von Anfang aufgrund der ihr innewohnenden Dialektik scheitern mußte (wie die Kritische Theorie dies tat) oder daß die Aufklärung nur eine weitere Epoche in der Geschichte der Verstellung und des Entzugs des Seins (Martin Heidegger) sei. Vielmehr deutete sie wie auch Cassirer den Nationalsozialismus als einen Antihumanismus, der in der deutschen Tradition überhand gewann.

[22] Käte Hamburger, "Anachronistische Symbolik: Fragen an Thomas Manns Faustus-Roman," in *Kleine Schriften zur Literatur und Geistesgeschichte,* 2. erw. Aufl. (Stuttgart: H.-D. Heinz Akademischer Verlag, 1986), 309–33, hier 325.

[23] *Kleine Schriften,* 333.

[24] Thomas Mann wirft Käte Hamburger Kälte, mangelnde Einfühlsamkeit vor, ein vor dem Hintergrund des Motivs der "Kälte" in eben dem Roman recht signifikanter Vorwurf; ausführlich dazu Irmela von der Lühe, "Dienende Frauen — alternde Mädchen. Literarische Montage und biographische Konstruktion in Thomas Manns *Doktor Faustus*" (Antrittsvorlesung, Göttingen, 6. Mai 1998, unveröffentliches Ms.).

[25] Käte Hamburger, *Von Sophokles zu Sartre: Griechische Dramenfiguren antik und modern,* 4. Aufl. (Stuttgart, Berlin, Köln, Mainz: W. Kohlhammer, 1962). Behandelt werden Klytemnestra, Orest, Elektra, Iphigenie, Helena, Alkestis, Phädra, Medea, Ödipus, Antigone.

[26] *Von Sophokles zu Sartre,* 103.

[27] *Von Sophokles zu Sartre,* 112.

[28] Drei Festschriften wurden ihr gewidmet; sie erhielt die Ehrendoktorwürde der Gesamthochschule Siegen (Dr. phil., 1980) und die Ehrendoktorwürde der Georg-August-Universität Göttingen (Dr. theol., 1987) sowie das Große Bundesverdienstkreuz, die Verdienstmedaille des Landes Baden-Württemberg, die Stuttgarter Bürgermedaille, den Schiller-Gedächtnispreis des Landes Baden-Württemberg. Vgl. Günther Schweickle, "Käte Hamburger in Stuttgart," in *Käte Hamburger: Reden bei der Akademischen Gedenkfeier der Universität Stuttgart für Frau Prof. Dr. phil. habil. Käte Hamburger, 8. Dezember 1992,* hrsg. im Auftrag des Rektorats der Universität Stuttgart v. Jürgen Hering (Stuttgart: Universitätsbibliothek Stuttgart, 1993), 20.

Panelists' Commentary

RITCHIE ROBERTSON (OXFORD UNIVERSITY): We have heard two very rich papers and I think I shall respond to the title rather than to people themselves, in a somewhat tangential way. A Tradition in Ruins: it seems to me there are several traditions involved here and I think it is worth distinguishing in a very schematic way at least two traditions in the Weimar Republic in relation to which I think one could locate at least Susman, Arendt, and Hamburger. If I confine myself to three out of four writers, I hope that will be sufficient.

First, I want to be very schematic here and simply remind you of what you know. There was a tradition of conservative humanism to which one could assign Ernst Cassirer, for example, and Jakob Wassermann, and of which Thomas Mann was the exemplary figure. I will call this tradition the later stage of Jewish assimilation or of the German Jewish symbiosis, a term, as you were reminded this morning, which thanks to Michael Brenner and others has again become respectable. This tradition looks back to the aesthetic humanism of the late eighteenth century, especially to Lessing — think of Thomas Mann's essay on Lessing and of Cassirer's study of the Enlightenment, in which he tries very hard to choose Lessing as the typical figure of the Enlightenment and to make Voltaire into a kind of French Lessing.

On the other hand there is a more radical modernist and religious tradition of which key figures include Walter Benjamin and Gershom Scholem. For this tradition crucial experiences were first the rediscovery of Judaism by Martin Buber, and however rude Scholem and Benjamin were about Buber in their correspondence, with no doubt he is the important and enabling figure for them and their generation. Another important experience was the messianic activism of the immediate postwar period. And this tradition looks back not so much to the Enlightenment as to Romanticism and the Baroque. I am thinking here especially of Benjamin. And where the aesthetic humanism of Cassirer emphasized the symbol, the radical tradition emphasized more allegory. Now, Margarete Susman, I think, can clearly be located in relation to the latter tradition, and her preoccupation with

Job long predates the postwar book which we heard about, as is apparent in her early essay on Kafka, about "Das Hiob-Problem bei Kafka,"[1] an essay which was important, as Thomas Sparr recently pointed out, for Gershom Scholem and helped to inspire his *Lehrgedicht* on *Der Prozess*, which I think must be a very important document and piece of critical insight into Kafka's novel.[2] It was very interesting that instead of Lessing, both Susman and Arendt look back to Rahel Varnhagen as an important predecessor and seek to reconstruct her situation and her painful and torn conception of Jewish identity.

Finally, Hamburger: I think I'd be inclined to relate her to the first tradition, that of conservative humanism and to bear in mind especially her exile work on Thomas Mann and the Joseph tetralogy, which is after all a great statement of humanism, but as Gesa Dane made very clear, Hamburger went far beyond this tradition and in many ways revised it. I'll mention simply two to which she drew attention. Her argument that Goethe's *Iphigenie* was far less relevant to present time than Hauptmann's *Iphigenie*, and when you recall that in Hauptmann's *Atridentetralogie* Iphigenie appears as a blood-crazed priestess — that's a rather shocking judgment but understandable in the time. Second, the critical attitude to *Doktor Faustus*, which as we heard, she commented was a lamentation for Germany but not for German Jewry, a point that Egon Schwarz made more recently.[3] It is after all curious that in *Doktor Faustus* there are only three Jewish figures: one is a rabbi of whom we hear very little; the second is a rather objectionable salon charlatan; and the third is an international entrepreneur. So I think if we are going to consider Susman, Arendt, and Hamburger in context, you have there a very rough historical context in which they can be placed. Thanks.

DAVID SUCHOFF (COLBY COLLEGE): I also wanted to start by commenting on the title of the panel, but I had a very different reading of what the title suggested. In fact, rather than tradition in ruins, I understood much about a tradition in reconstruction, that is to say, the continuation of a tradition of Jewish reflection in Germany; and the complex ways this identity and this tradition is asserted in these writers, and I learned a lot from the papers. One thing I wanted to bring out was just the question of "ich," or assertion of identity. What was clear to me is that from the accounts of each of these figures, that reworking the tradition *is* an assertion of identity — that is, one can assert one's identity through a re-reading of figures and in fact by restoring different figures in the canon. Sometimes the paper sounded as if a counter-tradition were being constructed very much in a Benjaminian sense, a tradition of reflection on Jewish identity in Germany. The other question raised, or connections raised — the question of institutionalization, the question of whether one is inside the academy or not, whether that gives one more freedom to address questions of Jewish culture in Germany. I wanted to draw out the connection between, in this regard, the American context, that is Hannah Arendt and the New York intellectuals with whom she was associated. On the one hand the New York intellectuals were praised as the Jewish figures in the United States who were able to speak openly concerning Jewish issues. On the other hand if you read Irving Howe you'll find him reflecting on the constraints placed on that identity — that is, New York meant only one thing, New York intellectuals and that meant "Jew."[4] So there was an ambivalence to that position. So, the question inside the academy: I found the reading of Käte Hamburger very moving in that regard.

The other question I wanted to bring up was the relationship between a feminist perspective and a Jewish perspective — that is, how this works in Hannah Arendt, the way Hannah Arendt wrote about the private sphere and femininity and the connection between that and the way she wrote about European Judaism and the question of passivity, which comes up in *Eichmann in Jerusalem*. I wanted to bring the Eichmann affair up, because it was a crux for Arendt's career, and the issue itself became the public issue where questions of Jewish identity and politics became unavoidable for a whole generation of Jewish intellectuals in the United States. What I wanted to point out was that this question of Jewish passivity had a wholly different cast within the Jewish community and outside of it. So I wanted to raise the question of audience. Does Arendt's political theory change when, writing as a journalist, she decides to appeal to a larger, non-Jewish intellectual community? As far as addressing a Jewish audience goes: the question of the Jewish masses as depoliticized and passively accepting their fate was a hot-button issue in Jewish cultural politics that goes back to writers like Chaim Nachman Bialik; think of the furor his Hebrew poem, "City of Slaughter" caused, written in response to the Kishinev Pogrom of 1903, which expressed his outrage that Jews failed to fight. So I just wanted to bring out the contrast, audience-wise: what did it mean for Bialik to take a public stand as a Zionist in 1903, addressing a Jewish public, for Arendt to address a Jewish public as a Zionist during the Second World War, and for her to address a general audience as a "New York intellectual" in 1963 and after?

The last thing I wanted to point out was that biography is a way of writing cultural history: claiming the right of a certain kind of self to exist in a certain culture. This is what Arendt's re-reading of Rahel Varnhagen meant: underneath her compromises, she meant to assert the rights of a strong female Jewish self in German culture. The reading of Hamburger went in this same direction, which I find fascinating. So these are a few things that occurred to me.

GISELA HOECHERL-ALDEN: What you just said about inside and outside the academy: what to me was interesting was that Melitta Gerhard's (1891–1981)[5] and Marianne Thalmann's (1888–1975)[6] names did not come up at all. It is very interesting to me that they, once they were here, even though they did not, especially Melitta Gerhard, have a prestigious position, she did do a lot of publishing on Schiller, and Marianne Thalmann on Romanticism, and now I ask anyone to correct me, but I don't think she went back to Rahel Varnhagen. She was working more on Tieck and the male Romanticists. On the other hand, Bertha Badt-Strauss, and I would slightly disagree with Barbara Hahn, I think she did become much more political when she was here because I remember distinctly reading that she gave Harry Slochower (1900–1991), a Jewish and leftist Germanist from Brooklyn College in New York City, a forum in *Jewish Frontier* and other publications she was affiliated with, the opportunity to publish very critical Jewish and leftist articles, which in the end led to his downfall in the McCarthy era. He lost his job as a Germanist. But I do want to point out that not only did she, when she was here, work for publicizing exile literature in this country, works by Karl Wolfskehl and others, but also gave Jewish Germanists who were in the country and who had been in the country before 1933 a voice that was denied to them in the traditional Germanistic publication organs like *Monatshefte, Germanic Review,* or the *Journal of English and Germanic Philology,* and of course the *PMLA.* Thank you.

Discussion

BARBARA HAHN: Ich fange an bei der letzten Geschichte mit Bertha Badt-Strauss. Ja, sie hat sich in Amerika politisiert. Aber um noch einmal diese Lektüre von ihrer Trennung aufzunehmen, der Raum der Politik muß geschützt werden, damit der Raum der Kultur etabliert werden kann. Ich würde ein gewisses Unbehagen lesen nach der Emigration, weil diese beiden Dinge zusammenschießen. Wenn man ihre Artikel anschaut, dann schreibt sie jetzt nur noch über Texte und über Personen mit einer klaren politischen und kulturellen Identität. Das heißt, sie bringt genau die Dinge zusammen, die sie in Deutschland immer getrennt halten wollte. Und das tut sie mit einem gewissen Enthusiasmus und unten drunter lese ich ein gewisses Unbehagen, daß diese beiden Dinge plötzlich identisch sind. Die Frage, was das bedeutet für die amerikanische Gesellschaft, da meine ich doch, das bleibt offen. Es gibt die Demokratie, das ist ein wesentlicher Punkt, auf den sie auch immer wieder hindeutet, aber es gibt einen bestimmten Zwang zu einer kulturellen Identität, der ein Unbehagen hervorruft. So würde ich es lesen auch in diesem Buch *White Fire* über Jessie Sampter. Sie hat sich in Deutschland nie politisch geäußert und jetzt tut sie es.

Nun ganz kurz zu der Frage der "biography." Ich denke, wenn man Hannah Arendts Biographie der Rahel Levin auf dem Hintergrund ihrer Rezension von Peter Nettls Biographie der Rosa Luxemburg liest, dann wird sehr deutlich, daß sie das biographische Verfahren versucht zu verändern. Die Biographie darf nicht die Bruchstücke des Lebens zusammenführen. Das kann man tun, sagt sie über Nettl, wenn man in der Lage ist, Geschichte zu schreiben. Sie hat für sich selbst aber immer den Anspruch, daß sie das nicht kann und auch nicht können will, weil sie immer die Gefahr sieht, daß der, der das kann, sozusagen die Trümmer der Geschichte im Zug der Sieger mitführt, wie sie im Anschluß an Benjamin sagt. Das heißt, für sie ist die Biographie eine Herausforderung, insofern sie die Fragmentarik dieses Lebens, das zur Disposition steht, erhalten kann und nicht synthetisiert. Ob ihr das in dem Buch über Rahel Levin gelingt, das ist eine andere Frage, die man nochmal diskutieren müßte. Aber vom

Anspruch her, was eine Biographie sein soll, ist das für sie das Entscheidende.

Gesa Dane: Zwei Hinweise nur: Erstens zu Käte Hamburger und *Doktor Faustus.* Sie weist ja unter anderem auch zurück, daß eine solche Musikerfigur überhaupt eine Aussagekraft haben kann. Und sie weist auf die beiden anderen jüdischen Figuren hin, auf die dann später, sehr viel später, Ruth Klüger wieder hinweist, nämlich auf Meta Nackedey und Kunigunde Rosenstiel.[7] Sie weist ganz scharf diese Konturierung zurück. Darauf wollte ich hinweisen, daß sie da vielleicht sogar traditionsstiftend war. Und zweitens: Käte Hamburger, das habe ich in meinem Referat beiseite gelassen, hat in Schweden natürlich in schwedischer Sprache geschrieben. Sie hat immer versucht, die neuere deutsche Literatur, die ihr wichtig war, auf schwedisch in der schwedischen Öffentlichkeit publik zu machen. Da ist eine gewisse thematische Kontinuität im Schreiben, aber eben nicht im Schreiben auf Deutsch. Ihre Bücher, die sie über deutsche Literatur in Schweden publiziert hat, sind immer etwa zu einem Drittel der Auflage eingestampft worden, weil sie halt nicht nachgefragt wurden.

Willi Goetschel (University of Toronto): Ich spreche jetzt auf Deutsch, weil ich zu den beiden Papers eine Ergänzung machen möchte und zwar in Aufnahme des Vorschlags von David Suchoff. Ich glaube, es ist sehr wichtig, daß wir überlegen, daß es verschiedene audiences, d.h. Zielpubliken gibt. Das kann man, glaube ich, bei Margarete Susman sehr schön illustrieren. Sie hatten gesagt, Frau Dane, daß *Das Buch Hiob* ein Kaddisch ist. Ich glaube das nicht. Vielleicht habe ich Sie falsch verstanden. Ich würde behaupten, *Deutung einer großen Liebe* ist das Kaddisch. Das ist das Kaddisch auf die selbstzerstörte deutsche Kultur. Wenn Sie es lesen als die Kodierung der Liebe nicht Charlotte von Stein zu Goethe, sondern der Deutschen und der Juden. Und *Das Buch Hiob,* hier scheint mir doch sehr wichtig, daß man das als einzelnes Buch sieht, das sich unterscheidet von der frühen Kafkadeutung. Es gibt eine theologische Potentialisierung, die reinkommt und die eben nicht nur eine Trauerarbeit des Versunkenen ist, sondern die Pointe ist, darauf hat Hermann Levin Goldschmidt auch hingewiesen, es ist eines der Grundbücher der jüdischen Geistesgeschichte des zwanzigsten Jahrhunderts neben Martin Bubers *Gottesfinsternis,* was spät, nämlich 1953, erscheint, und neben dem *Stern der Erlösung* (1921). Die Metapher der Zerrissenheit, auf die Frau Hahn hingewiesen hat, ist übrigens direkt von Rosenzweig abgeleitet, die berühmte Stelle: "wenn das Leben mich einmal auf die Folter spannen würde und mich in zwei Stücke reißen, so wüßte ich freilich, mit welcher der beiden Hälften das Herz, das ja unsymmetrisch gelagert sei, mitgehen würde; ich wüßte auch, daß ich diese Operation nicht lebendig überstehen würde."[8] Da gibt es eine große Hermeneutik. Die einen sagen, es wäre die deutsche Seite, die anderen natürlich die jüdische. Im *Buch Hiob* geht es um eine Abnabelung von der untergegangenen deutsch-jüdischen Beziehung, ich sage bewußt nicht Symbiose. Es ist eine bewußte Besinnung zurück aufs Biblische, auf Hiob, und eigentlich ist es ein zukunftsgerichtetes Buch. Ich warte immer noch darauf, daß es neue Leser gibt, die das merken, denn ich meine, darum, um das geht's im *Buch Hiob*. Es ist ein positives Buch, es ist ein anti-theologisches Buch, es ist ein Buch, das zum Beispiel von der Gott ist-tot-Theologie völlig ignoriert worden ist. Weil genau Gottes Tod durch *Das Buch Hiob* ausgeschaltet wird. Ich denke, daß diese beiden Bücher, diese beiden Nachkriegsbücher, einen sehr schönen Kommentar zum Thema der Sektion "Tradition in Ruins" geben. Sie sind der Versuch, aus diesen Ruinen wieder herauszukommen. Und ich denke, dass dieser Zusammenhang eine schärfere Konturierung des Projektes ergibt, um das es bei Margarete Susman ging.

WALTER SOKEL: Ich wollte auf David Suchoffs Bemerkung über *Eichmann in Jerusalem* eingehen und kurz über *Eichmann in Jerusalem* sprechen. Es ist in gewisser Hinsicht ein antisemitisches Buch und es wurde ja auch als antisemitisch empfunden. Es kann als Beispiel des berühmten jüdischen, deutsch-jüdischen Selbsthasses angesehen werden. Die Juden werden nämlich in diesem Buch in nazistischer Weise gesehen, als Feiglinge. Das ist ja auch ein wichtiger Topos im Antisemitismus, besonders im deutschen Antisemitismus, der Jude als Feigling, als Wehrdienstverweigerer, als Anti-Held. Und das ist genau, was Hannah Arendt den Juden vorwirft. Sie hat also auch bei Heidegger gelernt.

DAVID SUCHOFF: The reason I brought that up was as a historical moment. There are other things to say about Hannah Arendt's book, but as a historical moment it was a point in at least American intellectual history where one had to take a position, and Jewishness became much more public for a whole generation of intellectuals. It was a landmark in that regard. One was identified as a Jew by that question, by the question raised by Hannah Arendt's book. Mary McCarthy in her defense of Hannah Arendt says this, she says that you could tell who was a Jew and not a Jew by the way they talked about this question. It was quite a moment, just generationally.

CHRISTOPH KÖNIG: Meine Bemerkung schließt sich an die Versuche an, die jetzt offenbar hier angestellt werden, zu zeigen, daß auch in der Abwehrung, der Distanz und der Kritik an der Tradition, die diese Frauen zerstört hat, diese ihre Denkhaltungen zum Teil aus diesem Raum beziehen müssen. Ich habe nur eine kleine Bemerkung, eigentlich eine Frage, weil Barbara Hahn das sicher dann viel besser beantworten kann. Die Frage ist, wie der Begriff der Entscheidung, der hier so emphatisch von Susman verwendet worden ist, gemeint ist. Ist er theologisch gemeint im Sinne einer Theologie, die von Kierkegaard herkommt und gerade in der Absurdität des Verhältnisses des Menschen zu Gott und seiner Übermacht den Glauben definiert. Wenn dem so oder so ähnlich wäre, dann würde sich wieder zeigen, wie schwierig es ist, selbst in der Absage noch eine eigene Sprache zu finden. Davon zeugen ja auch die Gedichte von Paul Celan.

DORRIT COHN: I want to thank Dr. Dane for her really very interesting paper on Käte Hamburger. This brings me to my comment, which is that Käte Hamburger in some ways is very different from the other women that we discussed. Her importance, international importance, is as a theorist and not as a belletristic critic the way the others are. I keep being astonished by the impact she has in France these days. Her book was translated some six years ago into French. She has acquired a tremendous importance and a tremendous respect among French literary theorists. And unfortunately this is not true in this country, but you may know that her book *Die Logik der Dichtung* which is translated as *The Logic of Literature* has been reissued now by Indiana University Press with a preface of Gérard Genette, which I translated for them.[9] I hope that this is going to stimulate interest in her theory here too. But perhaps she should not be lumped too easily or linked too easily with the other women that were discussed here. They have great interest as women writers, as women critics, great interest as Jewish critics, but I think that Hamburger's *Logic of Literature* is in a different world, as it were.

GESA DANE: Das ist auch der Grund, warum wir Käte Hamburger aus der Reihe herausgenommen haben. Sie ist auch die einzige, die wieder nach Deutschland gegangen ist. Sie ist auch die einzige, die zumindest nachweisbar seit dem Ende der zwanziger Jahre eine akademische Karriere anstrebte und an den unterschiedlichsten Hürden einfach gescheitert ist, bis sie dann eben als Sechzigjährige habilitieren konnte, was aus heutiger Sicht eigentlich glatter Irrsinn ist. Ihre Bedeutung in

Deutschland, glaube ich, war sehr groß. Wir profitieren von ihr heute noch, ohne daß sie immer im Mund geführt wird.

BARBARA HAHN: Ich würde gern noch einmal auf die Hiobsgeschichte zurückkommen. Was wir gerade in der Diskussion machen, wenn ich das einmal von einer anderen Perspektive ansehe, wir versuchen Kontexte zu ziehen und die Kontexte auch mit Namen zu belegen. Das finde ich falsch und richtig. Ich finde es richtig, weil es natürlich Zusammenhänge gibt, die man ziehen kann und die man auch ziehen muß. Auf der anderen Seite, denke ich, gibt es Texte, die ihre Kontexte nicht einfach mit sich tragen. Und das muß man, glaube ich, einfach aushalten. Um noch einmal auf Margarete Susman zurückzugehen. Was Sie, Herr Goetschel, jetzt getan haben, Sie haben dieses Bild von dem "mitten auseinandergerissen" mit dem Namen Rosenzweig übersetzt. Rosenzweig hat das gesagt, es gibt dieses berühmte Zitat. Interessanterweise hat Margarete Susman, als sie dasselbe Bild benutzt hat, den Namen Rosenzweig nicht genannt. Ich finde das interesssant, daß er an dieser Stelle einfach fehlt, obwohl das so nahe liegen würde. Ich beziehe das jetzt im weiteren Kontext auf das, was in dem Hiobsbuch geschieht. Das Hiobsbuch versucht in einem historischen Moment, der überhaupt noch nicht zu begreifen ist, auf eine Tradition zurückzugehen, die schon zerbrochen ist. Margarete Susman hat in der Rezension der Rosenzweig'schen und Buber'schen Übersetzung der Schrift ziemlich deutlich gesehen, daß damit die Ablösung von der Sprache der Akkulturation geschaffen wird. Sie hat das so formuliert: Das Deutsche ist uns in Fleisch und Blut übergegangen und plötzlich spüren wir, es gibt Deutsch, dem eine fremde Sprache, nämlich das Hebräische, anhaftet wie ein nasses Gewand. Es ist ein Deutsch, was so fremd ist in unserer eigenen Muttersprache, daß wir das fast nicht benutzen können. Sie hat, denke ich, in ihrem Kafka-Aufsatz versucht, diese Spannung zu konturieren. Sie hat Kafka gelesen als Umschrift der alten Hiobsgeschichte, aber sie hat sie fast so gelesen, als ob sie schon Buber hätte lesen können, nämlich Bubers Entfernung von der Luther'schen Tradition als Grundlage, als Tradition, die Kafka wiederum umgeschrieben hat. Als sie 1943 angefangen hat, sich mit Hiob zu beschäftigen, um überhaupt ein Muster zu finden, um darzustellen, wie sie die Shoah sah, hat sie sich auf eine merkwürdige, selbstverständliche Weise wieder zurück zu Luther begeben. Als ob man diese Tradition noch einmal für einen Moment konstruieren müsse, damit richtig deutlich wird, wie sie zerfällt. Ich denke, das ist bezogen auch auf die anderen Versuche, einen Kontext zu konstruieren, deshalb wichtig, weil gerade in diesen Bruchstücken, die wir in dieser Sektion versucht haben darzulegen, wir es mit Denkversuchen zu tun haben, die nicht einfach an die überlieferten Diskurse anschließbar sind. Und das finde ich wichtig, sich noch einmal klar zu machen. Es handelt sich nicht um einen Gegensatz. Hier ist Theorie und hier sind jetzt literarische Versuche, sondern es handelt sich um Versuche, eine Kulturtheorie zu entwickeln, die sowohl in Deutschland ohne Nachfolge blieb, die aber auch in anderen kulturellen Kontexten, zum Beispiel in diesem Land, nicht wieder aufgegriffen wurde. Worum es mir ging, auch im Kontext des Vortrags, um das nochmal deutlich zu machen: es gab andere theoretische Wege, die untergegangen, die verschwunden sind. Es wäre vielleicht interessant, sich noch einmal daran zu erinnern.

Ich greife noch einmal auf, was vorhin gesagt wurde, Margarete Susman war nicht die einzige, die versucht hat, darüber nachzudenken, wie die Emanzipation der Juden und die Emanzipation der Frauen zusammenhängt. Darüber gibt es bis heute, und das sage ich jetzt als These, keine Theorie, die das irgendwie deutlich machen könnte. Es gibt aber Ansätze, die damals gedacht wurden und denen man noch einmal nachgehen müßte. Die sind auf eine gewisse Weise namenlos geblieben. Man kann darüber nachdenken und dann sagt man Weininger. Bei Weininger ist es alles sozusagen negativ verbandelt. Es gibt produktivere Umgänge damit. Da wäre auch Hannah Arendt noch einmal einzuführen. Hannah Arendt hat sich immer geweigert, diesen Zusammenhang zu denken. In dieser Weigerung ist ein unglaublich produktives Moment, weil diese beiden Emanzipationsgeschichten zu sehr übereinandergelegt wurden. Hannah Arendt hat einfach noch einmal die Differenz deutlich gemacht. Die Differenz zwischen der Emanzipation der Juden und der Emanzipation der Frauen. Die Weigerung wäre auf diesem Hintergrund noch einmal zu lesen als Anforderung: hier ist etwas, worüber man noch nachdenken muß. Das ist nach wie vor offen, gerade in dieser Abwehr.

PAUL REITTER (OHIO STATE UNIVERSITY): This comment is for David Suchoff. I wanted to ask you to expand on the comments you made about the prospective links between Hannah Arendt's feminism and her reading of Jewish identity. I think it is precisely this connection that allows us to see her discussions of Jews that she perceives or portrays as feminized, as something other than Jewish self-hatred, as deeply sympathetic, and perhaps a sort of recuperative gesture.

DAVID SUCHOFF: The article I am thinking of there that really influenced my thinking is by Hanna Pitkin on "Justice."[10] It is one of the best things on Hannah Arendt and it really takes seriously her thoughts on the Jewish predicament in Europe as a passive predicament. She reads that against her later political theory which valorizes action before all else. In another essay Pitkin argues that action for Arendt, a supposedly universal category, is gendered male.[11] Pitkin suggests interesting links between Arendt's fear of a passive, apolitical Jewish tradition, her predicament as a female, German-Jewish intellectual, and the fact that the action she prizes in Jewish terms is also quite male-defined. These patterns preexist the Eichmann affair, which turned — at least in the public reception — on whether Jews had acted decisively enough, and on Arendt's suggestion that they hadn't. It is a very interesting essay that just opens up many connections. And during the war, Arendt wrote a column for *Aufbau*, the German-Jewish émigré newspaper in New York. In that column, she propagandized for the formation of a Jewish army, supporting a program of the *Irgun*, one of the right-wing Jewish underground groups in Jewish Palestine, though she eventually backed away.[12] Arendt was actually part of a long tradition of self-critique in modern Jewish culture that attacked the passivity of European, and particularly, traditional Eastern European Jewish life. This is the part of Arendt that really needs to be looked at, the connection in her thought between femininity and her excessive and often unfair attack on supposed Jewish passivity. These connections are particularly interesting, connecting her "private" predicament as a woman (in her own terms) with the public positions she took on Jewish politics and history, because in her political theory the split between the public and the private is absolute. And it makes you want to ask, does Judaism belong in the private, is Jewishness the private, is the female the private? So it is an interesting set of connections to think about.[13]

HASKELL BLOCK: I can't help commenting on this question of Jewish passivity, because there is a fine essay by Simon Epstein in the *Revue germanique internationale* in 1996 on just this question[14] where he argues that for reasons best known to themselves in Poland, France, and the United States there has been a completely false emphasis on so-called Jewish passivity and investigation of the history of the Jews in Germany particularly in the years immediately leading up to Hitler's accession of power would indicate that Jews were anything but passive, and this is documented in great detail in that study of Simon Epstein.

DAVID SUCHOFF: I am not really talking about the factual situation. I think *Eichmann in Jerusalem* is a deeply wrong and troubling book. But it is clearly one of Hannah Arendt's anxieties long before and it figures into her thinking about Jewish culture. There is a tradition for it in Jewish literature in Europe before her. Placing her as a Jewish thinker, I just think the history of this issue must be accounted for. It is not just something that suddenly arises with the Eichmann affair.

JONATHAN SKOLNIK: I meant to pose a question for all the speakers and the panelists. I was wondering if they would address the question of symbiosis, which came up again today. For a second time today we've heard the recent social histories of Michael Brenner and Shulamit Volkov used as works that have some moment of symbiosis,[15] have rehabilitated it. I understand their studies of German-Jewish subculture somewhat differently, as something that shows that it was an "authentic German-Jewish symbiosis" but one that nonetheless existed as a monologue rather than a dialogue. I am wondering in this context if it would be correct to say the following: that we have heard today three phases in relation of the critics to the object: the first came out indirectly in Amir Eshel's talk about the first generation of Jewish historians, who had a problematic relation of subject to the object of their research, that had some sort of alienation from Jewish sources that Scholem saw positively as "unmenschlich"; in Geiger, the relation to Goethe concentrated positively a tradition no longer in the Hebrew sources that the first generation looked for but rather in the Enlightenment sources of Sachs[16] and Abraham Geiger and others. But here it seems that the speakers have talked about a new tradition that seems to have been formed after the Holocaust, where the point of reference is no longer a traditional Jewish world, no longer a first generation of Jewish emancipation that's looked at positively as in Ludwig Geiger's foundation of *Zeitschrift für die Geschichte der Juden in Deutschland,* but rather Jewishness takes as a starting point the "Zerrissenheit" and the breaks that Gesa Dane described — no longer looking at Rahel as the founder of the Goethe cult but as someone that was now addressing two very different and now possibly irreconcilable traditions.

GERHARD AUSTIN (UNIVERSITY OF CONNECTICUT): I was just concerned about the previous remark because that shows, I think, the danger that we seem to be running into with all these discussions, it was the question of Jewish passivity and in the exchange of remarks it was: is it now Jewish passivity, is it not Jewish passivity? And I find that we are putting things here into groups as if there is the one phenomenon "Jewish passivity." I am just thinking of the moment when Hitler took over, as far as I know, Jews in general in Germany and throughout the world, were pretty much split and we have these documents of letters that went to Hitler in which orthodox Jews said, well, it's ok, it's ok, we have this little problem about your anti-Semitism, but we'll just get along fine. And observations have been made that it was not so much the Jewishness that determined the attitude towards Hitler, but it was much more the political attitude of the individual too.

DAVID SUCHOFF: I'll just say it one more time. The point I meant to make by bringing this up in Arendt, is that in Jewish culture, long before 1933, there was an autonomous tradition of reflecting on the Jewish position on modernity that has to do with passivity, that has to do with Jewish political action, that has to do with the traditional culture of the shtetl, and I raised this point to show Hannah Arendt's rootedness in the tradition of Jewish reflection, which then has to be taken into account, I think, when one considers the later controversies and her relation with things German. And that was the point I meant to make.

BARBARA HAHN: Eine Bemerkung zu *Eichmann in Jerusalem*. Was mich stört ist, wenn dieses Buch zu dicht an die anderen Bücher von Hannah Arendt herantritt. Es ist eine andere Art von Text. Ich denke, das sollte man ernst nehmen. Sie hat immer darauf beharrt, daß sie versucht hat, eine Art Protokoll zu schreiben. Und ich denke, in großen Teilen ist das Buch eine Art Protokoll. Die Frage ist, was wird da protokolliert? Wird Eichmann protokolliert? Wird der Prozeß protokolliert, wird der Kontext protokolliert? Wird Hannah Arendt's Nachdenken, wenn sie das hört, protokolliert? In dieser Perspektive bekommt das Buch auch noch einmal einen anderen politischen Einsatz. Dieses Buch, ich will nicht sagen, es ist ein falsches Buch, es ist einfach ein ungeheuer gewagtes Buch. Es ist ein Wagnis, von dem ich nicht weiß, ob man das eingehen darf. Das Buch beurteilt nicht, was da drinsteht. Dem Buch fehlt eine Ebene, das Buch stellt diesen Prozeß aus, ohne daß deutlich wird, wer jetzt hier eigentlich darüber redet. Und deswegen, denke ich, kann man auf eine gewisse Weise die Aussagen des Buches Hannah Arendt nicht pro oder kontra vorlegen.

Das funktioniert nicht. Bei den anderen Büchern, denke ich, muß man das tun.

Jetzt komme ich noch einmal auf diese Geschichte mit dem privat und öffentlich zurück. An dem Punkt wird es nämlich wirklich interessant. Es sieht so aus, als ob Hannah Arendt einen Ort des Privaten verteidigt, sozusagen als residualen Ort, damit es hier den öffentlichen Ort des Politischen gibt, von dem sie spricht als das Wagnis der Öffentlichkeit. Nur, ich würde denken, daß dieses Private, dieses Abgetrennte, dieser Raum, der da etabliert wird, mindestens so gefährlich ist wie der Raum der Öffentlichkeit. Denn, in dem Raum geht es um ein Denken, das sich der Verantwortung aussetzt, und diese Verantwortung muß man auf eine bestimmte Weise hinter sich lassen, insofern man in den Raum des Politischen geht. Dort kann man nämlich nur mit einer Stimme sprechen, man muß mit einer Stimme sprechen. Im Raum des Denkens darf man das nie tun. Das ist, glaube ich, Hannah Arendts großer Unterschied oder ihre Kritik auch an Heideggers Art zu philosophieren, wo Mehrstimmigkeit immer im Bereich der Verantwortungslosigkeit bleibt. Indem sie sagt, es gibt einen Unterschied, hier denken wir vielleicht privat und hier reden wir, wird deutlich gemacht, daß, wenn wir von dem einen Bereich in den anderen gehen, man sich verändern muß. In der Politik gibt es eine Stimme und wenn man die nicht wagt zu nehmen, dann hat man nichts zu sagen. Man ist unpolitisch, man ist verantwortungslos. Deswegen würde ich auch nicht mitgehen und auf dieses Modell die Frage nach Jude und Frau abbilden, weil ich denke, daß es hier um etwas anderes geht. Hier geht es um die Frage, wo ist das Denken zu situieren und wo der politische Einsatz.

Editors' Annotations

[1] Margarete Susman, "Das Hiob-Problem bei Franz Kafka," *Der Morgen* 5 (1929): 31–49.

[2] Thomas Sparr, "Gershom Scholem und die deutsche Literatur," *Germanic Review* 72 (1997): 42–56.

[3] Egon Schwarz, "The Jewish Characters in *Doctor Faustus*," in *Thomas Mann's "Doctor Faustus": A Novel at the Margin of Modernism*, ed. Herbert Lehnert and Peter C. Pfeiffer (Columbia, SC: Camden House, 1991), 119–43.

[4] Vgl. auch David Suchoff, "Irving Howe, The Cold War Canon Debate, and Yiddish, 1954–1992," in *Living With America, 1946–1996*, ed. Cristina Giorcelli and Rob Kroes (Amsterdam: VU UP, 1997), 211–22, and David Suchoff, "The Rosenberg Case and the New York Intellectuals," in *Secret Agents: The Rosenberg Case, McCarthyism, and Fifties America*, ed. Marjorie Garber and Rebecca L. Walkowitz (New York and London: Routledge, 1995), 155–70.

[5] Melitta Gerhard (born in Berlin); Dr. phil. 1918 in Berlin, Habilitation 1927 in Kiel; emigration 1938 to teach at Rockford College in Illinois (1938–1942); University of Missouri, Columbia, ASTP (Army Specialized Training Programs) 1942–1945, since 1945 Wittenberg College, Ohio, Emerita (1955); Festschrift 1965. — See Gesa Dane, "Melitta Gerhard (1891–1981): Die erste habilitierte Germanistin: 'In bunten Farben schillernder Gast' und 'uniformiertes Glied der Zunft,'" in *Frauen in den Kulturwissenschaften: Von Lou Andreas-Salomé bis Hannah Arendt*, ed. Barbara Hahn (Munich: Beck, 1994), 219–34.

[6] Marianne Thalmann (born in Linz); Dr. phil. 1919 in Vienna; Habilitation 1924 in Vienna, emigrated 1933 and taught at Wellesley College until her retirement in 1953, whereupon she returned to the Federal Republic.

[7] Ruth Klüger, "Jewish Characters in Thomas Mann's Fiction," in *Horizonte: Festschrift für Herbert Lehnert zum 65. Geburtstag*, ed. Hannelore Mundt, Egon Schwarz, and William J. Lillyman (Tübingen: Niemeyer, 1990), 161–72.

[8] Brief an Rudolf Hallo, Ende Januar 1923, in *Franz Rosenzweig, Briefe und Tagebücher*, ed. Rachel Rosenzweig and Edith Rosenzweig-Scheinmann, vol. 2 (The Hague: Martinus Nijhoff, 1979), 888.

[9] Käte Hamburger, *The Logic of Literature*, 2d rev. ed. (Bloomington: Indiana UP, 1993).

[10] Hanna Fenichel Pitkin, "Justice: On Relating Private and Public," *Political Theory* 9.3 (August 1988): 327–52.

[11] Hanna Fenichel Pitkin, "Conformism, Housekeeping and the Attack of the Blob: the Origins of Hannah Arendt's Concept of the Social," in *Feminist Interpretations of Hannah Arendt*, ed. Bonnie Honig (University Park: Pennsylvania State UP, 1995), 51–81.

[12] Hannah Arendt, "Die Jüdische Armee — der Beginn einer jüdischen Politik?" *Aufbau*, 14 November 1941, 1. The quotation is quite interesting: "unser nationales Elend beginnt mit dem Zusammenbruch der Sabbtai-Zvi Bewegung. Seither

haben wir Dasein als solches, ohne nationalen und meist auch ohne religiösen Inhalt, als Wert an sich proklamiert." The other article is Hannah Arendt, "Ganz Israel Bürget Füreinander," *Aufbau,* 24 April 1942, 18.

[13] For further reference see: David Suchoff, "Gershom Scholem, Hannah Arendt and the Scandal of Jewish Particularity," *The Germanic Review* 72:1 (Winter 1997): 57–76. (Special Issue on Gershom Scholem).

[14] Simon Epstein, "Les intellectuels mobilisés: Notes sur le combat des Juifs allemands dans les années 1928–1933," *Revue germanique internationale* 1996, 5:67–72, 258–59.

[15] Michael Brenner, *The Renaissance of Jewish Culture in Weimar Germany* (New Haven: Yale UP, 1996); Shulamit Volkov, *Die Juden in Deutschland 1780–1918* (Munich: Oldenbourg, 1994).

[16] Michael Sachs (1808–1864) religious conservative who served as rabbi and preacher in the Berlin community from 1844 until his death twenty years later, devoted his literary efforts to bridging the gulf between classical Jewish literature and contemporary taste.

4: German-Jewish Double Identity

Hermann Levin Goldschmidt, 1997 (© Willi Goetschel)

A Jewish Critic from Germany:
Hermann Levin Goldschmidt

Willi Goetschel

L ET ME START WITH AN OBSERVATION from Leo Baeck that highlights not only the work of Hermann Levin Goldschmidt but, I
would argue, the decisive point we must take in discussing the subject
of German literature and its Jewish critics. The statement occurs in the
concluding paragraph of Baeck's *The Essence of Judaism*. "Nicht nur
um uns handelt es sich, wo es sich um uns handelt." In English: "Not
only we are concerned when we become a matter of concern."[1]

To speak of identity means to speak of the intricately winding
road along which self-determinations are expressed in a cultural environment which, in all its contingency, determines the nature of the
discourse. The peculiar economy of self-explanation which comes into
play here forces a compromise that precariously navigates between a
heteronomous dictate and what we wish to view as authentic and
autonomous interventions. For identities, like traditions, do not
spring from pristine origins. Rather, they represent complex mediations of the crisis of modernity itself. Like symptoms, identities function as a compromise formation, and in the best cases, as a working-
through of conflicts. Instead of originary positions of sorts, they are by
definition fragile, precarious, strategic, and often dynamic.[2]

In modernity, Jewish identity is, like any other identity construction, a result of the epistemological crisis that marks the emergence of
modernity. This crisis meant that the social order had to be reinvented
from the bottom up. During the seventeenth and eighteenth centuries, the new political models of the absolutist state and, eventually,
the nation state were introduced to replace the model of the Holy
Roman Empire, which had become increasingly precarious in the face
of the new science and the emerging philosophies of nature and natural rights. This watershed marks the Jews as a particular group left out
in the conceptual cold of societal reorganization. For the process of
transition to the modern nation state is realized on the grounds of a

Christian, if secularized world view that determines its outcome. The disintegration of the old Christian world order also meant that the place of the Jews had to be renegotiated. With the demise of the early modern Holy Roman Empire and the emergence of the nation state, there arose the new problem of nation building, and as one of its consequences, a problem termed the "Jewish question."

The introduction of conceptual individualism, of the social contract model, and of a secularized version of conscience and freedom ironically posed the problem of legitimation for the existence of groups that seemed to lack the qualifications seamlessly to dissolve into the modern nation state. Perceived as the primary example of anachronism in the West, the Jews were condemned to continue their bit part in the European imagination. While the question of what is Jewish functioned previously as the other question for what is Christian, the "Jewish question" takes now, with the Enlightenment, its modern, national turn. It starts to function now as the other question for what is German, French, British, and so forth.[3]

But to ask what and who the Jews were was at the same time to ask what and who, therefore, the Germans, the French, the British might be. This question was to take center stage in the development of the nineteenth-century notions of nationalism. The query "What is German?," as Nietzsche notes, would become one that would not go away.[4]

German Jewish modes of self-representation are therefore determined by the cultural parameters within which they are forced to operate. Considering their efforts for a discursive space, and thus, a place in society, means considering the role margins and mechanisms of inclusions and exclusions play in German culture. If, as Germans, Jews find themselves forced to address their position with regard to a framework that in principle seems to exclude any social, religious, or cultural difference, the attempt to join what excludes them places them in a double bind which undermines the very effort of national (or indeed any) self-determination which it nevertheless requires. In this situation, self-determination, before all else, has to rely on, and is expressed in terms of difference and alterity.[5]

Thus the formulations of Jewish identity are determined in such a way by the cultural paradigm of their environment that they represent its necessary supplement. In posing the "Jewish question," the European and German predicament receives its radicalized refraction and reflection. It is in the margins of the discursive space, outside of the proper frame, that is, decentered and at some times de-ranged, that Jewish self-determination is assigned its place.[6]

Speaking of dialogue — even if it may just have been, as Scholem so poignantly put it, a dialogue in which Jews were largely speaking among and to themselves[7] — speaking of such a dialogue is situated within a complicated and complex-ridden quagmire that before anything else warrants careful reconnaissance. For the cultural set-up in which the discussion of the — shall we call it dialogue, complex, symbiosis, or simply cultural reality? — has been fixed is one that because of its sheer transferential overdetermination has shadowed the debate. Unlike anyone else, Hermann Levin Goldschmidt has pioneered in pursuing the work of critical inventory by taking stock of the legacy of German Jewry in a fashion untrammeled by the ideological wars waged from all sides after 1945.

In the wake — I mean *wake* here in the double meaning of the word — of the Second World War, Auschwitz, the German destruction and tragic self-destruction of its very own culture,[8] Goldschmidt understood that reconstruction, if it was to be more than just the slogan of the day, had to attend to a principal recollection of the past. For Jewish recollection in the wake of Auschwitz this meant to ground recollection — as Margarete Susman had so impressively argued in her *Das Buch Hiob und das Schicksal des jüdischen Volkes* — in a reflection upon the Biblical sources.[9] Along with Helmut Plessner's *The Belated Nation*, Max Horkheimer and Theodor Adorno's *Dialectic of Enlightenment*, Erich Fromm's *Escape From Freedom*, Hannah Arendt's *The Origins of Totalitarianism*, and Martin Buber's *The Eclipse of God*, Susman's study was a groundbreaking attempt to come to terms with the destruction of Jewish life in Germany and German culture. Susman confronts the unspeakable by taking up the work of mourning, not by searching for a cause but by pursuing the existential question of how life itself would have to be conceived anew after Auschwitz. Only such a return to the origins of the Biblical sources, Goldschmidt realized (following Susman but also the line of thought from Mendelssohn to Cohen, Rosenzweig, Buber, and Leo Baeck) would yield the grounds and resources needed for a critical new beginning. Taking his cue from Hermann Cohen's *Religion der Vernunft aus den Quellen des Judentums*, Goldschmidt formulated his program of a contemporary philosophy after Auschwitz as one that would — intrinsically modern and critical — ground itself in a conscious reclaiming of the "sources of Judaism."[10]

Born in 1914 in prewar Berlin, Hermann Levin Goldschmidt emigrated to Switzerland in February 1938. After fourteen years of residence he was finally granted official permission to remain and work in Switzerland. Soon thereafter he founded the Jüdisches Lehrhaus Zürich. After the Second World War Zurich had the largest German-speaking Jewish community in Europe, and it was an ideal site for such an undertaking. It was here that Margarete Susman, who served as a kind of mentor to a circle of exiled Jewish intellectuals, published *Das Buch Hiob und das Schicksal des jüdischen Volkes,* one of the first attempts to come to terms with what had occurred in Germany.

For Goldschmidt, the "sacrifice of six million innocents," the greatest single disaster to befall the Jews in 4000 years of history, creates an entirely new situation after Auschwitz. Auschwitz, Goldschmidt realized, requires above all else a recovery of the traces of Jewish tradition and an inventory of the remains of Jewish life that had flourished in Germany, which had been the center of advanced European culture. The crucial insight guiding the work of the *Jüdisches Lehrhaus* was that the present and future of Judaism depends on the past, and a working-through of that past. Critical in its attitude toward public opinion, the *Lehrhaus* did not look to *Vergangenheitsbewältigung* as a solution, a term with negative connotations that gained wide currency in Germany, but which can also imply a wish to get rid of the past. The central idea of the Lehrhaus was instead that the present situation called for a rigorous *Aufarbeitung* of the past. Opposed to the attempt to draw a historical divide between a lost world of the past and the present, the Lehrhaus emphasized the continuing importance and contribution of Jewish life in Germany. This emphasis on continuity instead of destruction leads to a study of Judaism as something more than a relic of history. The Lehrhaus was thus able to address the reality of Jewish life in Germany after Auschwitz free of the trammels of theologically fraught discourse, unhindered by the particularly unfortunate tropes of God-is-dead theology.[11] Acknowledging the paradox that, as Goldschmidt put it, "the six million dead are the part of us that is most alive" makes any ideological construction of Jewish identity impossible.

For if Franz Rosenzweig's Jüdisches Lehrhaus in the Frankfurt of the 1920s sought to address the predicament of Jewish identity in a Germany alienated by its recent confrontation with modernity, post-Auschwitz consciousness faced a radically different and deeper dilemma. Judaism was now called into question in the most existential way. The depth of this challenge posed all questions of Judaism and

Jewish identity with a new and sharper sense of urgency. Life after Auschwitz could not avoid confronting the brute fact of Auschwitz. The sheer survival of Judaism required Jews to define their situation in a radically changed world.

The Jüdisches Lehrhaus began this task, and was directed by Goldschmidt from 1951 until it closed its doors in 1961. It was here that Goldschmidt developed the material that became his trilogy published in the 1950s: *Das Vermächtnis des deutschen Judentums* (1957, expanded 1965), *Die Botschaft des Judentums* (1960), and *Dialogik: Philosophie auf dem Boden der Neuzeit* (1964).[12] In 1946, *Hermann Cohen und Martin Buber* appeared. It examines each writer as a theorist of Jewish modernity. This study's subtitle *Ein Jahrhundert Ringen um Jüdische Wirklichkeit,* that is, "The struggle of a century for Jewish Reality," indicates the direction in which Goldschmidt will take the interpretation of the role of Judaism for modernity. Two years later followed *Philosophie als Dialogik,* which casts the problem of delimiting autonomous spheres for philosophy and religion in dialogical terms. The move to dialogics preserves the intricate complexity of the interdependence of each realm that resists reduction to any simple formula, an approach that was crucial to a new and critical conception of Judaism.[13]

Unlike Buber's "dialogical principle," Goldschmidt's dialogics operates without theological underpinnings as a strictly philosophical argument. The dialogical procedure settles the dispute between philosophy and religion with the resources of epistemology alone, in a manner sharply distinguished from Buber's deeply metaphysically tinged mode, which was part and parcel of his phenomenology of religion. Goldschmidt's sharp distinction between philosophy and religion typifies his concept of modernity committed to critical rationality while refusing to sacrifice religious and spiritual life where it has its legitimate place. His position argues for a critical conception of modernity that resists the one-dimensionality of instrumental reason, a critical perspective that in fact constitutes an unflagging commitment to scientific thought. In his project of *Dialogik* — always resistant to premature visions of dialectical solutions — Goldschmidt laid the groundwork for a modern understanding of Judaism. For the first time, it became possible to leave apologetics behind without having to resort to nationalistic or isolationist modes of thought. Instead, the history of the Jewish people was to be rethought.

German-Jewish historiography as well as the work of Simon Dubnow set the parameters for this project.[14] Rewriting Jewish history became the last but decisive step in the process of emancipation; an emancipation that aimed at liberating the Jewish self-image from subjection to mythologized shadow histories of the other. Previously silenced "others" now stepped forward to reclaim their past and write their own history.

In the year of his death, Leo Baeck recommended that the Europäische Verlagsanstalt publish *Das Vermächtnis des deutschen Judentums.* The book appeared in 1957, and the press became Goldschmidt's publisher until 1968. The revolt of the sons against the fathers who represented that Nazi past in the German cultural turmoil of 1968, had, however, the ironic effect of leading those radical sons to discard and ignore important work of cultural memory and recovery that had already been done. Swimming against this tide, Goldschmidt came to see 1968 as Germany's final repression of its past. *Das Vermächtnis des deutschen Judentums* forcefully argues for a dynamic interpretation of this legacy, an interpretation that neither fixes nor hypostatizes the past but liberates its critical content. Critical appropriation of the past transforms history into a site for negotiating one's identity and its determinants. Legacy becomes the name for what is specific, yet a specificity that is realized only in the process of interpretation. *Das Vermächtnis des deutschen Judentums* and *Die Botschaft des Judentums* occupy the boundary zone between historiography and reflection on history's theoretical implications. Both books reject the normative conventions of historiography; they keep open the space in which the conditionality of historiography can be addressed. Goldschmidt forces us to recognize that history itself requires a firm grounding in theory, because reflection on history — when history is not being altogether ignored — is always contested ground.[15] His first step in this project is to stake out the discursive and institutional bounds in which a history so long and effectively ignored, or at least relegated to the status of non-existence, can be represented.

In this view, culture transcends any univocal representation as "other"; nor can Jewish culture be defined in the biological, deterministic image conjured by the myth of symbiosis.[16] Now it can be recovered in its own terms, as a once thriving and vital reality. This experience presents, beyond theological strictures, an experience of crucial significance not only for Judaism but also for modernity itself. For Goldschmidt, Jewish modernity is not a theological problem but rather an inspiring contribution to modern culture, playing a constitutive role in the creation of modern culture as a whole.

It was Spinoza who first made it possible to conceive of Judaism as something more than a theological issue; his sociological and political interpretation of Biblical scripture led to a radically modern conception of Judaism. According to Spinoza, a critical reading of Biblical scripture is naturally resistant to any attempt to support a dogmatic or doctrinal interpretation. The Bible's mandate, Spinoza argues, is legislative, prescribing rules and laws guiding moral action. Thus according to Spinoza the Bible makes no truth claims whatsoever and is therefore free from theological pretension. This line of thought was carried on by Moses Mendelssohn, who formulates a modern liberal conception of Judaism whose fundamental outlines were shared by Leo Baeck, who in his *Essence of Judaism* defined at the beginning of the twentieth century a modern concept of Judaism.[17] It was this line of thought which Goldschmidt continued. Along with Buber and Scholem, Goldschmidt represents one of the rare instances of a German Jew taking on Baeck's legacy of a resolutely uncompromising modern Jewish self-understanding at a moment when many felt their Jewish heritage had betrayed them.[18] Instead, Goldschmidt's call was that this heritage — whose cultural contribution had been betrayed, rejected, and all but destroyed by the Germans — was not what betrayed culture but on the contrary what — ignored if not repressed, marginalized if not mutilated — called for its rescue. And a rescue that was needed not because of piety but on behalf of a future that without it would just be once more a repetition of repression and destruction.

Goldschmidt's argument is thus distinct from confessional attempts to read Jewish history in Christian terms, a trend so pervasive that even philosophers such as Hermann Cohen and Franz Rosenzweig find their positions determined by it. Instead, Judaism could now be freely treated in its own specific historical terms. Christianity was no longer the yardstick by which every other religion was to be measured. Only this assertion of the independence of Jewish historiography and hermeneutics made it possible to begin a Christian-Jewish dialogue that no longer sought to skirt the hard questions. Yet the frankness borne of his strong commitment to this project was not always met with congeniality.

Aside from the many essays Goldschmidt has written for anthologies published by Christian presses, two books, *Heilvoller Verrat? Judas im Neuen Testament* and *Weil wir Brüder sind* were published with Katholisches Bibelwerk, Germany's official Catholic publishing house. The press, however, made a less than full effort in its promotion of its "Jewish" books. Goldschmidt's study of Judas interprets

this figure as an attempt on the part of Christian theology to project
onto the Jews the Church's own guilt at having betrayed its Jewish
heritage. Goldschmidt argued that the perpetuation of this myth
served not only to fuel continued anti-Semitism (even in a secular,
post-Christian world where Christ may have disappeared but culprits
are still called Judas), but also prevented well-meaning Christians from
dealing with their religious genealogy. It was a critique that was
largely ignored.[19] *Weil wir Brüder sind* argues for a "heilsgeschichtli-
che Arbeitsteilung" (a division of labor in history's road to redemption). The admonition for Christians to become better Christians and
for Jews to become better Jews would strike too close to home to be
met with enthusiasm when what people prefer is talk of harmony,
good will, and reconciliation. The antifundamentalist thrust of Goldschmidt's critique may have lacked a certain appeal in this situation.
But his statement that "the holy land is everywhere," radically refuses
to attribute sacredness to land, nations, language, institutions or
whatever else might be considered itself part of the religious moment
in modernity. For in modernity, Goldschmidt argues, Judaism's uncompromising demand that rejects idolatry in any form should be
understood as a caution against any confused attempt to identify representation with what it represents.

For Goldschmidt as for Hermann Cohen, the essential contribution of Judaism is its call for universal liberation. Any kind of exclusiv-
ism or compromise with the powers that determine the status quo is a
betrayal of the prophetic impulse that promises historical redemption.
So long as any people stands deprived of freedom, Judaism can neither
forsake nor delegate its responsibility to bring messianic hope to frui-
tion. As long as exploitation and subjection seem the unquestioned
rule, the insistent call for liberation remains all the more necessary.
Judaism, according to Goldschmidt, represents the intransigent, historically specific call to reject any compromise in the pursuit of universal freedom. Its messianic mission can therefore be fulfilled only by the
universal establishment of peace on earth. Judaism is kept alive, so to
speak, sometimes even despite the efforts of its representatives, by the
sheer force of its radical message.[20] This future-oriented message is
what defines the timeless relevance of Judaism's message. The universal character of that message shapes the contingent particularity of
each of its interpreters. A paradox informs the messianic power of this
message: it is the particular alone, in all its contingency, that is capable
of representing the hope and promise of the universal. This messianic
conception keeps Judaism from falling into a temporal stasis. The

Jewish and philosophical impulses of Goldschmidt's thought meet in this insight. *Freiheit für den Widerspruch,* which began as a lecture in 1969 and was published as a book in 1976, argues for the importance of contradiction to philosophy, and thereby becomes an expression of the Jewish experience in modernity. The central tension of that experience is seen as the tension between the demands of the universal and the specific forms, for instance in Judaism, which those universals took. *Freiheit für den Widerspruch* argues that any conceptual attempt to harmonize the particular and the universal, whether by dialectical means or otherwise, would claim to fix precisely that which defies fixity. The dynamics of this tension result in ever new instantiations of this contradiction. To resolve such a contradiction would be to misunderstand it completely, silencing the insistent challenge and radical meaning of universalism. Judaism's aporetic solution to this existential contradiction stands as a signal contribution to this human struggle. To follow Jewish history is to observe an ongoing historical negotiation between the universal and the particular.

Thus while Jewish identity and philosophy mutually constitute one another, they do not do so in a way that leads to fixed definitions, but rather in a way that opens onto the complex nature of modernity itself. Goldschmidt's dialogics argues that the practical import of contradiction needs to be recognized as a counterweight to the philosophical notion of some absolute ground for experience. Such certainty had already been successfully challenged by Nietzsche, though was never fully abandoned by modern philosophical discourse. To acknowledge the insistence of contradiction offers a way out of the theoretical impasse that results from the hermeneutic circle, granting legitimacy only to that which one has already presupposed. It is precisely Goldschmidt's grounding of his philosophical reflections in the historicity of Jewish experience that gives it an open and unhindered prospect on the possibilities of a human universalism.

If one of the consequences of 1968 has been the forgetting of the legacy, in part due to the institutionalization of Jewish Studies in Germany and Austria, or if such subject matter has become an ethnic enclave or another rubric among others, a collection of obsolete tales important only to the abandoned fathers, the increasing importance of cultural difference has brought Goldschmidt's work a new attention. This growing interest in theorizing difference and contradiction as constitutive elements of the modern experience has led to the development of many new models for understanding alterity and identity in critical terms. Alterity and identity are now seen as central questions of philosophy. Goldschmidt's antidialectical impulse, like Theodor Adorno's *Negative Dialectics,* aims at the redemption of contradictions rather than their refashioning into elements of a dialectical system. Whereas Adorno's critical method carries out dialectics to a point of implosion, Goldschmidt, like Jacques Derrida, challenges the manipulation of contradictions altogether. Adorno, Derrida, and Goldschmidt all argue for an epistemological aporia that forces us to reflect on the critical limits of the power of concepts. Pushing conceptual claims beyond such limits leads to monological thinking and, as a consequence, to totalitarianism in theory and praxis. The persistence of this urge to do away with contradictions once and for all betrays some of the violence inherent in conceptual thought.

Goldschmidt's work combines a rare ability to reflect on the Jewish predicament after Auschwitz with systematic philosophic rigor. His decidedly liberal, middle position between Zionism and Orthodoxy makes him an exception in a postwar Europe characterized by increasing polarization. If the liberal tradition of German Judaism has all but ceased to exist for all practical purposes, and Zionism and Orthodoxy have claimed to be the only valid choices for a viable Jewish identity, Goldschmidt's contribution stands as an insistent challenge to such claims. At a time when vicarious religiosity, or vicarious patriotism, has become a way of life for many Jews, Goldschmidt's reminder that there is more to Judaism than the privilege of the persecuted has not always been enthusiastically received.

While Alain Finkielkraut's *Le juif imaginaire* (1980)[21] describes the problem of postwar Jewish identity in this regard, Goldschmidt responds that the problem has indeed become one of Jews without Judaism. For Goldschmidt the question of Jewish identity has never been primary but secondary to the work of recovering Jewish history for modernity, not as something to wallow in, but as a way of realizing the Bible's promise. Goldschmidt's ability to be equally at ease in things Jewish, Christian, or secular flows naturally from a coherently developed Jewish position that has long superseded the need for apologetics or self-aggrandizement. Goldschmidt has instead fully integrated the message of Judaism into his concept of modernity.

Goldschmidt embodies his perspective in detail in a number of readings of German literature, essays in which he again and again lays bare the productive but also at times tragic tension between Jewish self-assertion and its refusal by nationalism and other varieties of universalism. Hailing chiefly from the period of the mid-1940s to the mid-1950s, Goldschmidt's essays on Goethe's identification with

Moses, on Heine and Freud, Wassermann, Werfel, Zweig, Mann, and Kafka are energetic interventions in a discourse defined by containment, repression, and displacement. As literary criticism, these readings attend precisely to this fact by exposing, addressing, and challenging renewed or often simply continued attempts at the remarginalization and discursive exclusion of Jewish voices.

Let me just illustrate this perspective with a few examples selected from Goldschmidt's collection of essays on Judaism, brought together in volume four of the complete edition of Goldschmidt's works, a volume programmatically entitled *Der Rest bleibt* (The Remnant Remains).

In his 1956 essay "Heine and Freud," Goldschmidt traces Heine's sometimes offensive refusal of conventions that separate "the Jewish" from the "general," "universal," or "public" aspects of his poetry. In this, Goldschmidt joins Freud who calls Heine a Jewish poet, a claim that is valid, Goldschmidt points out, because "Heine breaks up the boundaries based on Mendelssohn's distinction between the confessional delimitation and, in general, any delimitation of Judaism as he pushes it [i.e., Judaism] once more to the fore and into the public. He breaks every form, including the Jewish form of hiding Judaism" (201).

In "Jakob Wassermann's Jewish Destiny" — a talk given in January 1945 — Goldschmidt addresses the problem posed by Wassermann's self-understanding, an attitude marked by the inability to break the spell of a repression that prevents him from consciously acknowledging his Judaism as a productive and inspiring chance. As he formulates it, Wassermann

> is the ideal example of an *un*conscious Jew whose entire life — which remains an expression of Jewishness without ever living this Jewishness in a conscious way — presents despite all its immanent consistency and even honesty one great mistake and suffering without end. Why are we concerned? It is our concern because it represents a danger, for us too, as far as we are never exempt from the seduction to deceive ourselves, intentionally or not, about the direction, the rights and obligations that come with our Jewishness. And this is our concern because it represents a threat due to the hatred of the world around us rekindled again and again by those Jews who, in the footsteps of Wassermann, work other fields as they refuse to harvest from their very own ones. (257)

In this fashion, Goldschmidt points out, Wassermann achieves quite a feat, writing an entire book without a single Jew in it, yet a book that speaks of nothing other than the Jew: Wassermann's *Caspar Hauser* (263). Yet as long as Judaism serves only as a shadow discourse, as the case of Wassermann illustrates, repression always threatens to return with a vengeance (cf. 264–65). Interestingly enough, Goldschmidt concludes his essay on Wassermann on a positive note, documenting the apparent waste of passion and talent that appears to exemplify his case: "How powerful [Jewish destiny] proves itself to be when we stay connected with it!" (271).

In his 1946 essay "Stefan Zweig's Jewish Legacy," Goldschmidt points to an allegorical dimension in Zweig's novels *Ungeduld des Herzens* and the posthumous *Schachnovelle,* where the precarious, marginal existence of Zweig's "world of yesterday" is powerfully depicted. As it turns out, the patient's treatment in *Ungeduld des Herzens* becomes with her incurable illness an allegory for the wrong approach to the cure. As Goldschmidt puts it: "for the Jew there is no cure from Judaism as paralysis, only the liberation of the Jew to enjoy himself, a cure that requires recognition: that he begin to view what seems from the outside to be disease as in fact his state of health" (285). In the *Schachnovelle* two different chess strategies come to represent productive and counterproductive possibilities for dealing with the other:

> This is Stefan Zweig's Jewish legacy. There is no need to perish when exposed to a difference with an opponent entirely different from us. For, instead, we can regain our ground through such a difference. If we abstain from attempting to force our way onto the opponent in evil impatience or to want to beat him in his own, different way, or if we are seduced to give up ourselves because of his impatience with regard to our way and, instead, patiently are who we are — free from being compelled neither to force ourselves to another, nor the other to comply with our way, that would be foreign to the others — then one day we not only will regain our own ground but also be able to accept the others in their otherness and will be, we might add, accepted by them in our otherness. (293–94)

The argument that German literature can only be properly interpreted if its treatment of Judaism is met with a critical eye is demonstrated by the essay on "Thomas Mann's Joseph and Moses." Goldschmidt's 1945 review of Mann's story "Das Gesetz" ("The Tables of the Law") took Mann to task for his harsh and even derogatory manner of dealing with Jewish history. Mann defended himself by claiming that he was just following the Biblical narrative which, by his lights, was the actual source of the nasty ridicule he dealt Moses and his people.

Goldschmidt shows that Mann must have had a rather loose understanding of textual accuracy, given the great liberties he took in in-
venting incendiary details in elaboration of Moses' mission, and more:
that ultimately Mann's ridiculously incendiary portrait of Moses turns
out to be his own self-portrait and wholly a projection at that. While
Mann suggests that Moses suffered from a lack of identity, Goldschmidt reminds his readers that it is the author Mann in exile who
has projected the symptoms of his own unease onto Moses and his
people: it is in fact a deracinated German who suffers a severe crisis of
self-understanding here. If we develop a self-conscious attitude towards our own history, Goldschmidt concludes, we will not only be
able to be ourselves, but also will be in the position to grant space
enough for the other self that belongs to others: to love them "like
ourselves."[22]

Let me conclude this short discussion of Goldschmidt's essays
with a passage from his Kafka essay. An English translation was published in *Commentary* in 1949. Here Goldschmidt makes an important point, often ignored in current approaches to our subject. In
trying to identify "Jewish" topics, aspects, or meanings in literature,
criticism too often leaves crucial questions of epistemological interests,
methodological sophistication, and critical self-examination unasked.
But asking these questions must be our primary concern if our discussion is to serve any critical purpose. In passing, Goldschmidt formulates this complex in the following way:

> I should like to avoid reducing Kafka's Judaism to a limited for-
> mula — which would also reduce Judaism to a formula; for the pre-
> cise sense in which Kafka and we who continue to share his epoch
> are Jews, will be determined only by our future history, when we
> have lived it to its end. But even so, it must be conceded that not a
> great deal is to be got from a special Jewish interpretation of Kafka.
> Not individual details — such as the family of the Castle messenger
> Barnabas, so easily seen as "Jewish" — but his whole work breathes a
> Jewish air. (305; *Commentary*, 134)

Inasmuch as history has been a somewhat one-sided affair, Goldschmidt's work shows how deeply, nevertheless, both sides have been
intertwined with each other. It is therefore not so much out of piety,
for the ends of historical justice or anyone's satisfaction, that the interdependence of culture must be acknowledged. But I would like to
argue that such conscious acknowledgment represents a necessity, if
only the better to understand our present, a present where the past

will return so long as it is not worked through, determining our future in ways other than we might wish.[23]

Goldschmidt's and other Jewish exile critics' call for working through the past might, in the end, seem less peculiar if transposed in a different environment. In that spirit let me conclude with the two versions of Columbus's prayer offered in Carlos Fuentes' story "The Two Americas." Fuentes uses these prayers to allude to the (historically unsubstantiated) assumption of Columbus's Sephardic descent and the Sephardic legend that Jews exiled from Spain took along the keys to the houses in order to have them ready on the day of their eventual return. But we might also bear in mind Goldschmidt's point: that despite such dubious legends, there is no need to claim Columbus as one of our own, as our history offers us a surfeit of great men and women already. These prayers pronounced by a fictional Columbus nonetheless express the unrequited longing of Jews for Spain, much the way Jews felt 400 years later for Germany. This same unrequited longing, one might add, seems the fate of those who, like Goldschmidt, dare to remind their contemporaries of the deep and powerful affection German Jews held for the culture they not only shared, but also nourished, cultivated, and helped to create. It is in this spirit that I would like to cite Fuentes, whose text illuminates the deep, perhaps unilateral, but finally emotional aspects of culture for us today. As Fuentes's Columbus explains, he would carry, alongside the key to the ancestral house of his forefathers, a prayer:

> Mother Spain, you have been cruel to your Israelite children. You have persecuted and expelled us. We have left behind our houses, our lands, but not our memories. Despite your cruelty, we love you, Spain, and we long to return to you. One day you will receive your wandering children, you will open your arms to them, ask their forgiveness, and recognize our fidelity to your land. We shall return to our houses. This is the key. This is the prayer.[24]

The second version of this prayer expresses the asymmetry of the predicament of the German-Jewish experience in even less ambiguous manner:

> You, beloved Spain, we call Mother, and during all our lives we will not abandon your sweet language. Even though you exiled us like a stepmother from your breast, we will not cease to love you as a most holy land, the land where our fathers left their families buried and the ashes of the thousands of their loved ones. For you we save our filial love, glorious nation; therefore we send you our glorious greeting.[25]

This talk was presented in September 1997. Hermann Levin Goldschmidt passed away in March 1998. For a more comprehensive discussion of his life and work see my prefaces and introductions in the edition of his collected works published by the Passagen Verlag, Vienna.

Notes

[1] Leo Baeck, *Das Wesen des Judentums,* 2d ed. (Frankfurt am Main: Kauffmann, 1922), 303.

[2] See Willi Goetschel, "The Differential Character of Traditions," *Telos,* no. 95 (Spring 1993): 161–70.

[3] Cf. also Amos Funkenstein, *Perceptions of Jewish History* (Berkeley: U of California P, 1993), esp. "The Political Theory of Jewish Emancipation," 220–34.

[4] Friedrich Nietzsche, *Jenseits von Gut und Böse,* in *Sämtliche Werke: Kritische Studienausgabe,* ed. Giorgio Colli and Mazzino Montinari, vol. 5 (Munich: Deutscher Taschenbuchverlag, 1980), 184.

[5] For a discussion of this issue see Willi Goetschel, "Models of Difference and Alterity: Moses Mendelssohn, Hermann Cohen, Franz Rosenzweig, and Hermann Levin Goldschmidt," in *The Dilemma: From Enlightenment to the Shoah,* ed. Edward Timms and Andrea Hammel (London: Edwin Mellen, 1999), 25–38.

[6] A telling case in point is the way in which the question of "Jewish philosophy" is tackled. Cf. Willi Goetschel, "'Gibt es eine jüdische Philosophie?' Zur Problematik eines Topos," in *Perspektiven der Dialogik: Zürcher Kolloquium zum 80. Geburtstag von Hermann Levin Goldschmidt,* ed. Willi Goetschel (Vienna: Passagen, 1994), 91–110. Jacques Derrida has recently described the relationship with the image of *psyche,* the double mirror, whose continual reflections betray something of the endless mutual mirroring of oneself in the face of the other. Jacques Derrida, "Zeugnis, Gabe," in *Jüdisches Denken in Frankreich: Gespräche mit Vidal-Naquet, Derrida, Thalmann u.a.,* ed. Elisabeth Weber (Frankfurt a.M.: Suhrkamp, 1994), 63–70.

[7] Gershom Scholem, "Wider den Mythos von dem deutsch-jüdischen Gespräch," in *Judaica* 2 (Frankfurt a.M.: Suhrkamp 1970), 10.

[8] Adolf Leschnitzer has captured the precarious interrelation of Germany's genocide with its cultural suicide in the title of his book: *Saul und David: Die Problematik der Deutsch-jüdischen Lebensgemeinschaft* (Heidelberg: Lambert Schneider, 1954). The figures of Saul and David evoke an intimate family resemblance and deep cultural affinity and, at the same time, the rejection and denial of the central role of the "minor" in one's own culture.

[9] Margarete Susman, *Das Buch Hiob und das Schicksal des jüdischen Volkes* (Zürich: Steinberg, 1946, 2d ed. 1948). First published in 1946, the preface of the second edition addresses in 1948 the question what the foundation of the State of Israel would mean with regard to Auschwitz. Cf. Hermann Levin Goldschmidt, "Margarete Susmans Buch Hiob," in *Aus den Quellen des Judentums: Aufsätze zur Philosophie, Werke 5* (Vienna: Passagen, 2000), 243–52.

[10] On Hermann Cohen see Goldschmidt's early discussion in *Philosophie als Dialogik. Frühe Schriften, Werke 1* (Vienna: Passagen, 1993), 101–29. For the coining of "philosophy out of the sources of Judaism" see Goldschmidt in *Das Vermächtnis des deutschen Judentums, Werke 2* (Vienna: Passagen, 1994), 108–14; *Die Botschaft des Judentums, Werke 3* (Vienna: Passagen, 1994), 170–71. For the hidden rejection of the concept of a "Jewish philosophy" this expression contains see Goetschel, "'Gibt es eine jüdische Philosophie?' Zur Problematic eines Topos."

[11] For Goldschmidt's last statement on the Lehrhaus see his speech "Das jüdische Lehrhaus und das Vermächtnis des deutschen Judentums," in *Das Jüdische Lehrhaus als Modell lebensbegleitenden Lernens,* ed. Evelyn Adunka and Albert Brandstätter (Vienna: Passagen, 1999), 61–69; for a contextualization see also Willi Goetschel, "Universalität, Partikularität und das jüdische Lehrhaus," *ibid.,* 47–59.

[12] These books have all been re-edited in the edition of the collected works published with Passagen, Vienna, with the exception of the last title whose original chapters now form parts of volume 1 and volume 5.

[13] This book is now part of volume 1. Some of its chapters became later also part of the 1964 *Dialogik.*

[14] For a discussion of the signficance of Dubnow see Goldschmidt, "Simon Dubnows Darstellung des deutschen Judentums," in *Der Rest bleibt: Aufsätze zum Judentum, Werke 4* (Vienna: Passagen, 1997), 223–37.

[15] Similarly, Leschnitzer argues in *Saul und David* that instead of offering a final interpretation of the German past, Auschwitz and its consequences remain subject to an open-ended process of interpretation that takes its cue from history's ever-changing course. Such an understanding recognizes the determining role of the future for an historical assessment of the past. This, Leschnitzer points out, may also include a future change of meaning of the concept of history itself. Cf. Leschnitzer, *Saul and David,* 196.

[16] It is interesting to witness the return of the use of the term "symbiosis," a term that seemed to have been abandoned long ago. It is as if the hesitations and strictures against applying such a biological term to the process of a complex cultural exchange faded over the decades. However, the term symbiosis in the context of culture still carries unwarranted implications, conjuring as it does a leveling metaphorization of historical experience that reduces the very complexity, richness, and productive tensions of cultural life as well as the far-reaching tensions produced in the course of this experience. Though Leschnitzer, for instance, uses the term symbiosis, his use is grounded in a model of cultural exchange in which "symbiosis" marks the penultimate step in the development of the process of complete absorption of Jews by German culture. Cf. Leschnitzer, *Saul und David,* 39. The polemical undertone in Leschnitzer's use of the term, however, is missing in most later critics.

[17] For a discussion on Mendelssohn's reformulation of Spinoza's conception of Judaism see Julius Guttmann, "Mendelssohns Jerusalem und Spinozas Theologisch-Politischer Traktat," in *48. Bericht der Hochschule für die Wissenschaft des Judentums* (Berlin, 1931) and Willi Goetschel, "Moses Mendelssohn und das Projekt der Aufklärung," *Germanic Review* 71 (1996): 163–75. See also Goldschmidt, "Moses Mendelssohns geschichtliche Bedeutung," in *Werke 4,* 165–79.

[18] Goldschmidt's discussion of Leo Baeck's work is prominently present through-out his writings. On Gershom Scholem see the special issue dedicated to the dis-cussion of his connection to German-Jewish intellectual tradition, *Germanic Review* 72.1 (1997).

[19] A brief summary of Goldschmidt's critical analysis of the figure of Judas can be found in his entry on Judas in *Theologische Realenzyklopädie,* vol. 17, 304–7.

[20] This argument is explicated in its full implications in *Das Vermächtnis des deut-schen Judentums, Werke 2,* and in a systematic way in a discussion of the key con-cepts of Judaism in *Die Botschaft des Judentums, Werke 3.*

[21] Alain Finkielkraut, *The Imaginary Jew,* trans. Kevin O'Neill and David Suchoff (Lincoln and London: U of Nebraska P, 1994).

[22] It seems ironic that Moses' command to love one's neighbor as oneself (Leviti-cus 19:18) is so often claimed to mark the progress to a distinctly Christian ethics when, at the latest since Hillel, it has come to be viewed as the content of Jewish ethics in a nutshell.

[23] For Goldschmidt's last public address, the introduction to the first Mary Levin Goldschmidt-Bollag Memorial Lecture, in which he underscores the necessity of the work of remembrance, see his "Words of Remembrance," introduction to *Im-perative zur Neuerfindung des Planeten, Imperatives to Re-Imagine the Planet,* by Gayatri Chakravorty Spivak (Vienna: Passagen, 1999), 16–26.

[24] Carlos Fuentes, "The Two Americas," in *The Orange Tree* (London: Picador, 1995), 219–20.

[25] Fuentes, "The Two Americas," 229.

Response to Willi Goetschel

Thomas Sparr

MEINE DAMEN UND HERREN, Steve Dowden hat am Beginn eine Typologie der Responses entworfen: Koreferate, richtig ausgearbeitete Referate, von denen wir ja ganz beeindruckende gehört haben, substantielle Fragen oder Improvisationen. Meines ist eine Schwundstufe des letzten, was daher rührt, daß ich durch einen Irrtum einen anderen Aufsatz von Willi Goetschel zur Response erhalten habe. Ich hatte es vorbereitet und nun — Hermann Levin Goldschmidt. Das ursprüngliche Thema, dem wir uns heute morgen stellen wollten, war die *Deutsch-jüdische Literaturinterpretation der Doppelidentität: eine jüdisch-israelische Perspektive* und als Hauptredner war Gershon Shaked vorgesehen. Shaked ist in Deutschland bekannt durch zwei Bücher. Ein Buch über jüdische Identität deutschsprachiger Autoren und seine im vergangenen Herbst erschienene Geschichte der hebräischen Literatur, eine Doppelperspektive, eine Verlängerung, der Amir Eshel nachher noch etwas nachgehen wird.[1]

Wichtig und das Aufschlußreiche an diesem Thema ist *das Doppelte*. Immer wenn von Juden in Deutschland, von Juden aus Deutschland die Rede ist, kommt etwas Doppeltes zur Sprache. Hinrich Seeba zeigte uns Heinz Politzer als Amerikaner und Deutschsprachigen, als Künstler und Gelehrten. Und wenn ich ihn richtig verstanden habe, so brachte diese Spannung etwas Doppeltes zum Ausdruck, nämlich ein deutschsprachiger Jude zu sein. Christoph König und Amir Eshel zeigten uns Ludwig Geiger als Interpreten von Goethe und den Juden, von deutscher Literatur und jüdischer Geschichte, eine Art Selbstinterpretation auch dies. Hannah Arendt schließlich hat eine ganze Reihe jüdischer Identitätsmuster entwickelt. Denken Sie an den Schlemihl, den Paria, all das, was sie in ihrem Aufsatz über jüdische Tradition entwirft als Identitätsmuster.[2] Auch das ist immer in einer Dopplung gedacht. Bei Margarete Susman hat Barbara Hahn uns gestern auf das Schlüsselmotiv des Zerrissenen hingewiesen. Von Käte Hamburger haben wir auch eine doppelte Identität, wenn nicht mehrfache Identität erfahren, als Philosophin und Germanistin, als Exilierte in

Schweden und deutschsprachige Literaturwissenschaftlerin. Hermann Levin Goldschmidt schließlich, auch hier etwas Doppeltes, nämlich der deutsch-jüdische Dialog, wie Willi Goetschel es uns gezeigt hat.

Ich möchte in den Gedanken, die ich äußere, etwas zu dieser Atmosphäre der fünfziger Jahre sagen und Ihren Blick darauf hinführen. 1959 erschien im Jüdischen Verlag in Berlin die Anthologie *Jüdisches Schicksal in deutschen Gedichten,* herausgegeben von Siegmund Kaznelson, dem langjährigen Leiter des jüdischen Verlages. Im Untertitel hieß dieses *Jüdisches Schicksal in deutschen Gedichten: eine abschließende Anthologie.* Juden würden fortan nicht mehr auf Deutsch, sondern in anderen Sprachen dichten. Es sei ein irreversibler Bruch, eine Zäsur entstanden. Wenige Jahre zuvor, 1955 war das Leo Baeck Institut in Jerusalem, New York und London gegründet worden, ein Institut zur Erforschung der Geschichte der Juden aus Deutschland bis 1933, keinesfalls darüber hinaus. Dazwischen, 1957, erschien Goldschmidts *Das Vermächtnis des deutschen Judentums.* Auch diesen Titel hat man, glaube ich, als eine Summe des deutschen Judentums zu lesen, als eine Summe, die man lesen und studieren kann, die aber so etwas wie eine Erbschaft bedeutet. Hermann Levin Goldschmidt hat, so ist meine These, in einem Augenblick für einen Dialog plädiert, als zwei kaum miteinander sprechen wollten. Das berührt zum einen Juden aus Deutschland, das berührt aber auch deutsche Kritiker. Wenn wir den Titel unseres Kolloquiums *German Literature, Jewish Critics* einmal umkehren und fragen *Jewish Literature, German Critics,* die Reaktion deutscher Kritiker auf jüdische Literatur oder jüdische Autoren, die in Deutschland publizierten, so ist das Ergebnis verheerend, was die Wahrnehmung von Autoren als jüdischen Autoren oder auch nur von Themen angeht. Sie finden da Dokumente, vor allem was Paul Celan angeht, aber auch Nelly Sachs und viele andere, ein völliges Verkennen eben dieser Erbschaft, dieser Summe, die Juden in den fünfziger Jahren für deutsche Leser noch einmal präsentieren wollten.

Nun ist dieser Dialog vorangegangen, weitergegangen. Ich möchte den Blick einmal auch auf diese Zäsur lenken und die Frage stellen, wie irreversibel die Zäsur war, wie ein Dialog fortgesetzt wurde. Es gab in den fünfziger und sechsziger Jahren drei Vertreter eines Dialoggedankens. Einmal Martin Buber, als eine sehr synthetisierende und zusammenführende Kraft. Martin Buber hatte 1953 gegen erbitterten Widerstand in Israel den Friedenspreis des deutschen Buchhandels angenommen und in Frankfurt erhalten. Es gab Margarete Susman, die beschlossen hatte, niemals wieder nach Deutschland zu kommen; sie ist dann 1959 zur Verleihung der Ehrendoktorwürde doch nach Berlin gereist. Und Gershom Scholem, der ein Plädoyer für die historische Erforschung des Judentums gegeben hat. Wir können eben nicht, so schreibt er in seinem Buch über Sabbatai Zwi, das 1957 auf Hebräisch erschien und erst vierzehn Jahre später auf Englisch, wir können eben nicht von vornherein sagen, was das Judentum ausmacht.[3] Es ist das, was zu bestimmten Zeiten, bestimmte Gruppen, bestimmte Gemeinden für ihr Judentum halten. Also ein sehr konkretes Paradigma vom Jüdischen, ein historisches Paradigma, kein substantialistisches Verständnis des Judentums. Das hat ihn in einen gewissen Widerspruch zu Hermann Levin Goldschmidt gebracht. Das zeigen seine Briefe auch in den späteren Jahren. Das waren die drei Vertreter eines deutsch-jüdischen Gesprächs, wenn man so will: Martin Buber als ein großer Befürworter, als eine zusammenführende Kraft, Gershom Scholem als ein Skeptiker, der gesagt hat, es habe diesen Dialog nie gegeben, weil zu einem Dialog zwei gehören, die aufeinander hören, aber es sei doch immer nur ein deutscher Monolog gewesen, und Margarete Susman.

Es gehört zu den großen Irrtümern der literarhistorischen Forschung, meine Damen und Herren, daß man immer glaubt, Juden seien Anwälte einer deutsch-jüdischen Symbiose gewesen, sie hätten diesem Gedanken einer deutsch-jüdischen Symbiose besonders angehangen. Das haben nicht minder Deutsche getan. Die Schlüsselgestalt in diesem Jahrhundert einer besonderen Wahlverwandtschaft zwischen Deutschen und Juden war Stefan George. Im Georgekreis, in seiner großen Wirkung war es dann Erich von Kahler, der in seinem 1933 erschienenen Buch *Israel unter den Völkern* noch einmal diesen Gedanken einer besonderen Nähe von Juden und Deutschen aufgestellt hat. Erich von Kahler wird den meisten von Ihnen bekannt und vertraut sein. 1875 in Prag geboren, 1970 in Princeton gestorben. Das ist auch ein Gedanke, den ich noch anfügen möchte, wenn wir über den Dialog sprechen, daß man auch dies im Auge behält, daß die Idee oder der Mythos, wie immer man das benennt, Willi Goetschel hat ja verschiedene Lesarten für Symbiose, Mythos, Komplex gegeben, daß wir also im Auge behalten, daß dies nicht weniger eine Konstruktion von deutschen Schriftstellern im 20. Jahrhundert war. Hermann Levin Goldschmidt hat geäußert, daß wenn es einen Widerspruch gäbe, würden wir denken, etwas sei nicht in Ordnung, in Wirklichkeit aber ist dort etwas nicht in Ordnung, wo es keinen Widerspruch gibt. Das ist natürlich sehr dialektisch gedacht, und ich wollte doch noch wenigstens auf einige Widersprüche hinweisen. Ich danke Ihnen für Ihre Aufmerksamkeit.

Panelists' Commentary

ABIGAIL GILLMAN (BOSTON UNIVERSITY): Willi Goetschel's paper has touched upon many, enormously important and difficult questions at the core of our enterprise here. And I wanted to just mention a few especially provocative points. First of all the notion of reclaiming Jewish historiography on its own terms, of trying to understand Jewish history in Jewish terms, what a challenge that is. Second, the notion of, to quote Willi, the German-Jewish *what*: "question?" "symbiosis?" "dialogue?" — the terms are not adequate and we could spend several hours talking about this. Third, the notion that the Holocaust calls Jewish identity into question in an existential way. Is this true? Is this the case? What are the implications of this? Fourth, the notion that the essence of Judaism is a call for universal liberation, is the messianic essence above all? And lastly, the challenge, I think, of Goldschmidt, the publication of Goldschmidt — and you remember that the first thing he did was to open the Jüdisches Lehrhaus — is a commitment to Jewish learning and a return to Jewish sources and Jewish texts in our quest for the answers to these questions. That seems to me the unspoken premise of Goldschmidt's whole project. Are we going to take it seriously, and what are the implications of that?

Now I wish to step back from Goldschmidt for a moment to talk a little bit more about the enterprise of the colloquium, and particularly about the question of what it means to be a Jewish critic of German literature. Or alternatively, I think a better question is: what is the legacy of the generations of German refugees, these generations that we have been talking about, Jewish and non-Jewish scholars, for those of us working in Jewish-German studies today? For those of us putting together syllabi on literature, for those of us trying to create German Studies curricula, German Cultural Studies curricula, for those of us struggling for our own methodology, and in our scholarship wrestling with various discourses of identity.

And this question was running through my mind during Professor Seeba's talk. There is no question that the legacy of these scholars he discussed and that have been discussed, as Germanists, as comparatists, as teachers and critics of literature has been tremendous. The trickier question is, I think, what was Jewish about their work? And in what way were they Jewish critics? Now, we talked a little bit about whether on the one hand, engaging in social issues, political issues was one kind of response. Alternatively, neutrality, silence on the topic of identity was another response. But I think that both of these are primarily reactions to the experience of exile and persecution, that is, to a largely negative experience of Jewish identity, or of Jewishness. Did any of them bring positive Jewishness, or Judaism, to bear on their teaching and scholarly work? And how? Now, I think that it is clear that Goldschmidt provides an extraordinary model in this regard, as has been eloquently spelled out for us.

I want to say a few more words, since one of the genres of response in the conference has been paying tribute to one's teachers, I wanted to say a few words about Gershon Shaked, who was my teacher. I think that it is a shame that his voice couldn't be heard in this context and in particular, pertaining to these questions that I just raised. I think it is uncannily appropriate, that in place of Shaked we were able to learn about Goldschmidt this morning. Both men have deep similarities. First of all, both men's lives and commitments were deeply shaped, irrevocably shaped by the Holocaust. Whereas Goldschmidt went to Switzerland, Shaked who was born in Vienna in 1929, went to Palestine in 1939. Whereas Goldschmidt made the province of history and culture his home, Shaked made Israel his home, and devoted his life to Hebrew letters and Jewish literature.

Gershon Shaked (© Dan Porges)

For Shaked, after the Holocaust, there was no other place, no other place besides Israel for a Jew.[4] Goldschmidt felt equally strongly about history, about his intellectual and spiritual enterprise, there was no other place to go. But for Shaked this idea of no other place is not about facile Zionism. The question that drives his work, as is the case with Goldschmidt, is the fragility of identity, the fragility of modern identity and of Jewish identity. He was fascinated with the condition of the deracinated European Jew who was deracinated even before the Holocaust, as he would say about Kafka or Wassermann, and he also wrote about Philip Roth, Bernard Malamud, S. Y. Agnon, Aharon Appelfeld.[5] These Jewish writers even in their new home couldn't escape shadows. And he felt this so powerfully that one cannot construct a new identity without being haunted by the shadows, without being haunted by memory. And again, also like Goldschmidt, Shaked is committed to negotiating the contradictions, not to synthesizing them, but to keep negotiating these tensions, a very important and difficult point that Willi was making about Goldschmidt's work.

And finally on the question of saying "I." I wanted to read a few words from the preface to one of Shaked's books, one of his collections of essays:

> Literary critics sometimes live under the illusion that they represent a rational conceptual approach to the realm of literary texts. In this conventional view, the texts themselves are regarded as intense fusions of unconscious primary processes and secondary conscious processes. The function of criticism seems to be only a secondary process: the objective reformulation of a fictitious world of imagination. Fiction has biographical and subjective sources, while criticism tries to be above and beyond the critic's personal life and biography.
>
> This is of course a concept that does not pass the test of reality. Genuine criticism originates from the same sources and resources as authentic fiction. The difference is only the genre of communication: The selection of texts, the extraction of critical issues, and the ideological arrangement of critical terms are as conditioned by the biographical, psychological, and ideological background of the critics as literary works are by those of the artist.
>
> I emphasize the subjectivity of criticism at the outset of this volume in order to make it clear to the reader that in my analyses of the texts and contexts of various Jewish writers — writers who wrote in at least three languages and on three continents — I am trying to understand my own, and my generation's, identity as it is influenced by the major issues of our Jewish and human existence. The texts to which I refer are the texts of my intellectual biography; the conti-

nents where these writers have lived and written are the locations of
my own physical wanderings; and the sources of the issues I evoke
are of my own emotional life as depicted and delineated by some of
the best Jewish writers of the last century.[6]

BARBARA HAHN: Ich möchte zwei Fragen stellen in Anschluß an Willi
Goetschels Ausführungen und noch einmal aufnehmen, was Thomas
Sparr ausführte. Goldschmidt gehört zu den Emigranten, die in einen
Sprachraum emigriert sind, aus dem sie kamen. Das heißt, Emigration
war nicht sofort Sprachwechsel und Kulturwechsel. Und das hat, wie
wir gestern auch an Margarete Susman gelesen haben, ein großes Pro-
blem aufgeworfen. Der Sprachwechsel, sofern er nötig war — das ha-
ben wir gerade auch noch einmal bei Shaked gesehen — hat auch die
Möglichkeit eröffnet, eine Distanz zu gewinnen, eine Distanz zum
Deutschen und zur deutschen Kultur.

Was ich irritierend finde an Goldschmidt, und darauf zielt meine
Frage, ist, daß im Abschied vom Deutschen, im Weiterschreiben auf
Deutsch, dieser Bruch so schlecht spürbar ist. Das finde ich irritierend
auch gerade noch einmal bezogen auf Margarete Susman, die an diesem Problem so sehr gearbeitet hat. Also um es noch einmal so zu
formulieren: man hat den Eindruck, daß er das weiche Deutsch, dieses
weiche Lutherdeutsch, von dem Margarete Susman als der Sprache
der Akkulturation spricht, als ob er das weiche Deutsch ohne große
Reibungen hatte mitnehmen können in die Schweizer Emigration und
in die Durcharbeitung dieses Problems, mit dem noch nie vorher jemand konfrontiert war. Das ist meine erste Frage: Wie kann man das
eigentlich verstehen, daß dieses Deutsch sich so hält?

Die zweite Frage war: Goldschmidt hat sich ebenso wie Rosenzweig mit der Frage beschäftigt, welche Orte des Wissens muß man
etablieren, damit man über Judentum in Deutschland nachdenken
kann. Und das heißt natürlich auch, daß der Ort, wo normalerweise
dieser Typus von Wissen produziert wird, nämlich die Universität
verworfen wird. Es muß ein anderer Ort sein. Dieser andere Ort, den
Rosenzweig in Deutschland etabliert hat, hat also diese Wende gegen
die Universität. Er versucht einen Ort zu etablieren, wo dieser Typ
von Fragestellung überhaupt erst einmal entwickelt werden kann.
Jetzt frage ich, wenn man in der Emigration ist, also sowieso schon
abgetrennt von dieser Kultur ist, was tut man, wenn man in der Emigration noch einmal diesen Sonderort des Wissens etabliert? Also was
heißt das, ein jüdisches Lehrhaus in Zürich, das sich nicht nur an die
Gruppe von Emigranten in Zürich adressieren kann, sondern auch ei-

nen anderen Kontext haben muß? Also worin besteht dieser, abgeschnitten von dieser Kultur, die man thematisieren möchte?

Und dazu jetzt noch eine kleine Unterfrage: Ich fand so sehr schön diesen Hinweis auf diesen Text von Goldschmidt *Freiheit für den Widerspruch*.[7] Freiheit für den Widerspruch würde auch noch einmal bezogen auf die Orte des Wissens eine Frage produzieren. Wie schreibt man das? Wie schreibt man einen Text, der nicht nur behauptet, daß er frei ist für Widerspruch, sondern der das praktizieren kann? Sie haben das bezogen auf Texttypen wie, nehmen wir einmal diesen Namen Derrida. Jetzt könnte man sagen, im Text Derrida gibt es eine Schreibweise, die diesem Problem korrespondiert. Also Widerspruch wäre nicht ein Thema, sondern ein Versuch, es zu praktizieren. Bei Goldschmidt scheint es mir so zu sein, daß es in einer bestimmten Weise ein Thema bleibt, daß also gerade auch da sich jetzt nicht noch einmal ein neuer Raum der Reflexion öffnet. Und das würde auch zurückführen zu meiner ersten Frage, nämlich was bedeutet das, mit der Sprache nicht zu brechen und doch mit der Sprache zu brechen und diese Weichheit zu halten?

AMIR ESHEL: Mir scheint eine unverzichtbare Perspektive, die uns gewissermaßen fehlt, die zu sein, auch nach Israel zu blicken und zu überlegen, welche Gestalten wir dort vorfinden, deren Biographien ähnlich wie die von Gershon Shaked einen solchen Bruch aufweisen. Durch diese Perspektive könnten wir hoffentlich die Frage deutsche Literatur und jüdische Identität, jüdische Identität und philologische Lektüre neu aufwerfen. Es ist also ein Plädoyer für eine vergleichende Perspektive, die über den auf unserer Tagung behandelten Bereich hinauszugehen will.

Ich denke dabei an mindestens zwei Philologen, Ludwig Strauss und Werner Kraft, die eben diesen Schritt (die Emigration nach Palästina/Eretz Israel) vollzogen haben. Ich denke gleichzeitig aber auch an Lyriker — das ist eher mein Gebiet —, die zwar aus deutschsprachigen Elternhäusern stammten, sich aber für die hebräische Sprache entschieden haben.[8] Lyriker wie Tuvia Rübner, Jehuda Amichai, Nathan Zach und Dan Pagis. Ein Vergleichsmoment dieser Philologen und Lyriker ist meines Erachtens die Suche nach einer Selbstbestimmung ihres Judentums. Nicht die Jüdischkeit oder eine sentimentale Identifikation mit der jüdischen religiösen Überlieferung bestimmte ihr Judentum, sondern was ich als Reflexion des jüdischen Daseins in der Moderne bezeichnen möchte. Wenn ich Reflexion des jüdischen Daseins sage, meine ich die Reflexion des eigenen Standpunktes: wo stehe ich angesichts, vor allem angesichts der Shoah in diesem Jahrhundert? Eine Reflexion, die den eigenen Standpunkt, aber nicht nur den eigenen, sondern auch den kollektiven immer mit im Blick hält. Man kann meiner Überzeugung nach diese Reflexion sowohl in der Lyrik als auch in der philologischen Arbeit vorfinden. Und Gershon Shaked ist wirklich ein sehr wichtiges Beispiel dafür.[9] Um die Bedeutung der Reflexion jüdischen Daseins in der Moderne aus lyrischer Perspektive zu erläutern, möchte ich abschließend auf den Lyriker Dan Pagis hinweisen.

Dan Pagis ist 1930 in der Bukowina geboren, in Radau, ungefähr fünfzig Kilometer entfernt von Czernowitz. Er ist in einem deutsch sprechenden Elternhaus, also in einer durch die deutsche Kultur geprägten Umgebung aufgewachsen. Deutsch war seine Muttersprache. Er kam in den vierziger Jahren in ein Arbeitslager in Transnistrien und entkam nur sehr knapp dem Tod. Dan Pagis kam mit siebzehn Jahren nach Palästina, traf dort Tuvia Rübner und über Rübner Lea Goldberg, Ludwig Strauss und Werner Kraft. Diese Bekanntschaften halfen dem jungen Lyriker Pagis zum eigenen poetischen Ausdruck. Im Laufe der sechziger und siebziger Jahre wurde Pagis einer der bedeutendsten hebräischen Lyriker. Gleichzeitig war Pagis Professor für mittelalterliche jüdische Dichtung in Spanien an der Hebrew University in Jerusalem. In ihrer poetischen Dichte, eigentümlichen Temporalität, unvergleichlichen Intensität und nicht zuletzt in ihrem Bezug auf das Jüdische kommen Pagis' Gedichte jenen von Paul Celan deutlich nahe. Ein Gedicht, das auf hebräisch "Juchasin" (deutsch "Herkunft") heißt, figuriert den im jüdischen Denken so zentralen genealogischen Bezug von Vater und Sohn und verortet dabei das Erinnern und das Schreiben als die wohl markantesten Modi jüdischen Daseins in der Moderne:

> Mein Sohn läuft zu mir und sagt: mein Sohn.
> Ich sage meinem Vater: höre, mein Sohn, ich.
> Mein Vater läuft zu mir und sagt: Vater
> hast Du gehört? Uns wurde ein Denkmal errichtet.
> Ich laufe zu mir und sehe: ich liege,
> wie üblich, mit dem Gesicht zur Wand, und schreibe
> auf die weiße Wand mit Kreide
> ihre Namen alle, damit ich
> meinen Namen nicht vergesse.[10]

Discussion

WILLI GOETSCHEL: I would like to respond briefly to a few points. I thank Abby Gillman for calling attention to some of the points I tried to make clear. One issue I wanted to make a little bit clearer is when Thomas Sparr tried to juxtapose Scholem to Goldschmidt. I thought actually that one of the points is — at least in my reading — that the whole project of his is close to Scholem's. The problem with Scholem, if you read his letters, is that he responds nicely to people who are on the other side of the gap, and he attacks people who are actually close to his position. One name for that is the Buber complex, a rather deep running complex in Scholem. The quotation I read from Kafka is exactly saying that: Judaism consists in the life, and this is very similar to Scholem's view that Judaism is the total sum of the traces it produces in history, that this is the only reliable way to arrive at specificity with regard to defining Judaism. According to Scholem, this means that there exist no normative criteria to determine or define Judaism. All history is willing to offer are ever better and more differentiated descriptions and interpretations of history. But this is not Scholem's invention — this is good Spinoza; this is good Mendelssohn; this is prime Leo Baeck. That's where Scholem is rooted. I think that it is important not to polarize Scholem, when his own position shows a profound affinity to the kind of thought from which he so emphatically wishes to distance himself.

Barbara Hahn's questions are very interesting. I never thought about them. With regard to the first one I would like to respond with an anecdote that highlights the conflicted resistance to Goldschmidt: He tells how he goes to Frankfurt and informs his audience, "My family tree reaches back to 1523 in Frankfurt," and then he is astonished when people don't like him there. The point is that when and where German language is denied from the outside, the particularities of Goldschmidt's writing stand to rebel against any attempts at cultural expropriation reclaiming his language as his own. This is why for many he is a scandal, and I think that this is an intervention we have to take seriously.

We have also to be careful in the terminology, which is taking over in Germany these days in Judaic studies, people talk about Jews in Germany. "Jews in Germany" is the Nazi terminology; but they were first German Jews, and Goldschmidt does this weird thing, maybe: he just remained a German Jew. And he is greeted as one; he is viewed as a fossil, maybe, but as long as it is a scandal, I would say he's making a point.

Of course one of the problems of his discourse is that there are different decades we are talking about. Goldschmidt starts publishing in 1939, with his first book on Jeremias Gotthelf,[11] and he goes through the forties, fifties, sixties, and he changes back and forth, then the different genres in which he writes also, and that must be put in perspective, but this option to not give up this identity, which is also extended to Austria (his mother is from Austria, that's why he got the honorary cross, a sort of ambivalent thing, from Vienna), which leads me to the second point, the place of learning. The Jüdisches Lehrhaus is separate because the university had no space. There was a conference in Vienna about the "Modell des jüdischen Lehrhauses": should there still be one in Europe? What I tried to point out was that one should not read the Jüdisches Lehrhaus as a sort of a positive, ideal model. We have to read the Jüdisches Lehrhaus as an insistent critique about the exclusion of Jews.[12]

If you read the history of the German university — which was anything but universal — Jews were excluded. Ironically the Frankfurt School continued that tradition. If you'll remember, the only chair in Jewish studies in the thirties was in Frankfurt; Adorno and Horkheimer made sure that Buber, the first holder of that chair, would not return to it. This is the '68 complex. What happened to Rosenzweig, to Buber, to Goldschmidt — institutionally there was just no space.

What does a Jüdisches Lehrhaus in Zurich mean? I must recall that when he started it in the fifties Zurich was the largest German-speaking Jewish community. Thanks to the Swiss foreign police, which did its work very well, the refugees were pushed out. But Goldschmidt had hoped to rebuild, with those Jews who would be staying in the country, a new place and space from which the legacy of German Judaism could be passed on.

STEVE DOWDEN (BRANDEIS UNIVERSITY): I have a short question for Thomas Sparr and I would like to ask Willi Goetschel for a clarification. At the beginning of your talk, Thomas, you said something about the inevitability of "das Doppelte." What went into the decision to call your Verlag "Der jüdische Verlag im Suhrkamp Verlag." It seems to embody this "Doppelte."

THOMAS SPARR: Das ist natürlich eine Firmenbezeichnung, die aber schon ein historisches Problem zu erkennen gibt, daß ein Verlag, der ursprünglich von Juden für jüdische Leser gegründet worden ist, als ein autonomer Verlag 1938 zerschlagen, 1959 noch einmal wiedergegründet als eigener Verlag in Deutschland ohne Erfolg, heute die Tochtergesellschaft eines großen deutschen, deutschsprachigen Verlages ist. Das zeigt auch so etwas Doppeltes an. Was mir wichtig ist an dieser doppelten Identität, ist, daß wir diesen Problemen anscheinend nie entgehen. Also ob wir nun sagen ein deutscher Jude oder ein Jude aus Deutschland. Das bedeutet in Deutschland heute enorme Probleme. Das heißt, die eigenen jüdischen Korporationen nennen sich eben nicht deutsche Juden, sondern lehnen diese Bezeichnung ab, weil es die historische Bezeichnung des Zentralvereins war, also der assimilierten Juden, sie sagen Juden aus Deutschland und in Deutschland. Das alles sind Verdoppelungen, auf die wir immer stossen, wenn wir über Juden aus Deutschland oder in Deutschland sprechen. Das ist, wenn wir zum Beispiel auf französische oder italienische Juden stossen, ganz anders. Diese Verdoppelung ist denen gar nicht zu vermitteln. Das war der Punkt, auf den ich Wert gelegt habe, und Sie haben völlig Recht, das beschäftigt mich jeden Tag.

STEVE DOWDEN: Thank you. I also want to pick up something that Abby said. It has to do with the notion of Jewish messianism in secularized form, which I think of especially in terms of the Frankfurt School, particularly Walter Benjamin and then Adorno viewing literature as the site of the "promesse de bonheur." Now, what you said about Goldschmidt's interpretation of Wassermann's Caspar Hauser as an encrypted Jewish figure is also something that Gershon Shaked has said about Kafka's K. in *Das Schloss* — K. embodies the Jewish historical experience without being explicitly depicted as a Jew. Are these then figures that in some sense have to be recovered for Judaism, so to speak? At what point, when you talk about a secularized messianism, does Jewish content become lost? Is Goldschmidt in danger of losing Jewish content in his secularized political, sociological messianism?

WILLI GOETSCHEL: Well, he reads Caspar Hauser as a symptom. So it is not that he would be interested in looking where there is no messianism. It is a symptom in a way that Wassermann tries to be a German writer, and the argument is — I think David Suchoff is going to quote

a very telling passage, so I am not going to talk about that now —
that what happens is the return of the repressed. While Wassermann
does not talk about Jews in his Caspar Hauser book, Goldschmidt argues that a closer look reveals an underlying Jewish theme at the heart
of this tale. Goldschmidt himself is not interested in messianism in
that way. He is interested in regrounding recollection and recovery
work of the biblical tradition in which messianism is sort of the here-
and-now, and you'll see in Mendelssohn and Spinoza while the older
generation of the Frankfurt School has a far less specific notion of
messianism, a messianism that lacks some of the specificity — and
bite — of historical memory of the Jewish experience. Toward the end
of the nineteenth century it becomes increasingly clear that emancipation is going to be denied. There is a shift and the messianism is projected into the future. One could read the Frankfurt School as a
tradition of thought that in that regard still follows a nineteenth-
century paradigm of secularized messianism.

CHRISTOPH KÖNIG: Ich möchte gerne etwas zurücktreten von dem,
was aktuell diskutiert worden ist, und mit Ihnen vielleicht die Frage
diskutieren, welchen wissenschaftsgeschichtlichen Stellenwert die Diskussionen haben, die wir seit gestern führen. Also ich frage mich, was
wir hier tun.

Wir befinden uns in einem wissenschaftsgeschichtlichen Kolloquium "Jewish Critics, German Literature," und ich denke, es könnte
hilfreich sein, wenn man sich die Frage stellt: welche Formen der wissenschaftsgeschichtlichen Betrachtungsweise sind möglich? Und wie
folgen sie oft in der Entwicklung der Wissenschaftsgeschichte aufeinander. Ich beobachte, daß wir gerade heute vormittag eine starke
Tendenz dazu haben, uns zu *erinnern,* um dieses Wort aufzugreifen.
Also wir erinnern uns an jüdische Gelehrte und versuchen, damit auch
eine gewisse Tradition fortzusetzen. Das ist legitim, und doch möchte
ich die Frage stellen, wieder auf die Wissenschaft bezogen, ob es nicht
sinnvoller wäre, sich zu fragen, ob wir mit den Ergebnissen dieser jüdischen Gelehrten etwas anfangen können oder nicht, also ob sich,
mit anderen Worten, die Resultate der Forschungen auf unseren heutigen Stand beziehen lassen und sie gewissermaßen auch innerhalb der
Wissenschaft diskutieren.

Ich möchte kurz erläutern, wie ich das meine. Ich stelle ganz allgemein fest, daß die Wissenschaftsgeschichte der Germanistik beispielsweise immer beginnt mit einem emphatischen Beschwören und
Erinnern von Heldengestalten. Es sind diese großen Biographien, die

die Söhne für ihre Väter schreiben oder die Schüler für ihre Lehrer, um die Erinnerung an die große Gelehrtengestalt wachzurufen. Die zweite Phase, die dann in der Regel eintritt, ist die Phase der Ideologiekritik. Da wird dann festgestellt, man hatte das in Deutschland in den sechziger Jahren, daß die politische Orientierung nicht korrekt oder eben korrekt war. Es wird also politisch geurteilt und es wird ausschließlich über die Werte verhandelt, die diese Gelehrten hatten. Sie werden in der Regel dekouvriert. Eine dritte Phase wäre dann die, in der man sich die Frage stellt, wie denn das Leben dieser Heroen funktioniert hat, und damit meine ich auch das Gelehrtenleben. Man versucht also, Verhältnisse herzustellen zwischen Öffentlichkeit, öffentlicher Funktion, zwischen Seminar, dem esoterischen Raum der Wissenschaft, mit ihrer Biographie usw. Es ist also etwas, was mit den Systemen spielt. Man entdeckt sehr viel, aber es bleibt immer noch unbefriedigend, weil die Hauptfrage nicht gestellt wird, wie man sich dazu stellt. Es werden also gewisse Systeme hergestellt, man versteht manches, aber man weiß nicht, ob man damit einverstanden ist. Daher sollte in der Wissenschaftsgeschichte eine vierte Phase hinzutreten, in der man dann das, was man hier versteht, wieder prüft, so wie es ideologiekritisch (in einer von mir als zweiten Phase genannten) geschehen ist, in der man prüft, ob das auch etwas taugt, ob man damit heute in der Wissenschaft etwas anfangen kann.

Ich denke, um jetzt zu unserem Thema zurückzukehren, daß die Thematik, die wir hier haben, die große Chance in sich birgt. Das zeigte sich auch in verschiedenen Vorträgen, daß man sofort in die Verhältnisse kommt. Also daß man sich sofort fragen muß, weil es eben dieses Heroische nicht gibt. Thomas Sparr sprach zu Recht von dem Doppelten, das man immer findet. Die Gefahr, die ich sehe, ist, daß man nicht nur ein großes Augenmerk, wie gestern vormittag bei den amerkanischen Emigranten, auf die großen Gestalten legt, die auch Erfolg hatten, sondern auch die Gefahr, daß die ambivalente Situation, in der sich diese Gelehrten befanden, in einer neuen Form sakralisiert wird. Daß also diese widersprüchliche Situation, in der sie sich befanden, plötzlich als Garant dafür genommen wird, daß hier eine höhere Wahrheit zugänglich geworden ist. Das sind die zwei Aspekte und Probleme, die ich sehe, und ich möchte darum bitten — oder auch dazu auffordern —, daß man sich vielleicht vermehrt die Frage stellt, ob die Jewish Critics, von denen wir heute sprechen, auch für die heutigen wissenschaftlichen Diskussionen wichtig sind. Danke.

Willi Goetschel: Yes, I think that is a very interesting question. My answer would be sort of retranslating my talk into the terms of that question. First, it is not about content, what we should look after, but it is the reflection, the challenge and the implosion partially and the redrawing of the disciplinary boundaries. I think that the nontrivial result, or what it could possibly be, of such a conference, is to realize that as much as this discussion is about Jewish critics of German literature, it should make us rethink the historical constructions of German Studies and these people who fit, or do not quite fit in here — because as you said, somehow they are *sperrig* — really should lead us to a critical rethinking. I think the point would be precisely not to limit our approach to the question of what kind of content can be found in the work of these "Jüdische Gelehrte" here or there, but what kind of strategic interventions they chose.

William Donahue (Rutgers University): I have a question for Barbara Hahn. It seems to me that you couched your criticism of Goldschmidt in terms of language and style. Maybe the assumption that he doesn't stand up to the Derridian standard is itself questionable. I wonder if I could provoke you to a more specific critique. In other words, are you saying that you just find him too conventional, or how does he differ from Susman in your mind?

Barbara Hahn: Es geht nicht um Stil und es geht auch nicht um Brillianz. Es geht um ein Problem. Und das Problem will ich so benennen: Wie kann man in einer Sprache, in der man aufgewachsen ist, mit der man gelebt hat, wie kann man in dieser Sprache etwas ausdrücken, was in dieser Sprache nicht mehr sagbar ist? Das ist eine Paradoxie. Dafür gibt es keine Lösung. Ich frage eigentlich nur danach: Welchen Umgang kann ich in diesem Text mit diesem Problem lesen? Und wenn ich noch einmal aufnehme, was Amir vorher sagte, wenn ich das vergleiche mit anderen, die in derselben Problematik waren, dann kann man in den Texten eine Spur dieses Problems lesen. Und was mich irritierte bei Goldschmidt war, daß ich diese Spuren nicht fand. Das war die Frage. Also ich fragte mich einfach, wie wird dieser Kulturbruch, wie wird dieser Sprachbruch bearbeitet, wenn der Text wirkt, als ob er eine glatte Oberfläche hätte? Es geht wirklich nicht um irgendwelche ästhetischen Kriterien, überhaupt nicht, das wäre eine ganz entsetzliche Verharmlosung. Genau darum geht es nicht. Es geht nicht darum, ob es schöne oder konventionelle Texte sind. Ich will es auch gar nicht bewerten. Es ist eine Frage außerhalb der Bewertung, es geht um ein Problem.

DAVID SUCHOFF: Just a quick observation: When Derrida was interviewed, I think in *Jüdisches Denken in Frankreich,* he roots his philosophical tradition in Hermann Cohen, so that he understands the question of the unassimilability of the particular to be a historical question of culture.[13] He does not himself see a dissonance between the insistence of the particular and its claims against the universal. That's in his style, but he sees the historical-philosophical place that gets worked out in precisely Goldschmidt's material. That's one. The other thing, the question of double identity: It's not just a question of double identity for Jewish critics, but it's the utopian claim for German culture to claim its double identity, that is, to give the particular its place, its voice, within a German language area. So it is German double identity that is as much the claim and not just Jewish identity.

WILLI GOETSCHEL: Concerning the question of unspeakability: I think the point is here in Goldschmidt, and I think it is a very important point, that first of all he is the one who had never used the word Holocaust or Shoah. He always takes at least a dependent clause when he mentions the terrible chain of events now referred to as Holocaust. What is important for Goldschmidt concerning the issue of unspeakability is that things are precisely sayable in human language and that what is really needed is not so much metaphysical speculations about the failure of language but the recovery of specifics; specifics that precisely defy even a lot that is said in the name of a discourse of unspeakability. There is a whole debate and that would be exactly my *Bilder* essay which Thomas Sparr prepared for discussion.[14] Goldschmidt himself stands for a historic and individual particularity, and he seems to say that as long as we can speak about these things, the only thing is to speak about them and resist prescriptions about what can be said or cannot be said, and that is what he has been doing. Goldschmidt's own discourse may strike many as couched in a language and style of an old voice, but I think we all share the idea that it is imperative to let everyone speak in their own voice and not deny anyone the right to the particularity of one's own voice.

HASKELL BLOCK: I was particularly struck by Willi Goetschel's account of the perspective that comes from the reshaping of boundaries for literary study. I think this is a very important aspect of the whole discussion. And I couldn't help thinking of Isaac Deutscher's essay called "The Non-Jewish Jew," where Deutscher argues that the margin can be the center, that there is a perspective that can emerge from marginalization, from alienation, from the edge of the boundary that results in a new view and a new positioning of the observer.[15]

To come back to the question raised about scholarly and critical approaches and the question of identifiability of a specific Jewish perspective with respect to German literature: I am sorry that we don't have more attention given in the course of our deliberations to Hans Mayer. When you think of Hans Mayer's collection of outsiders for example,[16] Mayer following Lukács, is leaning very heavily on the position of the alienation of the Jew in German life and the intellectual alienation. I think this is true to some extent of figures in the United States as well, and you can certainly see it in the emphasis on dissent, on criticism, on a conscious separation against the establishment, against the status quo, Irving Howe called his journal *Dissent* and so on, and all of this has to do, it seems to me, with the notion of alienation, as a critical stance and its redefinition. And it does seem to me this is one important aspect of the Jewish contribution to the discussion of German literature.

Editors' Annotations

[1] Gershon Shaked, *Die Macht der Identität: Essays über jüdische Schriftsteller* (Frankfurt am Main: Jüdischer Verlag, 1992); Gershon Shaked, *Geschichte der modernen hebräischen Literatur: Prosa von 1880 bis 1980* (Frankfurt am Main: Jüdischer Verlag, 1996).

[2] Hannah Arendt, "The Jew as Pariah: A Hidden Tradition," *Jewish Social Studies* 6 (1944): 99–122.

[3] Gershom Scholem, *Sabbatai Zwi: der mystische Messias* (Frankfurt am Main: Jüdischer Verlag, 1992); Engl.: *Sabbatai Sevi: The Mystical Messiah, 1626–1676* (Princeton, N.J.: Princeton UP, 1973); *Shabtai Tsevi* (Tel-Aviv, 1956/57).

[4] Gershon Shaked, "No Other Place: On Saul Friedländer's *When Memory Comes, 1979*," in *The Shadows Within: Essays on Modern Jewish Writers* (Philadelphia, New York, Jerusalem: The Jewish Publication Society, 1987), 181–89. Saul Friedländer, *When Memory Comes*, trans. Helen R. Lane (New York: Farrar, Straus, and Giroux, 1979).

[5] Shaked, *The Shadows Within*.

[6] Shaked, *The Shadows Within*, xii–xiii.

[7] Hermann Levin Goldschmidt, *Freiheit für den Widerspruch*, mit einem einführenden Interview von Alfred A. Häsler (Schaffhausen: Novalis Verlag, 1976); rpt., ed. Willi Goetschel (Vienna: Passagen, 1993).

[8] Amir Eshel, *Zeit der Zäsur: Die Rhetorik der Zeit in der Lyrik jüdischer Dichter im Angesicht der Shoah* (Heidelberg: Winter, 1999).

[9] Apart from Shaked, *The Shadows Within: Essays on Modern Jewish Writers* cf. also Gershon Shaked, *En makom aher: 'al sifrut·ve-·hahevrah* (Tel Aviv: Hakibbutz Hame'uhad, 1988).

[10] Dan Pagis: *Kol ha-shirim: "Aba" [pirke prozah],* ed. V. Chanan Chewer und T. Carmi (Jerusalem: hHa-Kibuts ha-meuhad: Mosad Byalik, 1991), 167 [Heb. *Collected Poems. 'Vater' (Prosa)*], 167 (Übersetzung von Amir Eshel).

[11] Hermann Levin Goldschmidt, *Der Geist der Erziehung bei Jeremias Gotthelf* (Berne and Leipzig: P. Haupt, 1939).

[12] Willi Goetschel, "Universität, Partikularität und das jüdische Lehrhaus," in *Das Jüdische Lehrhaus als Modell lebensbegleitenden Lernens,* ed. Evelyn Adunka (Vienna: Passagen, 1999), 47–59.

[13] Elisabeth Weber, ed., *Jüdisches Denken in Frankreich: Gespräche mit Pierre Vidal-Naquet, Jacques Derrida, Rita Thalmann, Emmanuel Levinas, Leon Poliakov, Jean-François Lyotard, Luc Rosenzweig* (Frankfurt am Main: Jüdischer Verlag, 1994).

[14] Willi Goetschel, "Zur Sprachlosigkeit von Bildern," in *Bilder des Holocaust,* ed. Klaus Scherpe and Manfred Köppen (Vienna: Böhlau, 1997), 131–44.

[15] Isaac Deutscher, *The Non-Jewish Jew and Other Essays,* ed. with an introduction by Tamara Deutscher (London and New York: Oxford UP, 1968).

[16] Hans Mayer, *Outsiders: A Study in Life and Letters,* trans. Denis M. Sweet (Cambridge, Mass.: MIT P, 1982).

5: Embattled Germanistik

Walter Sokel, April 1975 (© The Albert H. Small Special
Collections Library, University of Virginia Library)

Part of an Intellectual Autobiography

Walter H. Sokel

I PROPOSE TO DEAL HERE with this question: How was it possible for me, a nominally Jewish refugee from Nazi Austria to take up the study of German literature in America at a moment in history — the autumn of 1941 — when Germany was staging the most horrendous persecution and clearly threatening the destruction of Europe's Jews? What could possibly motivate me to begin the disciplinary study of the language and literature of a nation officially dedicated to the elimination of the people to which I belonged by birth?

Three years before, I had narrowly saved my life through a risk-braving escape — dizzying in retrospect — from the death trap that was Nazi *Mitteleuropa*, and thereafter had arrived in New York, my sole possession eight dollars cash and the clothes I wore. What, in such circumstances, could conceivably propel my intellectual and spiritual return to the cultural realm of the people whose elected regime would most certainly murder me should I attempt a physical return? And how did such a — in the circumstances — profoundly problematical decision shape the form my approach to the study of German culture would assume? What kind of professional work would result from an enterprise fraught with such momentous questionableness?

My choice of this profession at such a time constituted an enormous provocation to the milieu in which I lived. It would challenge me to justify myself for years and years to come. I vividly recall an encounter that epitomized this challenge. It occurred in New York in 1944, in the last phase of the war against Hitler's Germany. I was a graduate student in the Columbia University German department and a teaching assistant in Columbia's Extension School, teaching a second-semester German language course. As I was making a purchase in the little candy and soda-fountain store on upper Broadway, across from Columbia University, the aged Jewish store owner spotted our textbook, *Continuing German,* under my arm, and, quavering with indignation, bellowed: "Beginning German is bad enough, but *con-*

tinuing German is unforgivable." This incident, symptomatic at the time, shook me up, heaping fuel to feelings of shame and guilt, forever lying in wait in myself.

I shall use my experience of the first years of my professional study and career to show a particular perspective evolving from which to view German history and culture, Jewish-German relations, and, in general, the significance of historical context for the study of literature. When, in the summer of 1941, having obtained the B.A. in History and Philosophy at Rutgers University, I made the decision to take up graduate work in German, it did not appear to me by any means as problem-ridden as it would soon thereafter. I had never identified Germany with Nazism. I had viewed the Nazis as the, in all likelihood, very transitory victors in a civil war that had pitted Germans against Germans and was merely a local sector of a global strife between the right and the left. On one side I saw the desperate upholders of a dying class society and, on the other side, those who revolted against it to establish the worldwide classless society. For local historical reasons this civil war had assumed a particular urgency and virulence in certain countries, such as Germany and Austria. In the Soviet Union, it had already been decided, even though in a form that left much to be desired, while in Western Europe and the United States it would hopefully be decided at the ballot box and by gradual reform. When I first awakened to politics, in the summer of 1932, I became immediately involved in it as a most passionate observer. Every Sunday night I avidly followed the radio reports of the ferocious weekend street battles between Marxists and Nazis taking place in the cities of Germany. They impressed upon me the clear fact that the enemies of Nazism were Germans who seemed willing to risk their lives to prevent a Nazi takeover of Germany. I was deeply impressed by the significant defeat of the Nazis in the elections of November 1932. When Hitler finally did come to power, he was after all supported by a minority — although a very big one — of the German electorate, and his government had been installed by a maneuver of the ruling circles, an alliance of large landowners, high bureaucrats, and finance capital, backed by the military. The Nazis appeared to be the praetorian guard of the economic elite, who used the Nazis to impose their absolute rule upon the workers. I saw that the first inmates of the concentration camps were all Germans, only a minority among them Jewish, and continued to be so for years until the outbreak of the Second World War. German literature, art, and culture I held to be largely opposed to Nazism. Leading German writers, artists, and scientists had left Germany or were incarcerated or forbidden to publish, exhibit, and teach. My firm association of German culture with the anti-Nazi cause was, of course, decisive in making my initial decision to study German literature unproblematic for myself. Far from representing Nazism, German literature and culture, on the contrary, seemed to me to have been the first to unmask and combat not only Nazism itself, but the social forces and structures responsible for the seeds of Nazism in earlier German society.

One of the most influential books for my early adolescence had been Heinrich Mann's novel, *Der Untertan* (*Man of Straw* is the not very felicitous title of its English translation; *The Emperor's Subject* would be more appropriate.) I had read it at age fourteen, half a year before Hitler's accession to power. It had converted me to socialism, and I saw a triumph of social democracy as the only and ultimate hope for Germany. *Der Untertan* taught me to see the cradle of National Socialism in the society of Wilhelminian Germany. Far from seeing this continuity as some kind of innate corruption of the German people — a view increasingly fashionable near and beyond the end of the Second World War. I saw it as a result of the class structure of German society that had to and would be revolutionized. Neither did Germany seem to be unique in exhibiting the profound need for revolutionary change. The whole industrial world seemed to be in the throes of a deep chronic depression which only the advent of feverish preparations for and the final outbreak of total war ended, or rather, as I viewed it then, interrupted. The indictment of German bourgeois society issuing from *Der Untertan* was powerfully reinforced by a spate of left-leaning German authors of the Weimar Republic that became the staple of my extracurricular education in the authoritarian quasi-Fascist Vienna of my youth. The fact that these literary-political teachers were all Germans convinced me that German literature by and large formed an advance guard in the fight against the Nazis. Choosing German literature as a field of professional study thus would not merely contradict, but actually aid my struggle against Nazism.

Furthermore, many of the figures of identification in my teenage years, the literary characters in whom I, a lonely child, recognized with relief and delight my kindred souls and who enabled me to gain self-respect and self-assurance, showing me that my isolation and feeling of inferiority did not make me a unique monster, an absolute misfit, my forerunners and older siblings, — Tonio Kröger, Hans Castorp, Harry Haller — they were Germans, projected and written by German authors. They who gave me my identity by confirming it were Germans. To the extent that I had acquired an identity, it was — or felt to be — German more than anything else. Of course, that by no means precluded my identifying with members of many other ethnic groups. It meant only that among the figures who helped me decisively in shaping my identity Germans were prominent.

At the time I certainly did not think of identity in terms of nationality. In my late teens I was convinced that nations and national identities had to be overcome, and I considered myself neither German nor Austrian nor Jewish, but a human being, pure and simple, a member of humanity. My homeland was the world. In hindsight, however, it seems that my easy and spontaneous identification with characters in German books had made my subsequent professional choice of teaching German language and literature appear not unnatural to me.

The immediate cause of my decision to enroll in German graduate studies, however, was practical. As an undergraduate my major had been history with a minor in philosophy. In the philosophy course given by the inspiring, tweedily elegant, and somewhat bohemian Professor Houston Peterson, who commuted to Rutgers from the Village in New York and whose svelte wife occasionally came to class, wrapped in a fur coat, with a huge Russian wolfhound at the leash, the epic novels of nineteenth-century Europe were discussed.[1] Even though I was a passionate reader of fiction and had myself already twice attempted to write novels with a grand sweep and teeming casts of characters, during my undergraduate years my most absorbing interest had shifted to philosophy of history — an interest originally aroused by Spengler's *Decline of the West* which, read in the disaster-threatening atmosphere of Vienna in the second half of the thirties, had left a deep and lasting impression upon me. It had made me incline toward an apocalyptic view of history that the events of the following years seemed to confirm to a terrifying degree. I toyed with the project of writing a history of the idea of progress as originating in Judeo-Christian eschatology and presumably reaching its end in our own time. But to pursue such a plan was impossible in the history department of Rutgers University and, most probably, in almost any other history department at that time. Intellectual and cultural history had as yet hardly been established as legitimate fields of study, and the kind of historical study suggested to me by the Professor of European History at Rutgers did not appeal to me at all. A native of Greece, Professor Peter Charanis[2] was riveted on Byzantine history. For him everything in fifteen hundred years of Western history led back to

Byzantium. The project he wished to assign to me was a study of commercial treaties negotiated between Florence and Byzantium in the late thirteenth and early fourteenth centuries. That closed History as a graduate subject for me. Besides it was discreetly pointed out to me that to a Jewish immigrant like myself an academic career in History or Philosophy or Comparative Literature — the subjects I was most interested in — would probably be closed. My only chance would lie with German because there I enjoyed the advantage of being a native speaker. Since I knew that an academic career would be best suited for my type of mentality and personality, I chose the field that seemed to be open for me — German.

I was received with open arms and warm cordiality by the German department of Rutgers University. As an undergraduate I had, in my spare time, continued to read German literature voraciously, so that its formal study appeared to be extremely easy. My professors, Albert W. Holzmann[3] for older and Johannes Nabholz[4] for modern literature, seemed to welcome with obvious relish my incessant oral contributions to their classes, as they provided agreeable relief to them from having to fill the whole class period with their own lectures. Professor Nabholz in particular soon asked me to take over quite a few of his classes. They were tiny: four or five candidates for the M.A., with halting command of spoken German. I thoroughly enjoyed exhibiting to them my thoughts and feelings about the texts assigned and impressing them with what I knew. The approach to literature then practiced at Rutgers was traditional and, from a self-reflectively theoretical view of disciplinary method, astonishingly naive and elementary. It mainly consisted of biographical information, plot summary, rudimentary formalism, lay psychologizing about characters, and listing of influences. Literary history proceeded by unreflectedly received classifications by periods, schools, and movements. At Columbia, where two years later I began to study for the Ph.D., methods were basically the same. Only the bibliographies supplied at the beginning of each course grew longer. I received no essential enlightenment from my courses in either department.

However, two extracurricular discoveries united at the beginning of my graduate studies to give them a direction that proved decisive for my intellectual development and subsequent professional work. One was the chance encounter with Franz Kafka's *Metamorphosis,* one summer afternoon in the New York Public Library to which I owe a good deal of my education. The other was a showing of Jean Cocteau's surrealist film, *The Blood of a Poet,* in an art cinema on lower

Fifth Avenue, shortly before or after Pearl Harbor. Although the two experiences blended, I also have to distinguish between them.

My reading of *Metamorphosis* was a psychological and existential experience, an intensely personal and traumatic encounter at a level of great inner depth. However, it merely crowned, but did not fundamentally change my habitual way of mimetic reading, i.e., reading in which the reader identifies with a character. Gregor Samsa was simply the climax, the unsurpassable instance of self-identification that had begun with Tonio Kröger. The degree, the visceral intensity of identification was different, but not in kind. I still recognized myself in the outcast hero, the absolute misfit, the totally isolated reject of humanity. Of course, Kafka's work totally withheld the misfit's triumphant vindication in the earlier plots where artistic success or joining the Immortals redeems the outcast-hero in the end. They conformed to the Cinderella pattern of ultimate compensation Freud had drawn as the artist's fortunate fate in "The Poet and Daydreaming," which had been my guiding light when I projected myself into the future. This ultimate reassuring confirmation I felt missing in Kafka's tale or hinted at too vaguely in Gregor's self-imposed death to be of use. For that reason its effect was much more profound, because profoundly unsettling, than that of the earlier stories. And, beyond that, the enigmatic event that made Gregor an outcast opened the world of this story toward the literally meta-physical, absent from the earlier misfit plots.

The impact of *Metamorphosis* made me hunt for all other texts by its then still little known author. In my first semester of German graduate studies, at Rutgers, I read all the works of Kafka available in the university library. They included volume five of Max Brod's Mercy Verlag edition of Kafka's *Schriften* — the stories and short pieces from the *Nachlaß*. Those one- and two-page texts in particular acted as a revelation. Unlike *Metamorphosis,* these texts no longer offered mimetic identification. They left the recognizable world of waking life behind without, in most cases, giving up the scenery of humdrum contemporary reality for the wonderland of fairy tale or myth. There was magic in them, but it was magic left unexplained in the midst of everyday quotidian life. The strange transgressions and distortions of empirical reality in them could not be attributed to sorcerers, magicians, and supernatural beings. They remained unexplained and, for that reason, cried out for explanation, initiating a search that could never end. With their everyday settings and enigmatic distortions, they resembled dreams. It was this dreamlike quality that made these texts so liberating an experience for me. Kafka himself gave the aptest formulation of this feeling of sudden expansion of freedom with which a totally new mode of writing, beyond all limits set by tradition, suffuses one's life.

This vast exhilarating enlargement of the realm of inspiration and reference for the creative imagination came to me not only from Kafka. Reading him, as I mentioned before, coincided with my discovery of surrealism, first in Cocteau's film, and then in paintings in the Museum of Modern Art, which had a most faithfully devoted visitor in me. Shortly thereafter the experience of nonmimetic modernism was powerfully reinforced by my encounter with T.S. Eliot's *Prufrock* and *Waste Land*. I was reliving one or two generations later the fascinating process of consciousness raising and expanding that is now named modernism. Looking for its equivalents in my field of study, German literature, I naturally hit upon Expressionism which evoked distant echoes of scandalized conversations in our family that I had overheard in early childhood. I was engrossed in Albert Soergel's wonderful volume, *Im Banne des Expressionismus*. (Recently I was struck when I discovered that Soergel's now largely forgotten work had played a similarly decisive role in Heiner Müller's youth.)

The effect upon me of Kafka, Expressionism, and transmimetic modernism was two-fold: On one hand, it freed me from confinement to realistic description of waking life in my own creative efforts, while, on the other, it pointed clearly to my future field of concentration in graduate study. It would be the antimimetic tradition of which, as I quickly discovered, German literature from Sturm und Drang and Romanticism onward offered a particularly rich array of examples. Having done my M.A. thesis at Rutgers on distortion and deviation from mimetic representation in the poetry of Georg Heym, I planned to embark on a comparative treatment of the fantastic in E. T. A. Hoffmann and Kafka. However, Professor Henry Schulze[5] in the Columbia German Department, who taught E. T. A. Hoffmann, pooh-poohed my project right away: "Comparing Kafka to E. T. A. Hoffmann does not make any sense," he decreed. "For one thing, there are no points of comparison, and besides the difference in literary rank between them precludes it." What he meant, of course, was that the crazy Jew from Prague was so immensely inferior that one could not consider him an academic subject. Kafka simply did not count as German literature. More than ten years later, I learned from Wilhelm Emrich that Emil Staiger had held the same opinion of Kafka. He could not understand how an established Goethe scholar like Emrich could waste his time on such a weird and minor figure. I had men-

tioned my project to Professor Schulze in late 1944. It was a time
when Kafka was beginning to be recognized in the American intellectual community. Angel Flores had just brought out his influential
volume, *The Kafka Problem* (1946) in which serious critical literature
on Kafka was presented to the American public. Professor Schulze's
response was symptomatic of the attitude of the Columbia German
department, at least prior to the arrival of Professor André von
Gronicka, in late 1944.[6]

The department was chaired by an aged Virginia gentleman, born
shortly after the Civil War, of an old Charlottesville family, Robert
Herndon Fife, who, many years before, had published a small book on
Young Luther.[7] He taught the older and Classical period of German
literature. Professor Frederick Heuser[8] and Schulze shared the newer
field from Romanticism onward. Both were unabashedly old-
fashioned German nationalists. Although I never encountered overt
anti-Semitism, I interpreted Professor Heuser's initial attempt to dis-
suade me from pursuing graduate work in Germanistik as motivated
by anti-Jewish prejudice. Perhaps I was wrong. Perhaps it was sincere
solicitude for my future that prompted his efforts at discouraging me.
At American colleges, he warned me, hardly anyone could ever get
beyond teaching "der, die, das." Since I insisted on enrolling against
his advice, I could never get over a certain discomfort and unease in
my relationship to him.

Professor Heuser was not needed to make clear to me the discouraging prospect ahead for anyone beginning the Ph.D. in German
shortly after the fall of Stalingrad. The reasons speaking against it were
much more weighty than the likelihood of staying stuck with teaching
"der, die, das." It was rapidly becoming apparent that the German
language, and even the very words "German" and "Germany," had
turned into emblems of horror, arousing the most visceral disgust and
revulsion. Vansittart had already pleaded for the quarantining of Germany after the war, her permanent exclusion from the family of civilized nations. Soon thereafter, Morgenthau's plan of dismantling all of
German industry and pastoralizing the country forever became a seriously considered option. Any distinction made between Germans and
Nazis had become taboo. Even the physical extermination of all Germans above a certain age or the sterilization of all German males or at
least the cessation of Germany as a national and political entity were
earnestly debated. Anticipating Peter Viereck's popular study, *Metapolitics*,[9] which equated all of German civilization with the incubation
of Nazism, an acquaintance of our family, a Jewish refugee from Vi-

enna, assured me in a heated argument that anti-Semitism had always been active, even in the highest flowering of German culture. "They had always been Nazis in spirit — all of them. Do you think Goethe was a friend of the Jews? He could not stand them and he would be a Nazi, if he were alive today. And Schiller would have seen Hitler as a hero and glorified him in a drama. It's all there, anticipated, in his works. They were all Nazis. All Germans were Nazis, always have been, always will be. There will be Nazis as long as there will be Germans."

As a student of German literature, I felt morally damned, absurd, and perverse, a traitor not only to my fellow Jews but to humanity. As the news of the death camps thickened each day, a deep sense of guilt as well as shame took hold of me. How could I justify myself? How could I justify teaching the language in which the annihilation of my aunts, my cousins, and, had he not succumbed to a heart attack on the eve of his deportation, of my father was administered? Was there any treason worse than trying to mediate and thus, in a way, to "sell" the culture that had issued in such unimagined horror? And even more monstrous seemed the self-betrayal that I, a Jew, in preparing to teach German literature, associated myself, in some way, with my own would-be murderers.

Yet I was profoundly split. While I felt guilty and ashamed of the discipline I had chosen, I was, at the same time, angry, even furious at the indiscriminate equating of German-speaking people with Nazis. I argued vehemently against the persecutors of everything German, against this facile wholesale condemnation of a culture in which the fight against all that Nazism represented had been at least as important as those aspects in which one might see sign posts on the road to it. To be sure, I increasingly realized that the two could not always be neatly differentiated, that they sometimes interpenetrated and even depended upon each other, that there were trends in German culture and iconic figures, such as Nietzsche, equally seminal for Nazi and anti-Nazi attitudes alike. Yet, I fanatically insisted on the absolute need of saving in German civilization that which was different from Nazism, and moreover saving even the ambiguous. Indeed in my indignant reaction against the wholesale condemnation of everything German, which raged all around me, I even pleaded for the saving of Nazis who demonstrated a genuine change of mind and heart despite the enormous difficulty of verifying it. In my zeal against the over-zealous prosecutors of German civilization, I claimed a misdirected idealism in individual Nazis that could be used and made valuable if redirected toward the cause of humanism. In fact, as I discovered, with some horror at myself, my so passionate recoil from the inverted racism of the germanophobes was threatening to turn me into a kind of German nationalist myself.

I should like to dwell for a moment on that threat. Thinking back on those years of mind-boggling revelations of so many atrocities committed by Germans, culminating in the genocide against the Jews, I am struck by my lack of visceral reaction. Of course, I shuddered at the crimes of the Nazi regime and found them ghastly, but I had not expected anything else from Hitler's regime. Thus I did not experience that visceral rage that seized me when confronted with the advocates of the destruction of Germany. Strange and disturbing as it is to admit it, a much more spontaneous and intense anger welled up in me at the Allied fliers bombing German cities into oblivion than at the operators of the gas chambers. In the latter case, it was an abysmal sadness rather than anger that enveloped me. This difference puzzled and troubled me at the time, but I would not deny it, at least not to myself.

Of course, I am talking of a gut reaction. My rational self understood very well that any means, no matter how cruel and destructive, had to be used to extirpate Hitler's regime. But I also felt that Germany — the towns that Romantic art and literature had made precious to me, the people among whom there were many who loathed Nazism and all it stood for, and the many young Germans who supported the regime only because they had never known a real alternative — I felt that that aspect of Germany had been doubly victimized — first by the Nazis, and then by the Allied bombers that rained destruction upon her. There was for me no glee in that, but the sadness of tragedy. Destruction had to be wrought, but its necessity was a horrendous shame.

Certainly the destruction of Germany seemed to have much justification on its side. It could appear as a righteous retribution, a just punishment of unprecedented crimes committed in the name of and without effective protest by the German and Austrian peoples. It thus seemed quite plausible and fair that Germany should never again be permitted to exist as an entity, and that German culture, and eventually even the German language, should cease to be. Before the onset of the Cold War, such a scenario did not seem improbable. Fear for my professional future thus reinforced my ever-growing realization how much of my own identity, my memories, my roots were bound up with the language in which my imagination had been formed and the literature in which it had learned to unfold. Thus I felt the projected destruction of Germany as a threat to my own being.

I lacked a comparably strong attachment to my Jewish heritage. Jewish culture and Jewish lore had been peripheral to my development after I defected from my strong Old Testament-based childhood faith when, following my Bar Mitzvah, I had absorbed the message of Darwinian evolution in H. G. Wells' outline of world history. Having lost my faith in the God of my grandfather and father, I felt for many years that my identity was no longer bound to Judaism. My emotional investment in my professional commitment to German grew more intense, in direct ratio to the danger to Germany's continued existence as a nation. As a prospective teacher of German literature I considered it my primary task to present to the American public aspects of German culture that would make the popular identification of Germany with Nazism much harder to maintain and thus to help counteract that isolation of Germany which had to be the precondition of her destruction.

This task had become more and more difficult each day the war dragged on without signs of any effective German opposition to Hitler's regime. My earlier hope of a German revolution had proved to be totally deluded. Profound doubts arose in me as to whether my previously spontaneous distinction between German civilization and Nazism could be maintained in light of the fanatical devotion with which most Germans seemed to follow Hitler to their common doom. With grievous disappointment I witnessed the end of Nazism being totally imposed from outside without any participation by Germans inside Germany.

This necessitated a shift in strategy if I wished to continue to defend German literature and culture as fields worthy of study. This defense had to set itself a twofold goal. One was to move the focus of the distinction between German civilization and Nazism from the present to the past. The other was to seek to understand the peculiar appeal Nazism, or a thinking akin to it, could have for so many highly educated and cultured individuals, and why it proved particularly strong in German-speaking culture. These two tasks followed one another in time. The first was prominent during work on my dissertation in the late forties and early fifties. The second emerged and began to preoccupy me after I began to teach as a full-time faculty member at Columbia College in the fall of 1953. Since time will not permit me to do justice to both, I shall concentrate here on the first. The way the Second World War had ended showed the Nazis' success in having turned most Germans, who were neither in exile nor in concentration camps, into obedient followers, or at least non-resisting subjects of the Führer. Yet, not so long before, strong forces had existed in German culture and society fiercely opposed to all that Nazism espoused. Our task as teachers of German culture would have to be the unburying of their memory, and the highlighting of that not inconsiderable body of German literature that, beginning with the Enlightenment, had been engaged in radical social critique and subversion of authority. A counter-canon had to be developed in opposition to, or at least distinct from, the official literary canon approved and promoted by German nationalist Bürgertum.

Walter Sokel and Peter Heller

What made the choice of Expressionism as a subject of study especially attractive to me was the convergence in it of two modes of revolt. Expressionism had given a strident voice to a sociopolitical revolt not only against war and the military-industrial complex that had spawned and maintained it, but against all forms of domination, from the bureaucratic state to the patriarchal family; and it had expressed this revolt in forms that sabotaged traditional aesthetics. Thus it was for me a two-pronged assault on the established world. The forgotten moment of Expressionism seemed a topic made to order. Departmental approval was made possible only because a young professor from the University of Chicago had joined the Columbia German department. Born in Moscow and raised in Weimar Germany, the Russo-Baltic André von Gronicka had brought a much-needed breath of liberal modernity and cosmopolitanism into the department.

In the setting of the first years of the postwar period, researching Expressionism assumed a nostalgically utopian dimension for me. Reliving in the imagination the mutinous mood that had swept through Germany at the end of the First World War compensated to some extent for its non-occurrence at the end of Second World War. Expressionism had articulated the impulse to revolutionize German society. Its failure did not refute its significance. It bestowed a tragic aspect on the narrative on which I had embarked.

Expressionism, in which Jewish authors participated in a higher numerical proportion than in any other movement of German literature, offered a striking example of the close comradeship of Gentiles and Jews in German culture, subsequently to become a heatedly controversial topic under the heading of "German-Jewish symbiosis." In Expressionism I saw Gentile and Jewish Germans firmly united in a common struggle for shared goals. How exhilarating it was to discover that Hanns Johst, later poet laureate of Nazism, had satirized anti-Semitism in an early Expressionist play, and that one of the greatest Expressionist poets, Gottfried Benn, who in 1933 avowed his spiritual allegiance to National Socialism, had been erotically as well as artistically close to the Jewish poet, Else Lasker-Schüler, who two decades later was to die in Israel. I felt it should be the task of a teacher of German literature to highlight the prominence of the Jewish presence in German culture, but also to examine the strong attraction that German culture had exerted on the Jews of Central and Eastern Europe. I was eager to challenge the notion, prevalent then and revived today, that the so-called symbiosis had been a mere, and ultimately disastrous, self-delusion of the Jewish partner, because Germans allegedly had always been quasi-innate anti-Semites. Not that I had not come to realize the potency of anti-Semitism in German culture in terms of historical fact and final result. But I drew different conclusions from it. For me German-Jewish symbiosis was not a delusion, but a dream, i.e., a reality in the making, pregnant with enormous possibilities for the good of both sides, and the world. The fruits of German-Jewish collaboration had been real enough and abundantly evident, in the century and a half before the victory of Hitlerite reaction cut down the tree from which those fruits had come. Germanophobic Jews who decried the symbiosis as having led into the

Holocaust failed to see that they were abetting the Nazis' cause. Germanophobes and Nazis shared an identical goal — an absolute and everlasting separation of Germans and Jews. Both wished to see a glorious project that had begun with the Enlightenment undone.

Reminding the world of German movements in which Jews and Gentiles had joined forces in a shared vision of human emancipation, I sought to counteract both. I tried to illuminate a past that had projected a more inspiring future than the one now arising from the death camps of the most recent past and the hatred in the ashes and rubble that were present in Central Europe. My original dissertation project of a comparative study of Kafka and E. T. A. Hoffmann was to establish by literary scholarship a Jewish-German symbiosis of a kind that had not existed in actuality. I attempted to bring the "Aryan" Hoffmann, member of the Nazi-approved canon of German writing, into close association with the "degenerate" Jew from Prague by revealing striking similarities between them. Thus in a way I would not only Germanize the Jew, but also Judaize the German. For its enemies among the Jews, German-Jewish symbiosis had proceeded in only one direction — surrender of Jewishness to the German enemy. They ignored the opposite direction, equally, or even more, significant historically — the exposure of German minds to Jewish mentalities, the infiltration of German culture by Jewish ways of thought. As the wife of a famous Germanist once put it in a conversation: "With the Jews, the salt has gone out of Germany." The Nazis had seen that other direction of symbiosis very well when they decried the "corruption" of Germany by Jewish influence. They hated it and succeeded in extirpating it. Shedding light on the reciprocity of Jewish-German interchange thus turned out to be a weapon against Nazi thinking as well as against its germanophobic counterpart in fanaticism. It could subvert the ironclad boundaries, the polarizing dividing lines between the two ethnicities, erected by the Nazis and steadfastly maintained by Jewish germanophobes. Showing strong resemblances, family likenesses, to use Wittgenstein's term, in writers belonging to ideologically constructed opposites named German and Jewish would above all undermine the habit, deeply ingrained in the cultural discourse of Germany, of thinking in dualisms, of setting up absolute types or archetypes and ranging them against each other in polar opposites such as artist and burgher, idealist and materialist, Romantic and Classical, male and female, Aryan and Jew. Nazi racism was only an insanely consistent instance of this centuries-old tradition of seeing the world as a battleground of polar opposites. The same kind of thinking in terms of irreconcilable opposites that had led to the destruction of six million Jews I saw continued in those Jews who considered the barrier between Jews and German valid for all time and wanted it perpetuated.

Walter Sokel, 1999

Years later, in the mid-fifties, when I had begun teaching German intellectual history at Columbia College, I liked to use another example to subvert dualistic thinking. I tried to show how Arthur Schopenhauer, known for his anti-Semitic prejudice and a highly respected member of the Nazi pantheon, strikingly anticipated the thinking of Freudian psychoanalysis, branded by the Nazis as typically Jewish. And what could, from the Nazi perspective, be more "destructively Jewish" than Schopenhauer's deconstruction of Romantic love as purely sexual desire? Pointing out such "Jewishness" in a famous anti-Semite was a special pleasure to be savored.

Similar affinities to Freud, but also to American Pragmatism, I tried to make my students see in Nietzsche who, at that time, was still regarded as the most important forerunner of Nazism. In the same vein, I projected a course on German Romanticism, a movement extolled by Nazi scholars as Aryan-Nordic *par excellence,* linking it, as an important source of inspiration, to surrealism, for the Nazis a prime example of "degenerate" art.

Such re-readings of the official German canon in the light of its close relationships to what had been proscribed by Nazi ideology as dangerously subversive were to help not merely to rehabilitate German culture in the eyes of the democratic world, but likewise to undermine the German conservative outlook, prevalent in postwar Germany, as it had been under Nazism and before it. Authors revered by German nationalist Bürgertum had to be shown as having paved the way for that subversion of pieties for which Germans had been taught to blame the Jews and the French. It was to be eye opening for both camps of the recent war, and thus contribute to building a bridge across the abyss created by the projection of fated, mutually exclusive, and eternally hostile essences in human beings.

Editors' Notes

[1] Houston Peterson (b. Fresno, California 1897, d. Dennis, Massachusetts 1981) was a professor of philosophy who specialized in philosophical approaches to literature. He received his doctorate in philosophy from Columbia in 1929 and joined the faculty of Rutgers full time in 1938. He retired in 1963.

[2] Peter Charanis (b. in Lemnos, Greece, in 1908) was a distinguished Byzantinist on the Rutgers faculty from 1938 to 1976. He died in New Jersey in 1985.

[3] Albert William Holzmann (b. 1894 in Newark, New Jersey, d. 1975 in Highland Park, New Jersey) received his doctorate from Columbia University in 1935. As of 1923 he was instructor of German at Rutgers; Assistant Professor 1927–1931;

Associate Professor 1931–1947; Professor 1947–1960; head of department 1934–1960. He was the author of *Family Relationships in the Dramas of August von Kotzebue* (Princeton: Princeton UP, 1935).

[4] Johannes Nabholz (b. 1905 in Berne, Switzerland, d. 1983 in Vero Beach, Florida) earned a Ph.D. from New York University in 1936. From 1939 to 1974 he taught German literature at Rutgers University. He was the author of *The History of the Faculty of Arts in German Universities* (New York, 1936).

[5] Henry H.L. Schulze (b. 1882 in New York City, d. 1964) took his undergraduate degree from City College in 1903 and his A.M. from Columbia University in 1905. His career at Columbia followed this path: Assistant Professor 1915–1933, Associate Professor 1933–1945, Professor 1945–1948, emeritus 1948–1964. Schulze specialized in German literature of the nineteenth century.

[6] André von Gronicka (b. 1912 in Moscow, Russia, d. 1999 in Manahawkin, New Jersey) emigrated to the United States in 1926. He took his Ph.D. in German from Columbia University in 1942. After teaching at the Universities of Kansas (1937–40) and Chicago (1940–1944) he returned to Columbia where he rose through the ranks until leaving for the University of Pennsylvania in 1962. He retired in 1980. He was the author of publications in the area of Russo-German literary relations, Thomas Mann, and modern drama and novella.

[7] Robert Herndon Fife (b. 1871 in Charlottesville, Virginia, d. 1958) earned his M.A. at the University of Virginia in 1895 but took his doctorate at Leipzig in 1902. He was instructor of German at St. Alban's School in Radford, Virginia and then at Western Reserve University, Cleveland, 1901–1903. Beginning in 1903 he was at Wesleyan until 1920, when he left for Columbia University at the rank of full professor. Fife founded the *Germanic Review* in 1926 and served as president of the MLA beginning in 1944. He edited E. T. A. Hoffmann's *Meister Martin* (1907), Heinrich Heine's *Harzreise* and *Buch Le Grand* (1912). He wrote *Der Wortschatz der englischen Mandeville* (Leipzig, 1902); *The German Empire between Two Wars* (New York, 1916); *Young Luther: The Intellectual and Religious Development of Martin Luther to 1518* (New York: Macmillan, 1928); *Summary of Reports on the Modern Languages* (New York, 1932); *The Revolt of Martin Luther* (New York, 1957).

[8] Frederick William Justus Heuser (b. 1878 in Silesia, Germany, d. 1961) came to the United States in 1889. After studies at Columbia, Berlin, and Munich he joined the Columbia faculty in 1902 and stayed until 1944. He was Director of the Deutsches Haus (1928–1944) and served as an educational specialist to the State Department. His works include *Capitalization in German* (1928); *Gerhart Hauptmann's Trip to America in 1894* (1938); *Hauptmann's Germanen und Römer* (New York, 1942); *Gerhart Hauptmann: Zu seinem Leben und Werk* (Tübingen: Niemeyer, 1961); *German University and Technical Libraries: Report on a Tour of Inspection* (New York: Institute of International Education, 1949).

[9] Peter Viereck, *Metapolitics: From the Romantics to Hitler* (New York: Knopf, 1941).

Response to Walter Sokel

Marc A. Weiner

As always, Professor Sokel has provided us with a text that is both rich and thought-provoking, a text in which he elegantly and forthrightly employs the insights of cultural psychoanalysis — with which we all associate his groundbreaking work on Kafka and Expressionism — in a candid discussion of the trajectory of his own life and career. As someone who is two intellectual generations removed from Professor Sokel, I feel indebted to him and honored to have been asked to discuss some of the issues and questions that his reflections have engendered. In what follows, I wish to make some observations that I feel might serve to illuminate: (1) the degree to which Professor Sokel's experience is representative of his generation; (2) some of the methodological issues and assumptions underlying his reflections on his career; and, above all (3) the ideological implications, whether intended or unacknowledged, of his approach to the material he has chosen to discuss.

The first observation I wish to make is perhaps the most obvious and concerns the belief, harbored in Professor Sokel's youth, that the Germany represented in its literature and other arts may act as a model of a cultural, and perhaps communal, essence that is superior to the realm of politics, and indeed even a counter to it. Of course, such a belief has a longstanding tradition in the bourgeoisie of which Professor Sokel writes and is perhaps most emphatically and encyclopedically articulated in Stefan Zweig's classic *Die Welt von Gestern* (1944), in which time and again the author, like most of the writers Zweig cites of his generation, valorizes aesthetic production as the vessel in which the cultural essence of a nation might be preserved from the barbarous and more base political reality surrounding it. From this notion it is but a small step to the émigrés' investment in their identity as the "true" representatives of German-speaking culture, as "das andere, bessere Deutschland." It is worth asking whether we should view such a belief in hindsight as a kind of salvation for a generation of both

Germans and Jews, or as one of the hallmarks of a way of responding to political forces that tended to make the *Bildungsbürgertum,* to which so many Jews of this generation belonged, as Professor Sokel points out, all the more vulnerable to the enforcement of a political reality that viewed them not as a better Germany, but as a cause and a symptom of Germany's problems. What's more, the question emerges as to whether this belief is more discernible among the Jews of this generation than among their detractors.

The belief in the nonutilitarian value of the arts informs another feature of Professor Sokel's text as well, which is the substance of my second observation. While he characterizes — and rightly criticizes, though in a very gentlemanly way — part of the paradigm of intellectual life at Rutgers and Columbia as one based on identification as the means through which one approached a literary text, he acknowledges that he himself in his youth approached much literature in this very way. What's more, Professor Sokel's text also suggests that such an approach was a hallmark of others in his generation not only in their youth, but as they matured as well. He implies that such an identification is at once both uplifting or regenerative and, at the same time, delimited and perhaps even narcissistic. In terms of the question as to what degree Professor Sokel's reflections are representative of others — whether of his generation in general or, in light of this conference, of its Jewish critics in particular — one must ask whether his own later, mature attraction to Kafka, the early manifestations of which he describes so vividly, is not indebted precisely to this model, especially given his repeated suspicion that his Professor Schulze, as well as Emil Staiger, rejected Kafka because the author was Jewish. That is, the question emerges as to whether not only their vilification of Kafka, but Professor Sokel's own attraction to the writer as well was based on identification. If so, we should seek to identify more precisely, if we can, what is meant by such identification — what are its psychological features and the cultural-social parameters in which it emerges most forcefully? Is it comparable to the kind of empathic, subjective response of which Hinrich Seeba spoke in his enlightening and wide-ranging paper at the beginning of the conference?

We might ask whether this mode of exegesis — qua identification — was typical for both generations (Schulze's and Sokel's), and for both Jews and Germans, or are we to understand it as a singular experience? To what degree may we view Professor Sokel's identificatory approach as symptomatic? And more importantly, if it is based on identification, the question remains unaddressed as to whether we should view this model of exegesis as problematic in terms of the social function of literature, for pushed to its extreme (which I am doing only for the sake of discussion, and not to make a caricature out of Professor Sokel's text), this would suggest that a culture that views Germans and Jews as incompatible would assume that a writer such as Kafka would be best appreciated by Jews and not by Germans and that, conversely, German authors would be best understood by non-Jews. Thus the connection to the theme of this conference. Clearly it is not Professor Sokel's intention to endorse such a notion, but the absence of a commentary on the question of his own interest in Kafka as related to identification with the author not only for his psychological profile but for his cultural identity as a Jew, leads one to reflect upon the ramifications of such an approach. Professor Sokel's interest in problematizing the binarisms everywhere discernible in the culture of his youth is laudable, especially given its social and ideological agenda, but one might ask to what extent it remains based on an unacknowledged model of identification through culture — that is, on cultural identity — be it religious or ethnic.

My third observation concerns Professor Sokel's belief in scholarship and teaching as social engagement, one that may be discerned in much of his published work as well as in his reflections today. This belief is related to a specific and long-held conception of the Enlightenment project as one designed to effect personal, social, and moral development through aesthetic edification. He writes of "our task as teachers of German culture [as being] the highlighting of that not inconsiderable body of German literature that, beginning with the Enlightenment, had been engaged in radical social critique and subversion of authority." Time and again, Professor Sokel's text evinces his unabashed investment in the Enlightenment project as based on a belief in its goals of ethical-moral enhancement and improvement through education, and as one that strove, and perhaps for a time achieved, a German-Jewish symbiosis. In this context he writes that, in their mutual belief in the fundamental incompatibility of Germans and Jews, both germanophobes and Nazis "wished to see a glorious project that had begun with the Enlightenment undone." Such a conceptualization of the Enlightenment is complemented for those of my generation by the work of another Jewish émigré to this country which does not emerge in Professor Sokel's text, namely that of Theodor Wiesengrund Adorno, whose seminal contribution to the discussion of such a symbiosis revolved around the conviction that the *Bildungsbürgertum* of nineteenth- and early twentieth-century Germany and Austria participated in a culture whose investment in an ideology of Enlightenment values — progress, individuality, reason, moral rectitude — was based on the repression of the very psychic forces that would resurface in Nazism and the Holocaust. That is, what we might wish to consider is the question as to the degree to which the belief in the Enlightenment project so forcefully and elegantly presented in Professor Sokel's paper itself might not emerge from — that is, constitute an example of — the very cultural problem that Adorno addresses. The answer to this question, of course, will depend on one's opinion of the veracity of fundamental tenets of the Frankfurt School and of its ability to account for the relationship between what might appear to be incompatible cultural phenomena, in this case beliefs associated with the Enlightenment and the advent of the Holocaust. Clearly, this is of central importance to our examination of Jewish critics responding to much of German literature from the late eighteenth century onwards. Perhaps this helps to explain Professor Sokel's desire to fuse a harmonic union of Kafka and Hoffmann that had never existed in reality. And what, we might ask, would Adorno have made of that?

Finally, much of Professor Sokel's text evinces the conviction that there is much in German culture that is good, that opposes Nazism, and that thereby transcends the baser motivations that propelled and attracted Hitler's followers, as well as the forces that led to the cultural context in which he and they could flourish. This assumption, I think, bears reflection — not the assumption that there may be nobler and morally finer thinkers in Germany's literary and cultural pantheon than Hitler and Goebbels, but the assumption that we must state this fact in order to justify our interest in German culture. Why must we do so? Why do so many scholars today feel — and this is something I hear often — that we must defend the study and teaching of what most people would agree are aesthetic documents replete with questionable or even reprehensible attendant ideas? Do we feel that only ideologically pure art is appropriate for study and education? If so, what literature and artworks would qualify for such scrutiny? While I do not wish to join Daniel Goldhagen and the various germanophobes cited in Professor Sokel's text in claiming that all of German culture somehow led to the Holocaust, I do wish to question the need to justify our intellectual and professional undertaking by pointing to those features of German-speaking culture not blatantly protofascist, or to those that could potentially act as signs of another, better Germany. After all, the anti-Semitic imagination is a fascinating cultural phenomenon and one well worth investigation. The attendant question emerges for this conference as to whether the need to justify German culture by accentuating its more glorious moments is represented especially prominently or pervasively among its Jewish critics (though, personally, I doubt this is the case), or whether it is perhaps a generational phenomenon discernible in the culture of which Professor Sokel speaks. If this is not the case, what accounts for its perpetuation today?

I applaud Professor Sokel's refusal to view Nazis and Jews in black-and-white terms and his ability to uncover the gradations of German cultural history, as suggested by his remarks on Schopenhauer and, to a lesser extent perhaps, on Gottfried Benn. What I wish to draw attention to for the sake of further reflection and discussion is what I believe is a widespread assumption in the academy today that we must highlight such "positive" aspects of Germany's cultural past so as not to scare away or alienate students and administrators in a time of institutional transition. This is not to say that I believe such motivations propelled Professor Sokel's remarks (I don't think that's the case), but it is to point out that an assumption may be discerned therein that has widespread ramifications in our own daily experience as educators of the relationship between Germans and Jews, and of our work as, for some of us, Jewish critics of German literature.

Thus, in summary, my concerns, questions, and the themes and/or areas that I believe would benefit from more extensive discussion are:

(1) the degree to which we wish to view Professor Sokel's reflections as representative of his generation in general or of the experience of his generation of immigrant Jewish scholars in particular;

(2) reading as privileged when it is based on (affirmative) identification;

(3) the investment in what we might call an uncritical model of the Enlightenment project; and

(4) the implied assumption that it is our duty to underscore the fact that there is such a thing as a superior German cultural history.

That Professor Sokel's reflections have raised such questions and issues as these is a testimony to his candor, to his position among his generation of Jewish émigrés who have worked in German Studies in this country, and to the intellectual and ethical quality of the life he has lived. I have spoken out of genuine respect for his professional accomplishments and for the personal experiences he and others of his generation have passed through, for I am well aware that those of us in my own generation, who have entered his profession, have benefited from both.

Panelists' Commentary

HASKELL BLOCK: I too came away from Walter Sokel's challenging and interesting paper with the question how far can we generalize from his experience. These are after all pages of an autobiography and all of us would have individual stories perforce that would shape our own situation. I discussed the program of the meeting before coming up with my good friend in New York, Ludwig W. Kahn, who is a retired professor of German at Columbia University.[1] Ludwig pressed on me the fact that one must make a distinction between refugee scholars who came over with their studies completed — people like Erich Heller or Oskar Seidlin and Ludwig himself — who had their Ph.D. by the time they came to this country as refugees, and those like Walter Sokel who represent another level in the generative process. These situations are essentially different, and it is important to keep these differences in mind. Maybe we could talk a little bit more about that.

I think, too, one could make a further distinction among Jewish refugee scholars who came over before completing their studies and with the development of Comparative Literature, from about the mid-1940s, somewhat after you began your studies, but programs did develop notably at Harvard under Harry Levin (1912–1994), and then Renato Poggioli (1907–1963), and at Yale under René Wellek (1903–1995), there were a few other programs in place. In the late 1940s and in the 1950s the field expanded very considerably and quite a number of the young graduate students who entered comparative studies were in fact from German-speaking lands. I think of people like Ralph Freedman, or Ulrich Weisstein, or Wolfgang Holdheim, or Geoffrey Hartman.[2] The list could go on and on, and it seems to me in an earlier situation these young men might very well have become students in German departments but for reasons not unlike those you indicate and also for the fact that does after all offer a way of bringing the study of literature into closer accord with the way in which we actually apprehend literature and live with it. One can understand the very rapid development in the 1950s and 1960s of Comparative Literature in both private and public universities. I would say more strongly in the public sector, in the large state universities where a number of the people I mentioned had their initiation into the field. The result of this again was to provide some point of interaction with an established tradition in certain areas of European culture.

I went myself, after some work at Harvard, to the Sorbonne where there was an Institut des Littératures Modernes Comparée and where even though the methods were somewhat mechanical, relying heavily on studies of source and influence, there were also new departures that were underway and there was a very decent humanistic concern and genuine preoccupation with the situation of the individual in our time. I illustrate this by just one little anecdote. My mentor Jean Marie Carré (1887–1958) had been at the Sorbonne for many, many years. He did his dissertation on *Goethe en Angleterre*[3] under Fernand Baldensperger (1871–1958), he came from the Alsace-Lorraine, he was a highly cosmopolitan man himself. When shortly after the establishment of the Vichy regime the Sorbonne faculty was assembled for the purpose of listening to the promulgation of the anti-Jewish decrees, whereby all Jewish members of the faculty were forthwith to be dismissed, only one man among that audience rose to his feet and protested with all of the energy in his power, and that man was Carré.

Now, was this because he was a professor of Comparative Literature? I would not go that far, but it does seem to me to tell something about the man who had exemplary courage — which he passed on to his children. His daughter was caught as a courier for the resistance and suffered a rather brutal punishment as a result. But one cannot help thinking of the French experience and the French situation, and we are still living with the aftermath because parenthetically it does seem to me that the Germans have made a far more serious and sustained attempt to face their own history than in some ways have the French. We are beginning to catch up to the Vichy syndrome, and the French are also, I think, becoming much more aware of the enormities of the past.

Well, all this has to do with the refugee scholar. There is also the question of the American scholar in the American university context, and I am very much indebted to Professor Klingenstein's work.[4] Though it discusses much more professors of English studies, there is some attention to comparative literature and the early history, for instance, Joel Spingarn (1875–1939) at Columbia. Harry Levin once commented to me that he thought Spingarn was the greatest comparatist that the United States had yet produced, and that's a very challenging observation and certainly one that is worth reflection. But the discussion is mainly on people like Lionel Trilling (1905–1975), who were professors of English studies. There is a glance at Ludwig Lewisohn's (1892–1955) abortive career as a Germanist, but there isn't much concern really with German studies and perhaps partly because there were very few chairs in German. It was a small field, there were very, very few Jewish professors of German literature in the first four decades of the century and that situation changed. But this would further explain, it seems to me, the reluctance of Jewish scholars. Now, there were some. One thinks of Sol Liptzin at City College in New York.[5] He wrote well on Heine, on Schnitzler,[6] but when he learned of the atrocities perpetrated in Germany in the early 1940s he abruptly stopped teaching German literature and began teaching Yiddish literature instead. He never went back to German studies. He retired to Israel and died not too long ago. But it is, I think, an interesting history. I came to know Harry Slochower (1910–1991).[7] He had been fired at Brooklyn College (1957) during the McCarthy period, and his political record was stridently Marxist, and I don't think Harry ever abandoned Marxism as a faith, but in 1974 he published a little paper in a quarterly called *Judaism* on "What It Means To Be Jewish."[8] Harry was a Germanist. He did his Ph.D. at Columbia, he published his dissertation on Richard Dehmel in 1928,[9] he wrote extensively on modern German literature. He is probably best known for a book, *No Voice is Wholly Lost,*[10] but much of his criticism is myth criticism with a very strong psychoanalytic orientation. This won't take long:

> I was born in Bukowina, a small multi-national state of the old multi-national Austro-Hungarian Empire and came here at the age of thirteen, one year before the outbreak of the First World War. I was raised in the Jewish tradition and at first lived on the lower Manhattan Jewish East Side. While my parents were alive, I participated in religious rituals. Pesach, in particular, was a heart-warming and joyous family gathering. Now, the family is dispersed and I no longer observe any of the religious rituals. Yet, today, I feel more than ever that I am a Jew. For me, then, being Jewish is not related to being religious. It is, rather, an expression of the heart and spirit, probably reaching back to deeply buried unconscious roots. Two historic events cemented this feeling for me: Hitlerism and the recent Yom Kippur attack. (462)

And he goes on to emphasize what seemed to him to distinguish characteristics of the Jewish intellectual:

A critical questioning temper. This temper begins with Hebraic prophetic literature, most eloquently expressed in The Book of Job, and
appearing in Jewish writers, such as Marx, Freud, Kafka, Ernst
Bloch. . . . This attitude has been acclaimed by non-Jews as well, by
Thorstein Veblen who valued Judaism as "a disturber of the intellectual peace." (462)

That's a fine essay of Veblen on the intellectual preeminence of the
Jews in modern Europe.[11] And Veblen was himself not a Jew. Slochower continues:

The second principle is the quest for communal alignment with our
own people and, beyond that, with all peoples. This longing is a
dialectical "corrective" of our historic alienation. (462)

And Slochower goes on to conclude:

Israel once lived in tents and its history begins with exile, as Erich
Kahler put it. Exile begets critical consciousness as well as a yearning for
harmony with others, a longing to be treated as a Mensch. (464)

Well, I think Harry Slochower is reacting here precisely to the enormity of recent history, to the problem of coming to terms with it, and
it seems to me this goes well beyond any doctrinaire communist
apologetics and it would be a mistake, I think, to pigeonhole Harry in
that way. But it does seem to me significant, that the New York Jewish intellectuals, particularly those engaged with German literature,
were passionately committed to social reform. I think of John Gassner
(1903–1967), of his work and the study of world drama and modern
drama, and Gassner's relentless insistence on the social origins and social consequences of dramatic experience. This again, is something
that comes out, it seems to me, of life in New York, of participating in
life in New York, not limited to it, but entirely characteristic of the local scene, and I think that some of this also comes from your experience, Walter.

PETER HELLER: In large agreement with Walter Sokel's talk, I feel
somehow the need to act here as a "Grobian" and to make some remarks that maybe seem obvious, but I feel I must point to some
problematic implications inherent in the theme of this conference.

There is, as we all know, a tradition of German-Jewish criticism of
German literature, going back to Mendelssohn, Rahel Levin Varnhagen, Börne, Heine, the "quarter-Jew" Hofmannsthal, Harden, Kraus,
Kerr, Polgar, Benjamin — down to Reich-Ranicki, including Germanists and scholar-critics like Gundelfinger/Gundolf, Lukács, Erich

Heller, some present here. That Jewish assimilationists — the most significant segment of Jews in terms of contributions to German culture, namely: outsiders striving to be insiders — should develop a special affinity to criticism is not surprising. Moreover, given the unprecedented German persecution and murder of Jews *and* the foundation of a Jewish state claiming to speak for all Jews as a nation with its own language (though one alien to Jews outside that state), and given the resurgence or continuity of German natives claiming that Jews don't belong in their country, it is also understandable that there should be perceived a need to *justify* the interest of Jews in German language and culture.

Peter Heller teaching at SUNY Buffalo, 1988

Yet, speaking at least for those who grew up in that German language and culture, I think it nonetheless *astonishing* that this issue (which is, in some sense, implicated in this conference) has been raised and continues to be raised. For nothing is more natural than the bond to one's mother tongue and its culture, the native country which is the country of one's childhood. And I don't think it would ever occur to anyone to question, or make an issue of, or demand the justification of an exiled Russian or exiled Chinese or exiled American for their being concerned with Russian or Chinese literature and culture, or the American language, culture, and country.

I regret that the challengingly impertinent questioning of the interest of Jews in German language and literature by Jewish chauvinists (or, say, by severely moralizing American Jews who have no inkling of what that bygone German-Jewish culture was like) has not been made explicit so far at this conference which, I believe, would never have come into being, had there not been felt the *need* to respond to the persistent question that Sokel's paper is the first to address, the question: "How could you, as a Jew, still be concerned (and concerned in a *positive* sense) with German language and culture?"

For it seems that what is hardly waiting in the wings any longer is a new intolerance in the name of ethnicity (if not race or religion); and unless this intolerance is repudiated, even the benevolent attempt to single out an allegedly specifically Jewish contribution to the criticism of German literature might seem to provide grist on the mill of invidious discrimination. Once more: given memories of the Holocaust, given Israel, and given resurgent or continuing anti-Semitism, we should acknowledge that we are on problematic grounds, in a still traumatic sphere, which is at the same time ridden with clichés, open to political exploitation, media hype, hypocrisies, resentments buried under heaps of "Wiedergutmachung," self-righteous claims, protestations of guilt and of innocence, and lies, lies, lies. We should take this into account with a view not only to the restricted though sympathetic, if woefully isolated and ever-shrinking contexts of our German departments, but with a view enlarged, say, to the wider screen of an explicitly Jewish-American university like Brandeis and the American-Jewish contexts, with a view to the German-speaking countries with their tiny remnants of Jews, and the state of Israel that, by and large, I believe, is fairly predicated on the conviction — and the imperative — that one cannot be a Jew *and* German (or Austrian for that matter); a conviction shared, it seems, by many or most Germans (or Austrians for that matter).

Peter Heller in the 1940s

I just felt I needed to say this, in response to Sokel's sincere account, untarnished by the sterile and narrow-minded pretense to political correctness; and as a reminder of where we are now.

SUSANNE KLINGENSTEIN (MIT): My response to Walter Sokel is that of an outsider, an Americanist, who is working on American-Jewish literary critics. I left Germanistik and my special love, *das Wiener fin de siècle*, about ten years ago. I would like to respond very briefly to four different areas Professor Sokel touched upon in his talk:

1. Identity Formation in Vienna

Professor Sokel's intellectual development seems to me unexceptional, if not typical for Jewish literary academics of his generation in two interconnected ways. First, in the lack of Jewish knowledge (or literacy) and Jewish identification.[12] His assertion that in the 1930s, "I considered myself neither German nor Austrian nor Jewish, but a human being, pure and simple, a member of humanity. My homeland was the world," could have been made, *mutatis mutandis,* by American-Jewish literary critics of his generation, especially by men such as Harvard's first Jewish professor in the English Department, Harry Levin. Second, as a youth Sokel identified not with the Jews but with a strong nation (Germany) along two trajectories: he recognizes himself in the misfits, outcasts, and artists of modern German literature, and he sympathizes with the literature of the enlightened political left.

What *surprises* about Professor Sokel's development is how radical Sokel's nonidentification with the Jews and Jewishness is (he confesses having been angrier at the Allies bombing German cities than at the operators of the gas chambers) and that Austrian literature never comes into view as a vehicle of identification (one could enter into fascinating speculations why that should be so). Here is my way of making sense of these phenomena: Professor Sokel's nonidentification with Jewishness may be due to the extensive negative stereotyping of Jews in Vienna he witnessed during his childhood and adolescence. Moreover, Sokel describes himself as a "lonely child," and speaks of his "isolation and feelings of inferiority." His self-perception was perhaps due to a confluence of culture (negative stereotypes, incidences of anti-Semitism), unsupportive parenting, and personality. In any event such a self-perception makes it unlikely that as a child or youth he would identify with a beleaguered people (the Jews); rather, he would wish to identify with a strong people who could make him feel secure. Indeed, Sokel finds strong offers of identification in the artists and outcasts portrayed in German literature, because *they* are eventually redeemed into a strong master culture.

It would be interesting to know here why exactly Professor Sokel was turned off by Jewish Orthodoxy, as he indicates, and what his Jewish education consisted of.

2. The Importance of Kafka

Professor Sokel's decision to study German was made for understandable emotional and pragmatic reasons. The overpowering effect of Kafka's *Metamorphosis* seems to me entirely unsurprising. Kafka's novella presents a misfit who is not redeemed and who reflects more closely than Thomas Mann's heroes Walter Sokel's own situation in the 1930s and early 1940s. Indeed, Professor Sokel asserts, "I still recognized myself in the outcast hero, the absolute misfit, the totally isolated reject of humanity." Unrecognized by Professor Sokel at the time is what I believe to be the Jewish element in Kafka's sense of self that transforms Gregor Samsa into a roach ("Ungeziefer"), and which I suspect plays itself out in Sokel's own self-perception as shaped in the anti-Semitic Vienna of his youth.

But Kafka is important not only because Sokel recognizes himself in Kafka's non-heroes, but also, as Professor Sokel points out, because of the surrealism of Kafka's settings: a "dreamlike quality . . . made these texts so liberating an experience for me." What is the liberating element? Kafka's surrealism allows an escape from German reality to which Sokel was tied by the German literature he admired. In fact, Kafka is the answer to a lot of problems for the young literary scholar Walter Sokel in America: Kafka wrote in German, the mother tongue to which Sokel was so attached in exile; Kafka was a Jew whose Jewishness did not seem to matter, and he was a writer who during the late 1940s and 1950s was one of the stars of high modernism in America and for a while became the dejudaized epitome of the intellectual's alienation from mass society.

3. Academe

During the 1940s and 1950s Jewish professors at Columbia (and elsewhere) were characterized by a general desire to be seen as members of high culture, not as Jews. It was alright then to be Jewish by birth but not by cultural or political affiliation. This would change with Israel's victory in the Six-Day War of June 1967, which for American Jews ushered in a period of re-ethnicization.

Lionel Trilling said in 1944 at a symposium organized by a Jewish magazine: "I do not have in mind to serve by my writing any Jewish purpose. I should resent it if a critic of my work were to discover in it either faults or virtues which he called Jewish."[13] This was a fairly typical attitude at the time.

With the expansion of colleges and universities due to the GI Bill Jews were hired in large numbers. However, Jewish instructors hired to teach in American humanities departments did not do Jewish cultural work until the late sixties (among the rare exceptions is Sol Liptzin, a professor of German at City College who wrote on Yiddish and other Jewish literatures).[14] I was somewhat surprised to learn that at Rutgers University, which is close to New York City with its large Jewish population and the example of many Jewish professors at City University and Columbia, pressure was exerted on Walter Sokel not to become a literary academic. I am wondering whether Jews were similarly advised at history departments in the country at a time (around 1940) when reservations vis-à-vis Jews were beginning to wane at major universities such as Harvard and Columbia.

4. German-Jewish Symbiosis

Finally, I would like to comment on Professor Sokel's claim that a reciprocity existed in the cultural exchange between German and Jewish thought. For Professor Sokel the German-Jewish symbiosis is a "dream, that is, a reality in the making, pregnant with enormous possibilities for the good of both sides." He argues that "the same kind of thinking in terms of irreconcilable opposites that had led to the destruction of six million Jews [he] saw continued in those Jews who considered the barrier between Jews and Germans valid for all time and wanted it perpetuated"; and he asserts that the "germanophobes and Nazis shared an identical goal — an absolute and everlasting separation of Germans and Jews."

It seems to me that Jews who deny the existence of a German-Jewish symbiosis (as did Gershom Scholem, for example) do not necessarily deny its theoretical possibility. And they most certainly do not share the goals of the Nazis. They do not consider the "other" inferior, or vermin that needs to be exterminated. There is precious little evidence for Professors Sokel's claim that the Germans were susceptible to Jewish thought before the Second World War. I see no evidence that the German-Jewish symbiosis was a reciprocal affair.

Professor Sokel's term "germanophobes" for Jews who question the reality of a German-Jewish symbiosis seems to me purely polemical. Rather, these Jews became indifferent to Germans and German culture. His identification of the doubters of a German-Jewish symbiosis (germanophobes) with Nazis implies that the former would be obsessed with what they have turned away from (just as the Nazis were really obsessed with the Jews). This reveals that Professor Sokel does not think about Jewishness in terms of positive content, that is, as something that can take the place of German culture. Yet doubters of the German-Jewish symbiosis, intellectuals such as Gershom Scholem (or Cynthia Ozick in this country) turned away from German culture and put in its place Jewish culture.

The notion of a German-Jewish symbiosis seems to me entirely erroneous because it posits two irreconcilable entities, Jews and Germans, who become interdependent for pragmatic purposes. This was (and is) clearly not the case. Jews born and raised in Germany think of themselves quite naturally as German Jews. Whereas I do not know of any Germans before 1945 who as Germans would wish to embrace Jewish ways of life and thought. That, since the early 1960s, *Germans* have expressed an interest in the reality of a German-Jewish symbiosis is quite understandable but misleading in its implication that there had been a special receptivity among Germans for Jewish thought and culture when this was clearly not the case.

Discussion

TOM KOVACH (UNIVERSITY OF ARIZONA): I would like to take up from Susanne Klingenstein in questioning the reassertion of a German-Jewish symbiosis. Just for a humorous anecdote, I met Walter during the break after the morning session, and I said that I had been a little distressed about what I perceived of yesterday's attempt to rehabilitate the notion of German-Jewish symbiosis, and I was so glad to hear that being problematized again this morning. And he said, oh well, you are going to hate my talk. I didn't hate it, but I found it very inspiring and moving. But I do want indeed to question that — if this seems ungracious then at least you're prepared. Two things that I would really like to raise. One is the biological origin of that metaphor and the other is its utopian content. I simply feel that to perpetuate anything, any biological discourse, in reference to the encounter between German and Jewish culture, mentalities, or whatever in light of the history of our century is just very, very troublesome. And I think that not to discredit what is wanted in the use of that phrase but just to discredit that metaphor, I think we would all do well to leave it behind us. And the other is precisely its utopian content; that is, I think we all agree on wanting to rescue something of the encounter between these two cultures and not to regard it as a one-way street leading to Auschwitz and that being its sole meaning, but yet to talk about the symbiosis, isn't this so much a product of an earlier age in which one could think that the Nazis were an aberration, that this really never was going to happen, and if we want to rescue not only the heritage from Mendelssohn and Heine onward through 1933, but also (and others have alluded to this) the potentiality of a new and not all that tiny Jewish life in Germany today, shouldn't we use a discourse that points in new directions and not try to revive that?

WALTER SOKEL: I would like to respond just very briefly. Talking in biological metaphors, just because the Nazis talked about it, I should desist from it because they did it? Because after all we are biology and the biological discourse is a very important one, it seems to me, even though it has been abused by racists. So I feel perfectly all right. Now, I also used it in a way in quotation marks, because it is being bandied about and I simply used something, but one would have to go into this in great detail, what is meant by symbiosis, but I would like to make one point that also answers Professor Klingenstein, namely that it seems to me that I would still insist on the similarity between the Nazis and the, what I call germanophobes (that's an exaggeration, but I would still stick to that term), in their aim. Because the aim is the same, namely a "German-rein" or "Judenrein" Germany and a "German-rein" Jewishness. And I think that's really a terrible kind of program.

NOAH ISENBERG (WESLEYAN UNIVERSITY): I would like to apply a bit more pressure to this question of German-Jewish symbiosis in referring to Moritz Goldstein's very famous polemic of 1912 in the *Kunstwart* entitled "Deutsch-jüdischer Parnass."[15] In the later, the subsequent writing in the *Leo Baeck Year Book* (1957) he refers to this as precisely what Professor Sokel has just described for us.[16] The most famous passage of the 1912 essay is: "We Jews are administering the spiritual property of a nation which denies our right and our ability to do so." But in his retrospective remarks on this piece, Goldstein points out that the reception, and there was an enormous debate, and some of you may be familiar with it, in the reception of the piece, it was criticized, or assumed rather, that the article could have been written by a Nazi, a protofascist, or an exclusionary political Zionist. I would be very curious, how you, Professor Sokel, would read this very important text, a polemical text, that may in some way bear, I think, on your reading of the problematic notion of German-Jewish symbiosis. So I thought I should evoke this text to apply as I said a bit more pressure to this vexed problem of a German-Jewish symbiosis.

WALTER SOKEL: My answer is very brief. Unfortunately I must admit I am not familiar with it, so I can't comment on it. But perhaps you can enlighten me on it and then we can discuss it.

HANS WETZSTEIN: So far this symposium has carefully avoided any political implication that would be behind a criticism of German literature, be Jewish or otherwise which would be helpful in explaining how something like Hitler happened in Germany. Now, that's for the political department. But I don't think we literature departments can be that puristic. And I mention two German authors who were very critical. One is Emil Ludwig. He wrote in 1942 the history of *The Germans,* not published in German until 1945.[17] He published it in English, French, and Spanish. And it's very critical of the Germans but it's also an attempt to explain why these waves of power supremacy happened. And another author is Lion Feuchtwanger who in 1930 wrote a book called *Erfolg* about the first attempt of Hitler to succeed in Munich.[18] Whenever Americans ask me what to read which explains how something like that could happen in Germany, I recommend Lion Feuchtwanger. There is a closing here. I asked Harry Levin at Harvard once whether he had ever seen it. And his reply shocked me. He said: "Feuchtwanger (it was at the time of McCarthy) Feuchtwanger, isn't he a leftist?" For a professor of literature, I didn't think that was a very good answer.

FRANK TROMMLER: I have a compliment and a comment and a question for Walter Sokel. The compliment is certainly something that is not only for the presentation but also for the openness with which Walter Sokel has received younger scholars from Germany, including myself. He also helped to open up a pretty narrow American German-istik towards a more comparative view, towards modern authors, not just Kafka, but also others, especially with Expressionism. And when I came in the later 1960s that was very important, almost a project of renewing Germanistik, and I had seen the German university scene was going on in the United States, so that the later feedback towards German Germanisten from the United States has started with a lot of opening the field that could happen thanks to Jewish and to some extent non-Jewish immigrants of your generation. So this is the compliment.

And the comment, I would like to also say, has to do with the first part. One has to see it institutionally. American Germanistik was, let's say, a very sedate enterprise and with a lot of problems keeping out the political implications that the gentleman just mentioned, that in 1945 certainly the last anti-Semite finally kept his mouth shut when the news of the concentration camps reached German departments. And one shouldn't misunderstand that the late forties and fifties were the period of McCarthy. A lot of political commitment among immigrants could not be expressed, so that it was a double, or triple problem to be Jewish, to be Jewish in German departments, and then the German within the American surroundings, and then also being sometimes left in the McCarthy era. So I think there are many reasons for a less politicized German studies or Germanistik at that time.

And now comes my question. I would like to know, because I have a lot of contacts with younger people and Jewish Americans who study and deal with Germany. Professor Sokel, I would like to ask about your very strong statement for German culture and not dividing out the Jewish part of it. Did you in your later work from the fifties and sixties onward stress the Jewish components in the teaching of German literature? That would be one part, and the other, how have your views changed in the last thirty years, because there are many younger American Jews studying and teaching German whose acculturation to German culture is really very different from yours. And this is my question: what is your advice or your point of view towards these younger generations?

WALTER SOKEL: Thank you very much. For the first question I would say that I treated the Jewish component of German literature marginally. That is, in giving courses, in discussing Jewish authors, I did mention, never left it out, the Jewish background, but I never made a big issue of it. So it was marginalized in my treatment. But it was marginalized together with the biographical in general, you see. So it wasn't just the Jewish that was marginalized. I marginalized the biographical element to some extent. But to the second, it is difficult, I didn't quite understand the gist of our question, what advice would I give to Jewish-American students of today on what? I mean, I am not sure how I should address this. I don't understand the question. I mean I understand your words, but I don't know what the point of the question is, you see. [*Frank Trommler clarifies his question, but does not use a microphone, so his words could not be transcribed.* EDS.] Well, I would say it's a very important field, and I certainly would not inhibit it, but I would not necessarily go out of my way to encourage it, but would merely say, encourage it wherever it is found to be desired. I would not promote it actively to a terrible degree.

PETER DEMETZ: I have one comment and a few remarks, very short. First of all I would say I am very dubious in a discussion, in a theoretical discussion for "erkenntnistheoretische" reasons, about the terms "typical" and "representative." It is too difficult to say what is typical. Statistical? Or representative? What is typical? That is all I have to say about that. Typical is often that which appeals to our own attachment, that's my suspicion. Second, I would say that when I continued my education at Columbia, I really received an education in Walter Sokel's apartment. I remember we were sitting there together, and we had totally different opinions. Walter always stressed historic context and philosophy, and I always said, syntax, syntax, syntax, because I came from the formalist end of the spectrum. But I always thought of Walter as representative of a new course that Lionel Trilling introduced at Columbia. I think you were teaching that, and that I think deeply impressed me. But we were of two opinions and I think we have kept these two opinions. Thirdly, and now I am beginning to be a little polemical I think, the question of the past of National Socialism and fascism. I really think — and I don't want an answer, because you will clearly prove that I am wrong — I think the specificity of fascism and National Socialism, etc. is not such that we can establish an "Ahnenreihe" of high philosophers and poets who then, as it were, flow into the mouths of Goebbels and Hitler. What we have to see is a history of the pragmatism of power. National Socialism had no philosophy, had no ideology except two, destroy the Jews and take the East. Otherwise everything was on the table and could be manipulated. There was one section early which said nationalize the department stores, because they were Jewish, or nationalize the big banks, there was a very leftist wing, which was totally sacrificed in the course of electoral campaigns. I simply doubt that for instance Walter's concern with finding out who are the philosophers and who are the poets who could have been protofascists, really pays. I think it is a "Systemzwang" coming from the old "Geistesgeschichte," assuming that if I have a political phenomenon, I have to have a grandfather in philosophy. I *radically* doubt that. I think if you look at fascism and the National Socialists, it is a matter of the political departments, or if you are interested, of establishing what it is to have power and to manipulate ideas that can be taken from almost a postmodern repertory.

SUSANNE KLINGENSTEIN: Do you think you could establish though an "Ahnenreihe" for the two goals that you have identified for Nazism to kill the Jews and take the East.

PETER DEMETZ: To my mind the relationship of the Nazis to these ideas was purely pragmatical. And if this concern with their philosophical antecedents doesn't bring out a totally cynical and pragmatical attitude to these ideas, it's on the wrong track.

JEFFREY SAMMONS (YALE UNIVERSITY): I just felt the need to defend our field a little bit against the charge of political abstinence. If there's been anything wrong with our field in the last twenty years, that is certainly not it. I wanted to say that I thought that the two examples raised were not the best ones. Emil Ludwig was after all the biographer of Mussolini.[19] When he was in the exile community in the United States he became very alienated from it because of a feeling of an over-identification of American right-wing politics. Feuchtwanger is on the other side. There could be a reason why Feuchtwanger's persistent and naive Stalinism might get on somebody's nerves, and as far as *Erfolg* is concerned, it has kind of a standard Marxist interpretation of the inflation as being caused by rich farmers starving the city. And the representative who is supposed to be the person who acts and looks like Hitler in the situation is really a pathetic, a comical figure, who is being raised beyond his justification. He is a kind of novelistic counterpart to Charlie Chaplin's Great Dictator. And although I think we can understand how this would happen in the circumstance, I am rather doubtful of the explanatory power of that particular novel.

BRITTAIN SMITH: I would like to make a brief commentary expressing my personal gratitude to Professor Sokel for all that he has taught us, and me, not only about Kafka and Expressionism, and Musil, but also about the grace of critical writing. And I wholeheartedly endorse his attempt here today to break down dualistic thinking. But I was a little troubled by some parts of the talk, for it seems to me in that attempt to break down, it might have also upheld some sorts of dualistic thinking. And partly having been trained by reading Professor Sokel I am used to paying attention to metaphors. I was struck by two metaphors that entered. One was that of *infiltration*, Jewish culture has infiltrated German culture, the other was the metaphor of *salt*. German Jewish culture as "das Gewürz, die Zukost." It seems to me if we are going to break down dualistic thinking, we need at least to give as a preliminary stage equal brain to both parts of the topic and discussion, and I say this with great respect.

WALTER SOKEL: Can I make just a brief comment, factually. The metaphor came from Ruth Martini, about salt, not from myself. I put it in quotes.

ABIGAIL GILLMAN: Thank you for sharing your experiences. As an American Jew from New York City who entered the field forty years later than you did, I can still say that many of your experiences ring true for me, many of your feelings and questions strike chords within me and my own experience. Quickly on the question that Marc Weiner raised, identification versus non-identification. This may be another false dualism. It seems to me that when you turn to modernism and surrealism, it's precisely that which enables a nonmimetic identification. That's exactly the point. And on dualism: I was thinking about the ways in which you in your teaching tried to subvert dualism, for example, looking at the affinities between Romanticism and

Expressionism, or surrealism, or Freud and Schopenhauer. It's not just the Jewish and the German, but much can be Jewish without being called Jewish or even being Jewish. There can be an affinity between Christian and Catholic romanticism and Jewish modernism and it's neither Jewish nor Christian, but the labels are the problem. And finally, I was thinking, while you were speaking, of a text that my friend Bill Donahue first showed to me, which is a letter that Ernst Toller, the Expressionist writer Ernst Toller (1893–1939), sent to Goebbels after the book burning.[20] It is an extraordinary letter where he in fact says: you claim to represent German culture and act in the name of German culture, well, you are not. You are not the representatives of Goethe and Schiller, you are not their heirs, *we* are. You are trying to claim it, but instead you are trampling it, you are distorting it, you represent the antithesis of what that tradition represents. It's a very powerful text and also a very powerful pedagogical tool for our students today to see.

Editors' Annotations

[1] Ludwig W. Kahn (b. 1910 in Berlin) emigrated first to Switzerland, where he received his doctorate from the University of Berne in 1934, and then from England to the United States: University of Rochester (1936–1940), Bryn Mawr College (1940–1942), Vassar College (1942–1945), City College, New York (1944–1967), Columbia (1967–1979). He wrote *Shakespeares Sonette in Deutschland* (Strassburg: Heitz, 1934); *Social Ideals in German Literature, 1770–1830* (New York: Columbia UP, 1938); *Literatur und Glaubenskrise* (Stuttgart: Kohlhammer, 1964).

[2] Educated at the University of Washington and Brown University, Ralph Freedman (b. 1920 in Hamburg) took his Ph.D. in Comparative Literature from Yale in 1954. He taught for many years at Princeton University, until retiring in 1988. Ulrich W. Weisstein (b. 1925 in Breslau) studied originally (1947–1950) at the University of Frankfurt. In 1954 he took his doctorate in Comparative Literature from the University of Indiana, Bloomington, where he also did most of his teaching until retiring in 1990. Comparatist Wolfgang Holdheim (b. 1926 in Berlin) took undergraduate and graduate degrees at UCLA but earned his Ph.D. at Yale in 1956. Most of his career was spent at Cornell University (1969–90). Leaving Germany in his teens and coming to the United States via England, Geoffrey H. Hartman (b. 1929 in Germany) took his Ph.D. from Yale in 1953. Nearly all of his teaching years were spent there. He retired in 1997.

[3] Jean Marie Carré, *Goethe en Angleterre: Etude de littérature comparée* (Paris: Plon-Nourrit, 1920); *Goethe en Angleterre: Bibliographie critique et analytique* (Paris: Plon-Nourrit, 1920).

[4] Susanne Klingenstein, *Jews in the American Academy, 1900–1940: The Dynamics of Intellectual Assimilation* (New Haven: Yale UP, 1991).

[5] For more information see *Identity and Ethos: A Festschrift for Sol Liptzin on the Occasion of his 85th Birthday*, ed. Mark H. Gelber (New York, Berne, Frankfurt am Main: Peter Lang, 1986. Sol[omon] Liptzin (b. 1901 in Satanow, Ukraine, d. 1995 in Jerusalem) taught at City College from 1923–1963 as a professor of Comparative Literature. Of particular interest in the present context is his *Germany's Stepchildren* (Philadelphia, 1944), which explores the attitude of German-Jewish writers toward their origins.

[6] Solomon Liptzin, *Heine* (Richmond, Atlanta [etc.]: Johnson, 1928; rpt. New York: City College P, 1962); *Arthur Schnitzler* (New York: Prentice-Hall, 1932; rpt. Riverside, CA: Ariadne, 1995).

[7] For more information see *Myth, Creativity, Psychoanalysis: Essays in Honor of Harry Slochower*, ed. Maynard Solomon with the assistance of Sophie Wilkens and Donald M. Kaplan (Detroit: Wayne State UP, 1978). In 1952 Slochower was called before a Senate Internal Security subcommittee charged with the investigation of subversive activities. When asked if he had been a communist, he invoked the Fifth Amendment and was dismissed from his post in Comparative Literature at Brooklyn College. Slochower subsequently worked as a psychoanalyst and taught at the New School of Social Research from 1964 until 1989.

[8] Harry Slochower, "What It Means To Be Jewish," *Judaism: A Quarterly Journal of Jewish Life and Thought* 23 (Fall 1974): 462–64.

[9] Harry Slochower, *Richard Dehmel, der Mensch und der Denker: Eine Biographie seines Geistes im Spiegelbild der Zeit* (Dresden: C. Reissner, 1928).

[10] Harry Slochower, *No Voice is Wholly Lost: Writers and Thinkers in War and Peace* (New York: Creative Age P, 1945).

[11] Thorstein Veblen, "The Intellectual Pre-Eminence of Jews in Modern Europe" (1919) is reprinted in Thorstein Veblen, *Essays in Our Changing Order*, ed. Leon Ardzrooni (New York: Viking, 1934), 227–29; the passage quoted by Slochower is found on p. 227.

[12] In a conversation with Walter Sokel after the panel discussion I learned that he had been very observant as a boy and wanted to become a rabbi. He became disillusioned with Judaism when he encountered the writings of H. G. Wells. [SK]

[13] "Under Forty: A Symposium on American Literature and the Younger Generation of American Jews," *Contemporary Jewish Record* 7 (February 1944): 15. Cf. for the larger context Susanne Klingenstein, *Enlarging America: The Cultural Work of Jewish Literary Scholars, 1930–1990* (Syracuse, New York: Syracuse UP, 1998), 207–16.

[14] Liptzin's published works include *The Flowering of Yiddish Literature* (New York: T. Yoseloff, 1963) and *A History of Yiddish Literature* (Middle Village, NY: Jonathan David, 1972).

[15] Moritz Goldstein, "Deutsch-jüdischer Parnaß," *Der Kunstwart* 25 (1912): 281–94 where he wrote: "Wir Juden verwalten den geistigen Besitz eines Volkes, das uns die Berechtigung und die Fähigkeit dazu abspricht." — For the context of this article cf. Steven E. Aschheim, "1912. The publication of Moritz Goldstein's

'The German-Jewish Parnassus' sparks a debate over assimilation, German culture, and the 'Jewish spirit,'" in *Yale Companion to Jewish Writing and Thought in German Culture, 1096–1996,* ed. Sander L. Gilman and Jack Zipes (New Haven and London: Yale UP, 1997), 297–305.

[16] Moritz Goldstein, "German Jewry's Dilemma: The Story of a Provocative Essay," *Leo Baeck Institute Year Book* 2 (1957): 236–54.

[17] Emil Ludwig, *The Germans* (London: H. Hamilton, 1942); *Geschichte der Deutschen: Studien über Geist und Staat* (Zürich: C. Posen, 1945).

[18] *Erfolg: Drei Jahre Geschichte einer Provinz* (Berlin: Kiepenheuer, 1930); English edition: *Success: Three Years in the Life of a Province,* trans. Edwin Muir (London: M. Secker, 1930).

[19] Emil Ludwig, *Talks with Mussolini,* trans. Paul Eden and Cedar Paul (London: G. Allen & Unwin, 1932).

[20] Ernst Toller, "Offener Brief an Herrn Goebbels," *Aufruf: Streitschrift für Menschenrechte 1* (Prague, 1933), reprinted in Ernst Toller, *Gesammelte Werke I: Kritische Schriften, Reden und Reportagen,* ed. John M. Spalek und Wolfgang Frühwald (Munich: Hanser, 1978), 76–77.

6: German Literature in the Public Sphere

J. P. Stern, St. John's College, Cambridge
(© Cambridge University Library)

An Appreciation of the Work
of J. P. Stern, Siegbert Prawer,
and George Steiner

Ritchie Robertson

S OME YEARS AGO Jeffrey Sammons published his considerations on the invisibility of German scholars in the United States, maintaining that for all the impact they had on the reading public at large, their conferences might as well be held in Klagenfurt.[1] I assume that in a civilized society there is interest in and discussion of literature, carried on through university courses, literary journals, newspaper book reviews, and that the major literatures of the world should feature in this discussion. In offering an unavoidably sketchy appreciation of the work of three critics, J. P. Stern, Siegbert Prawer, and George Steiner, I want to stress their contributions to stimulating among the wider reading public an interest in German literature and in the wider cultural and historical questions which the study of German literature, especially that of the twentieth century, inevitably raises. For I also assume that German studies in universities cannot in the long run retain their vitality if they are detached from the interests of intelligent people outside universities.

The Jewishness of my three chosen critics is relevant in varying degrees. For Prawer, the author of *Heine's Jewish Comedy,* and for Steiner, with his many reflections on Jewish identity and indeed the status of Western culture after the Shoah, it is an unignorable aspect of their work: in Steiner's case, clearly central. It is a major topic in his most recent collection of essays, in his autobiography, and in the collection of tributes to him compiled a few years ago by his admirers.[2] The late Peter Stern is not so easily classified. A biographical tribute by his pupil Michael Beddow begins: "Joseph Peter Maria Stern was born in Prague on Christmas Day 1920 into a Czech-speaking family of Jewish descent and Roman Catholic beliefs."[3] He would not have been defined as a Jew but for the catch-all character of the Nuremberg Laws. In this he resembled two of his own intellectual heroes and ex-

emplars, Ludwig Wittgenstein and Erich Auerbach; another comparison might be with Hugo von Hofmannsthal. To these writers, however, their Jewish descent was not something to be wholly expunged
and forgotten.

> Ganz vergessener Völker Müdigkeiten
> kann ich nicht abtun von meinen Lidern

Many readers, including Prawer, have taken these lines from "Manche
freilich . . ." as Hofmannsthal's reflection on his Jewish ancestry; be
that as it may, concern over Jewishness can certainly be found in his
work, as in that of Auerbach and Wittgenstein.[4]

Next, what is the specific contribution of Jewish refugees to the
place of German literature in British literary life? Can one say, indeed,
that there is a specific contribution made by such people? A well-
known attempt to characterize the specific contribution to British
culture by Central European émigrés was made some thirty years ago
by Perry Anderson. Considering such figures as Wittgenstein, Popper,
Gombrich, Berlin, and Namier, he argued that they formed a "White
Emigration" (in contrast to the "Red Emigration" of the Frankfurt
School to the United States). They came especially from Austria and
found congenial the empiricism, the anti-intellectualism, and the conservatism of a British culture which at that time was badly in need of
new blood. "A White Emigration rolled across the flat expanse of
English intellectual life, capturing sector after sector, until this traditionally insular culture became dominated by expatriates of heteroge-
neous calibre."[5] They shared the English antipathy to any totalizing
theory of society and culture such as those offered by Marx and
Hegel. Unlike such continental anti-Marxists as Weber, they did not
reply with a counter-theory. Instead, they concentrated on the conventions of language use (Wittgenstein and ordinary language philosophy), on political history as determined by immediate material
interests instead of ideology (Namier), on art history as an unexplained succession of styles (Gombrich). I do not necessarily want to
endorse Anderson's polemical term "White Emigration" or to associate my three critics with it, but it must be said — and I shall return to
this at the close of my paper — that the political implications of their
work are staunchly liberal and, in undoctrinaire ways, anti-Marxist.

Anderson's paper also reminds us that since the war British society
has been extremely free from anti-Semitism and hospitable towards
Jews. Not only have many distinguished Jews earned high honors —

one thinks of Sir Karl Popper, Sir Ernst Gombrich, Sir Isaiah Berlin, and of the many Jews in the House of Lords and in successive Cabinets, especially under Margaret Thatcher — but there is in present-day Britain little interest in identifying Jews. The Jew-sniffing of Edwardian times, found in the novels of Hilaire Belloc and the letters of T. S. Eliot, is largely a thing of the past.[6] In German studies one can find a curious form of Jew-sniffing in the once much-read survey of modern German literature by Jethro Bithell, Head of the German Department at Birkbeck College, London, from 1910 to 1938: this survey was first published in 1932 in the book *Germany: A Companion to German Studies* and reprinted many times with remarkably few changes.[7] He reveals a conservative literary taste with a weakness for "Heimatdichtung."

He provides half a sentence on Kafka (307), and half a sentence on Brecht (shared with Bronnen, 312); nothing on Musil; Heym, Trakl, and Stadler get one uninformative sentence each; Rilke is represented only by *Das Stunden-Buch* (282). He dislikes Jewish Vienna: "Voluptuous Vienna, between the nations, takes into its literature moods from all its neighbours and becomes international, the more easily as its greatest writers are Jews or half-Jews who have the typical Viennese mentality (soft and cynical and half-despairing — Vienna is the city of suicides), and are yet, with their limitless receptivity, half-Italian, or half-French, or half-Slav" (283). In 1932 Hofmannsthal is "half a Jew" (283), in the revised text of 1955 he is "the great-grandson of a Jew."[8] "To go from Jewish Vienna to Carl Spitteler . . . is like an escape to mountain heights," we are told (287–88). But Jews from outside Vienna fare no better: "The historical novels of Lion Feuchtwanger . . . owe their sales to their massed filth" (301); "since Wassermann is a Jew, his native province is not so much Franconia as a world of ideas, unctuously oriental to a great extent in substance and presentment" (291–92).

The conservative tastes and also the political naïveté too often found among British Germanists in the 1930s are reflected in the early issues of the journal *German Life and Letters,* founded by L. A. Willoughby in 1936 at a time when relations between Britain and Germany were thought to be improving. They include lectures by two writers favored by the National Socialist regime, Erwin Guido Kolbenheyer and Hans Grimm, originally delivered on tours of Britain, and an account of a "Dichtertreffen" held in Grimm's house at Lippoldsberg to which Willoughby and other British professors were invited and where they met Rudolf Binding, R. A. Schröder, Börries von

Münchhausen, E. E. Dwinger and other pro-Nazi writers.[9] It is a relief to learn that, though an antifascist exile in London, the socialist writer Fritz Gross, described *German Life and Letters* as "stark angebräunt," Goebbels's agent in London reported that despite the journal's professed neutrality, its rejection of Nazism was unequivocal.[10] However, it does seem that British professors of German were somewhat naive about German politics and out of touch with modernist currents in German literature.

In the 1930s German studies in Britain were a small-scale affair and could accommodate few refugees. As an additional hindrance, some Jewish refugees found themselves confined in camps on the Isle of Man as a result of the catch-all internment policy introduced in panic by the British government in May, 1940. Internment, as is well known, affected many anti-Nazi refugees, such as Renate Scholem, niece of the Kabbalah scholar Gershom Scholem and daughter of the German Communist Werner Scholem who was approaching his death in Oranienburg while she was confined on the Isle of Man.[11] After the war, however, native German speakers were needed in German departments, though sometimes viewed with unease, and numerous immigrants were employed, often people who had already studied at British universities. "By the late sixties," Rodney Livingstone tells us in his informative survey, "the immigrants occupied many of the important chairs in Britain," especially in London (Claus Bock, Ilse Graham, Siegbert Prawer, Charlotte Jolles, Werner Schwarz).[12] Their achievements included solid work in familiar areas, e.g. medieval studies (Schwarz, Peter Ganz, Marianne Wynn); research on Goethe and the classical age (Hans Reiss); Fontane and politics (Charlotte Jolles). Some, however, were instrumental in drawing British attention to aspects of German modernism. Richard Samuel published in the 1930s, jointly with Richard Hinton Thomas, an academic account of Expressionism which is still valuable. Above all, Erich Heller, a refugee from Prague, gave a pathbreaking series of lectures at Cambridge in 1946 entitled "German literature from 1914 to 1933," an area not yet covered in the very conservative syllabus. Some of these lectures, whose subjects included Kafka, Kraus, and Spengler, were published in the *Cambridge Journal,* a wide-ranging periodical edited by the conservative philosopher Michael Oakeshott, and again in Heller's stimulating book *The Disinherited Mind.*[13]

Unlike the figures discussed in Anderson's paper, Prawer, Stern, and Steiner arrived in Britain at earlier stages in their lives and completed their education there. Prawer's family came from Poland via

Cologne to Britain at the late date of 1939, when he was fourteen. He studied first English and then Modern Languages at Cambridge, demonstrating the width of his interests by his first two publications — again in Oakeshott's *Cambridge Journal* — one on Burton's *Anatomy of Melancholy,* the other on Jewish jokes.[14] He pursued an academic career as a lecturer at Birmingham University, Professor of German at Westfield College, London, and finally, in 1969, Taylor Professor of German at Oxford. Stern was born in Bohemia in 1920 and partly educated in Germany; he narrowly escaped via Poland after the German invasion in March 1939 and joined his father in London. He interrupted his study of Modern Languages at Cambridge to serve in a Czech squadron of the RAF; in 1942 his plane was shot down over the sea, and he spent fourteen hours, injured, in a lifeboat before being rescued. His studies and his career were at Cambridge, where he became a Fellow of St John's College, until his appointment in 1973 to the Chair of German at University College London. Steiner was born in 1929; his father left Vienna in 1924, so that he was brought up in France, and he arrived in America safely in January 1940, a few months before Hitler's forces overran Western Europe. After studying at Chicago and Harvard, he first went to Britain as a graduate student at Oxford, and received in 1955 the degree of D.Phil. for a thesis on "The Decline of Tragedy: A Study of Romantic Drama, 1790–1820," later to become the basis of *The Death of Tragedy.* After working on *The Economist* and some brief university appointments in the United States he stepped onto the academic ladder of Cambridge as a Fellow of Churchill College, eventually leaving Britain to become Professor of Comparative Literature at the University of Geneva.

In their literary studies, all three have attempted a synthesis between Anglo-American and Continental approaches to literature, but with markedly different emphases. Prawer's absorption of New Criticism is evident in his first book, *German Lyric Poetry,* a series of close readings of German poems from Klopstock to Rilke, which is still fresh and rewarding. Stern's approach to literature also focused from the outset on language and style, but instead of Richards and Empson, his mentor was Erich Auerbach, who in each chapter of *Mimesis* moves from the detailed analysis of a literary passage to conclusions about the representation of experience possible in the culture and period in which the text originated. Accordingly, Stern's review of Prawer's first book in the *Cambridge Journal* was critical of what he considered its narrow focus.[15] His own conception of stylistic analysis was illustrated in his own first book, which dealt with Ernst Jünger,

Siegbert Prawer, Queen's College, Oxford 1989

his hortatory and embattled style.[16] Steiner also reacted against what he considered the narrowness of New Criticism in order to address large questions of ethics, politics, and metaphysics posed by literature. His approach to literature has from the outset been comparative. One of his first publications, written when he was twenty-one, dealt with Shelley's translation of Goethe's *Faust*.[17] He has always assumed an intimacy with at least three literatures as well as a background awareness of the Hebrew and Hellenic roots of Western culture, and his literary work has been correspondingly enriching. Stern and Prawer have a similarly wide experience of literature and range of unforced reference, and both have supported comparative literature, Prawer through a book on the subject, Stern by editing a series of introductory studies called "Landmarks in World Literature"; though neither would probably give or have given unqualified support to comparative literature as a discipline, in view of the uncertainty of its aims and methods and the practical difficulty of institutionalizing it other than at universities with large graduate schools.[18]

All three have written not only for academics but for a wider audience. They have been much in demand as lecturers. Their successful communication has depended on writing accessibly, and while their individual styles differ widely, all are entirely free from the pretence that literary studies form a quasi-scientific specialism with a technical jargon intelligible only to initiates. While Prawer and Stern address primarily an audience of colleagues and students, however, Steiner directs his work at the nonacademic reading public and has found a wide resonance, especially with his early books *The Death of Tragedy* and *Tolstoy or Dostoevsky?* However, all three have been active in literary journalism, an important way of interesting nonacademics in what academics do. The scope for literary journalism has diminished in Britain since the 1960s: the *Listener* and *Encounter* have vanished, and the literary section of the *New Statesman* is now inconsiderable; the scene has been enriched, however, by the arrival of the *London Review of Books,* even though it tends to be mid-Atlantic rather than British, and the *Times Literary Supplement* continues to lead the field of literary reviews. For many years Steiner wrote long and informative reviews in *The New Yorker,* providing intellectual journalism of a very high order.

It may now be best to take, as representative of each author, a book in which the author's distinctive approach and his imagination seem most intensely present. I shall look briefly at Prawer's book *Heine, the Tragic Satirist* (1961); Stern's *Re-interpretations: Seven*

Studies in Nineteenth-Century German Literature (1964); and Steiner's *After Babel: Aspects of Language and Translation* (1975). These are far from being their authors' first books. Prawer had already published, besides his precocious *German Lyric Poetry,* a reception study of Mörike written in elegant German and an introductory study of Heine's *Buch der Lieder.* Stern had produced his early study of Jünger and his book, originally his doctoral thesis, on Lichtenberg. And Steiner, after publishing in rapid succession *The Death of Tragedy* and *Tolstoy or Dostoevsky?,* had restricted himself to journalistic publication while collecting material for the massive *After Babel.* The books I want to focus on are therefore those into which years of increasingly mature reflection and experience (literary and otherwise) have been condensed.

The first thing that struck me on re-reading *Heine, the Tragic Satirist* was its lightness of touch. A great deal of substantial learning is delicately handled and used to illuminate two centuries of poetry with uninsistent precision. Early on, Prawer comments on the "lightness, grace and deadly accuracy" of Heine's political satire, terms which could apply to this study — except the word "deadly." And it is significant that Prawer uses this phrase after quoting, in his own elegant translation, the passage from *Die Harzreise* where Heine affects to interpret the political meaning encoded in ballet. For the dance is an image that Prawer continually uses to express literary enjoyment.[19] But he is of course also aware of the ambivalence of the dance in Heine, of how it often signifies demonic and Dionysiac energies, and it seems no accident that one of the fullest readings of a single poem in the book is devoted to "Schelm von Bergen," where an executioner insinuates himself into an aristocratic masked ball and introduces a menacing atmosphere of night and death.

The reading of "Schelm von Bergen" also illustrates a valuable lesson that Prawer constantly inculcated as a teacher: that you can have access to a work of literature only by experiencing it as literature; if you try to bypass that experience for the sake of the work's presumed historical or philosophical content, you will be left with nothing. Hence he guides us through the dance-measure conveyed by Heine's meter and shows how subtle metrical and phonic changes gradually introduce the atmosphere of menace; but he ends by warning against the danger of simplification and tries to direct us towards the whole experience of the poem. In doing so, however, he is far from the tedious technique of extended paraphrase practiced by some German commentators on poetry. Prawer presents himself as a guide, a cicerone, stimulating us to look afresh at the poems for ourselves. And this modesty, unusual among critics, is also shown in the adroit use of quotations. Each section of the study begins with a beautifully chosen epigraph: that on "Neuer Frühling" with a quotation from a well-known poem by Brentano, "Mich erbarmte sich noch keiner / Von den Frühlingen der Erde"; the section dealing with some of the late Heine's most arresting poems, those in which he wrangles with God, begins with an epigraph from Yeats: "Now his wars with God begin; At stroke of midnight God shall win." These epigraphs accomplish a great deal of critical work economically by suggesting new perspectives from which to view Heine and inviting us to apply to Heine's poetry the rest of our literary experience. Similarly, when Prawer invokes Jung, Freud, and Kierkegaard (*Heine*, 60, 67, 147–48) to illuminate aspects of Heine's poetry, he is not proposing anything so flat-footed as a Jungian interpretation, but opening up further perspectives in which to see Heine. One could call this an exceptionally subtle use of intertextuality; but such a jargonistic term would seem heavy-handed and inappropriate to Prawer's agility, evoking that Nietzsche-an "Geist der Schwere" against which, as he reminds us, Heine campaigned in *Atta Troll* (*Heine*, 73).

The section on "Schelm von Bergen" also illustrates how Prawer emphasizes the pleasure gained in reading literature and maintains that the whole experience of a poem, and of Heine's poetry, is positive and even harmonious. Although "Schelm von Bergen" ends by reminding us of the stony death of the pleasure-seeking aristocrats —

Ein stolzes Geschlecht! Es blühte am Rhein.
Jetzt schläft es in steinernen Särgen

— more than extinction is hinted at. "Life has somehow prospered, in that remote world the poet has conjured up; it has somehow refused to be terrorized by night and death and has left an impressive monument of itself" (*Heine*, 155). Early in the book, Prawer undertakes to show how, in the poetry of his middle years, Heine reconciled the lyrical self of the *Buch der Lieder* with the politically aware self who wrote the *Reisebilder* (*Heine*, 11). Now, Heine might seem a peculiarly difficult poet in whose work to find harmony and reconciliation; it would seem easier to find dissonance everywhere. And Prawer is well aware of the half-buried terrors in Heine's life and writings, and also very aware of the Romantic exploration of the night-side of nature, for which his touchstone is Chamisso's tale *Peter Schlemihl*, "that greatest and deepest of all romantic tales" (*Heine*, 8); though I think he somewhat underplays the morbid interest in, and disturbing imaginative affinity with, the cruelty and sensuality of paganism that Heine conveys in the Wild Hunt episode of *Atta Troll* and in "Vitzliputzli." Prawer differs from most critics of Heine in his understanding of the Lazarus persona adopted by Heine in the poems written from his mattress-grave. While "Lazarus," a composite of the man restored from the dead in John 12 and the beggar in Luke 16, certainly suggests "deepest humiliation and most abject suffering," Prawer argues that it "suggests also insight and triumph. It conveys the triumph of a beggar who was destined to rest, ultimately, in Abraham's bosom; and the triumph of a man who had been declared dead and yet returned to sit beside his Lord" (*Heine,* 180–81).

But does this positive reading find any support in Heine? Surely the emphasis is all on the degradation. I might add that for Christians the story of Lazarus being raised from the dead has often been found disturbing, for to many readers, as to Tennyson in section thirty-one of *In Memoriam,* it seems to make death more, not less, mysterious.[20] Then again, Heine, as is well known, loves to end individual poems on a note of dissonance, the much-discussed "Stimmungsbrechung," as when the traveller in "Seegespenst," absorbed in his Romantic vision of the city under the waves, is restrained from plunging in by the ship's captain with the gruff words "Doktor, sind Sie des Teufels?" Heine's last poem, "Für die Mouche," a survey of history as a conflict between Judeo-Christian spiritualism and pagan sensualism, ends with the disruptive braying of Balaam's ass; and as Prawer admits in a chapter on the design of *Romanzero,* the book ends with the Queen's conclusion in "disputation," that both disputants — the rabbi and the monk — are equally smelly. Prawer accepts this dissonance as a sign of completeness and an indication that Heine would not settle for an artificial world of artistic illusion: "Heine could not, would not console himself with comfortable illusions; if consolation was to be found at all, it had to be found within a fully apprehended reality" (208). While one can only agree with the stress on Heine's artistic honesty, one may wonder whether, in this interpretation, Prawer is trying to have it both ways: to credit Heine with achieving artistic completeness and also with rejecting the illusion of artistic completeness. Despite such occasional doubts, Prawer's predilection for aesthetic harmony is doubly valuable: it guides us towards as complete as possible an appreciation of Heine's poems; and it offers a counterweight to those critical doctrines which would read literature negatively, at one time as documents of existential despair, more recently as empty vessels without intrinsic meaning.

Stern's *Re-interpretations* centers on realism, to which Stern assigned a special value. He conveys his understanding of the concept not through a definition or a formula but by considering a number of literary examples. From this exploration there emerges the conviction that of the three spheres into which human experience can be divided — the personal and private, the public and political, and the metaphysical and religious — realism deals especially with the second, "the realm of the Leviathan, the area of experience in which men are bound together not by love but contract, not by worship but agreement."[21] He describes realism as "an author's readiness to shape his tale not by what shall be or should be; not by the single man's unshaped experience of God and His commands; not by the author's spiritual fears, hopes and passionate injunctions; not by the content of his faith — *except* as these are realized, modified and alas worsted, in the living contact with contemporary reality, with other men" (*Re-interpretations,* 21). Realism can thus be contrasted with allegory, with an abstract apprehension of life as shown in Klopstock's *Messias* or in Schiller's dramas when these are interpreted as conflicts between personified abstractions.[22] Realism is not concerned with "the interpreted world" but with the world as we find it prior to interpretation. Hence he speaks of the realist's "creative assent" to the surrounding world, shown among other things in a commitment to narrative: "To invest creative energy in 'plot' and 'story' is to accept as meaningful, and care for, the *social* sphere in which alone a plot's convolutions and proliferations are enacted."[23] Stern examines how the well-known German aversion from the political placed limitations on realism in nineteenth-century German literature; but he also examines the strengths arising from these limitations. Thanks in part to German classicism, which defined the novel as an inferior genre, German writers of the nineteenth century were uneasy about descending to prose and often dignified their work with the label "poetic realism." When Grillparzer resorts to prose in *Der arme Spielmann,* he shows a failed artist whose purity of heart can never find acknowledgment from the world; Stifter's beautiful landscape descriptions are a consolation for the inevitable disappointments of social life; even the realist Fontane shows a disjunction between social and moral values. These — and also the appreciation of Büchner as anticipating existentialism — are unsurpassed and deservedly famous critical explorations. But Stern also explores the tensions and incoherencies that arise, for example, when

Stifter tries to invest nature with a meaningfulness which neither Romantic natural philosophy nor Christian providentialism will permit (*Re-interpretations*, 271). Far from trying to subsume his authors under a formula or a neat interpretation, Stern remains alive to the uniqueness of each and of their writings. Accordingly, his own writing is tentative, exploratory, and inevitably frustrating for anyone who expects a critical book to provide a handy message rather than guidance towards a new experience of literature.

In *After Babel*, Steiner dazzles and overwhelms the reader by his display of encyclopaedic information about language in its literary, philosophical, and musical relations. It has two principal theses, but I think its real claims on our attention are independent of its theses. The first thesis is that language is essentially a means of communication, that all language use involves translation, and that the study of translation is central to the study of language. The second is that an essential aspect of language is the capacity for concealment and fiction given by grammatical forms like the conditional mood and the future tense; while this capacity initially had survival value, it now enlarges the imagination. The first of these claims has been queried sharply by professional linguists who point out that a theory of language is independent of any actual use, even communication, to which language is put.[24] The second claim seems to me partly a Darwinian fable with no more authority than any other just so story, partly a contention about human intellectual powers rather than specifically about language.

However, the value of the book does not depend on the persuasiveness of its theses. It is, first, testimony to Steiner's own imagination. We should not treat the book as a collection of data, any more than we treat Burton's *Anatomy of Melancholy* as a medical textbook, but rather as an invitation to reflect on the many ways in which language makes us human. It is of course easy to catch Steiner out, as with the author of any highly ambitious book. For example, he reports it as an established fact that Indo-European languages differ radically from Semitic languages in their treatment of time, since the former has a threefold system of past, present and future, whereas the Hebrew verb distinguishes only between incomplete or perfected action (*After Babel*, 157). This distinction makes one wonder whether linguistic differences encode different experiences of time and make possible different cultural achievements, so that their language predestines the Greeks to be historians and the Hebrews to be prophets. For these speculations Steiner relies, though not uncritically, on Thorlief Boman's book *Hebrew Thought Compared with Greek*, evidently unaware that Boman's methods and conclusions had been tactfully but comprehensively demolished in 1961 by James Barr.[25] But nobody, even Steiner, can read everything, and I think his attraction to Boman's conjectures tells us something crucial about Steiner's imagination. For while his appetite for knowledge shows his fascination with human possibility, his interest in how our thoughts may be determined or restricted by our language suggests a countervailing interest in the boundaries of human possibility, in the limits set by our finite natures to exploration and change. And this is part of a debate between culture and nature. If culture is all-important, as the dominant paradigm in the humanities now assumes, then human nature and human society are indefinitely malleable and our problems can be set right by social engineering. If, on the other hand, our possibilities are constrained by our biological nature, as popularizing neo-Darwinists tell us, the political consequences mean placing severe restraint on our natural impulses and a constant struggle with nature. Since nowadays the culturalists are in the ascendant, Steiner is unusual in being prepared to contemplate the boundaries which may be destined to frustrate human possibility.

Second, Steiner's interest in translation means that *After Babel* contains more close reading of literary passages than any other of his books, and for many readers, including myself, these sections are the most rewarding. And here Steiner is wonderfully omnivorous in his reading. It was from this book that I first learnt about Stefan George's invention of a secret language, of which only two lines survive, and of Rudolf Borchardt's translation of the *Divine Comedy* into a version of Middle High German that never existed but ought to have. Steiner discusses extracts from Browning's translation of Euripides in *Aristophanes' Apology;* French translations of *Paradise Lost* and of Hopkins's "Pied Beauty"; Hölderlin's versions of Pindar; and versions of Dante by Rossetti and Littré as well as Borchardt; translations of Shakespeare's sonnets by Kraus, George, and Celan. Here he exemplifies what he often asserts, that culture is the loving and intimate acquaintance with older literature and that translating, transforming, renovating is an essential part of cultural transmission. And he conveys an enthusiasm for the sheer variety of literature, an enthusiasm best conveyed by detailed discussion. For these reasons, *After Babel* is a book one can return to with profit and pleasure, however much one may wish to question its major arguments.

George Steiner (© Jacques Sassier, Editions Gallimard)

Bearing in mind Stern's insistence on moving outward from literature to experience and history, I want now to compare briefly the treatment by these critics of certain large themes. First, inevitably for a Germanist, there is the presence of the Third Reich and the Holocaust and the question of what if any relation they bear to the high achievements of German culture.

While Prawer — and who can blame him? — has evidently not wanted to address these matters, Stern and Steiner have devoted much attention to the connections between culture and the inhuman. Increasingly, one of the principal themes of Stern's work became the task of understanding the manifold connections between "high" literature stemming from the intellect or spirit and the catastrophic political realities of the twentieth century. Stern faced this question notably in *Hitler: The Führer and the People,* which probably reached a wider audience than any other of his books. But one of his key ideas is already present in his first book, where he quotes Jünger's denunciation of the Weimar Republic for being out of touch with tragedy — "thus seeking" (Stern says) "inside the political and economic arrangements of a society that which man must face outside organized society, alone" (*Jünger,* 11). The search for metaphysical solutions in the political sphere was one of the temptations to which German intellectuals succumbed. Another was the idea of the "dear purchase," a conception Stern outlined first in an essay of 1968.[26] This, Stern argues, is an ideology that dominates early twentieth-century German literature and provides common ground for writers whose declared ideologies were widely separate. It is the idea that man needs to be redeemed, and can only be redeemed by the most arduous, most demanding exercise of the will, or by the most costly sacrifice — and even that utmost effort may, tragically, bring one only to a point just short of one's goal. Stern's key example is Leverkühn in Mann's *Doktor Faustus.* In order to achieve his breakthrough into a new music that is free from irony and pastiche, Leverkühn forfeits his health, his sanity, the possibility of love, even his salvation; all this is part of his pact with the Devil. It does enable him to produce what we are assured is a supreme work of art, *Dr. Fausti Weheklag;* yet the material of this art is Leverkühn's lament that he is damned. To Leverkühn, damnation is the condition of achievement. The novel leaves open the possibility that the intensity of his effort, or the very depth of his despair, may redeem him.

Next comes the Gretchenfrage: "Wie hast du's mit der Religion?" It would be impertinent to inquire into private beliefs, but one need

not do so, for Prawer's devout Judaism is apparent from his response
to the Sabbath atmosphere lovingly if ironically recalled in Heine's
"Prinzessin Sabbat" (*Heine*, 190–92). He writes finely and discrimi-
natingly about the late Heine's "return" to God, as based on the concept of Teshubah, generally translated as "repentance" but literally
meaning "return," which Heine sensed within the Christian parable of
the Prodigal Son (*Heine*, 187). Prawer observes that Heine's late poems contain little Christian charity, nor do they show trust in the Divine love and benevolence; and Prawer does not accept the
paradoxical claim that blasphemy is a sign of faith (234–35). Similarly,
Stern's Christianity is never thrust on the reader, but discernible everywhere: it figures most strikingly in a superb appreciation of Mörike's
religious poetry, and in reflections on Nietzsche's view of Jesus and
Paul.[27] Steiner is somewhat mysterious. Although he describes himself
as an unbelieving Jew, he has shown, especially in the last ten or fifteen years, a fascination with religion, and has clearly read extensively
in theology. A theological concept provides the title of his book *Real
Presences*, in which he opposes the dreary claim that in literature we
encounter empty words instead of a real "otherness." Despite the title,
nothing is said about the doctrine of the Real Presence. The impression persists, however, that Steiner is implying something more than
punning resemblance between the aesthetic experience and the actual,
not merely symbolic, presence of the body and blood of Christ in the
sacrament. Yet any analogy between aesthetic experience and the sacrament is questionable, not only on grounds of taste, but because the
reception of the sacrament is not primarily an experience but an action
whose efficacy is independent of the mental state of the believer. The
point of Steiner's reflections on religion remains opaque. Perhaps the
forthcoming text of the Gifford Lectures on Natural Theology, which
he delivered in 1990, will enlighten us.[28]

Something should be said about the conceptions of Jewish history
and identity expressed by these critics. Prawer has never, to my knowledge, reflected explicitly on this subject, but clearly the author of
Heine's Jewish Comedy and *Israel at Vanity Fair* has much to say indirectly about the matter. It is striking how recurrently Prawer's imaginative sympathies call him back to the nineteenth century, which looks
in retrospect like the golden age of emancipation. In Germany, Jews
were able to take a large though not a full part in social and public life;
the complete legal emancipation granted in Austria under the constitution of 1867, and in Germany with the founding of the Empire in
1871, was only too soon to be clouded by the outspoken anti-Semitism

that became current in the 1870s. Looking back, some German Jews spoke of a "German-Jewish symbiosis," though others, especially from a Zionist standpoint, hotly disputed the notion on the grounds that while Jews admired and adopted German culture, the Germans showed no reciprocal interest in the Jews. While this is not the place to argue the point, I think the concept of a German-Jewish symbiosis does have value. It draws our attention at least to the loving and inward absorption of German culture shown by very many cultivated German Jews and summed up by Joseph Roth in 1933: "We come from emancipation, from humanity (*Humanität*), from humanism, rather than from Egypt. Our ancestors are Goethe, Lessing, Herder, no less than Abraham, Isaac and Jacob."[29] Prawer's books on Heine and Thackeray increasingly explore a German-Jewish, Anglo-Jewish, and Anglo-German symbiosis. Hence also his emphasis on humor, on comedy, seen in his translations and discussions of Heine's verbal caricatures of his Jewish acquaintances, and in his reproduction of Thackeray's many visual caricatures of Jewish figures. The authorial persona of *Israel at Vanity Fair* is, once again, a cicerone, guiding us through Thackeray's work and cautioning us against premature judgments, but a guide who is prepared to be outspoken when necessary.

In writing about Thackeray's depictions of Jews, Prawer has entered into a current controversy. For, to judge from popular caricature, anti-Jewish animus seems to have been as strong in Britain as in Germany, and probably stronger. Karl Philipp Moritz, who visited England in 1782, recounts how a Jewish stagecoach passenger encountered contempt for not wishing to travel outside: "Here in England I have noticed this prejudice and contempt for Jews much more frequently than among us."[30] Anti-Jewish caricatures current in England have recently been described in detail, and with indignation, by Frank Felsenstein.[31] Yet anti-Semitic prejudice did not lead to violence. The emancipatory legislation that came by fits and starts in Germany was not even needed in Britain, where Jews were citizens by virtue of being born in the country. Jewish "emancipation" in the British context means political representation. Jews were allowed to elect members to Parliament in 1835, and on 26 July 1858 Baron Lionel de Rothschild became the first Jew to take his seat in the House of Commons. It would be difficult to find a counterpart by a German Gentile to Macaulay's forceful plea, "On the Civil Disabilities of the Jews" (1831). How then are we to judge these caricatures? Do they show that anti-Semitism was as powerful in Britain as on the

Continent? Or should we treat them lightly, since they seem to have done little real harm? The issue is still being debated.

Thackeray's antipathy to Jews and other foreigners is often expressed in terms which are at the very least excessively robust and have earned him condemnation as a Victorian racialist.[32] A notorious example, from *Notes of a Journey from Cornhill to Grand Cairo*, is the description in prose and verse of "greasy" and verminous Jews travelling on the deck of the ship taking Thackeray's persona, Michael Angelo Titmarsh, to Cairo. The verse runs in part:

> Strange company we harboured;
> We'd a hundred Jews to larboard,
> Unwashed, uncombed, unbarbered,
>   Jews black, and brown, and grey.
> With terror it would seize ye,
> And make your souls uneasy,
> To see those Rabbis greasy,
>   Who did nought but scratch and pray.
> Their dirty children puking,
> Their dirty saucepans cooking,
> Their dirty fingers hooking
>   The swarming fleas away.[33]

Prawer is blunt about these passages: they form "the most physically revolting picture of a group of Jews ever to appear in Thackeray's writings."[34] Generally, however, Prawer sensibly reminds us that we cannot expect modern liberal tolerance from somebody of Thackeray's time and class; also that Thackeray presents many people of his own class, upper middle-class Englishmen, behaving quite as badly as his Jews, and that he shows greed and selfishness to be omnipresent: "Instead of showing predatory Jews corrupting Gentile society, as revenge, perhaps, for past injuries, Thackeray's work shows a predominantly Gentile society exhibiting predatory behaviour at every level and forcing such behaviour on anyone who has not inherited wealth and who wants to make his way towards social position and esteem" (*Israel*, 413). This seems a sane and judicious answer to the question I posed earlier. After all, Thackeray always views society in a harsh, satirical light, and he was not the sort of person to present a critical analysis of anti-Semitism such as Maria Edgeworth undertook in her remarkable novel *Harrington* (1817).[35] Nevertheless, on occasion Thackeray's vitriolic anti-Jewish prejudice puts Prawer's tolerance under some strain.

Stern reflects on the German-Jewish relationship in the final and culminating chapter of his book *Hitler: The Führer and the People.* Here he gives a nuanced and compressed account of the tragic irony whereby German Jews increasingly discarded their traditional culture in order to absorb German culture, of which they provided many of the most creative members. In the arts, scholarship, and the sciences, they were "Germany's European conscience."[36] But the abandonment of a specifically Jewish culture, the retention of at most a nominal Jewishness, meant that "as time went by, their Jewishness was sustained less and less by what they really had in common with each other, and increasingly by the names others gave them" (*Hitler,* 207) Their host people ceased to welcome them and finally turned on them and annihilated them:

> The "emancipation" of the German Jews was a child of the Enlightenment, of the German Enlightenment. On its altar their ancient faith was sacrificed, and their traditional ways became a matter of embarrassment to them and to their friends. It was the secularising spirit of enlightened tolerance which opened German society and culture to them; and it was the intolerance of tolerance which caused them to abandon all religious and national cohesion, and thus rendered them defenceless in their hour of need. The history of Western thought knows no crueller irony. (*Hitler,* 204–5)

Stern emphasizes that the German Jews had, in their own estimation, become German. "In philosophy and the humanities, Jewish authors closely followed prevailing modes of German thought; in music and the visual arts, they frequently anticipated them; and even in their literary treatment of Jewish themes — one thinks of Heine's late poems, of Else Lasker-Schüler, of Paul Celan — German-Jewish poets followed and enriched an unmistakably German tradition" (*Hitler,* 206). Now, this is broadly right and it needs saying at a time when criticism, understandably, is focusing on the distinctively "Jewish" character of these writers at the risk of underplaying their "German" aspect. Even so, Stern seems to be exaggerating a little. For while one recognizes the continuity of Heine's "Jehuda ben Halevy" with his other late seriocomic poems in trochaic meter (like *Atta Troll* and "Bimini"), the close affinities between Lasker-Schüler and Expressionism, and Celan's debt to Rilke, surely their combination of elegiac mode and Jewish imagery do establish a distinctive atmosphere which makes their poetry markedly different from that of, say, Droste-

Hülshoff, Trakl, or Bobrowski. Celan not only stressed the "Jewish-ness" of his poems, not just those like "Todesfuge" that thematized the Shoah, but described himself as "one of the last who must live out to the end the destiny of the Jewish spirit in Europe."[37] Here Stern seems to be underplaying the distinctively Jewish note in German lit-erature.

Very different from either Stern or Prawer is Steiner's remarkable essay in which he formulates his self-understanding as a Jew, "A Kind of Survivor." He tells us that the memory of the Holocaust defines his sense of himself: "the black mystery of what happened in Europe is to me indivisible from my own identity."[38] Contrasting himself with the Orthodox, he tells us that he is not a believing Jew (Orthodoxy is not the only way of practicing Judaism, but it is the only one Steiner con-siders). He contrasts himself also with the Zionists who are building up a new and hopeful Jewish society in Israel. Instead, he affirms his intention to continue living in the Diaspora and to remain loyal to a Central European humanism that he associates with Marx, Freud, Kafka, and Schoenberg. Many readers have found this eloquent essay deeply inspiring. The Yiddish scholar David Roskies tells us that for "a number of years I identified with George Steiner's essay 'A Kind of Sur-vivor,' a cosmopolitan manifesto."[39] But, while attracted by the cosmo-politanism Steiner expresses, one might worry about the initial move in which he claims that his Jewish identity is inseparable from the Holocaust. A number of recent commentators have voiced concern about the tendency, among Jews whose religious Judaism is residual or absent, to make the Holocaust instead the foundation of their Jew-ish identity. Michael Goldberg has provocatively described a "Holo-caust cult" in which Elie Wiesel, the dedicatee of Steiner's essay, plays the role of High Priest.[40] By highlighting the achievements of the Di-aspora, Steiner avoids the extreme implications of this attitude. Nev-ertheless, and with all piety towards the victims of the Shoah, his essay does seem to require as a response the message Thomas Mann trans-mits through Hans Castorp in *The Magic Mountain:* "For the sake of goodness and love, man shall let death have no sovereignty over his thoughts."[41]

Steiner also remarks that he is a Jew in part because the Nazis would have labelled him one. This is a reactive definition of Jewish-ness. Sartre summed it up by asserting: "The Jew is one whom other men consider a Jew."[42] Would it not be better for Jews themselves to decide what makes them Jewish? However, this is not the main thrust of Steiner's essay. His retrospective identification with the cosmopolitan Jewish culture of Central Europe implies a partial blindness to that culture. Its members rarely thought of themselves primarily as Jews. They regarded themselves rather as Germans who were steeped in German and European culture; and so they were. The generation that particularly interests Steiner — that of Kafka, Schoenberg, Benjamin — did indeed explore aspects of Judaism and Jewish culture, partly because anti-Semitism made them feel unwelcome in Germany. The "renaissance of Jewish culture" sprang in part from a feeling of rejection by German society.[43] It was a decisive experience for Schoenberg when in 1921 he and his family were obliged to leave Mattsee, a holiday area in Austria, on the grounds that non-Aryans were unwelcome there.[44] Kafka, already sympathetic towards Zionism, wrote to Milena Jesenská after witnessing anti-Semitic riots in November 1920 in Prague: "Ist es nicht selbstverständlich, daß man von dort weggeht, wo man so gehaßt wird?"[45] Benjamin's curiosity about Jewish mysticism has to be set against his immersion in German Romantic philosophy.[46] In his construction of Jewish identity Steiner underplays the identification with German culture that Stern described and emphasizes a conscious cosmopolitanism, a conscious acceptance of outsider status, which is surely more characteristic of Jewish self-awareness after the Shoah than before it.

Finally, all three of these critics, coming to adulthood in the mid-twentieth century and escaping from the threat of Nazism, were offered as an alternative its antithesis and mirror-image, communism, and to their great credit all three resisted this temptation and pursued staunchly liberal politics. Steiner travelled extensively in Eastern Europe in the 1950s and was in no doubt about the grim oppression practiced there. As a writer on *The Economist,* he was, I am told, the author of an article warning against Russian's professions of detente, entitled "The Smile on the Face of the Monolith." Stern, coming from Prague, knew only too well what sort of regime the communists had imposed, shared in the hopes and grief of the Prague Spring, and was able, just before the end of his life to visit what was still Czechoslovakia in the wake of the Velvet Revolution. His imaginative understanding of life under Communism is apparent not least from some late essays on Václav Havel.[47] Stern found the communist fellow-traveller Brecht uncongenial. But often critics produce their best work when dealing with a basically uncongenial author. In *The Dear Purchase* he finely describes the moments of compassion in Brecht's otherwise hard-boiled poetry where a hint of Christian feeling shines through: above all in the bleak poem from *Hauspostille,* "Von der

Kindesmörderin Marie Farrar," where Stern finds appropriate a hinted comparison with the compassion shown in the Gospels and the dignity they confer, as Auerbach showed in *Mimesis*, on "ordinary random persons."[48] But their most interesting engagement with Marx and his legacy is surely Prawer's book *Karl Marx and World Literature* (1976), which documents Marx's immense acquaintance with world literature from the Greeks down to Balzac and Dickens, and shows how literary allusions form an essential part of the texture of his writings. Prawer further shows that the humane view of literature, expressed in Marx's Paris Manuscripts of 1844, persisted throughout his career. He continued to believe that while imaginative literature can be made into an instrument of class oppression, it can also give us insight into the mechanisms of alienation and reification. Literature is produced by individuals in specific historical circumstances, but great literature can rise above a dominant ideology. We have here a much more humane Marx than the scientific socialist who was used or abused to underpin the Soviet Union. We have also a Marx who loves books, who is himself human as well as humane, who is especially indebted to the aesthetics of classical German culture. Prawer's Marx therefore illustrates the power of the literary imagination in promoting hard thought about such uninviting subjects as economics. Through Marx, literature helped to change the world. But, besides vindicating the power of literature, the book also illustrates the value of literary criticism when applied to such unfamiliar materials as *Capital*. And by its close attention to Marx's life as well as his writings it puts Marx back in the nineteenth-century Anglo-German-Jewish world which is very much Prawer's imaginative home.

Notes

[1] Sammons, "Some Considerations on our Invisibility," in *German Studies in the United States: Assessment and Outlook*, ed. Walter F. W. Lohnes and Valters Nollendorfs (Madison, WI: U of Wisconsin P, 1976), 17–23.

[2] Steiner, *No Passion Spent: Essays 1978–1996* (London and Boston: Faber, 1996); *Errata: An Examined Life* (London: Weidenfeld & Nicolson, 1997); *Reading George Steiner*, ed. Nathan A. Scott and Ronald A. Sharp (Baltimore and London: Johns Hopkins UP, 1994).

[3] Michael Beddow, "Joseph Peter Maria Stern, 1920–1991," *Proceedings of the British Academy* 84 (1993): 529–37. I have attempted a fuller appreciation of Peter Stern's work in "Difficult Truths: An Essay Review of J. P. Stern, *The Heart of Europe*," *Comparative Criticism* 16 (1994): 247–61.

[4] These lines are taken as evidence of Hofmannsthal's Jewish self-awareness in Willy Haas, "Hugo von Hofmannsthal," in *Juden in der deutschen Literatur: Essays über zeitgenössische Schriftsteller,* ed. Gustav Krojanker (Berlin: Welt-Verlag, 1922), 139–64 (145), and also by Prawer in "Jewish Contributions to German Lyric Poetry," *Year Book of the Leo Baeck Institute* 8 (1963): 149–70. See Jens Rieckmann, "Zwischen Bewußtsein und Verdrängung: Hofmannsthals jüdisches Erbe," *Deutsche Vierteljahrsschrift* 67 (1993): 466–83; Ranjit Chatterjee, "Judaic Motifs in Wittgenstein," in *Austrians and Jews in the Twentieth Century,* ed. Robert S. Wistrich (London: Macmillan, 1992), 142–61; David Damrosch, "Auerbach in Exile," *Comparative Literature* 47 (1995): 97–117.

[5] Anderson, "Components of the National Culture," originally in *New Left Review* 50 (July-August 1968), reprinted with revisions in his *English Questions* (London and New York: Verso, 1992), 48–10 (103).

[6] See David Lodge, "The Chesterbelloc and the Jews," in *The Novelist at the Crossroads and Other Essays on Fiction and Criticism* (London: Routledge & Kegan, 1971), 145–58; *The Letters of T. S. Eliot,* vol. 1, ed. Valerie Eliot (London: Faber, 1988), 205, 206, where he mentions "a youth named Siegfried Sassoon (semitic)" and explains to Ezra Pound that "[Lord] Burnham is a Jew merchant, named Lawson (sc. Levi-sohn?)."

[7] Bithell, *Germany: A Companion to German Studies,* 2d, revised and enlarged edition (London: Methuen, 1937). First published 1932.

[8] Bithell, *Germany: A Companion to German Studies,* revised edition (London: Methuen, 1955), 325.

[9] The symposium of June 1936 is described anonymously — presumably by Willoughby — in *German Life and Letters* 1 (Oct. 1936): 78–79.

[10] Charmian Brinson, "Sixty years on: *German Life and Letters* and the National Socialists," *German Life and Letters* 49 (1996): 479–87 (484, 479).

[11] Peter and Leni Gillman, *"Collar the Lot!" How Britain Interned and Expelled its Wartime Refugees* (London: Quartet Books, 1980), 136–40, 259–60.

[12] Livingstone, "The Contribution of German-speaking Jewish Refugees to German Studies in Britain," in *Second Chance: Two Centuries of German-speaking Jews in the United Kingdom,* ed. Julius Carlebach et al. (Tübingen: Mohr, 1991), 137–52 (143).

[13] See Stern's tribute to Heller, "The Enlarging and Enlivening Study of Literature," in *Versuche zu Goethe: Festschrift für Erich Heller,* ed. Volker Dürr and Géza von Molnár (Heidelberg: Stiehm, 1976), 343–60.

[14] Prawer, "Burton's *Anatomy of Melancholy,*" *Cambridge Journal* 1 (1948): 671–88; "The Jew and the General," *Cambridge Journal* 3 (1950): 345–55.

[15] Stern, "On Stylistic Analysis," *Cambridge Journal* 7 (1953–54): 67–80. Prawer gracefully acknowledges one of Stern's comments in *Heine, the Tragic Satirist: A Study of the Later Poetry 1827–56* (Cambridge: Cambridge UP, 1961), 171.

[16] Stern, *Ernst Jünger: A Writer of Our Time* (Cambridge: Bowes & Bowes, 1953).

[17] Steiner, "Shelley and Goethe's *Faust*," *Rivista di Letterature Moderne*, n.s. 2, ii (April-June 1951): 269–74.

[18] See Prawer, *Comparative Literary Studies* (London: Duckworth, 1973).

[19] See especially his "Dada Dances: Hugo Ball's *Tenderenda der Phantast*," in *The Discontinuous Tradition: Studies in German Literature in Honour of Ernest Ludwig Stahl*, ed. P. F. Ganz (Oxford: Clarendon P, 1971), 204–23.

[20] See Michael Wheeler, *Death and the Future Life in Victorian Literature and Theology* (Cambridge: Cambridge UP, 1990), esp. 16–21.

[21] Stern, *Re-interpretations: Seven Studies in Nineteenth-Century German Literature* (London: Thames & Hudson, 1964), 31.

[22] *Re-interpretations*, 29, quoting Gundolf; it is only fair to add that Stern acknowledges Schiller's *Wallenstein* to be an outstanding dramatic presentation of leadership, power, and politics.

[23] *Re-interpretations*, 139. For "creative assent," see *ibid.*, 91. And see 345 for a qualification of the "plot" argument in respect of Fontane's *Der Stechlin*.

[24] See Samuel Jay Keyser, "The steely trimmers strike again," *New Review* 2.14 (May 1975): 63–66; and Steiner's reply, *New Review* 2.16 (July 1975): 54–55.

[25] Barr, *The Semantics of Biblical Language* (Oxford: Oxford UP, 1961).

[26] "The Dear Purchase," *German Quarterly* 41 (1968): 317–37. The idea is formulated also in *A Study of Nietzsche* (Cambridge: Cambridge UP, 1979), 140–41; in the opening essay of *The Heart of Europe* (Oxford: Blackwell, 1992), and in the posthumously compiled *The Dear Purchase: A Theme in German Modernism* (Cambridge: Cambridge UP, 1995).

[27] For Mörike, see *Idylls and Realities: Studies in Nineteenth-Century German Literature* (London: Methuen, 1971), 87–90; for Nietzsche, see *A Study of Nietzsche*, 153–57.

[28] George Steiner, *Grammars of Creation* (New Haven and London: Yale UP, 2001).

[29] Letter to Stefan Zweig, 22 March 1933, in Roth, *Briefe*, ed. Hermann Kesten (Cologne: Kiepenheuer & Witsch, 1970), 257. My translation.

[30] K. P. Moritz, *Reisen eines Deutschen in England im Jahr 1782*, in his *Werke*, ed. Horst Günther (Frankfurt am Main: Insel, 1981), II:56. My translation.

[31] Frank Felsenstein, *Anti-Semitic Stereotypes: A Paradigm of Otherness in English Popular Culture, 1660–1830* (Baltimore and London: Johns Hopkins UP, 1995).

[32] See J. A. Sutherland, "Thackeray as a Victorian Racialist," *Essays in Criticism* 20 (1970): 441–45.

[33] William Makepeace Thackeray, *The Paris Sketch Book; The Irish Sketch Book; and Notes of a Journey from Cornhill to Grand Cairo* (London: Smith, Elder & Co., 1894), 634–35.

[34] Prawer, *Israel at Vanity Fair: Jews and Judaism in the Writings of W. M. Thackeray* (Leiden: Brill, 1992), 150.

[35] See now the outstanding study by Michael Ragussis, *Figures of Conversion: "The Jewish Question" and English National Identity* (Durham, NC, and London: Duke UP, 1995).

[36] Stern, *Hitler: The Führer and the People* (Glasgow: Fontana, 1975), 206.

[37] Letters quoted in John Felstiner, *Paul Celan: Poet, Survivor, Jew* (New Haven and London: Yale UP, 1995), 55, 57.

[38] Steiner, *Language and Silence* (London: Faber, 1967), 164.

[39] Roskies, *Against the Apocalypse: Responses to Catastrophe in Modern Jewish Culture* (Cambridge, Mass.: Harvard UP, 1984), 9.

[40] Goldberg, *Why Should Jews Survive? Looking Past the Holocaust Toward a Jewish Future* (New York and Oxford: Oxford UP, 1995), ch. 3.

[41] Mann, *The Magic Mountain,* trans. Helen T. Lowe-Porter (London: Secker & Warburg, 1945), 496–97.

[42] Jean-Paul Sartre, *Anti-Semite and Jew,* trans. George J. Becker (New York: Schocken, 1948), 69.

[43] See Shulamit Volkov, "The Dynamics of Dissimilation: *Ostjuden* and German Jews," in *The Jewish Response to German Culture from the Enlightenment to the Second World War,* ed. Jehuda Reinharz and Walter Schatzberg (Hanover, NH, and London: UP of New England, 1985), 195–211; Michael Brenner, *The Renaissance of Jewish Culture in Weimar Germany* (New Haven and London: Yale UP, 1996).

[44] See Alexander L. Ringer, *Arnold Schoenberg: The Composer as Jew* (Oxford: Clarendon P, 1990).

[45] Kafka, *Briefe an Milena,* enl. edn, ed. Jürgen Born and Michael Müller (Frankfurt am Main: Fischer, 1983), 288.

[46] A point made by Prawer in his review of Robert Alter, *Necessary Angels: Tradition and Modernity in Kafka, Benjamin and Scholem,* in the *Times Literary Supplement,* 2 Aug. 1991, 8.

[47] "Havel's Castle," *London Review of Books,* 12, 22 Feb. 1990, 5–8; "Havel's Satirical Theatre," *Austrian Studies* 4 (1993): 139–49.

[48] Stern, *The Dear Purchase,* 334.

Jewish Critics and German Literature in the Public Sphere: A Response to Ritchie Robertson

David Suchoff

> The old woman, now a star hovering over the
> buildings.
> A Blue Piano, the city. A veiled bride.
> I walk on the carpet stone with Else,
> Drunk on the Blue Piano and spliced by her
> dazzling sight.
>
> — A. Sutzkever, "Else Lasker-Schüler"

THE PROBLEM OF "German Literature in the Public Sphere" posed by Ritchie Robertson focuses on two questions where twentieth-century Jewish critics are concerned. Prawer, Stern, and Steiner, Robertson rightly recognizes, have played a crucial role in engaging a critical reading public with "the wider cultural and historical questions which the study of German literature, especially that of the twentieth century, inevitably raises." The crucial contrary pull emerges in the appreciation of Steiner, calling our attention to a crucial caution. One might indeed be concerned, as Professor Robertson insightfully pointed out, about the supposed tendency of Jews whose religious Judaism is residual to make the Holocaust instead the cornerstone of their Jewish identity. While critics have articulated this concern in response to Steiner's landmark essay of 1965, "A Kind of Survivor," the excessive emotion and questionable judgment they display serves the useful function of making visible the double bind faced by Jewish critics who work with German literature in the public sphere in the late twentieth century.[1]

Such literature, Robertson notes, "inevitably" raises "larger historical questions": yet the Jewish critics who raise those questions run the risk of being seen as concerned with nothing but "identity," not history of public, historic dimensions, and an ersatz identity at that.

The bind pulls all the tighter by exerting pressure in the opposite direction: Jewishness clearly has an influence on the themes of J. P. Stern's work, a critic, whom Robertson reminds us, was a Jew by virtue of the Nuremberg laws but whose work seems to stray, in Robertson's description, from explicitly Jewish themes, like Steiner, whose identification with the victims of Auschwitz seems to produce an "imaginary" Jewish identification in his famous essay, "A Kind of Survivor."[2] Robertson's essay valuably raises this constraining construct to visibility: German literature unproblematically belongs in the midst of the public sphere of the late twentieth century, but Jewish critics can, seen from one extreme, represent an imaginary, diaphanous Judaism, as supposed acolytes of a "Holocaust cult"[3] thus letting their false particularity drown out the universal or on the contrary choose a suppressively universal culture, drowning out their Jewish particularity in an excessive desire to assimilate with the dominant culture. At worst, critics like Prawer seem to do both at the same time, trapped in a double bind that leaves them absorbed by a predilection for "aesthetic harmony" while weakly asserting their Jewishness as critics.[4]

This critical framework was known before the Second World War as "the Jewish question." The fact that Jewish critics are still forced into its constraining terms, moreover, says very little about the status of Jews writing or writing about German culture and very much more about German cultural criticism's continuing refusal — in 1997 — to accept Jewish writing as an integral, critical minority voice within German culture. As Willi Goetschel eloquently points out in his contribution to this volume, the question of Jewish identity, the question of who, precisely, the Jews might be, became a shadow language for the other European nationalities in quest of self-definition.[5] To put it more precisely in regard to the Jewish critic in German culture, the topic of the volume at hand: it is not so much Jewish identity that is "divided" in German culture — though the "Jewish problem" has provided a rich site of reflection and literary productivity for Jewish writers in the German tradition. The opposite is rather the case. German cultural criticism focuses on the "divided" Jewish critic, split between "untenable" alternatives, as a way of avoiding German self-criticism: as a projection onto Jewish material of the division, doubt, and cultural crisis that haunts the idea of "German" culture itself.

The constraining force of this critical grid is even more apparent in the polemics that the positions of Jewish émigré scholars have provoked. As one might well recall, Perry Anderson, writing in 1968 from a New Left position, introduced the concept of the "White Migration" to Britain to describe the politics of the largely Jewish émigré generation from Germany; Anderson contrasts the "red" migration of largely Marxist, Frankfurt School figures from Germany to America with supposedly more conservative positions taken by British refugee scholars, like Wittgenstein, whose families were under threat as Jews.[6] Anderson never mentions the Jewishness of these figures, whom he constructs in political-historical terms as "white," quintessential establishment figures whom he criticizes for having sacrificed that radical "outsider" status that Sigmund Freud attributed to his Judaism.[7] In exactly the same period in the United States, émigré Jewish scholars are subject to the opposite charge. George Steiner was attacked by Irving Howe, an opponent of the New Left, for being all too red and radically Jewish, albeit in a superficial way. Howe viewed Steiner's mediations on Auschwitz and Western culture as high mandarin identity politics, pitting the Third World against the Western tradition, inflating rather than diminishing his Jewish profile by using the Holocaust to identify with the Third World. While for Anderson Jewish émigré critics had assimilated all too well, for Howe, Steiner was the critic whose Jewish identity was all too prominent and who had broken too radically with belief in the West.[8]

The distinctive contribution of Prawer, J. P. Stern, and George Steiner breaks with this grid: rather than construct a silenced or "imaginary" ground for postwar Jewish identity, these three critics pay far more attention to the concept of the German, revising the very model of an integral German culture to which Jewish culture is symbiotically integrated or condemned to Ahasverus's wandering state. J. P. Stern's most public cultural interventions had not avoided Jewishness but rather directed themselves at the concept of an integral German nation. In "What is German?," an essay of 1985, Stern observes that the very notion of "*Kulturpolitik,* whereby literature, music, art, and philosophy are converted into instruments of national self-assertion in support of domestic and foreign policy, was a German accomplishment to start with," dating from defeats at the hands of Napoleon forward; the idea of cultural essence is for Stern both a German creation and the same time a cultural construction.[9] Stern's brilliant essays collected as *The Heart of Europe* (1992) decenter the idea of the German not by making Jewish claims to identity; indeed, his essay on "The Gypsies" is avowedly hostile to the term Holocaust and Jewish claims to a unique experience during the war. But it appears in a series of essays that question the very structure of German nationalism, thereby making space for Jewish culture in German thought.

"Revising the German Past?," his essay of 1989 on the Historikerstreit, quotes with approval "D.G. — that is, Daniel Goldhagen," then "a mere research student," for producing evidence, as Goldhagen puts it, that "the Jews were killed because they were Jews."[10] Stern's essay "On Prague German Literature" eloquently evokes the lost heritage of a transnational German literature, while "The Education of the Master Race" offers a bracing contextualization of Robert Musil. "Bitburg," a piece of surprisingly little renown, critiques the nationalist excesses of Rilke, Thomas Mann, Stefan George, and Ernst Jünger, about whom Stern wrote more fully, and is followed by the book's central piece. "What is German?" uses Wittgenstein's notion of "family resemblance" to critique the ideal of national purity, arguing that "Wittgenstein's method teaches us that there is no need to abstract one similarity, one 'essence' or 'spirit' of the nation."[11]

George Steiner's signal contribution to German literature's place in the public sphere similarly centers not on his claim to Jewish identity but on the extraordinary generalizations about German culture he has offered. Perhaps these statements have vanished from the public sphere, but they once catalyzed vociferous debate on German writing. Steiner, one might recall, once famously declared that "it is not merely that a Hitler, a Goebbels and a Himmler happened to speak German. Nazism found in the language precisely what it needed to give voice to its savagery."[12] Steiner then calls German literature to witness as evidence of this essentialism, with Heinrich Mann's *Der Untertan* offered as proof that "the essentially philological structure of German education" produced "loyal servants to Prussia and the Nazi Reich." Unlike these forgotten remarks, which helped secure Steiner's place as a public intellectual, Steiner's "A Kind of Survivor" (1965), his statement on Jewish identity and the Holocaust, has become a classic formulation only because it stated the obvious before almost anyone else: defining one's Jewish identity after the Holocaust, not to mention modern German culture, unavoidably involves confronting Jewish destruction, though certainly not facile identifications with its victims. This was precisely the rhetorical point of Steiner's dedicating his essay to Elie Wiesel. J. P. Stern similarly dedicated *In the Heart of Europe* to his friend and fellow Jewish émigré Erich Heller, who introduced his classic work on German modernism by reminding his audience that his rereading of Jacob Burckhardt and Oswald Spengler, to Nietzsche, Rilke, Kafka, and Karl Kraus could not be separated from "disasters that have befallen" its author, disasters that should not be seen as having imposed the limits of "identity" on his work but rather as having contributed to its "distinctive," and one might say, particularistic "virtue."[13]

Stern's mention of the concept of "alterity" in relation to German-Jewish writers in Prague — "a concept," to quote Stern "about which a fair amount of fuss is being made in present-day literary theory" — is thus a paradoxical reminder of the larger significance of particularistic questions of Jewish identity to contemporary public discussion.[14] The classic statement of this consonance of Jewish identity with the largest provenance of German culture belongs to Hermann Levin Goldschmidt's *Vermächtnis des deutschen Judentums*, first published in 1957:

> Only that scholar in the humanities who never and in no way denies his origin — which he can then make an explicit part of his research, or exclude altogether, whichever is more fruitful — can give his scholarship what it deserves. In the case of Judaism, a scholarship worthy of its people and all realms of scholarly inquiry whatsoever in which they are engaged, this means that only that Jew who is conscious of his Judaism from the ground up can devote his greatest strengths to scholarship, never led astray by what is best within him but instead always furthered by it.[15]

I have examined Stern and Steiner's positions in such detail because they demonstrate one moral to be drawn from Goldschmidt's point. Construct one's own Jewishness, he admonishes us, especially as a Jewish critic of German literature, for Sartre was partially right: Jewishness will always be subject to the larger culture's constructions. But Goldschmidt also reminds us that Jewish identity, whether brought to self-consciousness and renewal by acts of destruction or as the silent basis of the scholarly work so important to the Jewish tradition, remains a liberating, sometimes polemical, but always critical constituent of German literature's place in the public sphere.

In this spirit, I conclude with a quotation from Siegbert Prawer's *Heine's Jewish Comedy*. For Prawer, Heine is not Germany's "wound," as Adorno called him, nor a poet whose "predilection" was for "aesthetic harmony" but a Jewish writer whose "desire to be a full and useful citizen" was in no way opposed to but enriched by a "deep rooted wish not to deny a Jewish origin" and a "hatred of those who would force him to give it up."[16] The alternatives for the Jewish critic of German literature are thus neither Zweig's "wandering" of exile, on the one hand, nor an assimilation that denies Jewishness on the other, but a contradictory legacy that participates in and dissents from the notion of the German itself. Like every sentence of the Yiddish that was their historical linguistic ground, and like Wittgenstein, who argued against the monolithic concept of a national "spirit," Prawer places Jewish writers, and himself, not at the margin but the center of German literature's claim on the democratic public sphere.

Notes

[1] See for instance, Michael Goldberg, *Why Should Jews Survive? Looking Past the Holocaust toward a Jewish Future* (New York and Oxford: Oxford UP, 1995), chapter 3; and Lionel Kochan, *The Jewish Renaissance and Some of its Discontents* (Manchester: Manchester UP, 1992), chapter 4. 1 am grateful to Professor Robertson for these references.

[2] Alain Finkielkraut's *The Imaginary Jew* (trans. Kevin O'Neill and David Suchoff [Lincoln, Nebraska: U of Nebraska P, 1994]), makes the point that this "imaginary" postwar starting point is the unavoidable and necessary starting point for any deeper involvement with Jewish history and culture in the post-Holocaust era. For a positive reading of this "imaginary" stance, see my introduction to Finkielkraut's book.

[3] Goldberg, *ibid.*

[4] Robertson's critique of Prawer, in this regard, recognizes the great virtue and insight of Prawer's reading of Heine, not its limitation: "Prawer is trying to have it both ways: to credit Heine with achieving artistic completeness and also with rejecting the illusion of artistic completeness."

[5] See Willi Goetschel, "A Jewish Critic from Germany: Hermann Levin Goldschmidt," in this volume, for an analysis of the "Jewish" as in fact the German national question.

[6] Perry Anderson, "Components of the National Culture," originally in *New Left Review*, 50 (July-August 1968), reprinted in *English Questions* (London and New York: Verso, 1992), 97–117. Others listed include Ernst Gombrich, Isaiah Berlin, Bronislaw Malinowski, Melanie Klein, and Isaac Deutscher.

[7] See S. S. Prawer, *Karl Marx and World Literature* (Oxford: Clarendon P, 1976), 60–61.

[8] Irving Howe, "Auschwitz and High Mandarin," in *The Critical Point: On Literature and Culture* (New York: Horizon, 1973), 186. This is Howe's review of Steiner's book of essays, *In Bluebeard's Castle*. J. P. Stern, "What is German?" in *The Heart of Europe: Essays on Literature and Ideology* (Oxford and Cambridge: Blackwell, 1992), 300. Also Stern, "Revising the German Past?," in *The Heart of Europe*, 280–81.

[9] J. P. Stern, "What is German?" in *The Heart of Europe: Essays on Literature and Ideology* (Oxford and Cambridge: Blackwell, 1992), 300.

[10] Stern, "Revising the German Past?" in *Heart of Europe*, 280–81.

[11] "What is German?" 297.

[12] George Steiner, "The Hollow Miracle" (1959), in *Language and Silence: Essays on Language, Literature, and the Inhuman* (New York: Atheneum, 1967), 99.

[13] Erich Heller, "Preface to the Original Edition" (1952), *The Disinherited Mind: Essays in Modern German Literature and Thought,* expanded edition (New York: Harcourt Brace Jovanovich, 1975), xiii–xv.

[14] J. P. Stern, "On Prague German Literature," in *The Heart of Europe,* 62.

[15] Hermann Levin Goldschmidt, *Das Vermächtnis des deutschen Judentums,* vol. 2 of his *Werke,* ed. Willi Goetschel (Vienna: Passagen Verlag, 1994), 123, my translation.

[16] Siegbert Prawer, *Heine's Jewish Comedy: A Study of his Portraits of Jews and Judaism* (Oxford: Clarendon P, 1983), 76.

Panelists' Commentary

JEFFREY SAMMONS: I wrote out a few sentences in order to repress my loquaciousness to under five minutes. The first of these refers to a part of the presentation that is no longer in the version just presented, but I do hope that it will be in the printed version, because it goes into some of the darker moments of British Germanistik — which first of all makes us feel better and also diverts our gaze from its relentless focus on the Germans a little bit. Professor Robertson did mention here Jethro Bithell's 1932 survey of German literature in which he says he found a curious "Jew-sniffing" and gives some examples, and this caused me to look again at Bithell's poetry anthologies, on my shelf since my undergraduate days. Of Heine we are told that in the 1830s he is "no longer the romantic dreamer, he is the modern aggressive Jew," and the *Wintermärchen* "is narrated with corrosive wit marred by incredible coarseness," and while critic after critic identified "Jewish imitativeness" in *Buch der Lieder*, in *Romanzero* there is a "new and better Heine," "the laureate of his own race."[1]

In the other volume, from which Bithell in 1950 removed Nazi poets as no longer representative, he ascribes to Hofmannsthal "oriental smoothness."[2] Yet, I imagine all this is meant without malice since he attacks the "Jew-baiter," as he puts it, Adolf Bartels, as well as the Nazis.[3] Now obviously I look on these matters from the perspective of the Heine topic, and I won't have much to say about Steiner or Stern. Steiner seems to me the most enduringly Central European of them. I admire his cultural range, but I have suspected him from time to time of a language-usage fanaticism in descent from Karl Kraus, which always makes me uneasy when I encounter it. As for Stern, I value his studies of realism and found his book on the popular reception of Hitler interesting. But his Heine essay in *Idylls and Realities* in 1971 is so error-ridden and off-center as to suggest a distant acquaintance and a basic lack of real interest.[4]

With Prawer I have been most engaged, not without some, shall we say, dialectic. In my first Heine book I have thirty-nine index entries to Prawer, indicating my dependence on him, where I call *The Tragic Satirist* the very best that has ever been written on Heine's poetry — a judgment not much modified since.[5] I am also in awe of the grace and dignity of *Frankenstein's Island* (this is his book on Heine in England) and *Heine's Jewish Comedy*,[6] despite an occasional dissent, although I have had misgivings about a tendency to indiscriminate exhaustiveness and a doggedly chronological procedure that can obscure lineaments. This seemed true also of *Karl Marx and World Literature* and of the study of Thackeray and the Jews, which until a day or two ago I did not know had been published but which I read when it was still in manuscript.[7] Thackeray has a notorious capacity for amusing us against our better judgment. The lines quoted are impermissible but funny. The crazy rhymes may remind one of Heine, as Thackeray's appellation of Nathan Rothschild as "the Jew of the Kings" is something Heine might like to have said. Still, Thackeray's captious pungency, as Professor Robertson remarks, puts Prawer's tolerance under considerable strain. Professor Robertson has caught the irenic conciliatory manner, creditable to Prawer, but it was sometimes euphemistic, particularly in the case of Heine in England, where the forgiving account obscures the limits of Heine's vaunted cosmopolitanism. This perhaps un-German civility of scholarly discourse invites a more general consideration. Prawer's naturalization in Anglo-American critical habits corresponds to a lack of dialogue with German scholarship. He has paid little attention to contemporary German Heine study and, conversely, although the rising Judaistic interest in Germany leads to an occasional citation of *Heine's Jewish Comedy*, his other work including *The Tragic Satirist* is little acknowledged. That his 1970 Oxford inaugural lecture on Heine and Shakespeare is still the most perceptive essay on that topic has never been appreciated.[8] There may be a superintending issue of an alienation through Anglo-American assimilation of the White Emigration from the German intellectual culture in which it had its origin, exemplified most dramatically by the implacable fury with which the quondam Red Emigrant Adorno pursued Karl Popper.

PETER HELLER: Again I feel moved to make some nasty and perhaps unintelligible remarks — overly satiric no doubt — with some oblique pertinence I believe to one aspect of a problematic inherent in the exiles, including the exiled Germanists' acculturation. I have little Prawer and less Steiner but want to say something about Stern. Like Leslie Howard in *The Scarlet Pimpernel* — the facsimile of the epitome of the British aristocrat — J. P. Stern came from Czechoslovakia. Some Central European Jews, or individuals undeniably of Jewish extraction, responding well to the discreetly relentless pressure Britain put on its immigrants, were, it has seemed to me, occasionally quite well rewarded for their sustained effort to be as British as possible. Stern cultivated assiduously the manner to which he was not born, including a rather judgmental common sense that passed as British, at least at the time, though judiciously enriched and obscured by the admixture of a continental semi-philosophical essayism largely indebted to his older friend and occasional model, the far more original Erich Heller. Widely read, bright and urbane, Stern did not rock any boats. I recall a highly polished lecture comparing three models of adultery: Fontane's *Effi Briest,* Tolstoy's *Anna Karenina,* and Flaubert's *Madame Bovary.* Tolstoy fared reasonably well, but the prize went to the fine lovable *Effi Briest* for its balance and discreetly understated common sense and ethics, versus *Madame Bovary* which in its French way, its pitiless aesthetics, its symbolism, and its realism went as I recall a bit overboard. It seems unfortunately to be the habit of the truly great works of literature. There is much to be said for *aurea mediocritas,* even in literature (let alone in politics), but when the gold is largely painted on and wears off, it turns out, especially in the arts, to have been too dearly purchased, even though that *dear purchase* of gilded mediocrity was certainly preferable to the rabid fanaticized mediocrity which Stern had every right and reason to indict.

PAUL REITTER: Falling neatly into the space left open for me, I will speak mostly about Steiner. First I wanted to mention — just sort of a technical point — a reference to Steiner's theory of translation, or rather the criticisms that it has encountered from linguists and the linguistic community. More recently the work of cognitive linguists such as Berkeley's George Lakoff vindicates Steiner's conjectures. I just thought I'd throw that out since it does adumbrate what I am going to say about him, which is largely favorable. I would like to underline David Suchoff's call for more sympathy for Steiner's predicament. I read *Language and Silence* five or six years ago and, on a personal note, I was impressed by the intensity of his voice, of his confession, of his testimony. And though certainly I had some reservations about this absolute identification of Jewish identity with the experience of the Holocaust, it nonetheless is a compelling testimony, and I think it remains very widely read and influential. It does a great deal toward keeping German literature in the public sphere. Also, it is very important to point out that Steiner is alive to the dangers of that kind of identification and has spoken about it in various places — in the book on Heidegger for instance.[9] So it's not as if he makes this move unreflexively.

I also wanted to speak a little bit about *After Babel*. While Steiner in his explicit meditations on German-Jewish identity, for instance in the essay on Kafka, speaks of it as a difficult, uneasy, failed synthesis but certainly one that proved enormously productive, and one that he finds fascinating and continues to engage with, one which drives his interest, as he puts it. In *After Babel* he speaks of Jewish texts within the context of the German tradition without necessarily thematizing explicitly the Jewishness of these texts, the fact that they were written by Jews. He seems to present, in other words, a different narrative of the relationship between Judaism and the German tradition. He doesn't set them up as discrete categories that collide spectacularly in various places and ultimately cataclysmically at the end, but rather there is a sort of mutual influence that makes them almost inextricable. They are confluent in places to such an extent that it doesn't seem always to make sense of talking about a German linguistic tradition and a Jewish linguistic tradition. I refer here to the remarks on the Kabbalah with an extravagant emphasis on the influence of the Kabbalah on Romantic thinkers like Hamann and Herder, and then later on where he talks about the Rosenzweig-Buber Bible or Karl Kraus's translations of Shakespeare alongside Stefan George's. And these for him seem to be one linguistic phenomenon. So, perhaps that contradiction is worth talking about at some point — the idea that what Steiner does in practice may in some places contradict what he says when he speaks in explicit theoretical terms about the question of German-Jewish identity.

I wanted to also come back to the essays in *Language and Silence*, those programmatic essays, and mention also that while there is a kind of radical particularism there, he is claiming that his relationship as a Jew to German culture is, again, radically indistinguishable from his experience of the Holocaust and therefore nothing like what somebody else's relationship, a non-Jew's relationship, to German literature might be. At the same time, he does, like Adorno, call into question not simply the tenability of Jews studying German literature but the reason for reading literature *at all* after the Holocaust. He does that very forcefully. He says that people who operated the concentration camps were in some cases trained to read Goethe and play Mozart. So, in other words, his reflecting on the Holocaust calls the tradition of the humanities, generally speaking, into question — one of the few thinkers to do so, and of course in doing so, cutting a radical contrast to the prevailing New Criticism, which of course, posited literature as self-evident value.

While I am on the topic of justification for studying literature, and how and why Steiner has perhaps problematized it, I thought I would come back briefly to a discussion that we had this morning, where Professor Heller criticized what he perceived to be — if I understood him correctly — a demand that Jewish critics justify their involvement or engagement with German literature. The reason for this criticism being that such an emphasis can, or often does, emerge from a kind of chauvinism according to which Jews who were so victimized by German culture shouldn't spend their time with German culture; or it can come from a kind of identity politics that tries to privilege the relationship of Jewish critics to German literature and in doing so of course emphasizes the particularity of their relationship with German literature. (I hope that is clear. It sounded a little circular.) In any event, the point I wanted to make is simply that I think you make a good strong claim that we shouldn't have to necessarily justify our engagement with German literature beyond the kinds of justifications that other critics need to bring forth to justify their critical undertakings. Marc Weiner also made the point that it's in some ways wrongheaded to ask people to justify their engagement with a literature that's in some way connected with barbarism, because that implies that there are some literatures out there that don't have this connection. In any event, these are valid points. But the fact remains that as Walter Sokel pointed out this morning, there was an acute pressure, an experienced pressure, or rather the émigrés experienced that pressure, to justify their engagement with German literature, and they experienced it acutely and their ideas of involvement with German literature were forged by this pressure. And so, if we wish to understand their critical undertakings, we have to bring it into account, and I guess the challenge would be to do so without engaging in some sort of flaccid identity politics. I'll end on that note.

Discussion

PETER HELLER: If I recall, what I said there was rather to highlight that question. To say, yes, indeed, it has been raised, it needs to be raised, it also should be addressed from various points. Why there has been that felt need, and what it really implies both on the Jewish side, on the German side. I was very *grateful,* and very much in *agreement* with Walter Sokel for raising this question. I thought that this conference has been a little at fault in not breaking into this domain of traumatic issues, and sort of hovering above them somewhat. That was my point.

ANTONY POLONSKY (BRANDEIS UNIVERSITY): I'd like to make one observation on what Peter Heller said. He commented on the Czech origins of J. P. Stern. I think that the Prawers were first-generation from Poland, as far as I remember, and I think that was quite important. That's how they got out of Germany, because they were expelled as Polish Jews in 1938. That is certainly so in the case of Siegbert Prawer (and I think Ruth Prawer too) — he has several times referred to this. He once told me he speaks Polish. Many of these people — Stern, Prawer, Steiner — came from the German periphery, that is to say, from the German-speaking areas of Central Europe but not from the Second German Reich, which also perhaps illustrates something about them.

AMIR ESHEL: Ich hätte nicht gedacht, daß ich hier George Steiner sozusagen verteidigen würde, aber ich habe das Bedürfnis das dennoch zu tun. Zunächst ein kleiner Hinweis: 1959 erscheint sein Aufsatz "The Hollow Miracle,"[10] ein Aufsatz über das deutsche Wunder sozusagen. Dieser Aufsatz wurde natürlich ins Deutsche übersetzt. 1963 machte die Zeitschrift *Sprache im technischen Zeitalter* eine ganze Nummer mit Antworten auf Steiners und zwei weitere Aufsätze (von John McCormick und Hans Habe).[11] Man muß es heute nochmals lesen, um zu glauben, wie vor allem jüdische Kritiker auf Steiner reagierten. Ich möchte drei Namen nennen: einmal Marcel Reich-Ranicki, Hilde Spiel und Hans Weigel. Alle drei litten in der NS-Zeit, mußten ins Exil gehen oder wurden wie Reich-Ranicki deportiert, ich nehme an, daß das alles bekannt ist. Reich-Ranicki meint in seiner Replik, daß Steiner letztendlich ein Feuilletonist sei, zu salopp, zu vernichtend, seine Urteile unbegründet.[12] Hilde Spiel schreibt, daß Steiner vorsichtig sein solle, weil er nicht wie andere zu den Heimkehrenden gehört. Das ist sozusagen sein Fehler.[13] Und Hans Weigel geht wohl am weitesten und entwickelt eine ganze Theorie darüber, daß der eigentliche Niedergang der deutschen Sprache und der deutschen Literatur nicht erst im Zuge der NS-Zeit erfolgte, sondern *vor* der NS-Zeit.[14] Nach der NS-Zeit, sprich seine Gegenwart, sei die Blüte der deutschen Sprache, die eigentlich schöne Zeit sei die Zeit nach 1945. Die Zeit davor, die dreißiger Jahre und die zwanziger Jahre bedeuten nichts, da ist die deutsche Sprache korrumpiert und verlorengegangen und erst nach dem Krieg erleben wir sozusagen die neue Blüte der deutschen Sprache. Ich glaube, dass gerade anhand dieser drei Reaktionen von jüdischen Schriftstellern/Kritikern — alle drei waren Juden, obwohl sie vielleicht nicht in gleichem Maße dazu gestanden haben — es aus heutiger Sicht sehr interessant ist zu beobachten, wie gerade die drei auf Steiner reagierten. Auch hier könnte die vergleichende Perspektive hilfreich sein.

PETER DEMETZ: I just have a question to Professor Ritchie Robertson. It is a question about Stern, whom I knew for quite a while. The longer I listened to your apt characterization, the more it seemed to me that much in Stern's viewpoint can be explained using Ockham's razor, by his option for the Czechs. I don't think he was a German critic migrating to England. I think the Stern family was really firmly Czech-patriotic, and from that followed for instance his enlistment in the Czech Wing and not in the British Air Force. In my mind he would have had a choice, but he, I think, following his early attachment, enlisted in the Czech Air Force, the Czech Wing. Especially when you characterized J. P. Stern's view of Jewish-German closedness, which is so negative, I hear an old Czech argument against the German inclinations of the Jews and that goes back to 1843 or so, when Karel Havliček, the most outstanding Czech liberal, castigated a young Jew, because he dared to write Czech poetry. That's a very old argument there. I think much can be explained that way.

The second is really a question, namely, whether the English preoccupation with a political interpretation of Kafka and Kafka's world that is so strong in J. P. Stern and elsewhere, doesn't derive from Edwin Muir, whom you know better than me. I remember that in Edwin Muir's early translation there was a preface added in which this political interpretation for Kafka as anticipating a totalitarian system was very strong. And my question is whether subsequent English interpreters might not have been filling out the possibilities that were suggested by Edwin Muir.

WALTER SOKEL: I am answering Peter Demetz in connection with his discussion about Kafka's *Trial*, because it's not an English reaction only, it's also a Soviet Russian reaction — of dissidents. When *The Trial* first appeared in samizdat in the 1960s, the dissident intellectuals were asking, "Which one of us wrote this book?"

HASKELL BLOCK: I want to say a little bit about George Steiner. I once had the office of introducing Steiner when he came to the Graduate Center of the City University of New York. He was not very happy about his visit. He didn't care for the impression of either Bryant Park or Forty-second Street directly in front of the Graduate Center. He remarked in a rather supercilious way to us, well you may enjoy living in this place, but I don't have to. And he really felt that he was quite superior to the surroundings and very happy to come, make a brief statement, and then leave. Steiner's work, I think, is important in contemporary criticism. I've read several of his books, and I found some of his interpretive work quite valuable. When I had occasion to write on Paul Celan, I read some of Steiner's pieces. He has a couple of very long essays on Celan in the *Times Literary Supplement.* They are very much worth getting a hold of, because I think he writes of Celan with unusual understanding and sympathy and he has worked through Celan's poetry in a very careful, deliberate, and illuminating way.[15] This strikes me as one of the best things that he has done. But I also recall an old friend, a rather well-known Slavicist, who once complained to me about discussing literature with Steiner, about which he said, every time you try to make a point or engage in an argument, he hits you over the head with "what about six million Jews?" and this seems to be the only thing that Steiner can talk about, and he pronounces this with an air of proving something. Well, in a sense, Steiner was ahead, it seems to me, of the movement of historical consciousness. We were slow in the United States to realize the fullness, the enormity of the genocide. I found out in 1945 from the pictures in the newspapers, discovery of the camps, and so on. But even then, it didn't strike home until much later, when one realized just how awful and to what an extent this business was carried on. I think Steiner had a strong sense of that rather early. It is very much to his credit that he pressed as hard as he did. I think it is an important aspect of contemporary consciousness and has a lot to do with the fact that we have this conference here today. But Steiner, I think, emerges as a very mixed kind of critic. I have the feeling that some of his work like the *Tolstoy or Dostoevsky* book — that won't stand up, a highly journalistic and to my mind rather superficial performance.[16] But there are other things that Steiner has done that are at least in parts quite interesting, like his book *Antigones,* which is in a sense the old *Stoffgeschichte* but more literary and more sensitive.[17] He has read those plays, with the aid of Hegel, and thought very hard and illuminatingly about them. One has to reckon with George Steiner. I find him not a very attractive person simply because he is so full of himself, but he has a right to be so in a way, too, because he is a very wide-ranging and interesting and important critic.

Antony Polonksy: I think one of the things you have to remember about George Steiner is this: he was very badly treated for a very long time, and I think that this explains a lot of his behavior.

Paul Reitter: Well, as flippant as it sounds, I consider myself privileged not to have met Steiner, simply because I have a sort of fresh perspective on his works and I am not bogged down by unpleasant or pleasant encounters. One of the things that makes him so interesting is that he calls the humanities into question even as he affirms them, everywhere — affirms the study of literature everywhere, is obsessed with it, believes in its value and yet struggles to formulate its value in a way that reckons with the fact that people who, again, committed acts of barbarism were trained in the humanities, so that the traditional justification that the humanities somehow necessarily humanizes can no longer be used. Perhaps this is one of the things that pushed some of the émigrés to look at literature in new ways. Hence his emphasis on the communicative aspects of language — language and literature as a kind of cultural practice. You can say similar things about Erich Heller as well. He is also somebody who not quite as explicitly as Steiner also called into question in various ways the morality of our cultural accomplishment as far as its humanizing effect is concerned.

Ritchie Robertson: I am grateful especially to David Suchoff for complementing my paper by going out into wider questions and moving out from my focus on literary criticism to the cultural criticism practiced as well by Stern. One or two responses — I can't respond to all the points, but here are some. First, Walter Sokel was very kind in answering for me the question put by Peter Demetz. I do however want to answer it a bit. The political view of Kafka comes from several sources. One of them is Brecht, but I don't think that Edwin Muir is among them. Muir's prefaces to the translations of Kafka published by himself and his wife during the 1930s, contain, I think, very fine criticism. The center of Kafka's work for Muir was the aphorisms which Kafka wrote in 1917/18 when convalescing, or trying to convalesce, from tuberculosis in the Bohemian village of Zürau. And I must confess that these are also the center of my own understanding of Kafka, and it is from those that I move out to the novels and fiction. I associate Muir much more with the religious interpretation of Kafka.

I was very interested by Amir Eshel's information on the controversy aroused by Steiner's "Hollow Miracle" essay. I have never known what to make of that essay. And these responses are extremely interesting.

I want to say a little bit more about the situation of German Studies in Britain and the impact made by these new arrivals. It is indicative, I think, not of malice but of a quite deep cluelessness about events in Germany that the house journal of British Germanistik, *German Life and Letters,* was founded in October of 1936, at a time when, as the editor said, relations between Britain and Germany seemed to be improving. The first issue contains an account of the visit of the editor and two other professors of German for whom they had paid, to the house of Hans Grimm who held a meeting for various poets including E. G. Kolbenheyer and Börries von Münchhausen. Everybody had a splendid time. Well, the private correspondence between Goebbels and his London agent, recently brought to light by a London journalist, shows that the Nazis regarded *German Life and Letters* as extremely unreliable.[18] So, I don't think we can assign the slightest of degree of malice or sympathy for the Nazis to these professors, but a considerable degree of out-of-touchness. That's the background for the "Jew-sniffing" remarks by Bithell, which Jeffrey Sammons quoted.

The German émigrés who came to Britain, many of whom completed their education in Britain, are very striking for the small extent to which they thematized Jewishness. Two examples who come to mind, Hans Reiss[19] and Charlotte Jolles,[20] the Fontane scholar, did very much traditional Germanistik, focusing on canonical authors. I think it is a matter of generation, in part, that Prawer and Stern had little to say about these matters. I shall make an exception for an essay by Prawer, which I already quoted from in passing. An essay on Jewish contributions to German lyric poetry, the word "contributions," I think, is very much of its time, which he contributed to the *Leo Baeck Year Book* in London in 1963.[21] It is also significant that the main focus of the *Leo Baeck Year Book* has always been on German-Jewish history. It has sometimes articles on German-Jewish literature, Walter Sokel has written for it, but these have been and still are very much in the minority. And that goes along with the fact that German-Jewish matters and Holocaust studies have only begun to make their entry into British Germanistik. A great landmark in this respect has been the foundation of the Center for German-Jewish Studies at the University of Sussex, of which the director is Edward Timms. And that links up with the recent immense growth, not only in Britain but worldwide, of interest in exile studies. And we are just in time to catch one or two exile writers in Britain who are still alive, although many, just as Erich Fried received very little attention from British Germanisten, and some like Gabriele Tergit none at all.[22]

In my paper, I was intent on concentrating on the published works and literary criticism of these writers. I didn't want to enter into any personal or professional gossip. Nevertheless, although I dissent, I understand what Peter Heller means by his comments on Stern's acculturation. I'll simply mention two things, because they are already in the public sphere, in the obituaries and published by people who knew him very well. One remarkable fact, which Nicholas Boyle mentioned in his obituary, is that Peter Stern was extremely fond of fox hunting, because it is a democratic sport.[23] And another that comes from the obituary by Noel Annan, is that in his career Stern did not have as easy a ride as one might think.[24] I won't say any more, but that is a quite important fact.

Another feature of British Germanistik, which is relevant to the present discussion I think is this: there is in Britain a very strong homegrown tradition of literary criticism, especially that associated with William Empson, I. A. Richards and T. S. Eliot, which migrated to America and became known as the New Criticism. And it is partly because both British Germanists and émigrés found that tradition so congenial that we have not always paid the attention that we should to debates in Germany. And German Germanists, it must be said because the matter is reciprocal, have not always paid as close attention as they might to British Germanistik. That I think is changing. But it does help to explain why Siegbert Prawer's work on Heine bears only a tangential relation to the great growth of Heine studies in Germany from the early 1970s onwards. And I would say also that the work of Nigel Reeves in Great Britain, has received a shamefully small degree of attention in Germany. Although it is true that one of his finest essays was published in *Euphorion,* his book however, *Heine: Poetry and Politics,* seldom figures in bibliographies of German books on Heine.[25] There has been a matter of mutual neglect, which needs to be rectified. And it may well be that Prawer's work on Heine does not export well — a pity, but it may well be the case.

I'm coming to an end, but I want to mention another feature that has very much held up developments in British Germanistik and indeed put them on ice, and that is the almost complete dearth of academic jobs from the late 1970s to the late 1980s, a very disheartening time to the Germanist. That has now changed. I think the three growth areas, the three areas where British Germanistik is extremely lively are: exile studies, German-Jewish studies, and women's studies. It is now an exciting time to be a British Germanist, and I can only say that it took a long wait. Now, I've said my piece, and I am very grateful for having had the opportunity to say something about the British angle on the fascinating and thorny subject of this conference.

Editors' Annotations

[1] *An Anthology of German Poetry 1830–1889,* ed. Jethro Bithell, 2d ed. (New York: Rinehart, n.d.), xix–xxii. The preface is dated 1946.

[2] *An Anthology of German Poetry, 1880–1940,* ed. Jethro Bithell, 5th rev. ed. with additional poems (London: Methuen, 1951), xxxix. The preface is dated 1950.

[3] Bithell, ed., *An Anthology of German Poetry, 1880–1940,* 5th rev. ed., xl, lviii. — A prolific writer, though not an academic Germanist, Adolf Bartels (1862–1945) was the author of a literary history that went through nineteen editions between 1901 and 1943: *Geschichte der deutschen Literatur,* 19th ed. (Braunschweig: G. Westermann, 1943); he was also the author of *Rasse: Sechzehn Aufsätze zur nationalen Weltanschauung* (Hamburg: Verlag der Hanseatischen Druck- und Verlags-Anstalt, 1909); *Rasse und Volkstum: Gesammelte Aufsätze zur nationalen Weltanschauung,* 2. verm. Aufl. (Weimar: A. Duncker, 1920); *Der völkische Gedanke: Ein Wegweiser* (Weimar: F. Fink, 1923).

[4] J. P. Stern, "Contentious Muse," *Idylls and Realities: Studies in Nineteenth-Century German Literature* (New York: Ungar, 1971), 53–75.

[5] Jeffrey L. Sammons, *Heinrich Heine, the Elusive Poet* (New Haven: Yale UP, 1969), viii. The complete title of Prawer's book: Siegbert S. Prawer, *Heine, the Tragic Satirist: A Study of the Later Poetry, 1827–1856* (Cambridge: UP, 1961).

[6] Siegbert S. Prawer, *Frankenstein's Island: England and the English in the Writings of Heinrich Heine* (Cambridge: Cambridge UP, 1986) and Siegbert S. Prawer, *Heine's Jewish Comedy: A Study of his Portraits of Jews and Judaism* (Oxford: Clarendon P, 1983).

[7] Siegbert S. Prawer, *Karl Marx and World Literature* (Oxford: Clarendon P, 1976) and Siegbert S. Prawer, *Israel at Vanity Fair: Jews and Judaism in the Writings of W. M. Thackeray* (Leiden and New York: E. J. Brill, 1992).

[8] Siegbert S. Prawer, *Heine's Shakespeare: A Study in Contexts.* An inaugural lecture delivered before the University of Oxford on 5 May 1970 (Oxford: Clarendon P, 1970).

[9] George Steiner, *Heidegger* (Glasgow: Fontana/Collins, 1978).

[10] George Steiner, "The Hollow Miracle (1959)," in *Language and Silence: Essays on Language, Literature, and the Inhuman* (New York: Atheneum, 1977), 95–109.

[11] "Deutsch — gefrorene Sprache in einem gefrorenen Land?" *Sprache im technischen Zeitalter* 6 (1963). — Cf. Amir Eshel, "Die hohle Sprache. Die Debatte um George Steiners 'Das hohle Wunder,'" in *Deutsche Nachkriegsliteratur und der Holocaust,* ed. Holger Gehle, Doron Kiesel, Hanno Loewy and Stephan Braese (Frankfurt am Main and New York: Campus, 1998), 317–30.

[12] Marcel Reich-Ranicki, "Nicht der Schimmer eines Beweises," *Sprache im technischen Zeitalter* 6 (1963): 464–66.

[13] Hilde Spiel, "Für und wider die deutsche Literatur," *Sprache im technischen Zeitalter* 6 (1963): 450–52.

[14] Hans Weigel, "Blühende Sprache in einem aufgetauten Land," *Sprache im technischen Zeitalter* 6 (1963): 453–58.

[15] George Steiner, "A lacerated destiny," *Times Literary Supplement,* No. 4809, June 2, 1995, 3–4; "Paul Celan," *TLS,* No. 4480, Feb. 10–16, 1989, 135–36; cf. also "North of the Future," *The New Yorker* 65 (Aug. 28, 1989), 93–96.

[16] George Steiner, *Tolstoy or Dostoevsky?* (New York: Knopf, 1959).

[17] George Steiner, *Antigones* (Oxford and New York: Clarendon P, 1984).

[18] L. A. Willoughby, "Hans Grimm," *German Life and Letters,* o.s. 1 (1936): 78–79. — For the context see Charmian Brinson, "Sixty Years on: German Life and Letters and the National Socialists," *German Life and Letters* 49.4 (October 1996): 479–87.

[19] See Hans Reiss, "Exil oder Akkulturation? Zur Kontinuität der britischen und irischen Germanistik in der Zeit des 'Dritten Reiches' und in der frühen Nachkriegszeit," in *Modernisierung oder Überfremdung? Zur Wirkung deutscher Exilanten in der Germanistik der Aufnahmeländer,* ed. Walter Schmitz (Stuttgart, Weimar: Metzler, 1994), 55–70. — Hans Reiss was born in Mannheim in 1922. Following the Reichskristallnacht in 1938 he fled Germany. He took his doctorate at Trinity College, Dublin, in 1945. After holding various teaching posts at British and Canadian institutions he settled at the University of Bristol in 1965, where he remained until his retirement in 1988. For a full list of his publications see *Texte, Motive und Gestalten der Goethezeit: Festschrift für Hans Reiss,* ed. John L. Hibbert und H. B. Nisbet (Tübingen: Niemeyer, 1989).

[20] Charlotte Jolles (b. 1909 in Berlin) earned her doctorate in 1937 with a thesis under the direction of Julius Petersen entitled *Theodor Fontane und die Politik.* In 1939 she emigrated to England, where she worked aiding refugees for several years. From 1955–1977 she held a post at Birkbeck College, University of London. A full list of her publications can be found in *Exilanten und andere Deutsche in Fontanes London: Charlotte Jolles zum 85. Geburtstag,* ed. Peter Alter und Rudolf Muhs (Stuttgart: Hans-Dieter Heinz, 1996), 463–69.

[21] Siegbert S. Prawer, "Jewish Contributions to German Lyric Poetry," *Year Book of the Leo Baeck Institute* 8 (1963): 149–70

[22] Gabriele Tergit (b. 1894 in Berlin–d. 1982 in London) was the daughter of Berlin industrialist Siegfried Fritz Hirschmann. She studied history, philosophy and sociology from 1919–1923, taking a doctorate in 1925. During the twenties and early thirties she was active as a reporter and feuilletonist for the *Vossische Zeitung,* the *Berliner Börsen-Courier,* and the *Berliner Tageblatt.* Her first novel, *Käsebier erobert den Kurfürstendamm* appeared with Rowohlt Verlag in 1931 (rpt. Berlin, 1988). She fled to London via Palestine and Czechoslovakia in 1938. Her works include the novel *Effingers* (Hamburg: Hammerich & Lesser, 1951); *Atem einer anderen Welt: Berliner Reportagen,* ed. Jens Brüning (Frankfurt am Main: Suhrkamp, 1994); *Blüten der zwanziger Jahre: Gerichtsreportagen und Feuilletons 1923–1933,* ed. Jens Brüning (Berlin: Rotation, 1984); *Der erste Zug nach Berlin: Novelle,* ed. Jens Brüning (Berlin: Das Neue Berlin, 2000); *Im Schnellzug nach Haifa* (Berlin: Transit, 1996).

[23] "He had a boyish taste for fast cars and neat suits of surprising colours, wrote a characterful semi-italic hand, and was an enthusiastic horseman, with a precise Viennese style, who loved the classlessness and misty winter romance of local fox-hunting." Nicholas Boyle, "The Essentials of Criticism: Obituary of Peter Stern," *The Guardian* (London), 21 November 1991.

[24] Eulogy of February 29, 1992, published in the *Cambridge Review*, May 5, 1992.

[25] Nigel Reeves, *Heinrich Heine: Poetry and Politics* (London: Oxford UP, 1974). For a list of his publications see *Vermittlungen: German Studies at the Turn of the Century. Festschrift für Nigel B. R. Reeves,* ed. Rüdiger Görner und Helen Kelly-Holmes (Munich: Iudicium, 1999), 267–75.

7: Peter Demetz:
On Marcel Reich-Ranicki

Marcel Reich-Ranicki
(© ZDF Bilderdienst)

On Marcel Reich-Ranicki

Peter Demetz

POSTPRANDIAL TALKS ARE a tricky business at the best of occasions, and I confess that I feel a few uncertainties about my promise to speak about Jewish critics and German literature as such, at large, no less.[1] I have been long unwilling to dabble in generalities and I would rather speak, tonight and now, about *one* prominent critic whom I have come to know in recent years, if not decades. Marcel Reich-Ranicki of Frankfurt was unable, unfortunately, to attend our conference in person, and in his absence I would like to say something about his attitudes, ideas, and achievements — not in an impersonal way but keeping in mind my own experiences which probably qualify me, as least as his contemporary between societies, to understand him more clearly. I hasten to say that I am not going to indulge in the popular sport of Marcel Reich-Ranicki bashing, by now an established literary genre in Germany and elsewhere, especially among the younger generation. Reich-Ranicki bashers have been working with clubs or, as did Peter Handke,[2] ironic condescension, but rarely with the more delicate stubbornness used in Count Franz Czernin's little book.[3] I think Count Czernin would have argued more convincingly if he had not touched on the questions of Marcel's Jewishness (I am using the term with hesitations) in a few lines and with elegant kid gloves saying that Marcel's life has been shaped by "certain forces of disasters that are usually described in political terms."[4] It would be easy to suggest that younger Austrian and German intellectuals have a difficult time calling a spade a spade, but they are not the only ones (as our conference attests), and Hans Mayer once suggested that speaking about himself as a Jew among Germans he would do better to tell the story of an individual life than theoretically to discuss ideas, however pure and well-defined. I would like to follow his advice, at least in part.

I do not know of any American critic who is as widely and prominently visible as is Marcel Reich-Ranicki to German-speaking audiences. Harold Bloom is happily greeted by his friends when he is walking down

Das Literarische Quartett, October 21, 1993:
Sigrid Löffler, Ruth Klüger, Marcel Reich-Ranicki,
Hellmut Karasek (© ZDF Bilderdienst)

Das Literarische Quartett, November 18, 1996:
Sigrid Löffler, Marcel Reich-Ranicki, Hellmut Karasek
(© ZDF Bilderdienst)

Linden Street in New Haven, but Marcel has become a national figure and a star of literature, easily recognized from Kiel to Klagenfurt by all readers of his essays, his many books, and, above all, by the viewers of his television talk show. In the United States, a *New York Times* review on Sunday may increase print orders (I hope so) but a few enthusiastic remarks uttered by Marcel Reich-Ranicki on his show *Literarisches Quartett* may push a title, languishing on the overcrowded market, close to the top of the bestseller list, as happened to the memoirs of our colleague Ruth Klüger.[5] Just to speak about visibility: about seven weeks ago I had lunch with Marcel and his wife Tosia at *his* Italian restaurant (all German intellectuals have *their* favorite Italian restaurant because there are no German places left) and when we entered, he was ceremoniously welcomed by the owner, the maître d', and the waiters in impeccable white aprons. A hush fell on the crowd of the other Sunday guests who started to whisper to each other and began casting "yes-we-know-you" glances in our direction. Ach, what is literary glory! Sometime ago, the *Literarisches Quartett* was held in Prague, and shortly before the broadcast I walked down Wenceslas Square with Marcel. The town, as usual, was full of German *Bildungstouristen* who nearly formed a *Spalier* to let Marcel and Mrs. Reich-Ranicki pass through their admiring ranks, in the outdoor cafés heads were turned, and, suddenly, a Czech taxi driver came sprinting from the other side to address Marcel in impeccable Czech German: "Ich kenne Ihnen von der Television." Alas, his admiration did not extend to the other members of his guild. Taking us from the hotel to the Goethe Institute, he overcharged us one hundred percent.

In an essay first published in 1971, Marcel Reich-Ranicki suggested that Jewishness, or *das Jüdische,* was a rather vague concept, as was *das Deutsche* or *das Preussische,*[6] and, on various occasions, he comes close to approaching a self-definition of being Jewish by negation and exclusion rather than by inclusion; I find similar attitudes among a few of his contemporaries including Hilde Domin or Jurek Becker: a series of no's with a yes at the end. Marcel Reich-Ranicki readily admits that he is not religious at all, reveals that he last attended services at a synagogue sixty or more years ago, does not feel himself to be a member of a Jewish community, whether described in metaphysical, legal, or political terms; and yet he asserts very often that it is impossible not to be shaped, at least partly, by Jewish family origins, historical experiences, and by his non-Jewish contemporaries who reminded him and his family that they were Jewish — as happened to Heine, Börne, and many other Jewish liberals, baptized or not, in

Germany. When Nathan is asked by Saladin why, in spite of so many of his emancipated ideas, *ich bin mein Volk,* he still wears the Jewish garb, Nathan speaks about his loyalty to his forebears, for he cannot tolerate the thought of being disloyal to them; and he thus anticipates important reasons why so many irreligious Jews outside their communities hesitate to call themselves people totally freed of their origins; if, in our century, loyalty to mother and father lived on, it turned, after the Shoah, into an assertion of ineradicable solidarity with all those who perished in the camps. I believe that Marcel Reich-Ranicki would assent to a definition of his Jewishness not on religious, metaphysical, legal or linguistic grounds but would feel closer to an individuation based on solemn loyalty to his kin and his continued solidarity with those, past and present, who have been humiliated, disadvantaged, persecuted, and killed.

Thinking about these questions was useful to me when I asked where I stand myself, and not only in my assumptions of literary criticism. My situation may have been even more complicated than Marcel's, at least legally and nationally, and I thought that it would be easier to account for my early experience of European history if everybody knew what it meant to have a Jewish mother and a non-Jewish father who made my education more interesting because they belonged not only to different religious traditions but also to different political and linguistic societies which were definitely not interchangeable. The European thirties and forties were not a propitious time for young boys who were of such contradictory origins and yet wished to realize themselves, as young people usually do. I wanted to be another Thomas von Aquinas, Leo Trotsky, and Fred Astaire (not necessarily in that order) and I had a difficult time listening to what *others* said about me. Most of the time I was busy withholding my assent to classifications that did not emerge from my own anarchic experiences. Visceral liberals will have little difficulty in understanding my youthful opposition to any kind of *Fremdbestimmung,* whether implied in the halachic laws declaring the son of a Jewish mother to be a Jew, no matter what he wanted to be himself, or in the aberrations of a Darwinism gone astray in the Nuremberg Laws that were specific about the incorrigible importance of the maternal womb, and told me that I was a "Mischling ersten Grades" who had to bear the consequences, like it or not, of that earliest moment of extraction. The alternatives were troublesome; if I withheld my assent to my origins or proclaimed that I was that miraculously and perfectly free human being of the philosophical textbooks, I would be guilty of a failure to feel the most essential compassion with my mother and her relatives (most of whom died in the camps) and all who died with them.

Peter Demetz, Klagenfurt, June 1993

Perhaps it is too high a price to pay for an abstract freedom of all origins, yet I am somewhat skeptical about the new efforts in our profession to reconstitute (as it happens in a recent intelligent article in the *German Quarterly*) a category of the "hybrids" ("half-Jews" of yesteryear will welcome the more elegant appellation) as another minority to be defended against the claims of a tradition disinterested in roots, origins, and the blood of *Herkunft*.[7]

Jewish citizens living in West Germany, it is widely believed, more publicly asserted their interests in the late seventies and early eighties (be it that the anti-Zionist attitudes of the radical student movement demanded an answer or that the American Holocaust movie on TV challenged millions of viewers). It should be said that Marcel Reich-Ranicki was among the first who wanted to clarify the role of Jewish writers in Germany. His collected essays *Über Ruhestörer: Juden in der deutschen Literatur* (1973) asked what Jews shared in German literary history from the eighteenth to the twentieth century. It promises to enlighten us about history, but it is also an intensely personal book by a critic who wants to speak about his own experiences without moving his ego to the center of the stage; and even when he, about ten years later, answered questions about his earlier life, put to him by Joachim

Fest, he avoided all sentimentality and self-dramatization and insisted that he wanted to differentiate.[8] Taking his stand against anti-Semites and unreflecting philosemites, growing in numbers, in his essays he looked at the biographies and achievements of Heine, Börne, Schnitzler and a few recent writers, among them Friedrich Torberg or Jurek Becker, and noted that he fully agreed with Lion Feuchtwanger who had come to the conclusion that it was impossible to discover a linguistic element common to all German writers of Jewish origin — yet he felt dissatisfied with Sigmund Freud's late remark that what Jews shared was "das geheimnisvolle Etwas" difficult to analyze.[9]

Marcel Reich-Ranicki believes, or rather postulates, that there must be a specificity that contributes in a "high degree to shaping" what Jewish writers have done and thought; and after he has put aside language, he prefers to speak about "a shared perspective" created by the social experience of living on a kind of island, *eine Art Inseldasein*,[10] enabling these writers to see what is well-known and what is usual in a new and surprising way — though formalist readers of Victor Shklovsky like myself may object immediately that it is the glory of any good poet, whether Jewish or not, to see events newly and to articulate insights in an unusual way. There is always trouble brewing when a critic looks for specification in the search for generalities; as long as Marcel characterizes Heine and Börne, he moves on firm ground but perhaps less so when he cannot resist the temptation to declare that Heine's and Börne's striking characteristics anticipate later Jewish writing as a shared combination of lucid skepticism and a strong trust in reason and logic, also to be found, e.g., in Alfred Kerr, whom he greatly admires, and in others. He certainly goes a little too far when he suggests that Moritz Heimann fuses the severity of the Prussian with the lucidity, the skeptical passion, and the intense *engagement* of the Jews (1971),[11] as if these attitudes could be ascribed to all — certainly against Lessing's warning, in his mid eighteenth-century comedy that we never speak about, *Die Juden* (plural), as do the most dubious characters in his play. It would be far less difficult to argue, as does Marcel Reich-Ranicki, that Heine's achievements are the "fragments of one great provocation"[12] and that the function of many Jewish writers in German was to challenge, to provoke, to disturb the suffocating peace of the social and cultural consensus precisely because they wrote within the language but lived at a certain distance to the majority of its speakers who looked askance at them, to say the least.

I do not doubt that speaking about exemplary Jewish writers and critics of the German past — praising their lucidity, skepticism, rational engagement, and celebrating them as productive *provocateurs* and restless "Ruhestörer" — Marcel Reich-Ranicki defines the intentions and norms according to which he measures himself. Yet every moment unfolds within the flow of history, and it may be one of the paradoxes of Marcel's indisputable achievements that he has become a *Ruhestörer* of the most gentle kind, saving, protecting, and shielding important literary events that do not really provoke anymore, except orthodox members of yesterday's avant-garde or experimenters unaware of the long traditions of experiment. He is certainly not concerned with radically substituting one canon of texts for another; he is one of the most incisive defenders of Lessing's authority yet has kept strangely away from Moses Mendelssohn, the first semiotician among the Germans; for many decades he has admired the best (not the worst) novels of Anna Seghers rather than Christa Wolf's "Innerlichkeit"; he has come to love Goethe more deeply than Schiller; and his ancient admiration for Thomas Mann has prevented him from fully engaging with Alfred Döblin, the really modern writer among the German novelists of our century.

Horst Krüger, an intelligent observer of the literary scene, vividly remembers what happened among the young German intellectuals, very much left of center, when Marcel Reich-Ranicki was called to edit the literary pages of the *Frankfurter Allgemeine Zeitung:* their screaming about the Tendenzwende, the ultimate shift to the right, new fascism rampant.[13] I would recommend that his adversaries read his early essay on Friedrich Nicolai, who radically changed the literary institutions of the Enlightenment; his noble essay on Heinrich Mann; or his loyal essay on Franz Kafka's letters to his sister Ottla;[14] and I would like to list some of the names of the writers who received awards at Klagenfurt when he was the speaker of the jury: Gert Jonke, Ulrich Plenzdorf, Hans J. Fröhlich, or Hermann Burger. Surely, these essays and decisions have not left our usual canon untouched.

I cannot simply talk about Marcel's literary preferences without returning to his younger years. It is not exactly a topic for after-dinner entertainments but it is important for any understanding of why he feels at home in German writing, in an almost metaphysical sense. After 1945 a number of aging exiles returned to West or East Germany to write or to make movies (Kortner succeeded, Peter Lorre unfortunately failed) but Marcel's homecoming differs from that of the older generation. Actually he returned twice, in 1945 as a member of the

Polish military mission in Berlin and nearly thirteen years later as an unemployed and disillusioned Polish intellectual looking for work. The linguistic complexities of his education are not easily described; he was born in a small Polish town where his Jewish father owned a little factory; his mother came from a rabbinic family in Germany (many relatives in Prussia) who put him in his Polish hometown into a German school managed by Protestants; and when he was sent in 1929 to Berlin (his father went bankrupt in the economic crisis) he had little trouble attending the Werner-Siemens Gymnasium in Berlin-Schöneberg and later the Fichte-Gymnasium in Berlin-Wilmersdorf. He was lucky enough to have had many decent teachers who did not give him trouble when the Nazis came to power; he was, however, excluded from school excursions and sporting events, and much later complained to me that, when teaching summer school at an American college,[15] he felt lost when he was asked to participate in the daily sing-along of German *Volkslieder*, which he really did not know). He used his time to read the German classics and Thomas Mann and to go to the opera and the theater, during the early years of the dictatorship still run by talented disciples of Reinhardt, Jessner, and Piscator. His mother believed that he should go on to Berlin University (in Paul Celan's family, too, it was the mother who was close to the German cultural tradition) claiming the privileges of his Polish passport. He was even received by the Rektor who told him that the university was overcrowded and that there was no place left.

Yet it was not only a matter of a university place denied. In October 1938 the German police rounded up all Jews with Polish passports and deported them to Poland (Marcel reading a minor Balzac novel on the train), and thus he found himself, speaking Polish with some difficulty, with his German school certificates and his enthusiasm for Thomas Mann and Richard Wagner, *malgré tout*, in his father's country promptly overrun by Hitler's armies. He worked as a translator for the Jewish *Ältestenrat* in the Warsaw ghetto and fortunately escaped, together with his young wife from Lodz, to a hiding place in the house of a Polish typesetter who was not always certain that he wanted to continue hiding Jews in his cellar, especially when the Germans, at times, stopped the advance of the Soviet armies (a few details can be learned from Günter Grass in his *Tagebuch einer Schnecke*). I would rather speak about his decision after he had been liberated by the Soviet army to free himself, as he believed, once and for all, from all his past burdens of being a mere object of history, to become a subject able to participate boldly in the shaping of a new world order by working for a military mission, join the Communist Party, be of serv-ice to the Polish State as its representative in London, and being po-litically committed to a life in which literature, German or any other, was not of importance at all. His self-deception did not last for long; he was unable to accept the disparities between his ideals and Stalinist practices, asked for a transfer from the West back to Poland where he was promptly arrested, expelled from the party, and forced to make a meager living by occasionally interviewing visiting GDR luminaries for the State radio. Writing in Polish he slowly returned to his first literary attachments and wrote essays about the major figures of East German literary life (he must have been Poland's first GDR expert) and in the later fifties turned to West German writing, including Böll, Andersch, Walser, and Siegfried Lenz. He was even allowed to go on study trips to the two Germanies and in 1958 decided not to return to Poland. It was his third arrival in Germany, the moment of his ultimate return to writing in German, which I would call the mother tongue of his mind, and the beginning of an astonishing path through the media.

I have always been fascinated by Marcel's vicissitudes, particularly by his resolve to be active among other active human beings rather than to be victimized; and when it could not have been done other-wise in the allotted time and place, to do it by joining another society that offered a better chance to struggle against those who victimized other people. Marcel Reich-Ranicki threw in his lot with the Polish Republic, not an easy decision, considering endemic Polish anti-Semitism and his difficulties with his father's idiom. I, on my part, was put in the years before Munich by my mother in a Czech school and was welcomed coolly by a few nationalist professors while my new Czech-Jewish schoolmates wondered why I came so late. Here it has to be said that Masaryk's republic was an island of liberal attitudes sur-rounded by authoritarian and fascist states, including the Poland of the generals and Dollfuss's Austria; anti-Semitism was proscribed by law and definitely disliked by those citizens who wanted to emulate the enlightened example of Masaryk; and there was a strong move-ment of Czech-speaking liberal Jews, often but not always leaving their religious communities, who strongly supported the military Re-public — among them the Korbels, parents to one Madlena Korbe-lová, now Mrs. Madeleine Albright. I think I had a much easier time than Marcel identifying with the Republic ranging its citizens against Hitler.

Marcel Reich-Ranicki, reviewing
Günter Grass' *Hundejahre*, 1963

I was sixteen when the Republic mobilized against the Wehrmacht in late September 1938. Since I was too young to volunteer in the regular army, I enlisted immediately in the National Guard, instantly received a green and scratchy uniform, an old Russian rifle from 1917 and a long bayonet, and quickly went through basic training in a little forest in the suburbs. My schoolmates (whose fathers had been mobilized overnight) were astonished to see my new outfit and my pride, and suspected me of wanting to become a super-Czech overnight, rather than laughing over my quixotic attempt to fight Hitler right-then and there. Yet there must have been some difference between my and Marcel's joining the Slavs or, more precisely, our memories of doing so. I am enjoying going back to Bohemia to teach at a Moravian university regularly, and to edit or translate Czech lyrical or philosophical texts of importance.[16] Marcel continues to speak Polish at home with his wife Theophila (Tosia) yet does not feel attracted by the idea of seeing Poland again. He published an anthology of new Polish writers[17] soon after arriving in Germany and has written reviews of many of his Polish contemporaries but he has never been back again. Writing about Heine, his favorite, Marcel Reich-Ranicki often returns to the question of the lost fatherland, of exile, and of the effort to create new certainties to compensate for all the losses; and while Heine remains fully aware of the biblical refractions, his interpreter rather confronts the literary experience and asserts, more than once, that German literature, and only German literature, has become his "portative" homeland. We suddenly understand more sharply his attachment to German writing *durch dick und dünn,* from Berlin where the boy began to read to Warsaw and from there (after an unsuccessful attempt to distance himself from literature) to Germany again.

As a critic he has German literature on his mind, and I do not know anybody of his erudition and range concentrating on German with such passion and exclusive loyalty (his wife Tosia is the movie expert, and I always enjoy talking to her about films which he, I suspect, has never seen). He has done a good deal of writing about American novelists, especially for the *Frankfurter Allgemeine Zeitung,* for "hygienic reasons," as he recently told me. There are two separate spheres of the German novel, he suggests, one of the high kind, exemplified by Kafka's *Castle,* and another, low one, incarnated in Ludwig Ganghofer's *Schloss Hubertus;* and he misses a mediating kind, the interesting, well-written and entertaining piece (let's say Kurt Tucholsky's *Schloss Rheinsberg*). For these reasons, he likes John Updike, Philip Roth, Richard Ford, or Vladimir Nabokov whom he counts among the American novelists. The truth is that German readers lap up new American and British novels eagerly, sharing his view that the German novel is not particularly willing to illuminate and entertain a reading audience in the sense of *prodesse et delectare*. We often forget the great media change of the fifties and early sixties, or the simple fact that Marcel Reich-Ranicki has become the first to take the cause of German literature to national television, not as self-appointed judge (as his adversaries argue) but as a counsel for the defense who, justifying high standards and disqualifying the shoddy and trivial, appeals to a jury of all concerned readers. Yet there is yet another circumstance, or qualification, to make him unique on the scene; it is not only that he totally lives and breathes German literature but that he does so publicly at a historical moment when he is able to do so for the millions. Marcel once suggested that Thomas Mann was something of a *Komödiant* playing out his representative role, and the critic would be less qualified to discern the playacting talents of the Olympian hypochondriac of Kilchberg if he did not share some of these histrionic gifts in the service of the best of causes. I like him most when he restlessly wiggles in his chair, TV cameras rolling, hardly hides his fatherly impatience with Frau Sigrid Löffler, expansively extends his arms as if wanted to embrace a new good author, tells me "mein liebe*rr* He*rr* Demetz" (strong *r*'s) before dealing me an uppercut that should send me reeling to the floor, or shamelessly confesses that he reads with gusto and a joy almost as intense as lust. We teachers of German literature facing fewer people in our classes may learn a good deal from his performance.

Editors' Annotations

[1] The text printed here follows an audio tape of Peter Demetz's spoken remarks on the evening of September 20, 1997. His speech was held at the conference banquet well before the appearance of Reich-Ranicki's memoir *Mein Leben* (Stuttgart: Deutsche Verlags-Anstalt, 1999); translated into English as *The Author of Himself: The Life of Marcel Reich-Ranicki*, with a foreword by Jack Zipes (Princeton: Princeton UP, 2001). Though Peter Demetz's talk was informal, the editors have taken the liberty of annotating remarks that readers may care to explore more fully.

[2] Cf. Peter Handke, "Marcel Reich-Ranicki und die Natürlichkeit" (1968). See also "Wer einmal versagt im Schreiben, hat für immer versagt. André Müller spricht mit Peter Handke," *Die Zeit*, 3.3. 1989, 77–79; Reich-Ranicki is also a presence in Handke's *Die Lehre der Sainte-Victoire* (1980) and his *Mein Jahr in der Niemandsbucht* (1994). — For a fuller treatment, see Volker Hage, Mathias Schreiber, *Marcel Reich-Ranicki: Ein Biographisches Porträt* (Munich: dtv, 1997), 97–99, which also contains bibliographical references to secondary literature and a bibliography of Reich-Ranicki's published works.

[2] Franz Josef Czernin, *Marcel Reich-Ranicki: Eine Kritik* (Göttingen: Steidl, 1995).

[4] Czernin, 139: "Bei allem Verständnis für Reich-Ranickis biographische Prägung durch bestimmte Formen von Katastrophen, die üblicherweise in politischen Kategorien beschrieben werden. . . ."

[5] Ruth Klüger, *weiter leben: Eine Jugend* (Göttingen: Wallstein, 1992).

[6] Marcel Reich-Ranicki, "Moritz Heimann, Der träumende Praktiker," *Neue Rundschau*, Heft 1 (1971): 127–43; reprinted in Marcel Reich-Ranicki, *Die Anwälte der Literatur* (Munich: dtv, 1996), 144–66, here 149.

[7] Todd Herzog, "Hybrids and *Mischlinge*: Translating Anglo-American Cultural Theory into German," *German Quarterly* 70.1 (1997): 1–17.

[8] *Zwischen Diktatur und Literatur: Marcel Reich-Ranicki im Gespräch mit Joachim Fest*; nach d. Sendereihe d. ZDF "Zeugen des Jahrhunderts" (Frankfurt am Main: Fischer, 1987).

[9] Marcel Reich-Ranicki, "Im magischen Judenkreis," in *Über Ruhestörer: Juden in der deutschen Literatur* (Munich: Piper, 1973), 36–56, here 37f.

[10] Marcel Reich-Ranicki, "Aussenseiter und Provokateure," in *Über Ruhestörer: Juden in der deutschen Literatur* (Munich: Piper, 1973), 13–35, here 15.

[11] Reich-Ranicki, "Moritz Heimann," 149.

[12] Marcel Reich-Ranicki, "Zum Fall Heine," in *Über Ruhestörer: Juden in der deutschen Literatur* (Munich: Piper, 1973), 57–72, here 60.

[13] Horst Krüger, "Das heilsame Ärgernis: Brief an einen jungen Studenten der Literatur (DDR)," in *Über Marcel Reich-Ranicki: Aufsätze und Kommentare*, ed. Jens Jessen (München: dtv, 1985), 58–68, hier 65. Originally published in Fest-

schrift *Literatur und Kritik: aus Anlass d. 60. Geburtstages von Marcel Reich-Ranicki,* ed. Walter Jens (Stuttgart: Deutsche Verlags-Anstalt, 1980).

[14] Marcel Reich-Ranicki, "Friedrich Nicolai: Der Gründer unseres literarischen Lebens," *Frankfurter Allgemeine Zeitung,* Dezember 2, 1989, enlarged reprint in *Die Anwälte der Literatur* (Munich: dtv, 1994), 32–52; "Heinrich Mann. Ein Abschied nicht ohne Wehmut," *Thomas Mann und die Seinen* (Stuttgart: Deutsche Verlags-Anstalt, 1987), 109–51, partial printing in the *Frankfurter Allgemeine Zeitung,* August 15, 1987; "Kafka, der Liebende," *Frankfurter Allgemeine Zeitung,* March 15, 1975, enlarged reprint in *Nachprüfung: Aufsätze über deutsche Schriftsteller von gestern* (Munich and Zurich: Piper, 1977), 128–41.

[15] In 1969 Reich-Ranicki taught at Middlebury College.

[16] E.g. *Der Herrgott schuldet mir ein Mädchen: Tschechische Lyrik des 20. Jahrhunderts,* ed. and with a afterword by Ladislav Nezdařil and Peter Demetz (Munich and Zurich: Piper, 1994); *Polemiken und Essays zur russischen und europäischen Literatur- und Geistesgeschichte: Dostojevskij, von Puškin zu Gorkij, Musset, Byron, Goethe, Lenau, T. G. Masaryk,* ed. Peter Demetz (Vienna: Böhlau, 1995).

[17] *Sechzehn Polnische Erzähler,* ed. Marcel Reich-Ranicki (Reinbek bei Hamburg: Rowohlt, 1962).

Contributors

HASKELL BLOCK is a professor of Comparative Literature emeritus at Binghamton University, State University of New York. He has edited many works of and about both French and German literature, including *The Poetry of Paul Celan* (1991) and Voltaire's *Candide and Other Writings* (1984).

GESA DANE is a Wissenschaftliche Mitarbeiterin on the project "Zeter und Mordio! Vergewaltigung in Literatur und Recht vom 17.–20. Jahrhundert" at the Seminar für Deutsche Philologie der Georg-August-Universität Göttingen. She is the author of *Die heilsame Toilette: Kosmetik und Bildung in Goethes "Der Mann von funfzig Jahren"* (1994) and editor of *Anschlüsse: Versuche nach Michel Foucault* (1986). She has written many essays on German and feminist topics from the eighteenth century to the present as well as studies in the history of Germanistik.

PETER DEMETZ is Sterling Professor Emeritus of German and Comparative Literature at Yale University. He has edited many works of fiction and scholarship and written prolifically on German and European literature from Lessing to the present. His most recent books are *Prague in Black and Gold: The History of a City* (1997) and *The Air Show at Brescia, 1909* (2002).

STEPHEN D. DOWDEN is an associate professor of German at Brandeis University. He is the author of books and essays on modern German literature, including *Sympathy for the Abyss* (1986), *Understanding Thomas Bernhard* (1989), and *Kafka's Castle and the Critical Imagination* (1995). His most recent publication as editor is *A Companion to Thomas Mann's "Magic Mountain"* (1999; paperback 2002).

AMIR ESHEL is an associate professor of German at Stanford University. He is the author of *Zeit der Zäsur: Jüdische Lyriker im Angesicht der Shoah* (1999) as well as numerous essays in the area of German, Hebrew, and German-Jewish literature and intellectual life. He has co-edited special issues of *New German Critique*, *Germanic Review*, and *German Quarterly*. He is currently at work on a book entitled *Narra-*

tives of History: Historical Narratives and Political Discourse in Contemporary German Culture.

ABIGAIL GILLMAN is an assistant professor of German and Hebrew at Boston University. Her research and essays include work on German-Jewish literature and thought, Austrian literature, modernism and memory (literary, religious, cultural), and Biblical and Rabbinic texts.

WILLI GOETSCHEL is an associate professor of German and Graduate Coordinator at the University of Toronto. A prolific essayist, his areas of special interest are German-Jewish literature, philosophy, and intellectual life. He is an editor of *Germanic Review* and president of the Stiftung Dialogik. He is the author of *Constituting Critique: Kant's Writing as Critical Praxis* (1994) and has edited the nine volumes of Hermann Levin Goldschmidt's *Werkausgabe* for Passagen Verlag.

BARBARA HAHN is a professor of German at Princeton University. She has published widely, especially on German-Jewish topics and on the history and theory of women's intellectual traditions. She is the author of many essays and books, including *"Antworten Sie mir": Rahel Levin Varnhagens Briefwechsel* (1990), *Unter falschem Namen: Von der schwierigen Autorschaft der Frauen* (1991), and most recently *Die Jüdin Pallas Athene: Auch eine Theorie der Moderne* (2002). She has also edited scholarly works such as *Frauen in den Kulturwissenschaften* (1994) and volumes of letters, including *Pauline Wiesels Liebesgeschichten* (1997).

PETER HELLER was a professor of German and Comparative Literature emeritus at the State University of New York, Buffalo, where he founded the Graduate Group in Modern German Studies and directed graduate studies in German. He was known for his writings on Nietzsche, Lessing, Mann, Kafka, and Freud, among others. A last, posthumous book entitled *Exile and Displacement: Survivors of the Nazi Persecution Remember the Emigration Experience* appeared in 2002. It is a collection of memoirs by various hands, the editing of which was continued by Lauren Levin Enzie after Peter Heller's death in 1998.

GISELA HOECHERL-ALDEN has worked as Language Program Director and TA-Coordinator and is currently an assistant professor of German at the University of Maine. Her dissertation investigates the impact of antifascist refugee intellectuals on the field of American German studies. She has published articles on the history of Germanics and language pedagogy, is co-author of the elementary textbook *Deutsch heute,* and is currently working on narrative styles in exile biographies.

SUSANNE KLINGENSTEIN is an associate professor at MIT in its Program in Writing and Humanistic Studies. Her books include *Jews in the American Academy, 1900–1940: The Dynamics of Intellectual Assimilation* (1991) and *Enlarging America: The Cultural Work of Jewish Literary Scholars, 1930–1950* (1998).

HANNE KNICKMANN was a Wissenschaftliche Mitarbeiterin at the Deutsches Literaturarchiv from 1994–2002, where she was engaged in the "Internationales Germanistenlexikon 1800–1950" that has been undertaken by the Arbeitsstelle für die Erforschung der Geschichte der Germanistik at Marbach. She was responsible for scholars of German literature at American institutions of higher learning. She has published works on the history of Germanistik, on literary Expressionism, on Eduard Berend and the writings of other German scholars in exile. She is currently finishing a dissertation on Kurt Pinthus.

CHRISTOPH KÖNIG directs the Arbeitsstelle für die Erforschung der Geschichte der Germanistik at the Deutsches Literaturarchiv in Marbach and is a Privatdozent at the University of Stuttgart. He is the author of numerous essays on German literature and on the history of Germanistik and has edited many works, including *Jüdische Intellektuelle und die Philologien in Deutschland 1871–1933* (2001). He is the author, most recently, of *Hofmannsthal: Ein moderner Dichter unter den Philologen* (2001).

PAUL REITTER is an assistant professor in the German Department at Ohio State University. He has written essays and articles on a number of topics, including Walter Benjamin's reading of Karl Kraus, Franz Kafka's "The Judgment," the erotics of Viennese modernism, the Heine monument controversies, Victor Klemperer's diaries, and Pierre Bourdieu's feminism. He is currently completing a book on modernism, journalism, and German-Jewish identity.

RITCHIE ROBERTSON, Professor of German at Oxford University, is tutor in German at St. John's College. Besides German language (especially translation into English and essay-writing in German) he teaches a broad range of German literature from the Enlightenment to the present. He is the author of *Franz Kafka: Judaism, Politics, and Literature* (1987), and his most recent books are *The "Jewish Question" in German Literature, 1749–1939* (1999) and, as editor, *The Cambridge Companion to Thomas Mann* (2002).

Jeffrey Sammons is Leavenworth Professor of German Emeritus at Yale University. His scholarship concentrates above all on the nineteenth century and especially on Heinrich Heine. His many publications include *Heinrich Heine, The Elusive Poet* (1969); *Heinrich Heine: A Modern Biography* (1979); *Wilhelm Raabe: The Fiction of the Alternative Community* (1987); *Ideology, Mimesis, Fantasy: Charles Sealsfield, Friedrich Gerstäcker, Karl May, and Other German Novelists of America* (1998).

Egon Schwarz is Professor Emeritus of German and Rosa May Distinguished Professor Emeritus in the Humanities at Washington University, St. Louis. His research focuses on nineteenth- and twentieth-century German literature, and he has made important contributions to the study of German literary figures such as Rainer Marie Rilke and Hermann Hesse. His book *Verbannung* (1964) was the first major study of the literary exiles who left Germany because of Hitler's regime, and his autobiography, *Keine Zeit für Eichendorff* (1979), details Schwarz's life after he and his parents were forced to flee Europe during the Second World War. His most recent books are *"Ich bin kein Freund allgemeiner Urteile über ganze Völker": Essays über österreichische, deutsche und jüdische Literatur* (2000) and *Die Japanische Mauer: Ungewöhnliche Reisegeschichten* (2002).

Hinrich C. Seeba is a professor of German at the University of California, Berkeley. His publications include books on Hofmannsthal, *Kritik des ästhetischen Menschen* (1970); on Lessing, *Die Liebe zur Sache* (1974); and, as editor, two volumes of Kleist's dramas in the *Deutscher Klassiker Verlag*. His current projects include studies in the literary images of historical discourse, the German concept of a "Kulturnation," the role of language in identity formation, academic emigration and paradigms of intercultural history, and the cultural topography of the city (Berlin).

Walter H. Sokel is Commonwealth Professor Emeritus of German and English at the University of Virginia. Best known for his studies of Kafka and of German modernism, he is the author of *The Writer in Extremis: Expressionism in Twentieth-Century German Literature* (1959), *Franz Kafka: Tragik und Ironie* (1964), and *The Myth of Power and the Self: Essays on Franz Kafka* (2002). A novella he wrote in 1942, "Die Liebhaber hässlicher Mädchen," appeared in the February 2002 number of the Viennese journal *Zwischenwelt*.

THOMAS SPARR, currently editor-in-chief of Siedler Verlag in Berlin, is the author and editor of numerous works concerned especially with German and Jewish culture and history. Together with Christoph König he edited Peter Szondi's *Briefe* (2001). He is the author of *Celans Poetik des hermetischen Gedichts* (1989).

DAVID SUCHOFF is an associate professor of English at Colby College. He is the author of *Critical Theory and the Novel* (1994) and editor, together with Mary Rhiel, of *The Seductions of Biography* (1996). He has also translated works by Hermann Levin Goldschmidt and Alain Finkielkraut. His research and essays focus especially on Jewish intellectual, literary, and cultural life in the twentieth century.

FRANK TROMMLER is a professor of German and Comparative Literature at the University of Pennsylvania. He has written and edited books on modern German literature as well as on issues of youth, socialism, Germanistics, thematics, and German-American cultural relations. They include *Die Kultur der Weimarer Republik* (1978), *America and the Germans* (1985), and *Germanistik in den USA* (1989). In 1994 Professor Trommler was appointed by the American Institute for Contemporary German Studies to direct its Harry and Helen Gray Humanities Program.

REGINA WEBER is the author of *Gottfried Benn: Zwischen Christentum und Gnosis* (1982) and has written numerous essays on writers and scholars who were forced into exile during the Third Reich — including, among others Werner Vordtriede, Richard Alewyn, Bernhard Blume, Heinz Politzer, and Karl Gustav Vollmoeller — in *Exilforschung: Ein internationales Jahrbuch* (1995; 1996) and in John M. Spalek, Konrad Feilchenfeldt, ed., *Deutschsprachige Exilliteratur seit 1933* (2001).

MARC A. WEINER teaches at Indiana University where he is professor of German Studies and Director of the Institute of German Studies. He is the author of *Arthur Schnitzler and the Crisis of Musical Culture* (1986); *Undertones of Insurrection: Music, Politics, and the Social Sphere in the Modern German Narrative* (1993); and *Richard Wagner and the Anti-Semitic Imagination* (1995), which won the Eugene M. Kayden National University Press Book Award for best book in the humanities in 1996.

MEIKE G. WERNER is an assistant professor of German at Vanderbilt University, where she specializes in nineteenth- and twentieth-century literary and cultural studies. She has written articles on a wide range of topics, including the culture of modernism (especially publishing), turn-of-the-century reform movements, Sophie von LaRoche, Rahel Sanzara, and the history of Germanistik. She has also co-edited *Romantik, Revolution & Reform: Der Eugen Diederichs Verlag im Epochenkontext 1900–1949* (1999), and *Karl Korsch: Briefe 1908–1939* (2001). Her book on *Moderne in der Provinz: Kulturelle Experimente in Fin de Siècle Jena* is scheduled to appear in the spring of 2003.

BERND WIDDIG teaches German Studies at MIT with a focus on nineteenth- and twentieth-century German literature and culture. Since 1996 he has been Director of the MIT-Germany Program. He is the author of *Männerbünde und Massen: Zur Krise männlicher Identität in der Literatur der Moderne* (1992) and *Culture and Inflation in Weimar Germany* (2001). He has also written articles on the representation of National Socialism in German postwar literature, on fashion and modernity, on Elias Canetti, and on Thomas Mann. He is currently involved in a book-length study entitled "The Germans and Their Money: A Cultural History."

Index